A Guide to the Indian Tribes of Oklahoma

D1258306

THE CIVILIZATION OF THE AMERICAN INDIAN SERIES

A GUIDE TO THE
INDIAN TRIBES
OF OKLAHOMA

MURIEL H. WRIGHT

FOREWORD BY ARRELL MORGAN GIBSON

UNIVERSITY OF OKLAHOMA PRESS

NORMAN AND LONDON

by Muriel H. Wright

A Guide to the Indian Tribes of Oklahoma (Norman, 1951, 1986)

The Story of Oklahoma (Guthrie, Oklahoma, 1949, fifth edition)

Our Oklahoma (Guthrie, Oklahoma, 1949, second edition)

Springplace, Moravian Mission, Cherokee Nation (Guthrie, Oklahoma, 1940)

Oklahoma: A History of the State and Its People
4 vols. (with J. B. Thoburn) (New York, 1929)

Mark of Heritage
(with George H. Shirk and Kenny A. Franks) (Norman, 1976)

Library of Congress Cataloging-in-Publication Data

Wright, Muriel H. (Muriel Hazel), 1889–1975.
A guide to the Indian tribes of Oklahoma.

(The Civilization of the American Indian series; v. 33)
Bibliography: p. 274.
Includes index.
1. Indians of North America—Oklahoma.   I. Title.
II. Series.
E78.045W7   1987   976.6'00497   86–14678
ISBN 0–8061–0238–1
ISBN 0–8061–2041–x (pbk)

11   12   13   14   15   16   17   18   19   20   21   22   23   24   25

Dedicated to

the Indian leaders who guided their people

in the formation of Oklahoma

1807–1907

Foreword

Arrell Morgan Gibson

A Guide to the Indian Tribes of Oklahoma, first issued in 1951 as Volume 33 of the eminent Civilization of the American Indian Series, has passed through eight printings, a ringing confirmation of its inherent value as a scholarly reference. Its republication is timely. The *Guide* will appear on the threshold of the centennial of the passage of the General Allotment Act. Adopted in 1887 by the United States Congress and popularly known as the Dawes Act after its author, Senator Henry L. Dawes of Massachusetts, this statute drastically altered the cultures and life-styles of all the Indian tribes in Oklahoma. Its application by federal officials to each of the nations and reservations in Indian Territory, preparing American Indians for transition to the future state of Oklahoma, necessarily is a dominating theme of the *Guide.*

As the *Guide* appears in its ninth printing, its compelling essence must be the author's nonpareil credibility as spokesman for the sixty-seven tribes she profiles in the volume. Muriel Wright brought to the enterprise the advantage of her ethnic heritage, her exposure to learned mentors, her lifetime of productive research, and her literary experience as editor and author.

Muriel Wright descended from Choctaw tribal lineage. Her paternal grandfather, Allen Wright, served as principal chief of the Choctaw Nation in the period 1866 to 1870, a traumatic time for the Choctaws and other tribes of Indian Territory, the future Oklahoma, the aftermath of destructive involvement in the Civil War on the side of the Confederacy. His uncommon leadership ameliorated for the Choctaws

the pain of war's defeat and Reconstruction and prepared them for the new order that federal officials prepared to inflict on all tribes in Indian Territory. Principal Chief Wright also proposed the name Oklahoma for the state eventually carved from Indian Territory. Muriel Wright brought to her research and writing the strength, pride, and creative tradition of this distinguished genealogy.

She was additionally blessed with the tutelage of the triumvirate of Oklahoma history—Joseph Thoburn, Grant Foreman, and Edward Everett Dale—who transformed the Sooner epic from simplistic tradition and lore to objective scholarship. With this trio the Choctaw woman served a demanding apprenticeship in historical research, editing, and writing that yielded a prime bibliography of articles, essays, and books, the final major work being her *Guide to the Indian Tribes of Oklahoma.* She devoted her professional lifetime to the Oklahoma Historical Society, serving most of her tenure as editor of the *Chronicles of Oklahoma,* the state's historical quarterly. Her ethnic heritage and enlarging knowledge of the state's American Indian roots enhanced her qualifications for undertaking the monumental task of producing the *Guide.* Another strategic advantage, derived from her tribal heritage, that of an Indian viewpoint, she applied to this enterprise, infusing instinctive, properly placed sympathy into each tribal sketch.

The *Guide's* format follows the pattern of Frederick W. Hodge's *Handbook of American Indians North of Mexico;* Hodge had introduced readers to many of the tribes included in Muriel Wright's *Guide.*

As she points out, however, the forty-one intervening years between publication of Hodge's *Handbook* (1910) and the appearance of her *Guide* (1951) had been a time of "great changes" for Indians and "the country in which they live." And each tribal sketch in Wright's *Guide* stresses the impact of these changes on American Indians residing in the old Indian Territory.

The sketches depicting Oklahoma's sixty-seven tribes are arranged in alphabetical order—Alabama to Yuchi—providing ready reference. Each entry includes an explanation of the origin of the tribal name and linguistic affiliation, typical physical characteristics of members, and their location in Oklahoma and population in 1951. In addition the vignette for each Indian group contains a survey of tribal history, a description of ceremonials and public dances observed by members, and a statement of tribal organization and government. At the conclusion of each sketch is a useful listing of books and articles containing other detailed information about the tribe.

Several engaging themes permeate the tribal sketches and capture the reader's attention. One is the commonality of the removal experience. Much of the literature depicting the exile of tribes from their ancient homelands in all parts of the United States to the Indian Territory emphasizes the ordeal of the Five Civilized Tribes (Creeks, Seminoles, Cherokees, Choctaws, and Chickasaws). The *Guide* sketches make the salient point that virtually every tribe exiled to Indian Territory endured a Trail of Tears, suffering unnecessary travail and near-inhuman imposition in the merciless uprooting from each tribal homeland by federal officials and United States Army units and dreaded passage to the southwestern wilderness.

Each sketch evolves on a positive note, however, emphasizing the courageous, de-termined adjustment by the tribes to their new home in Indian Territory. And their heroic recovery is confirmed by their energetic transformation of the frontier into productive farms and ranches, the restoration of tribal governments, and the creation of villages, towns, and schools. The author makes the point that Indian immigrants were carriers of American civilization to this new land (schools, churches, constitutional government, law-and-order systems, and successful economic enterprises) in many respects just as surely as were their non-Indian neighbors in the peripheral states of Missouri, Arkansas, Kansas, and Texas.

A study of the sketches also provides the reader with a satisfying explanation, rarely found, of the exceedingly complex land-partitioning process carried out under the aegis of the General Allotment Act, which transformed Indian tribal estates (nations and reservations), each communally owned, to individual allotments (fee simple ownership) of from an average of 160 acres to over 200 acres assigned to each Indian whose name appeared on the tribal roll or census. The complicated work of the Dawes Commission accomplished this revolutionary economic and cultural change for the tribes of the eastern half of Indian Territory. Another federal commission which prepared the surplus land after allotment assignment in the western half of Indian Territory for settlement by homeseekers under the Homestead Act through the anomalous procedures of land runs, lotteries, and auctions is described in satisfying detail.

Another feature of the *Guide* is an explanation of how members of each of the tribes resident in Oklahoma adjusted to the "great changes," including the shift from tribal citizenship to United States citizenship and participation in the collective life of the new state of Oklahoma, formed from the partitioned nations and reservations and admitted to the Union in 1907. These include revelations of substantive cultural, economic, and social changes made by Indians adapting to the "new order." The author has singled out the Indians who provided leadership and direction as their people moved into Oklahoma society. The sketch for each tribe concludes with a persuasive presentation of the creative role that Indians from each of the sixty-seven resident tribes play in the educational, political, religious, and social life of modern Oklahoma.

Preface

Not since the publication of Frederick Webb Hodge's *Handbook of American Indians North of Mexico,* issued in two volumes in 1910 and 1911, has there been printed a comprehensive guide to this important segment of our population. The intervening forty years have brought great changes to the Indians and to the country in which they live, and students of the American Indian everywhere have felt the need of a readily available single source which brings the facts up to date. With this need in mind, I have attempted to present in compact form authentic accounts of all the Indian tribes and parts of tribes living in Oklahoma, which is the home of one-third of the Indians of the United States.

The United States Indian offices and agencies still record twenty-nine tribes in Oklahoma, most of them located here under the auspices of the government during the last eighty years of the nineteenth century. Within these tribal groups are the remnants of tribes once powerful on the American frontier, whose names even have been all but forgotten, yet who are significant in any account of Oklahoma Indians. For example, there are the Anadarko, well known in Texas and Oklahoma history, who are called Caddo today, their name perpetuated only by the town of Anadarko. And, locally, only one Indian in the Anadarko Area region was pointed out to me as an Anadarko, although in a census in 1857 that tribe constituted about 47 per cent of the people commonly included as Caddo. Because of the importance of their early history and traditions, I have included tribes such as this under their original names, with cross-references to the inclusive group. Thus, all in all, sixty-seven tribes are listed and described in this volume.

To make the guide serviceable and easy to use, I have listed the tribes alphabetically, discussing each under these headings: Name, Present Location, Numbers, History, Government and Organization, Contemporary Life and Culture, Ceremonials and Public Dances, and Suggested Readings. The suggested readings, of course, do not include all that has been written about the tribe, but they are, in my opinion, the most important and the most interesting of the easily accessible books and articles.

The compilation of the population data for each tribe posed peculiar problems. Except in a very few instances, census figures for all Indian tribes in America, from the first enumerations in Colonial days to the most recent census compiled by the United States Indian offices, have been at best only approximations. Federal census records are incomplete and fall far short of recording the actual Indian population in a given area at any one time, and the 1950 census does not provide enumeration by tribes. The reasons for the difficulties in obtaining an accurate count of the Indians are discussed fully in the introduction. The figures in this volume are also of necessity estimates, although every effort has been made to arrive at reasonably accurate numbers. Some figures are based on reports sent directly to me by the Indian leaders living in their tribal communities in the state. Others have been calculated on a percentage basis from the last separate enumerations of the tribes in their respective agency records. I believe that they represent, as accurately as is possible at this time, the approximate number of Indians in each Oklahoma tribe described.

In the preparation of this book, Hodge's *Handbook of American Indians* has, of course, been indispensable, just as it has been for every student of the North American Indian since its first issuance. However, it has been used cautiously, with due attention to later research and more recent volumes in the fields of Indian history, anthropology, and archaeology.

I have made full use of the original letters, records, laws, and other documents in the Indian archives and the library of the Oklahoma Historical Society. The rare documents in the Phillips Collection at the University of Oklahoma and in the Union Agency files in the office of the superintendent of the Five Civilized Tribes at Muskogee have also been fully utilized. Original Indian materials in my possession and notes from private collections of friends in Oklahoma have furnished valuable additional data. The bound volumes of the old Indian Territory newspapers in the files of the Oklahoma Historical Society have yielded interesting facts. Special field research provided information on present-day conditions and locations of the Indian tribal groups.

The Indian laws and treaties issued under United States government auspices have been basic texts used constantly in preparing the manuscript, and the compiled laws and session laws published under the authority of the governments of the Five Civilized Tribes have likewise been valuable.

I am indebted to many friends and colleagues who have contributed authentic data and allowed me to use documents and other source materials, and I am happy to acknowledge their aid, without which my book would have been sadly deficient. Professor Edward Everett Dale, research professor of history and director of the Frank Phillips Collection in the University of Oklahoma, pointed out special documents and source materials in the Phillips Collection; indeed, without his encouragement I would never have undertaken this volume. Mr. Grant Foreman of Muskogee kindly lent me some rare reports from the United States Indian Office. Mr. Dover P.

Trent, acting district director of the former Oklahoma City Indian Office, was generous in supplying reports on Oklahoma Indian census figures and on the work relating to the Indian credit associations organized among some of the tribal groups. Indian Office officials and agents replied in full detail to my letters of inquiry relating to Indian matters. Among them are the late John T. Montgomery, superintendent of the former Western Oklahoma Consolidated Agency at Anadarko; Mr. W. O. Roberts, director of the Muskogee Area Office; Mr. William W. Head, director of the Anadarko Area Office; Mr. Royal B. Hassrick, curator of the Southern Plains Indian Museum, Anadarko; Mr. T. B. Hall, superintendent of the Osage Agency; Mr. A. B. Caldwell, educationist, Five Civilized Tribes Agency, Muskogee; Mr. John L. Johnson, district agent, Pawnee Subagency; Mr. H. A. Andrews, agent, Quapaw Subagency, Miami; Miss Eva Lewers, principal, Eufaula Boarding School, Eufaula; and Mrs. Leila Black, principal, Wheelock Academy, Millerton.

Many Indian friends have been prompt and generous in response to requests for information and for materials. Special thanks are due former Chief Jeffie Brown and Rev. Wilsey Palmer of the Seminole Nation, Chief S. W. Brown and Mrs. Ella Burgess of the Yuchi, Mr. Joe Bartles of the Delaware, the late Chief Roly Canard and Dr. Fred S. Clinton of the Creek Nation, Mr. Andrew Dunlap of the Caddo, Rev. Robert P. Chaat of the Comanche, Mr. A. A. Exendine of the Delaware, Mr. McKinley Eagle of the Ponca, Mr. Robert Goombi of the Kiowa, Mr. John Haddon of the Kichai, Mr. Claude Hayman of the Modoc, the late Chief William Durant of the Choctaw Nation, Miss Lillian B. Mathews and Mr. George V. Labadie of the Osage Nation, Governor Floyd E. Maytubby of the Chickasaw Nation, the late Chief J. Bartley Milam and Rev. Eli Pumpkin of the Cherokee Nation, Mr. George H. Roberts of the Pawnee, Mr. Jesse Rowlodge of the Cheyenne, Mr. Carl Sweezey of the Arapaho, the late Chief Don Whistler of the Sac (Sauk) and Fox, Mrs. Sallie Tyner and Mr. Dan Nadeau of the Potawatomi, and Hon. William G. Stigler of the Choctaw, member of Congress from the Second Congressional District.

Nearer home, I wish to thank the members of the staff of the Oklahoma Historical Society for their interest and assistance. Dr. Charles Evans, secretary, Mrs. Rella Looney, Mrs. Helen Gorman, Mrs. Grace Ward, Mrs. Louise Cook, Mrs. Dorothy Thurston, Miss Martha Mulholland, Mrs. Edith Mitchell, Mrs. Mary Jeanne Hansen, Mrs. Hazel Beatty Hale, and Mrs. Myrtle Jeanne Cook have all been generous with their help during my research and work in their departments.

A special word of appreciation goes to my sister, Mrs. Guy C. Reid of Oklahoma City, for her continued interest and her assistance in typing many pages of the manuscript.

The preparation of this volume has been made possible through a grant from the Rockefeller Foundation awarded by the Rockefeller Committee of the University of Oklahoma in 1947, and I want to express my deep gratitude to the Foundation, the committee, and the University for the opportunity to carry on the necessary field work and research.

MURIEL H. WRIGHT

Oklahoma City, Oklahoma

Contents

The Indian Tribes

Illustrations

Maps

A Guide to the Indian Tribes of Oklahoma

Introduction

More Indian tribes have retained their character and identity in Oklahoma than in any other state of the Union. At the same time, the American Indian in Oklahoma is generally a highly respected colleague of his white contemporary in the professions, art, music, and every other walk of life. Quite as important as this may be, it remains that recognition also exists for the fine contributions the Indian has made to a developing culture in Oklahoma, which today is only three-quarters of a century advanced from the period of white settlement.

The Indian population constitutes approximately 5 per cent of the total population of the state. Many native Oklahomans are descendants of the Indian pioneer families who lived in the Indian Territory. Nowhere else in the United States can be found such blending of the blood and the civilization of the Anglo-American and the American Indian.

A resident of another state, coming to Oklahoma for the first time, was introduced by a relative to a group of friends on the platform of a railroad station while en route in Oklahoma. Later she remarked that she was disappointed in not having seen any Indians. "You have met several," was the reply. "Those friends to whom I introduced you were Indians." The newcomer was further surprised to learn that this group of five persons represented different tribes—Cherokee, Choctaw, Osage —and that the fair-haired, blue-eyed girl was a part Chickasaw.

Most Indians in Oklahoma are modern Americans in customs, habits, and dress, and have all rights and privileges as citizens of the state. Some of the outstanding leaders in business and professional life as well as officials of the state have been and are of Indian descent. Indian children attend the public schools under the general classification of "white children" by the Oklahoma constitution, and many Indian men and women are among the graduates of the state's institutions of higher learning.

There are no Indian reservations in Oklahoma like those found in some states to the west and north. All tribal lands were allotted in severalty by provisions of the Dawes Act of 1887 and other, later, Congressional acts. The surplus acres were subsequently ceded to the United States in agreements with the tribes of western and north central Oklahoma and opened in tracts to white settlers, the last great Indian land opening being the Kiowa-Comanche and the Wichita-Caddo reservations (3,232,503 acres) in 1901. Osage County is sometimes erroneously referred to as the "Osage Reservation," even though three-fifths of the land in the county has been sold and is now generally individually owned, just as other lands in the state are, with the exception of the subsurface (mineral) rights, which the Osage retained under tribal ownership in their last agreement with the United States.

There are a great many problems and questions to be considered in determining the number of Indians in Oklahoma. The main problem, of course, is who is Indian and who is not. There are all degrees of Indian blood (and the Indian blood itself is frequently mixed), from full blood to one-sixty-fourth or even less, and the Indian population has been so thoroughly absorbed into the general population of the state that many "Indians" themselves, if asked to answer the question of "race," would very likely reply "white" without considering that their Indian ancestors should be mentioned. Hence any count of the Indian population is at best an approximation.

Oklahoma is the home of approximately one-third of the total population of the American Indians in the United States. The federal census for 1940 reported 63,125 Indians in Oklahoma, of whom 7,454 were urban and 55,671 (or 88 per cent) rural. This number includes the individuals readily identified as Indian in comparison with members of other races (the census does not state what basis was used for comparison), but falls lamentably short of giving the actual population of all individuals of Indian descent in the state.

The reports of the United States Bureau of Indian Affairs usually include only those tribal members whose property is restricted and under the supervision of an Indian agent. As a result, these reports, especially since the allotment of tribal lands, do not give the total number in each tribe outside agency control, but even so, they are more accurate in giving the actual number of Indians than the federal census.

A report issued in 1945 by the Bureau of Indian Affairs listed 110,864 Indians in Oklahoma, an increase of 46,739 over the 1940 federal census. The population included in it is confined strictly to those Indians who are eligible to receive benefits from the government through the Indian Service program; namely, adults of one-half or more Indian blood and minors of one-fourth or more Indian blood. Even this number would be exceeded if persons from one-eighth to one-thirty-second or even one-sixty-fourth, Indian blood were counted. Individuals of this latter group, identified as "white" in a federal census, more often than not retain affiliations with their tribal relatives and are proud of their Indian ancestry. From the foregoing statements it should be clear that, counting all individuals from the full bloods to those of the smallest accepted degree of Indian blood who remain close in their ties of kinship and association, Oklahoma's Indian population exceeds by many thousands

even the 1945 census by the Indian Bureau.

A report made in 1944 by the District Indian Office at Oklahoma City showed that forty counties of the seventy-seven in Oklahoma had an Indian population of more than 1,000, twenty counties had between 100 and 1,000, and eleven counties had less than 100. The six counties listed with no Indian population were Woods, Alfalfa, and Ellis in the northwest, and Cimarron, Texas, and Beaver in the Panhandle. The seven counties with the largest Indian population were Adair (6,601), Cherokee (6,298), Delaware (6,066), Caddo (4,919), Seminole (4,577), Osage (4,375), and McCurtain (3,949).

Many Indian tribes were brought to Oklahoma from other parts of the United States under the auspices of the federal government. The five largest of these tribes, namely the Five Civilized Tribes—Cherokee, Chickasaw, Choctaw, Creek, and Seminole—were removed from their lands in the Southeastern states and settled in this region in the eighteen thirties. Twenty-nine tribes listed under the general jurisdiction of United States Indian agencies in Oklahoma today have retained their identity and are still known by their tribal names. Merged with these in past years are people from a number of small tribes and parts of tribes that have lost their identity, yet have a place in history and make a total of sixty-seven tribes represented in the Indian population of the state. Even the name of the state is a part of Indian history and is a memorial to the dominant characteristic of the region since prehistoric times.

The name *Oklahoma* is synonymous with the word "Indian" in the former name, Indian Territory, and is from the Choctaw *okla-homma,* meaning "red people" (from *okla* meaning "people" and *homma,* or *humma,* meaning "red"). This name was first applied to the Indian Territory by Allen Wright (principal chief of the Choctaw Nation, 1866–70) in the Choctaw-Chickasaw treaty of 1866, in

The Buffalo Hunt, from a painting by John Mix Stanley in the Smithsonian Institution

which plans were set forth to organize all the nations and tribes within the boundaries of the present state into one representative government titled the "Territory of Oklahoma." These plans for an Indian state did not mature, but the name became popularly known throughout the country and was given to the western half of the Indian Territory when it was organized separately in 1890, and to the forty-sixth state seventeen years later.

Indian tribes in Oklahoma represent two divisions discovered living throughout wide regions in North America at the beginning of the historic period. The "Hunters of the Plains" were the tribes that lived in the West between the Mississippi River and the Rocky Mountains; the "Woodsmen of the Forests," or "Woodland tribes," lived east of the Mississippi to the Atlantic Coast. Since there is no clear line of demarcation between the two divisions in Oklahoma, it is easier to show on paper the areas they formerly inhabited than it is to give their location today. The term "Plains tribes" is used in Oklahoma, although in its present sense it does not include all the tribes in the state that may have been originally classed "Hunters of the Plains," the term generally referring to five tribes in western Oklahoma—Kiowa, Comanche, Apache, Cheyenne, and Arapaho.

The division "Woodsmen of the Forests" is represented in eastern Oklahoma by a number of tribes and parts of tribes that were removed to the Indian Territory from east of the Mississippi River. Most of the small tribes that settled in the extreme northeastern corner of Oklahoma, now Ottawa County (former Quapaw Country or Quapaw Agency), were "Woodland tribes." The Five Civilized Tribes are the best known of this division in the eastern part of the state. All Indians in Oklahoma today are civilized from the point of view of Anglo-American culture, yet the term "Five Civilized Tribes" has been continued in use since 1866 by the Office of Indian

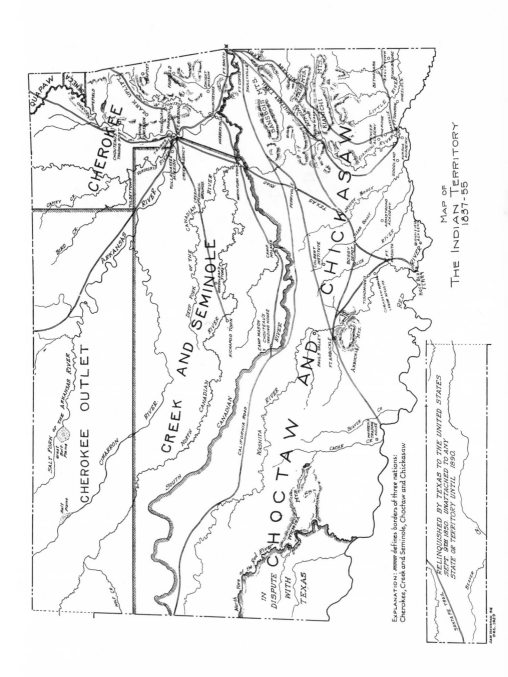

MAP OF
THE INDIAN TERRITORY
1837-55

EXPLANATION: *mmmm* defines borders of three nations:
Cherokee, Creek and Seminole, Choctaw and Chickasaw.

RELINQUISHED BY TEXAS TO THE UNITED STATES
SEPT 9TH 1850. UNATTACHED TO ANY
STATE OR TERRITORY UNTIL 1890.

Affairs to designate specifically the Cherokee, Chickasaw, Choctaw, Creek, and Seminole—who by that date had made remarkable advancement, each tribe having established its own government and referred to itself as a "nation" in written laws.

The Indian peoples in Oklahoma can best be identified according to language groups, all tribes in North America having been classified into a comparatively few linguistic families or stocks. There are approximately 58 linguistic stocks and more than 225 different Indian tribal dialects and languages in North America, grouped by similar basic words discovered in scientific study by ethnologists. For example, the Chickasaw, Choctaw, Creek, and Seminole tribes are classified in the Muskhogean linguistic stock. The Chickasaw and the Choctaw languages are almost identical except for some dialectal differences. Their written languages are the same, established by Protestant missionaries through the use of nineteen letters of the English alphabet. On the other hand, the Maskoke or Creek language, which was also reduced to written form by the missionaries, is close to that of the Seminole, and neither one is understood by the Choctaw and the Chickasaw. The Cherokee (Iroquoian family) have their own written language, the work of their famous tribesman, Sequoyah, who had perfected his wonderful invention of the Cherokee alphabet and placed the name of his people on the roll of the literate nations of the world by 1822.

There are proofs that some of the tribes now living in the state are the descendants of prehistoric Indian peoples who once lived here but whose names are not known. This region, like other parts of the United States, was inhabited by Indian tribes in prehistoric times, although their identification and number are difficult to determine since Oklahoma was in the path of a long series of mass migrations, probably from the west. Remarkable discoveries by archaeologists within the last twenty-five years have disclosed the dwelling places,

culture, and industries of the Indian peoples who lived in the Oklahoma region long before the tribes discovered by early explorers and mentioned by name in the first written records, beginning with those of the Coronado expedition in 1541.

The most spectacular archaeological discoveries were made from 1936 to 1938 in the excavation of a large mound near the town of Spiro in Le Flore County, through the interest of the Oklahoma Historical Society and under the direction of the University of Oklahoma. Many mounds of this type may be seen in eastern Oklahoma, a region particularly rich in archaeological remains. Some of the mounds are thought to have been erected for tribal religious purposes; others may have been built, and bark or skin lodges placed on top, as a protection against floods, since even after the weathering of centuries, some mounds forty feet in height and nearly always located in river valleys are found.

The Spiro Mound yielded objects that show the development, crafts, and culture of the people who laid them away in the earth possibly more than one thousand years ago. Among these objects are large ceremonial pipe bowls beautifully carved from stone, perfectly shaped arrowheads and bird points of flint, pottery jars and bowls, pieces of woven cloth and basketry, copper ornaments, and large conch- and sea-shell ornaments and gorgets etched with designs strangely like those of the old Mayan culture in southern Mexico. Some scientists claim that the Muskhogean tribes with their exotic village culture centering around high mounds in the Southeastern states were descendants of the Mound Builders. Exhibits from the Spiro Mound are on display in the Museum of the Oklahoma Historical Society at Oklahoma City, in the University of Oklahoma at Norman, and in the Philbrook Museum at Tulsa.

Other prehistoric tribes have been designated "Earth House People," the low mounds formed from the ruins of their dwellings seen on level or gently rolling uplands and occasionally on the steeper sides of hills and mountains in eastern Oklahoma, which is a part of the general region where such mounds are found. This region extends from the southern and southeastern parts of Missouri through Arkansas and includes all of East Texas and nearly half of Louisiana (from southwest to northeast). The late Joseph B. Thoburn after extensive research, prepared a manuscript on the subject, "The Northern Caddoan People of Prehistoric Times and the Human Origin of the Natural Mounds, So Called, of Oklahoma and Neighboring States," which is on deposit with the Oklahoma Historical Society. This paper points out that archaeologists have shown a measure of willingness to admit that these mounds are the work of human hands. In careful excavation of mounds of this class in Oklahoma, there was often found, at the center and near the bottom of the mound, "an ancient fireplace, containing wood ashes and bits of charcoal, with occasional fragments of pottery, flakes of flint, and bones" that had been split to extract the marrow. Study of these ancient dwellings suggested that the descendants of the Earth House People are represented by the Caddoan linguistic stock, whose ancient mass migration seems to have come at a later time than that of the Mound Builders.

The Caddoan was the most largely represented linguistic family in Oklahoma in the early historic period and included many tribes, large and small, that ranged over the eastern part of the state as far north and west as present Kay County and south to Love County. These people were sedentary in their habits, tilled the soil, and lived in villages composed of lodges, part of which were grass-thatched and part timber-framed and sod-covered. A lower type of circular mound, reported in archaeological study of western Oklahoma as ruins of dome-shaped, earth-covered dwellings of the Quiviran (Wichita) peoples in their

emigration from the Northeast, can be seen in Major, Garfield, Kingfisher, and Canadian counties. The Caddoan peoples had a comparatively dense population; and their culture, arts, crafts, and customs were remarkably uniform. The Caddoan linguistic family represented in the state today includes the Pawnee and a number of remnant tribes known under the names of Caddo and Wichita.

Other linguistic stocks than the Caddoan found in this area by the earliest European explorers included the Athapascan, the Shoshonean, and the Siouan. The Athapascan was represented by the Apache people, who depended on the buffalo for food, clothing, and shelter, following the vast herds that migrated north in summer and south in winter feeding on the prairie ranges. Apache tipi villages were found in Oklahoma near the western boundary. Wars with the Mexicans and the Indian tribes on the Southwestern plains in the eighteenth and nineteenth centuries pushed the Apache back into what is now New Mexico, where they are classed among the "Mountain tribes." These were the Apache proper, some of whose members are living among the people of the Plains tribes within the jurisdiction of the Anadarko Area Office in southwestern Oklahoma. These Apache should not be confused with the Kiowa-Apache, or Prairie Apache (referred to in some records as the Kataka), who came to the Plains from the Northwest and have long remained associated with the Kiowa. The Kiowa-Apache is a small Athapascan tribe that was never connected with the Apache proper in the historic period.

The Shoshonean linguistic family came out of the far Northwest in recent centuries and is represented in Oklahoma by the Comanche. Indian tradition and historical records refer to wars in western Oklahoma between the Plains tribes and the Ute, who are also of the Shoshonean family but do not live in the state today, though they formerly ranged south from

OKLAHOMA HISTORICAL SOCIETY

Indian police at Anadarko in 1894

the Panhandle on hunting expeditions. About the time the last great herd of buffalo was killed within this region, the Ute mounted their ponies and rode back to their old home country in the Rocky Mountains.

The Siouan linguistic family is represented by a number of tribes moved from other territories and states and settled in this region by the federal government. Among these Siouan tribes, the Osage and the Quapaw are indigenous to the country within the boundaries of the state.

Early colonial history reveals the pattern for relations with the Indian tribes, begun under British rule and later inherited and carried on by the United States. Administration of Indian affairs underwent changes and progress from time to time in the eighteenth and nineteenth centuries, yet the system remained and has had a vital place in the history of Oklahoma. Rivalries in trade in their American colonial empires had early led the French and the English to seek the Indian tribes as allies. During the Revolutionary War, former Indian trading posts became British military camps, a development which made friendship with the tribes on the frontier important to the colonies.

The Continental Congress provided for control of Indian affairs by passing an act on July 12, 1775, which divided the Indian country into departments or geographical divisions—Northern, Middle, and Southern. Commissioners were appointed for each department to treat with the Indian tribes, preserve peace and friendship, and watch British movements and intrigue. Under this organization, the first treaty made by the United States government was with the Delaware at Fort Pitt in 1778.

At the close of the war, because conditions necessitated further control of the Indian tribes, the Articles of Confederation gave Congress exclusive power and jurisdiction over Indian affairs. Two districts were designated in 1786, each under the supervision of a bonded superintendent: the Northern District included all the tribes living west of the Hudson and north of the Ohio rivers; the Southern District, all tribes south of the Ohio. Every tribe in these two districts laid claim to a region with definite boundaries recognized as tribal land, occupancy being the determining factor in fixing Indian title. The cession of tribal lands was to be secured through the consent of the tribal owners in return for payment of either money or goods or both. This principle of easing the Indian title was held the only just and right way to deal with the tribes and had been promoted through early Christian influences while the colonies were still under British rule.

The British system of making treaties with the Indian tribes was indirectly established in the United States in 1789, when the Constitution gave Congress the power to regulate trade with the Indians. Also, Indians not taxed were not counted as a part of the population in the states in apportioning representatives to Congress. The Dawes Act of February 8, 1887, providing for the allotment of certain tribal lands in severalty, declared every Indian born within the territorial limits of the United States a citizen, "entitled to all the rights, privileges, and immunities of such citizens." This act was amended on March 3, 1901, when "every Indian in the Indian Territory" was expressly declared a citizen of the United States. On June 2, 1924, Congress conferred citizenship upon all Indians born in the United States, yet today a few states still bar Indians from voting in state elections. In Oklahoma, however, all Indians can vote, and they have full rights as citizens under the state constitution.

Federal relations with the Indians were in the hands of the Secretary of War from 1789, when the War Department was created, until 1849, when the Indian Bureau was transferred to the newly established Department of the Interior. Today the Secretary of the Interior is the responsible administrator of the United States in the management of all property belonging to Indians classed "incompetent." This trust is administered through the Commissioner of Indian Affairs, the executive head of the Bureau of Indian Affairs (organized in 1824), which is divided into two coordinating parts: the Indian Office at Washington and the Field Service, whose personnel is in direct contact with the Indian people throughout the country.

Congress authorized the President in 1793 to appoint agents to live among the Indian tribes to hold their friendship and overcome any English influence. Three years later, at the suggestion of President Washington, Congress authorized the establishment of trading posts under the direction of the President, with the hope that through fair dealing and fair prices the Indians could be induced to trade with government stores, thus overcoming the evil influence of non-government traders who sold intoxicants to Indians.

The trading posts on Indian lands grew into industrial centers, and rights for public highways from one to another were soon granted in treaties with the tribes. Next the Indians were called upon to cede their lands adjoining these trading centers to the federal government. Finally, as white settlements advanced the frontier, the Indian tribes were forced to give up all their lands and move westward.

The movement that brought relations with the Indians into prominence in the Oklahoma region in the nineteenth century was promoted in Thomas Jefferson's administration. Even before this time, trading and hunting bands from the eastern tribes had crossed the Mississippi River. A Chickasaw trader was bartering with the Caddoan tribes living on the Arkansas River in Oklahoma in 1719. A band of Cherokee had been on the St. Francis River in what is now the state of Arkansas as early as 1775, and other Cherokee came to this location in 1794. A band of Delaware came west from Ohio and settled in Missouri in 1789. Choctaw hunting and war parties ranged west in the region between the Arkansas and the Canadian and the Red rivers as far as the Great Plains long before 1800.

Trade with the Osage brought about the first step toward establishing permanent settlement of Indian tribes within the boundaries of Oklahoma. The Chouteau fur-trading company of St. Louis, in rivalry with Spanish interests, induced a large band of Osage to move their permanent village in 1802 from the Osage River in Missouri to the Verdigris River in northeastern Oklahoma, a region that had long been claimed as Osage tribal hunting ground.

With the purchase of the vast territory of Louisiana in 1803, President Jefferson was convinced that the removal of all the eastern Indian tribes to this new western land was humanitarian and would contribute to their development and advancement. The cession of tribal lands in the East was to be secured from the tribes, and they were to locate permanently in a country to be set aside for them west of the Mississippi River. A Congressional act of March 26, 1804, authorized the President to make such a proposal to tribal authorities. Before the purchase of Louisiana, General William Henry Harrison had been delegated by President Jefferson to negotiate with the tribes living north of the Ohio River for the cession of their lands. Between 1803 and 1809, General Harrison completed treaties of cession for millions of acres in Wisconsin, Illinois, and Indiana from the Delaware, Piankashaw, Sauk, Fox, Potawatomi, Wea, and the "Kaskaskia tribe" that included remnants of the Kaskaskia, Michigamea, Cahokia, and Tamaroa. Eventually, after the Civil War, the last of these tribes were settled in the Indian Territory.

A band of Cherokee who visited Washington to interview President Jefferson in 1808 expressed their desire to move west. When the plan was approved, this Cherokee band moved beyond the Mississippi to the St. Francis and White rivers in present Arkansas, where a few of their kinsmen had already settled, and formed the division known as the Western Cherokee, later called Old Settler Cherokee when they moved to Oklahoma. In fulfillment of promises made in Washington for an exchange of a part of the tribal land in the East, the Western Cherokee were granted a large tract on the White River in Arkansas (then Missouri Territory) by the terms of the treaty of 1817.

This brought another problem since the tract assigned the Western Cherokee, as well as a promise to them of a hunting outlet to the west, encroached upon the Osage lands. Treaties with the Osage finally secured in 1818 and 1825 the cession to the United States of all Osage lands in what is now northern Arkansas and Oklahoma. Government commissioners unfamiliar with the country were also under the impression that the Western Cherokee lands affected the Quapaw, at that time living south of the Arkansas River; and a treaty with this tribe in 1818 secured the cession of all Quapaw lands extending into southern Oklahoma. Thus two treaties with indigenous tribes, the Osage north and the Quapaw south of the Arkansas River, cleared the way for the settlement of eastern tribes in the Oklahoma region; and by the treaty in 1828 the Western Cherokee exchanged their Arkansas lands for a country in northeastern Oklahoma and a hunting outlet extending west on the Plains.

The first eastern tribe assigned a country within the borders of the present state was the Choctaw, under the terms of a treaty made at Doak's Stand, Mississippi, in 1820, with General Andrew Jackson serving as United States commissioner appointed by the Secretary of War. Ten years later, on May 30, 1830, as President of the

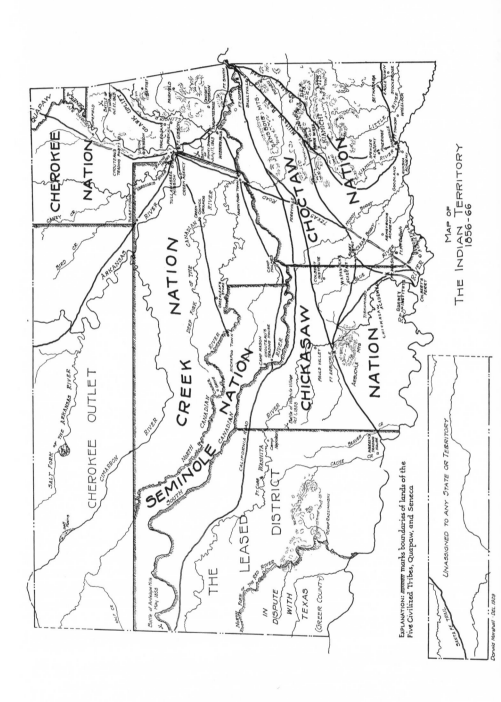

United States, he approved an act of Congress formally adopting the policy of removal of the eastern tribes and assigning them lands in the western part of the Louisiana Purchase. The country lying west of the state of Missouri and Arkansas Territory became known as the Indian Territory, bounded on the north by the Platte River and on the south by the Red River and extending to the limits of the United States on the west. The southern part of this original Indian Territory was unique in its development. After the Civil War, with further concentration in the Territory of many Indian tribes from Colorado, Nebraska, and Kansas, the present Oklahoma region became the real Indian Territory.

The decade following this Congressional action saw treaties made with each of the Five Civilized Tribes that provided for the cession of all tribal lands in the Southeastern states and the removal of the Indian people to the Indian Territory. This was a tremendous task for the federal government, attended by difficulties and trials for the army officers and government agents in charge, besides untold suffering, sickness, and death for thousands of Indian men, women, and children who were leaving their homes and country. The tragedies along the "Trail of Tears," as they ever afterward called this journey, and the many problems arising during the first years in the Indian Territory provided an unfavorable beginning, and proved almost disastrous, to the government's policy of removal.

The removal of the five tribes from the Southeast has had no parallel in United States history. Plans for an Indian state had been discussed with the foundation of the Republic and had been an inspiration to some Indian leaders, the Cherokee having all but attained the high goal. All of the five tribes had made remarkable progress by 1831, many families among them living in comfortable circumstances, owning good homes, Negro slaves, farms and plantations, and livestock. Some of the leaders owned trading establishments, ferries across large streams, stretches of turnpike roads, and inns on public highways. In some of the tribes, Christian churches and mission schools, supported largely by funds from the Indian governments, were flourishing. Wiping out all this high endeavor and attainment by removing these Indians to the wilderness beyond the Mississippi was a tragedy in their history.

One hope for a better future, obscured by the troubles of the time, was the provision made in the removal treaties with the Choctaw, the Creek, and the Cherokee guaranteeing their western lands under a patent issued by the United States to each nation. All of Oklahoma except the extreme northeastern corner was owned under one or another of these three patents: the northern part by the Cherokee, the central part by the Creek, and the southern part by the Choctaw. The northeastern corner of Oklahoma, now within the limits of Ottawa County, became the home of the mixed band of Seneca and Shawnee, including remnants of several other eastern tribes who came from Ohio in 1832; and the next year the Quapaw from the Red River region were ceded 150 sections in this region with a fee-simple title. The change from the old colonial policy of occupancy to the practice of granting the Indians patents in fee simple to their land was one of the most progressive and important steps in federal relations with the tribes. It made possible the holding of the lands under the Indian title for a comparatively long period—seventy-five years—during which a new, regional civilization, partly Indian and partly Anglo-American, grew and flourished. The establishment of their own institutions and laws by the Five Civilized Tribes eventually proved their settlement in the Indian Territory a successful experiment in government on the part of the United States.

The Chickasaw purchased the right of settlement among the Choctaw, and the

Seminole were settled among the Creek. The Choctaw and the Cherokee were the first nations established under republican forms of government in Oklahoma, with written constitutions and laws printed in both the native languages and English, forming something of a pattern for the separate governments finally organized by the rest of the five nations. Success of the venture was largely due to the influence and work of Protestant churches and mission boards, for the people of the Five Civilized Tribes took kindly to the Christian religion. Education based upon Christian principles and teaching was the ideal striven for in all the nations. Schooling in elementary subjects was promoted for both old and young. Courses in advanced subjects, besides homemaking for girls and improved methods of agriculture for boys, were required in the tribal academies or boarding schools operated under the supervision of the various church boards. Young men and, later, young women of ability and promise, after completing their work in these schools, were sent to schools and colleges in the East at the expense of the Indian governments, returning home in many instances trained as artisans or as teachers, preachers, lawyers, and physicians. The laws, newspapers, and books were published on printing presses in the nations, both in the Indian languages and in English. Substantial dwellings, from log cabins to handsome residences, were scattered throughout the country; individually owned herds of livestock fed on the open range; plantations were fenced and operated by some of the wealthy Indian citizens who were owners of Negro slaves. The general development of the Five Civilized Tribes in Southern ways and the recognition of Negro slavery under their laws finally involved them in the Civil War, in which most of the people of the five tribes sided with the Confederacy, although there were large factions, especially among the Cherokee and the Creek, who remained loyal to the Union.

The war retarded all progress in the Indian Territory, and its close brought changed conditions and a period of rehabilitation in the Indian nations. The people had been impoverished and the land laid waste, especially in the Cherokee Nation. Homes had to be rebuilt and schools and churches re-established. In addition, the building of transcontinental railroads and the advance of white settlement in the bordering states brought new problems in government.

New treaties demanded by the federal government from each of the Five Civilized Tribes at the close of the war were approved in 1866. These treaties allowed railroad building through Indian-owned lands and the settlement of Indian tribes from other parts of the United States within the borders of the nations. The latter movement had begun before the war, when lands owned under the Choctaw patent west of the ninety-eighth meridian had been leased to the government for the settlement of other tribes under the terms of the Choctaw-Chickasaw treaty of 1855. The Caddo and other small tribes seeking escape from the Texans had been moved in 1859 from their reservation on the Brazos River in Texas to land on the Washita River near present Anadarko.

During and immediately after the Civil War, the tribes in the West, including the Navaho, Cheyenne, Arapaho, Kiowa, Apache, Comanche, Kickapoo, and Sioux, were continually on the warpath, roused by the atrocities perpetrated on the tribes in California and by the surge of white immigration farther and farther into the Indian country. Wars, raids, and reprisals kept the United States Army busy throughout the West. Such widespread hostilities finally caused grave concern at Washington, for the warring Indians were seriously interfering with the construction of the first transcontinental railroad. An act of Congress provided for a peace commission —its members appointed by President Andrew Johnson in 1867 including several

MURIEL H. WRIGHT

Medicine Lodge Council, 1867

eminent army officers—to establish peace with the hostile tribes, remove the causes of war, and provide a plan for the civilization of the Indians. The following year, the Peace Commission made public its report setting forth a shameful record of Indian treaties broken by the government, of savage wars instigated by unprincipled white men, and of wanton massacres of Indian women and children by white people. In the meantime, the Commission had met the leaders of the Kiowa, Kiowa-Apache, Comanche, Cheyenne, and Arapaho in council on the Medicine Lodge River, in Kansas, and negotiated a treaty in October, 1867, providing reservations for these tribes in western Indian Territory, where their people were to take up farming for a living.

Colonel J. H. Leavenworth, appointed agent for the Kiowa and Comanche, established his agency near Fort Cobb, in present Caddo County, with the high hope of making farmers out of the Indians by peaceful methods. But the warriors, sea-soned in fighting, surly and angered over conditions, were not easily led into submission. Bands from all the tribes of the Plains, including those north in Kansas and Nebraska, went on the warpath during the late spring and summer of 1868. Some hostile Comanche made an attack on the Wichita Agency west of present Anadarko and threatened trouble in the western part of the Chickasaw Nation. In the autumn, many Indian war parties brought their families and established their villages on the Washita River near friendly bands who had had no part in the summer raiding. This time the government did not try peace talks and negotiation. Instead, the largest United States military expedition ever seen in the region came to western Oklahoma under the command of General Phillip H. Sheridan to break the power of the Indians in a winter campaign.

On the morning of November 27, 1868, during a heavy blizzard, a band of the friendly Cheyenne chief, Black Kettle, was suddenly attacked and annihilated by a

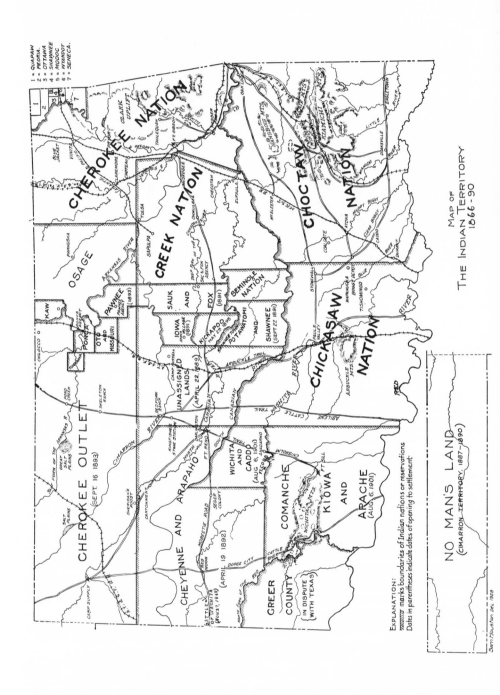

MAP OF
THE INDIAN TERRITORY
1866-90

EXPLANATION:
▨▨▨▨ marks boundaries of Indian nations or reservations
Dates in parentheses indicate dates of opening to settlement

NO MAN'S LAND
(CIMARRON TERRITORY, 1887-1890)

force of United States soldiers commanded by Colonel George A. Custer, in the so-called "Battle of the Washita," the site of which is about two miles west of the present town of Cheyenne in Roger Mills County. Black Kettle was killed, men, women, and children were mercilessly slaughtered, the village burned and destroyed, some Cheyenne captured, and 900 Indian ponies shot on the spot by order of Colonel Custer. News of the atrocity roused the Indians far and wide, and a special document signed by leaders of the Five Civilized Tribes was dispatched to Washington protesting such a massacre perpetrated under the excuse of war in the land where peaceful Indians were settled. Thereafter, the spirit of war and the hatred of white people were the prime motives of the Plains tribes in Oklahoma and elsewhere in the West, until retribution came with Custer's last stand on the Little Big Horn in Montana nearly a decade later. It is only in the light of such events that Indian life on the reservations in western Indian Territory into the early eighteen eighties can be interpreted.

Other tribes that had lived for a generation on reservations in the states and territories of the North and West moved to the Indian Territory by the terms of treaties with the federal government made shortly after the Civil War. The new reservations were located in the north central and the western parts of the Indian Territory. The end of Indian wars and the disappearance of the buffalo brought restricted living conditions and abrupt changes from the old tribal ways, along with close supervision under United States agency control.

Through the influence of the peace policy formulated and promulgated by President Grant in 1869 as the direct result of the report of the Peace Commission, Congress in 1870 barred the employment of army officers "in any civil capacity." President Grant then called upon religious organizations to supply agents for the Indian Service. The hearty response of the Orthodox Friends, or Quakers, resulted in the appointment of agents from their number for ten reservations in northern and western Indian Territory. Their promotion of the peace policy was criticized by outsiders who favored the continuation of military control over the Plains tribes, yet the employment and administration of Quaker agents until the early eighteen eighties accomplished much that promoted the welfare of the tribes. It should be noted, too, that a Quaker agent did not hesitate to call upon the military at Fort Sill before 1876 when trouble threatened at the Kiowa and Comanche Agency in one of the last outbreaks. Many army officers stationed at western military posts were interested in the Indian leaders and their people and made constructive contributions to the development of western Indian Territory.

Eventually the Indian Service replaced politically appointed agents with superintendents appointed through the United States Civil Service Commission. Then, by the Congressional act of March 3, 1871, treaty-making with Indian tribes and nations was abolished, and tribes were no longer recognized as "independent nations." This act brought transactions with the Indians under the immediate control of Congress, and henceforth what was formerly set down in "solemn treaties" was accomplished in simple agreements approved by the tribes.

Twenty years saw the marvelous settlement of the West, the creation of more territories and states leaving the Indian Territory as the last unorganized region. The driving of great herds of cattle north from Texas across the western Indian reservations to market in Kansas, the need for railroads in the industrial development of the Southwest, the demands of the "boomers" for opening the central part of the Indian Territory (unassigned to any Indian tribe) to white settlement—all foreshadowed the end of tribal life. The first step in breaking up Indian reservation life in this region was a Congressional act in

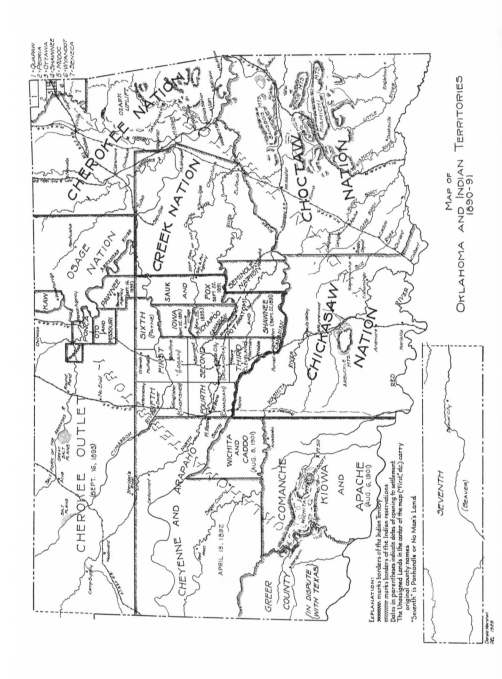

1887, known as the Dawes Severalty Act, which provided that lands belonging to certain Indian tribes should be allotted in severalty. Throughout the next ten years similar acts were passed that affected the remainder of the Indians in the Territory. This legislation eliminated tribal control of any area and left surplus lands to be opened to white settlers.

Political development of the Indian Territory under federal law had begun in 1834 when Congress provided for the extension of the jurisdiction of the United States courts in Arkansas to the Indian Territory, and eventually Fort Smith became a famous court town. All United States citizens who were arrested for crime in the Indian Territory were tried at Fort Smith, but Indian courts in the different nations tried their own citizens. However, if an Indian committed a crime with or against a United States citizen, he was tried in the United States court at Fort Smith. The first United States court for the Indian Territory was established in 1889 with headquarters at Muskogee, the law based upon the legal code of Arkansas. In nearly every session of Congress from this time until statehood in 1907, changes were made in the United States courts in the Territory.

The Unassigned Lands, a tract of approximately two million acres in central Indian Territory, were purchased from the Creek Nation and opened to white settlement in 1889. The next year Oklahoma Territory was organized in western Indian Territory with the provision that as soon as the Indian reservations were opened to white settlement, these lands should be annexed to the new commonwealth.

Another important act passed by Congress in 1889 authorized creation of a government commission to treat directly with the reservation Indians for the purchase of their surplus lands and with the Cherokee Nation for the purchase of the Cherokee Outlet (approximately six million acres), popularly (though erroneously) called the Cherokee Strip. This commission, known as the Cherokee Commission or the "Jerome Commission," was not favorably received by the tribes, but finally secured agreements for the purchase by the United States of the Cherokee Outlet lands and the surplus lands on the reservations. Seven openings of these land tracts to white settlement within a period of ten years added approximately fourteen million acres to Oklahoma Territory.

The Cherokee, Chickasaw, Choctaw, Creek, and Seminole nations to the east in the Indian Territory, in the meantime, had a separate history. The agencies in the nations had been consolidated at Muskogee in 1874 as the Union Agency, the name later changed to the Five Civilized Tribes Agency. In 1893 Congress provided for the creation of the Commission to the Five Civilized Tribes to secure agreements to extinguish tribal title to all their lands in Indian Territory. This commission, better known as the Dawes Commission, met strong opposition from the Indian citizens in all the nations, their officials and councils even refusing to meet the commissioners. It seemed that no agreements could ever be reached, and the Dawes Commission reported adversely to Washington. Word soon came back to the Territory, unofficially, that if no agreements were possible, Congress would arbitrarily confiscate all lands belonging to the Five Civilized Tribes. The press generally throughout the Indian Territory, most of the United States court officials, government appointees, and thousands of white people who had settled in the towns along the railroad favored taking over the Indian lands and dissolving the Indian governments. The Indian citizens, many of whom were persons of education, experience, and ability, were the proud owners of the land and had little respect for many of the white people who had no business in the country. These conditions imposed a great strain on the Indian governments and officials, and it is to their credit that they conducted themselves with dignity and maintained order among their people.

After four years of bitter political struggle, an agreement made at Atoka, Choctaw Nation, between the Dawes Commission and delegations from the Choctaw and Chickasaw nations, together with an agreement with the Creek and other provisions relating to all the Five Civilized Tribes, was incorporated in the Curtis Act of 1898 which provided that the Dawes Commission prepare a roll of the members of each tribe and complete the allotment of lands in severalty.

The work of the Dawes Commission covered a period of twelve years, during which thousands of clerks and other workers in the field were employed at the Commission headquarters in Muskogee. Approximately twenty million acres of land owned by the Five Civilized Tribes, or nearly half of the present state of Oklahoma, were surveyed and appraised. More than 250,000 persons appeared as claimants for a share in the tribal properties, many of whom had never seen the Indian Territory before nor had a part in tribal affairs. Reviewing the records of all claimants to de-

termine the actual members of each of the five tribes proved a tedious, slow work. When the rolls were finally closed in 1906, including all the "new born" (Indian children who were minors on March 4, 1905), the enrolled members of the Five Civilized Tribes totaled 77,942. Also, rolls for the Negro freedmen (former slaves in the nations and their descendants) had been made, and 23,325 of these people had been allowed limited allotments of land, although they did not share in the proceeds from other tribal-owned property in the Cherokee, Chickasaw, and Choctaw nations.

The Commission to the Five Civilized Tribes was abolished on July 1, 1905, the work of completing all its unfinished business devolving on the Secretary of the Interior; subsequently, a commissioner was appointed to take over this job at Muskogee. The Curtis Act had provided that the five Indian governments be dissolved on March 6, 1906, but when that date arrived, the tasks undertaken by the Dawes Commission were far from completed. Millions of acres of land were still unallotted, hundreds of thousands of acres of

MURIEL H. WRIGHT

Selection of allotments at Muskogee, April 1, 1899

tribal-owned coal and asphalt lands and rich timber lands were unsold, the funds from which were to be divided on a per capita basis among the Indian citizens of the respective nations. An enormous volume of business was handled by the commissioner's office at Muskogee in 1906, including supervision of millions of dollars coming in from leases and sales of coal, oil, gas, asphalt, marble, stone, gravel, town lots, and timber. Another act of Congress, approved on April 26, 1906—the most important law relating to the Five Civilized Tribes after the Curtis Act—provided for the continuation of the Indian governments in limited form until the tribal affairs were settled. Some of these matters are still in the process of settlement more than forty-four years later.

The allotted property of half-blood to fullblood Indians in Oklahoma was held in trust by the federal government from the time of allotment, the management and disposition of the land and the proceeds from it to remain under the supervision of the Indian agencies for a period of twenty-five years. The Burke Act of 1906 abolished this twenty-five-year period, individual Indians being allowed full management of their property when they were able to secure certificates of competence. Indians considered "incompetent" were held dependent for an indefinite period. In Oklahoma, there have been a number of cases of Indians—even some full bloods—who were successful in professions and in business who have never applied for certificates of competence for the management of their inherited Indian property. These persons have made their own way, aside from this restriction, yet they are still in "incompetent" class. Thus the term does not always indicate the real ability of the individual Indian.

Discovery of oil in commercial quantities brought great wealth to the members of the Osage Nation and to some individuals in other nations and reservations, especially the Creek and the Seminole. The further discovery of oil and gas and the opening of lead and zinc and coal mines in certain localities, together with the rapid agricultural and industrial development of Oklahoma, created a great demand for Indian-owned lands. The first two decades after allotment (1902) saw crime, graft, and sharp dealing by unprincipled persons against many Indians. Pressure from such people brought about liberalization of the government's policy of holding Indian property, and thousands of Indians who secured certificates of competence either gained little or lost all and were left impoverished. Over 27,000,000 acres of the 30,000,000 originally allotted are no longer owned by Oklahoma Indians. A significant percentage of the Indian people, however, have used their property to advantage, educated their children, and become useful citizens of the state. Those individuals who have been restricted in the use of their property under government supervision— the so-called "incompetent" class—in many instances are now land poor. The wholesale removal of restrictions and the granting of certificates of competency were stopped by the Indian Office in recent years and the trust period extended until 1956.

Reorganization for economy in the United States Indian Service was effected in July, 1947. Necessary reductions in the services least needed in Oklahoma were made, but basic services were continued for full bloods who remained under supervision, including medical service, education, extension and credit, soil and moisture conservation, road construction and maintenance. The Indian hospitals and eleven boarding schools in different parts of the state were continued in operation, including Chilocco Indian Agricultural School at Chilocco in Kay County, an institution that recently celebrated its seventy-fifth anniversary in the education of Indian boys and girls from many parts of the United States. In addition, these boarding schools were in operation in Oklahoma in 1951: Carter Seminary, Ardmore; Eufaula Boarding School, Eufaula; Jones Academy, Hartshorne; Wheelock Academy, Millerton; Sequoyah Vocational Training School, Tahlequah; Seneca Indian School, Wyandotte; Pawnee Indian School, Pawnee; Cheyenne-Arapaho Indian School, Concho; Riverside Indian School, Anadarko; and Fort Sill Indian School, Lawton.

In its reorganization in 1947, the Bureau of Indian Affairs made a number of administrative changes designed to limit long-range supervision of Indian matters from Washington by delegating greater authority to the Field Service, whose members are familiar with local problems and needs. Cash accounts of individual Indians involving $500 or less, hitherto kept under agency supervision, were closed at the agencies and the money turned over to the owners. For the first time in their lives, thousands of Indians were allowed to lease their own land, collect rents, and handle their money. Some have managed their business to advantage and have been successful in good jobs in industry in the cities and towns of the state. Others, after spending the money collected in advance from the one- to five-year leases made on their land, are in difficulty. Development of oil fields in southwestern Oklahoma has recently brought wealth to many individual Indians in the Anadarko Area region, among whom are seen comfortable homes, well-stocked ranches, and the latest models in automobiles—a situation comparable to that of the Osage people in their richest days.

In 1951, Indian Office supervision in Oklahoma was divided into two areas: the Muskogee Area Office for the east side of the state, and the Anadarko Area Office for the west side. Within the Muskogee Area Office are the Five Civilized Tribes Agency at Muskogee and the Quapaw Subagency at Miami. Within the Anadarko Area Office are the Kiowa-Comanche-Apache and the Wichita-Caddo agencies at Anadarko, the Cheyenne-Arapaho Subagency at Concho, the Pawnee Subagency at Pawnee, and the Shawnee Subagency at Shawnee. The Osage Agency at Pawhuska is a separate office, maintained by Osage tribal funds, for conducting all business relating to the Osage tribal properties.

Although there are no tribal reservations in Oklahoma like those before 1900, there are settlements in different parts of the state, generally in the region of the agencies, in which the fullblood Indians are in majority—where relatives and friends selected adjoining land at the time of allotment or have purchased land since. The tribal language may still be used in such a community, and generally there is an Indian church—Baptist, Methodist, Presbyterian, Friends—where services are conducted by a native preacher. The older people in these settlements oftentimes dress in a way that recalls the last tribal days, the women wearing gay-colored shawls in summer or bright blankets in winter—both men and women in some instances still wearing their hair in two braids over their shoulders. In some localities in central and western Oklahoma, the tipi, wickiup, or willow-brush arbor may be seen in the yard of the modern frame house.

Life in these communities is rural, and in many of them, especially in the hill country of eastern Oklahoma, the people are very poor. These Indian settlements are isolated, often accessible only by worn wagon trails. Their problems concern poor land or soil erosion, health, and education. For many years, special Indian day schools were operated by the United States Indian Office in the more isolated Indian areas, where there were no public schools because of the lack of state funds in communities with large tracts of nontaxable Indian-owned lands. (It should be noted here that all Indians with supervised land holdings pay taxes on personal property and income under the law of the state; and that those who purchase or inherit land are subject to full taxation on such property just as any other citizen is.) Today, the only Indian community with a special day school is

Mt. Zion, in McCurtain County, under the supervision of the Office of Indian Education in the Oklahoma Department of Public Instruction.

For a long period, schools in Oklahoma enrolling Indian pupils of one-quarter or more Indian blood have been enriched by funds from the federal government, the distribution of the money being handled through the various Indian agencies and supervised by a number of educational field agents. In August, 1947, the United States government entered into a contract with Oklahoma for the distribution and supervision of these Indian education funds by the state Department of Public Instruction. As a result the Office of Indian Education was established in this department on September 1, 1947. Orphans and children from broken homes, especially older boys and girls (of one-fourth Indian blood or more) who have no high school opportunities, attend the Indian boarding schools operated by the federal government in the state, preference being given to fullblood applicants. These schools offer home training and other advantages that cannot be given in public schools.

Indian tribal life was regarded as contemptibly backward for many years, and the suppression of old customs and habits was encouraged by government agencies in their effort to fit the tribes into patterns of civilized life. Added to this suppression was the scorn for everything Indian expressed by the civilian population that soon dominated the frontier. These attitudes, carried to the extreme, had a disspiriting effect upon the individual Indian, racial pride suffered, and much that was worthy of preservation from tribal ways was lost. The old ceremonials were abandoned as survivals of barbarism, tribal dances were outlawed on the reservations, and Indian languages were prohibited in the Indian schools. The native arts and crafts deteriorated and in many instances disappeared entirely. The older Indians, who had seen the last treaties and agreements made with

the United States government which had brought the final dissolution of tribal organizations and governments, came more and more to think their plight due to the "broken treaties" on the part of agencies representing the United States. Soon after World War I, the more enlightened and forceful Indian leaders and other persons who were members of national organizations interested in Indian welfare publicized conditions in the tribes and brought pressure on the Indian Bureau at Washington for alleviation of existing conditions. Congress enacted a number of laws promoting Indian life, and a nationwide study by a specially appointed board of the Institute for Government Research finally succeeded in turning the tide into constructive channels.

One of the basic problems for all Indians living in isolated communities or on reservations was economic—there were no jobs or opportunities to make a living at home and no system of credit for improving conditions in the community. To remedy this situation, Congress passed the Wheeler-Howard Act, approved June 18, 1934, the principal provision of which authorized the creation of a special revolving fund to be loaned for co-operative purposes to the organized tribes under government supervision. When it was found that this act did not fit the conditions and needs of the Oklahoma Indians, Congress passed the Oklahoma Indian Welfare Act (49 Stat. 1967), sometimes referred to as the Thomas-Rogers Bill, approved on June 26, 1936. It provides that any ten or more officially enrolled members of any Oklahoma Indian tribe, or their descendants, can organize for their common welfare, adopt a constitution and by-laws under certain rules and regulations, and secure a federal charter from the Secretary of the Interior as a local co-operative association. This charter conveys any powers properly vested in a body corporate under the laws of Oklahoma, the right to participate in the revolving credit fund, and other rights and

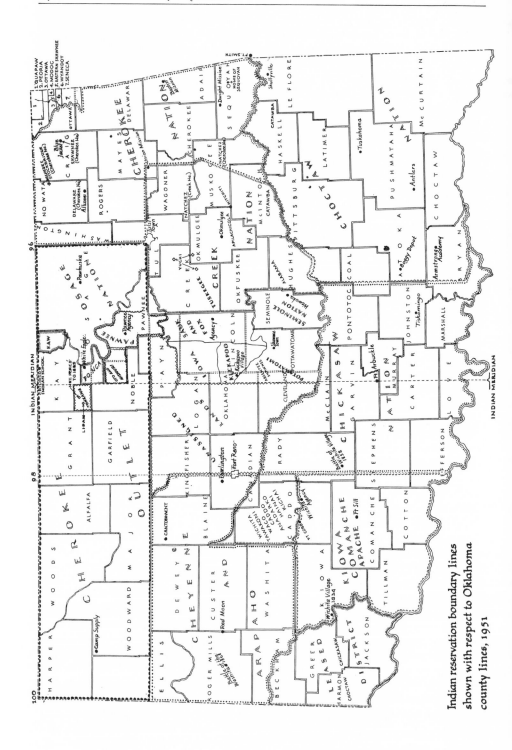

Indian reservation boundary lines
shown with respect to Oklahoma
county lines, 1951

privileges secured as an organized Indian tribe under the Wheeler-Howard Act. Aside from tribal organization, the Oklahoma Indian Welfare Act also provides that Indian community groups can organize credit associations for participation in the revolving credit fund under government supervision.

Oklahoma Indians were conservative in taking advantage of this legislation, eighteen tribes and parts of tribes, comparatively small groups, finally organizing and receiving charters for incorporation from 1937 to 1942. Other Indian groups were subsequently organized, making a total in 1949 of fifty-one tribal and credit associations in Oklahoma. Several have been closed because of an inadequate volume of business or for other reasons. Among the most successful of these associations are the Adair County Association, Cherokee County Association, Choctaw County Association, Le Flore County Association, Muskogee County Association, and McCurtain County Association. Five tribal groups are in operation: Seneca-Cayuga Tribe of Oklahoma; Wyandotte Indian Tribe of Oklahoma; Caddo Indian Tribe of Oklahoma; Kiowa, Comanche, Apache Tribal Business Committee; and Iowa Tribe of Oklahoma. The official report on the agricultural credits allowed in these organizations showed a good record on June 30, 1947: of the $1,899,414 loaned to 2,827 individuals, a total of $1,294,712 had been repaid on the principal, with $597,216 outstanding on long-term loans. A total of 1,821 individuals had repaid in full, 976 were in process of payment on long-term loans, and 30 had been written off with loans cancelled in whole or in part as uncollectible. The tribes and associations borrow money from the revolving credit fund established by Congress at 1 per cent and make loans to individual Indians at 4 or 5 per cent. Most of the loans made are for financing farming operations, a limited number have been made to buy farms, and some have been made to buy out the property interests of heirs in complicated inheritance cases.

The records of the negotiations for many of the treaties and agreements, particularly for closing the reservations in western Oklahoma after 1890, reveal a shameful chapter in the history of federal relations with the Indians. Legislation enacted in Congress in 1946 seeks to mend the "broken faith" with the tribes by adjusting through the Indian Claims Commission all tribal claims arising out of treaties and agreements. This commission, consisting of three members appointed by the President, will have the same powers as a court to review claims of any tribal group against the government in the United States and Alaska. Its work is to be completed within ten years and its final determinations reported to Congress. The Indian Claims Commission Act, termed "one of the most important, equitable, and constructive laws dealing with Indian affairs," gives Indian tribes the opportunity to be heard on the question of enforcement of the treaty rights of which they were deprived in the past.

Within the past twenty years, general interest in tribal history and traditions and arts and crafts has revived and grown among the Indians themselves, and a deeper appreciation and understanding have been aroused among the white citizenry, especially in Oklahoma. The development of Indian arts and crafts has been promoted since 1935 through the Indian Arts and Crafts Board, which consists of five members appointed by the Secretary of the Interior for terms of four years each. Through the work of the board a well-planned program of native weaving and basketry is making progress among the Cherokee and the Choctaw in eastern Oklahoma. The Sequoyah Weavers' Association with headquarters at the Sequoyah Indian Vocational School near Tahlequah is gaining a national reputation for its beautiful homespun materials. A new building has been opened at Anadarko to display the arts and crafts and historical exhibits of the tribes in western Oklahoma, with the idea of reviving interest in the native arts among these people and of furnishing a center for the commercial distribution of authentic Indian workmanship. In the field of Indian painting, the Art Department in the University of Oklahoma accomplished a great work in the late nineteen twenties in the training of five Kiowa artists who have won worldwide fame. Their accomplishments have been an inspiration in the revival of Indian art and the development of Indian artists throughout the United States.

In some towns and cities, social clubs and other organizations have been formed, with membership limited to enrolled Indians and their descendants, to study tribal history and traditions, to promote the welfare of underpriviledged Indian groups, or to secure the final settlement of tribal-owned properties and claims due under former treaties and agreements. The people in some fullblood Indian settlements meet annually or at specially designated times to participate in tribal dances and ceremonials, some of which are open to the public. Even the more primitive tribes in Oklahoma, with many old people still living who were born and reared in the customs and habits of the Stone Age, have made a creditable record. Indian life was always one of development and changing ways through the centuries; today, it continues to bring greater promise in art and culture and other accomplishments in meeting the new order of life in America.

An outstanding event in Oklahoma, developed within the past fifteen years, is the American Indian Exposition, directed exclusively by Indians of southwestern Oklahoma and held annually in August at Anadarko. Indians from Oklahoma and other states participate. The Exposition is serving to promote a better understanding and knowledge of Indian life; entertainment features based on Indian history and customs and exhibits of arts and crafts and of agricultural and industrial products draw

U. S. INDIAN SERVICE

William Karty, a Kiowa from Comanche, Oklahoma, who was manager of the 1940 American Indian Exposition at Anadarko

thousands of visitors from all over the United States and from foreign countries.

Since the founding of the first mission station in Oklahoma, Union Mission among the Osage in 1820, Christian missions and churches have had a far-reaching influence on all the tribes. Religious meetings and continuing educational work among the Indian people in the state, under the auspices of the different denominations, are remarkable. The annual association among the Cherokee, held near Tahlequah under the auspices of the Southern Baptist Convention, with as many as 1,500 fullblood Cherokee congregated and singing the old hymns in the native language is an affecting sight. Among the special Indian schools is Bacone College at Muskogee, operated under the auspices of the Northern Baptist Convention and attended by young men and women from many tribes in Oklahoma and other states. The Indian Mission Conference of the Methodist church holds annual conferences at appointed places in Oklahoma, attended by a large representation of Indian members of the church from different tribes over the state.

The Presbyterian church, U.S.A., carries on work generally in north central and eastern Oklahoma, and until 1948 operated the Dwight Indian Training School in Sequoyah County, the outgrowth of Dwight Mission established among the Cherokee in Oklahoma in 1829. The Presbytery of Indian, Presbyterian church, U. S., counts some country churches in southern Oklahoma, from Beachtown in McCurtain County to Milburn in Johnston County, and sponsors the Goodland Indian Orphanage in Choctaw County, established in 1848, the oldest mission in continuous operation in Oklahoma. Comanche Mission, Dutch Reformed church, is a unique Indian community center on an Indian land tract near Lawton. The Catholic church has a number of small mission schools over the state, one of the oldest being St. Patrick's Mission at Anadarko. The majority of the Osage are members of the Catholic church. The Friends support works at Wyandot Mission, at Seneca Council House at a crossroads in the Ozark hills a few miles southeast of Wyandotte, at Hominy on the Osage Reserve, and at Kickapoo Friends' center near McLoud.

A charter was issued by the secretary of the state of Oklahoma to a religious sect called the "Native American church," organized by a group of Indians from western Oklahoma for the express purpose of promoting "their belief in the Christian religion" with the use of peyote for the sacrament and for the continuance of certain old tribal religious beliefs. This organization has scattered membership in western Oklahoma and holds meetings generally in special tipi lodges near the homes of members. The great majority of the people of every Indian tribe in the state, however, belong to the old Christian church denominations.

Both world wars saw the Indian people of Oklahoma active in the service of their country, the young people in the armed forces, the people at home investing heavily in war bonds and giving their time and service to the Red Cross and other war organizations. Indians from the state, from the highest-ranking officers in the army and navy to the enlisted soldiers and sailors, served their country with distinction and honor.

Indian life in Oklahoma reflects the strength of character of this ancient people, and our Christian democracy has furthered their development. The unique experiment of the removal of the Indian tribes to Oklahoma by the government, begun under inauspicious circumstances in the eighteen thirties, has resulted in a degree of mutual tolerance, understanding, and affection between two races which has no counterpart elsewhere in America.

ALABAMA

The name Alabama, sometimes spelled Alibamu, has been said to be a corruption of the Choctaw term *alba'lmo,* "thicket cleared," which is a contraction of the Choctaw words *alba,* "thicket," and *almoh,* "cleared." (Many old Choctaw names are highly abbreviated phrases or mnemonics of the original terms.) One of the earliest references to the Alabama calls them *Atilamas,* undoubtedly from the Choctaw *att'ilami,* "they live separately [from us]," from the Choctaw *atta,* "to live," and *ilaminko* or *ilabinko,* "separately." This meaning is in harmony with the main thread of Alabama tribal history to this day.

The Alabama are of the Muskhogean linguistic family. In Oklahoma, they have been counted as a part of the Creek Nation since their removal west, continuing their early alliance with the old Creek confederacy that once held sway in the Alabama-Georgia region. Down to the time of statehood in Oklahoma, they had their own town and square-ground, and were noticeably different in their appearance and customs from the Creek proper. Their language is practically identical with that of the Koasati (q.v.), nearly that of the Choctaw-Chickasaw.

Early writers described the Alabama as a warlike people, a description consistent with their record in later tribal history. They were industrious in growing their crops and engaged in raising cattle, horses, and hogs before their removal to the Indian Territory.

◆ **Present Location.** The Alabama live in the vicinity of Weleetka, in Okfuskee County, southeastward into Hughes County. The largest Alabama community is located approximately three miles south of Weleetka, and is known as the Bird Creek settlement, although there is no Bird Creek in the vicinity. The settlement was named for Fushut-Chee Yarhola, who represented Alabama Town in the House of Kings in the Creek Council. He also served as a lighthorseman and was a man of considerable importance in the old Creek Nation. His name *Fushut-Chee* means "Bird Creek" in the Creek language, hence the name of the settlement where he lived. A large number of Alabama live near Livingston, Texas, on the Alabama-Coushatti (i.e., Koasati, q.v.) Reservation.

◆ **Numbers.** 175 Alabama were estimated to be in Oklahoma in 1950. The United States Indian Office census for 1944 gives a total population of 152 for the "Alabama-Quassarte Tribal Town" (i.e., Alabama-Koasati), which does not include those tribal members not organized under the Oklahoma Indian Welfare Act. A special census of the forty-four tribal towns in the Creek Nation, by the Creek officials in 1890, lists the population of Alabama Town at 171. The Indian Office census for 1910 gives 192 Alabama, counting 111 in Louisiana, not including those who were among the Creek in Oklahoma. The total numbers of the Alabama are approximately 500 living in Oklahoma, Texas, and Louisiana (1950). A government census of the Creek Nation in 1832–3, before the removal west, gives two Alabama towns with an Indian population of 321. A French record one hundred years before this gives six Alabama towns with 400 men, indicating a total population of about 1,600.

◆ **History.** The Muskogee migration legend tells of a prehistoric migration of the "Atilamas" or Alabama from the West portraying them as one of the most ancient and valorous of four tribes that settled east of the Mississippi River. The tribe was discovered in northern Mississippi west of the Chickasaw (q.v.), by De Soto in 1541. A century and a half later, the Alabama were living on the Alabama River below the junction of the Coosa and the Tallapoosa within present Alabama, the river and the state perpetuating the name of this important tribe.

The Alabama began moving to new locations at the close of the French and Indian War (1763), the main part of the tribe remaining among the Upper Creek at the Red Ground or Kanchati. During the next half-century tribal bands settled at different times among the Seminole of Florida, among the Koasati on the Tombigbee River, and among the Caddo in Louisiana.

The Alabama at Red Ground were counted among the fiercest warriors in the Red Stick War, or Creek War, in 1813–14. After their defeat by the armed forces of the United States, they were compelled to move north of their old location on the Alabama River, some settling in a village that took the name Tawasa, and others, among the Upper Creek in the vicinity of present Wetumpka, in Elmore County, Alabama. The people of these villages moved west to the Indian Territory with the recently hostile Creek in 1836. They finally settled in the vicinity of Weleetka, in Okfuskee County, Oklahoma, where Alabama Creek bears the name of the tribe.

The most prominent man of Alabama descent in the Creek Nation, Ward Coachman (Cochamy) was principal chief of the Creek Nation in 1876–79, serving at different times as member of the Creek National Council and as delegate to Washington in behalf of the nation. He spoke Alabama, Creek, and English, was an able administrator, and had a political organization of his own that counted among its members several of the leading mixed-blood Creek. Chief Coachman's maternal grandmother was Sophia Durant, a re-

markable woman in Creek history and a sister of the noted Alexander MacGillivray, the "Emperor of the Creeks" (*see* Creek).

Under the terms of the agreement between the United States and the Creek in 1901, all the Alabama living in the Creek Nation were enrolled as citizens of the nation, and each received an allotment of 160 acres from the Creek domain.

◆ **Government and Organization.** Until the close of Creek government in 1906, the Alabama were considered one of the forty-four Creek towns, with representation in the House of Kings and the House of Warriors under the constitution and laws of the Creek Nation. Alabama Town was in 1951 entitled to two members of the Creek Tribal Council, elected by their town members and sworn into office by the principal chief of the Creek.

Members of the tribal towns, Alabama and Quassarte No. 1 (*see* Koasati), living in northeastern Hughes County, were organized in 1938 as the "Alabama-Quassarte Tribal Town," with a charter from the Secretary of the Interior under provisions of the Oklahoma Indian Welfare Act of 1936. A constitution was adopted by vote of the town members, certification being signed by Sandy Wesley and Daniel Beaver, the Alabama Town chief, serving as the "Alabama-Quassarte Governing Committee." The charter was ratified by a vote of the adult members of the "Tribe" (thirty-six for, three against, more than 30 per cent voting) on May 2, 1939, with certification signed by Henry Scott, town king, and Porter Coachman, secretary, of "Alabama-Quassarte Tribal Town."

Baptist missionary work flourished among the Alabama, and resulted in the organization of the Alabama Church in 1874, some miles north of present Weleetka. Outgrowths of this work were the Arbeca Church in the Creek town, "Abihka in the West," near the site of Bryant, in Okmulgee County; and Wetumka Church, near Wetumka, in Hughes County.

◆ **Contemporary Life and Culture.** Fullblood Alabama predominate in the tribe, including mixed Alabama-Creek-Koasati. There is some admixture by intermarriage with white people. The Alabama engage principally in farming and stock raising.

◊ **Ceremonials and Public Dances.** Most of the Alabama, if not all, are members of the Baptist church and no longer observe the "Green Corn Dance" and ceremonials at their old square-ground near Weleetka.

As a "red town" or "war town," the Alabama were formerly always classed the best players of Indian ball. Challenge for a game in the Creek Nation was made by one town to another, the team of each having an equal number of players, sometimes as many as sixty on a side. Running, dodging, and wrestling were the order in the play to catch the small ball with the ballsticks. Each stick was about twenty-seven inches long with a small cup-like loop at one end, a pair of sticks being carried by every player. The game began by tossing the ball at the center of the field, the object being to catch and throw the ball to the goal against interference by the opposing team. In the game played by the Alabama and other towns among the Creek, a goal formed by two poles planted from three to six feet apart, between which the ball was thrown to make a tally, stood at opposite ends of the ball ground (sometimes two hundred yards long). Ball games between the Alabama and Kialegee (Kealedji) towns near the present Hughes-Okfuskee County line are still remembered as the hardest-fought games in the Creek Nation. Suggested Readings: Swanton, "Social Organization, Creek," in *42 Ann. Rep.,* Bur. Amer. Ethnol.; ——, *Early History of the Creek;* ——, *Indians of Southeastern U. S.;* Debo, *The Road to Disappearance;* Meserve, "Chief Samuel Checote," in *Chron. of Okla.,* Vol. XVI, No. 4.

ANADARKO

The name Anadarko is from *Nadako* in the Anadarko language, signifying "those who ate of the honey of the bumblebee," an interpretation given in a Caddo origin legend. The spelling Anadarko is the approved anglicized form based on *Anadaca, Anadahcoe,* or similar phonetic forms of the tribal name found in early published records of the nineteenth century.

The Anadarko belong to the Caddoan linguistic family and were one of the southern group of eight tribes that made up the Hasinai confederacy (*see* Hainai), whose villages were south of the Sabine River in what is now East Texas when they were first noted in the seventeenth century. The language of the tribe is almost identical with that of the Kadohadacho, or Caddo proper, a closely related people.

Early records described the Anadarko as well built and robust in physique, somewhat darker in complexion than the Caddo. They were highly regarded for their honesty, industry, and good humor. They were agriculturists and engaged in the manufacture of salt. Their customs and habits were similar to those of the Caddo (q.v.).

◊ **Present Location.** The Anadarko are now a part of the Caddo in Caddo County, Oklahoma.

◊ **Numbers.** An estimated 449 descendants of the Anadarko live in Oklahoma, the remnant of the tribe having long been counted with the Caddo (q.v.), whose numbers have increased approximately 133 per cent since the close of reservation days in 1901. The last available separate census of the Anadarko in 1857 gives 210 members of the tribe living on the Brazos Reserve in Texas (*see* Caddo). An official report in 1851 lists the number of the tribe at 202, not including tribal bands among the Caddoan peoples north of Red River.

An enumeration for 1847 shows 450 Anadarko. Before this date, their census reports in government records are incomplete, but it was known that their numbers had been greatly diminished in the eighteenth century.

◆ **History.** The chronicles of De Soto's Expedition of 1541–42 give the names of a number of tribes west of the Lower Mississippi, among them that of the Nondacao, a people who have been identified in ethnological studies as the Nadako or Anadarko. The tribal range was southwest of the Kadohadacho or Caddo proper, in the region of the Angelina and Neches rivers in East Texas. Until 1763, the Anadarko were identified among the Caddoan tribes in French government relations in Louisiana.

Their ranks weakened as a result of European trade and political rivalries in the Southwest, the Anadarko became closely allied with the Kadohadacho, and most of them were living in the tribal villages not far south of the present southeastern limits of Oklahoma in 1800. Peaceful bands of the tribe were living in the vicinity of Nacogdoches, Texas, in 1828.

After the Caddo treaty of 1835, under the terms of which the "Caddo Nation" (*see* Caddo) surrendered all claims to lands in Louisiana and agreed to move beyond the limits of the United States, the Anadarko and their Caddoan allies left East Texas and settled west on the Brazos River. They were among the tribes who signed peace treaties with the Republic of Texas in 1843 and 1844, and were represented at a peace council in 1845. Friendly trading relations with other Indians were carried on at Torrey's Trading House, established by law of the Texas Republic in 1843 near present Waco, yet the animosity of the Texas settlers against them was a constant menace to the peaceful tribes on the Brazos.

With the accession of Texas in 1846, United States commissioners made a treaty at Council Springs (May 15, 1846) near the Brazos River, which was signed by the chiefs and leaders of ten tribes—Penateka Comanche, Hainai, Anadarko, Caddo, Lipan, Tonkawa, Kichai, Tawakoni, Wichita, and Waco—acknowledging the United States as their protector. This treaty, the only one signed by the Anadarko with the United States, was far reaching in the promotion of peaceful relations with the Texas tribes. It is a significant fact in the history of the development of the Indian Territory that bands of nearly all these tribes were living in this region at the time.

With the exception of a few bands north of Red River, the Anadarko, Caddo proper (Kadohadacho), and Hainai lived in a settlement or "village" on the Brazos River, forty-five miles west of Torrey's Trading House. In May, 1846, special United States Commissioner Robert S. Neighbors visited this village and reported the Indians here peaceful, healthy, and prosperous. The Anadarko chief, Iesh, better known in the annals of Texas by his Spanish name, José María, was principal chief of these tribes for many years. Writing about the Brazos tribes in 1851, Captain Randolph B. Marcy said: "They are commanded by a very sensible old chief, called 'José María,' who feels a deep interest in the welfare of his people; and is doing every thing in his power to better their condition."

Efforts on the part of government agents to set aside a reserve for the tribes that signed the treaty of Council Springs finally resulted in 1854 in the Texas legislature's authorizing United States officials to select such a reservation. The tract chosen consisted of 37,152 acres, known as the Lower Reserve, located about twelve miles south of Fort Belknap, in Young County (*see* Caddo). The Anadarko and Caddo proper under the leadership of José María, in addition to the Waco, Tawakoni, Kichai, Tonkawa, Lipan, and some Delaware and Shawnee were soon settled on the reservation, grouped in tribal villages.

While all the tribes on the Lower Reserve were commended for good behavior,

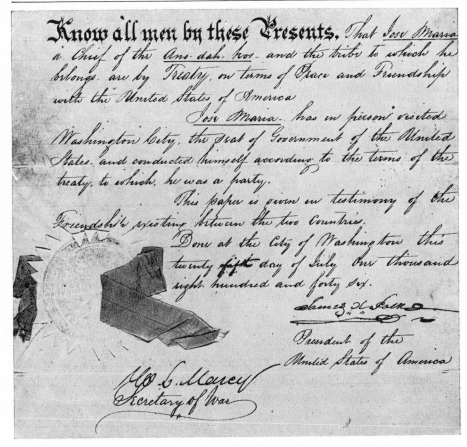

Know all men by these Presents. That José María a Chief of the Ana-dah-kos and the tribes to which he belongs are by Treaty, on terms of Peace and Friendship with the United States of America

José María has in person visited Washington City, the seat of Government of the United States and conducted himself according to the terms of the treaty, to which, he was a party.

This paper is given in testimony of the Friendship existing between the two Countries.

Done at the City of Washington this twenty fifth day of July One thousand eight hundred and forty six.

James K. Polk

President of the United States of America

W. L. Marcy
Secretary of War

President James K. Polk certifies that José María has conducted himself according to the treaty of peace and friendship. From the original document in the Oklahoma Historical Society

industry, and peaceable conduct, the Anadarko and Caddo were particularly noted in this respect. Through trading relations in Louisiana and Texas for more than a century, they had advanced in civilization and had adopted some conveniences in their homes.

These favorable conditions ended abruptly in December, 1858. Hostility of some of the Texans in the vicinity flamed up against the Indians of the Lower Reserve, apparently instigated through the jealousy and animosity of a former government employee who had been dismissed from the agency service. The situation became so tense from the fear and hatred that spread among the white settlers and from alarm among the Indians that leading Texas officials and United States agents immediately pushed plans to remove the tribes from the Lower Reserve to the Indian Territory north of Red River. In the spring of 1859, government agents selected new locations for the Texas tribes along the Washita River west of the ninety-eighth meridian, a region known in the Indian Territory as the "Leased District," since it had been leased to the United States for the settlement of "other Indian tribes" by the terms of the Choctaw-Chickasaw treaty of 1855.

A council to further the permanent settlement of the Texas tribes was called by government officers at Fort Arbuckle on July 1, 1859. The chiefs and leaders of nine tribes were present, José María representing the Anadarko.

About the time of this council, word suddenly came to the Brazos Agency that the Texans had set a day to massacre all the Lower Reserve Indians. Superintendent Neighbors immediately hastened preparations for the removal of all the tribes to the Indian Territory. Under the excitement of the time, the Texas troops on guard around the Reserve prevented the Indians from gathering up their horses and livestock from the open range. By the evening of August 1, 1859, 1,430 Indian men, women, and children, many of them on foot, had set out under military escort for the Washita River. They made the 170-mile journey by forced marches in fifteen days, arriving at their destination exhausted and sick from the stress of travel in the worst heat of August. All the tribes were in an impoverished condition, especially the Anadarko and the Caddo, their hurried departure from the Brazos Reserve having compelled many of them to come away empty-handed, leaving their personal belongings, household goods, and most of their livestock.

Their tribal affairs were under the supervision of the Wichita Agency, which was soon established on Leeper Creek about four miles east of the present town of Fort Cobb, in Caddo County.

The Anadarko had hardly recovered from their recent removal and were building their houses and breaking land for their new settlement on the Washita when they, with the other tribes of the Indian Territory, were drawn into the Civil War. On August 12, 1861, Commissioner Albert Pike secured a treaty in behalf of the Confederate States at the Wichita Agency, which bore the name of José María, principal chief of the Anadarko, along with the names of other tribal chiefs and leaders living in this region. A report by the Confederate Indian agent the following year stated that the Anadarko were prospering in their new location on the Washita. Chief José María remained loyal to the Confederacy until his death, which was not recorded but seems to have occurred about the time the war came to the Washita with the burning of the Wichita Agency and the massacre of the Tonkawa (q.v.) by Northern Indians in 1862. Soon afterward, a large part of the Anadarko went north with the Caddo to Kansas, where they remained as refugees behind the Union lines until the end of the war. From the time of their return to the Washita region in 1867, they were listed under the name "Caddo" at the Wichita Agency. As a part of the Wichita and Affiliated Tribes (*see* Wichita), they were allotted lands in severalty on the Wichita-Caddo Reservation in 1901.

◆ **Government and Organization.** All affairs regarding descendants of the Anadarko as a part of the Caddo are under the supervision of the Wichita-Caddo Agency in the Anadarko Area Office, only the name of the town in southwestern Oklahoma perpetuating that of the ancient Nadako tribe. In tribal times, their government was like that of the Kadohadacho or Caddo proper (q.v.).

◆ **Contemporary Life and Culture.** By intermarriage and close association with the Caddo proper, the Anadarko have lost their tribal identity and are now known under the name Caddo. Most of them live in rural communities in Caddo County.

Suggested Readings: Schoolcraft, *Historical and Statistical Information, U. S. Indian Tribes;* Swanton, *Source Material, Caddo;* Commissioner of Indian Affairs, *Report, 1859;* Grant Foreman, *Last Trek of the Indians.*

APACHE

The name Apache is probably derived from *apachu,* meaning "enemy," the Zuñi name for the Navaho, who were called "Apaches de Nabju" by the early Spaniards in New Mexico. Another possible derivation has been suggested in the Spanish from *'axwa'* (duo-plural *'axwa' ta*), an Apache Mohave (Yavapai) term meaning "man" or "people." The Apache call themselves *N'de,* or the variants *Tinde* or *Inde,* from the original term *tinneh,* meaning "people," which is the name of the tribal division including the Navaho. The fact that the Navaho call themselves *Dïnë* (pronounced "Din-neh"), nearly the original from *tinneh,* has been cited as one proof that the Apache left the much larger Navaho tribe in the prehistoric period.

The Apache are the southern branch of the Athapascan linguistic family. They formerly included many sub-tribes living in the Arizona–New Mexico region and eastward on the plains of Texas to the western boundary of Oklahoma. Two prominent groups in New Mexico are known by Spanish names: Mescalero, meaning "mescal people," and Jicarillo, "little basket." The Apache in Oklahoma belong to the comparatively large sub-tribe called the Chiricahua, their name taken from the Apache term for "great mountain."

The Apache are well proportioned and medium in height. They are generally good talkers, truthful, and industrious. The early Spanish explorers in the Southwest reported them "A gentle people . . . faithful in their friendships." Their wars and raids on the Spanish settlements of Mexico and New Mexico in the eighteenth and the nineteenth centuries and the determined resistance of a Chiricahua war party against superior numbers of United States troops won them a bad reputation which made even the name "Apache" synonymous with "savagery." All the tribal bands were more or less nomadic, a characteristic accentuated in the historic period by pressure from Spanish settlement in the Southwest and from the Comanche coming out of the Northwest.

◆ **Present Location.**   The Chiricahua Apache in Oklahoma live quietly on farms in the vicinity of the town of Apache in the southern part of Caddo County, about seventeen miles north of Fort Sill. Their tribal affairs are under the jurisdiction of the Kiowa-Comanche-Apache Agency of the Anadarko Area Office.

◆ **Numbers.** There are approximately 200 Chiricahua Apache in Oklahoma, out of an estimated total of 8,600 Apache in the United States today (Arizona, New Mexico, and Oklahoma). A total of 87 Chiricahua were allotted lands in severalty on the former Kiowa-Comanche Reservation in 1913.

◆ **History.** Chiricahua in Oklahoma belong to the former Eastern Division of the Apache that once roamed the region southward from the present Colorado–New Mexico boundary to the Río Grande River. They are not the same people as the Kiowa-Apache (q.v.) who have long been associated with the Kiowa tribe in Oklahoma. The Eastern Apache were first noted by Coronado on his expedition in 1540–41 when traveling eastward over the Staked Plains of Texas and on through western Oklahoma into Kansas in search of Quivira. Spanish records refer to the Apache as "Querechos." The name Apache was first applied to the tribe by Juan de Oñate, the founder of the colony of New Mexico, who led an expedition through western Oklahoma by way of the Antelope Hills in 1601.

Early Spanish records describe the Apache living in *"rancherías"* or tribal villages in the Canadian River region of Texas and western Oklahoma. Villages were moved from place to place as the

Apache camp on the Washita River in the 1890's

people followed the great buffalo herds feeding northward on the grassland ranges in summer, then southward in winter. The whole pattern of tribal living was dependent upon the buffalo for food, shelter, clothing, utensils, and implements. In the earliest historic period, the Apache were carrying on trade with the Pueblo tribes of New Mexico, bartering buffalo meat, hides, tallow, and salt for cotton blankets, pottery, corn, and a small green stone. Some of the salt, if not all, doubtless was procured by the Apache from the salt plains in western Oklahoma. Horses introduced by the Spaniards made great changes in the life of the tribe.

Historical records for more than two centuries tell about the Apache in large numbers savagely raiding the frontier white settlements and Indian villages of other tribes. Their strength and numbers were undoubtedly exaggerated, becoming almost legendary from their practices in war. A band of Apache would suddenly appear in a locality, strike their blows, seize any supplies in the way, and then quickly disappear, driving off horses and mules and leaving the inhabitants of the community in terrified uncertainty as to when they would strike again. One Apache scout could keep a whole settlement alarmed for days.

The Eastern Apache were reported hostile to the Plains tribes living east of them

even at the time of their discovery. By 1660, the Spanish settlements in New Mexico were losing horses in Apache raids. About this time, the Comanche (q.v.) from the Northwest were coming into conflict with the Apache, beginning a two-hundred-year period of hostilities between the two tribes. In 1723, the Apache were defeated by the Comanche in a nine-day battle on the Wichita River in Texas, after which they drifted southward from their earlier location on the Texas plains. There followed a period of relatively friendly relations between the Spanish settlements and many of the Apache bands, but this friendship ended in 1736. The sub-tribes of the Eastern Apache from this time carried on a struggle for existence against enemies on all sides: the Navaho to the west, the Spanish settlements to the south and southwest; the native tribes to the east in Texas, and the Comanche who were in the Red River region of present Oklahoma and North Texas.

The borders of "Apacheria"—the Apache country—lay some 260 miles northwest of San Antonio when a peace treaty was made on August 19, 1749, with some of the tribal chiefs visiting the settlement. This was an occasion for a great celebration at San Antonio, whose inhabitants dwelt in constant fear of Apache raids. The meeting for peace had been brought about by the efforts of the Catholic friars under the leadership of Father Santa Ana, who had long promoted the establishment of missions among the Apache to pave the way for the conversion of other tribes. San Saba Mission, established near Menard, Texas, in 1757, was visited soon afterward by a friendly throng of three thousand Apache on their way to hunt buffalo. The next year San Saba was destroyed by the Comanche (q.v.), who were jealous of any strength the Apache might gain in connection with the mission. Two other mission attempts on the Nueces River likewise failed, bringing the mission work to an end by 1769. Thus few Apache came under the early influence of the church. However, they became friendly with officials of the Texas government, both the Spanish and the later American.

The only treaty between the United States and the Apache of Arizona and New Mexico was signed at Santa Fé on July 1, 1852, providing for a tribal reservation, the boundaries of which were to be fixed by the government. Delays in designating these boundary lines and conflicts in authority between military and civilian control in the government's administration of Indian affairs in New Mexico and Arizona for many years meant a precarious existence for the tribe, in view of the advancing frontier and the disappearance of game for their food supply.

The comparatively large band of Chiricahua, known about this time as the "Wild Apache," had very little contact with the Americans in New Mexico until the Overland Mail route to San Francisco was established through their mountain country west of the Río Grande River in 1858. Late in the same year, the United States Indian agent held a council with the Chiricahua chief and his men at Apache Pass, after which it was reported that the Overland Mail stages always traveled in safety through this region.

The invasion of New Mexico by the Texans followed by activities of Confederate agents among the tribes encouraged some of the Indians to carry on depredations that terrorized the white settlements in this region at the beginning of the Civil War. Chief Cochise had been friendly to the Americans, but his enmity was aroused in 1861 when he was arrested while visiting a United States army camp for a parley under a flag of truce. Federal forces set out under the command of Colonel Kit Carson against the hostile tribes and soon defeated some of the Mescalero Apache.

The establishment of Indian reservations in the West was a major problem for the government after the Civil War, especially in more than one attempt to settle thousands of Indians from different tribes and sub-tribes within the confines of single reservations without regard to their former tribal relationships or enmities. The Chiricahua, now often referred to as the Southern Apache, were the hardest pressed among the tribes as an aftermath of the war. Chief Cochise steadily refused to accept a reservation in behalf of his people unless they were located in their former country near Apache Pass. Before the end of 1873, a total of 1,675 members of the tribe were settled on the Chiricahua Reservation which had been established in southeastern Arizona in keeping with the recent agreement. Today, Cochise County in Arizona perpetuates the name of the Chiricahua chief, who died on his reservation in peace in 1874. He was succeeded in the chieftaincy by his son Taza, who was friendly to the government. At Taza's death, Cochise's second son Naiche (or Nahche) became chief of the Chiricahua who later lived in Oklahoma.

The Chiricahua were making progress in establishing homes and farming operations on their new reservation when suddenly it was abandoned by the government in 1875, after the adoption of the policy of concentrating Indian tribes on one reservation in a region. The Chiricahua were now moved to the San Carlos Reservation on the Gila River, farther west in Arizona, much against their will. Following the discovery of coal on this reservation, there was an influx of miners into the region. Then the water rights on the Gila River were taken up by the white people, leaving the Indians without any means of irrigating their fields and gardens. In protest, a war party of Chiricahua began raiding expeditions, which were carried on at intervals during a ten-year period under various leaders—Victorio, Geronimo, and others—in the hope that their people would be allowed to return to their former location in southeastern Arizona.

General Nelson A. Miles took command of a final campaign to exterminate Geroni-

mo and his band, the operations forcing their surrender to Lieutenant Charles Gatewood in August, 1886. Chief Naiche and Geronimo and all his band, together with their families, numbering about 340 persons in all, were taken as prisoners of war to Fort Marion, Florida. They died here in such numbers within a year that they were transferred to Mount Vernon Barracks, Alabama, where they were kept for seven years, all the while never ceasing their pleas to be allowed to return to Arizona.

Persons interested in the welfare of the Apache prisoners for humanitarian rea-

GEN. CHARLES D. ROBERTS

General George Crook and the hostile Apache discuss surrender terms in Arizona, March 25, 1886. Mr. Fly, photographer from Tombstone, and his assistant, Chase, preserved the meeting for history.
Seated, left to right: Lt. W. E. Shipp, Lt. S. L. Faison, Capt. C. S. Roberts, Nachez (behind Roberts), Geronimo, Cayetano (behind Geronimo), Nana, Conception (behind Nana), Noche, Lt. M. R. Maus, José María, Antonio Besias, José Montoyo (interpreters), Capt. J. G. Bourke, Gen. Crook, Charley Roberts. In rear: Tommy Blair, pack train cook (holding up the mule), Josanie, Chihuahua, H. W. Daly, packmaster (behind José María), unidentified Indians, Mayor Strauss of Tombstone (behind Charley Roberts)

sons took up their cause, and by order of the Secretary of the Interior in 1894, a special train brought them from Alabama to Fort Sill, Oklahoma Territory. Upon their arrival at their first encampment about two miles northeast of Fort Sill on October 4, 1894, they were a pitiable sight, wretchedly poor, with few clothes or personal belongings. They numbered 296 men, women, and children, or about 70 families, among whom 50 men were able to work under military orders. They were placed in charge of Captain Hugh L. Scott, assisted by Lieutenant Allyn Capron, and were located separately from the other tribes living in the Kiowa-Comanche country around Fort Sill. They remained as prisoners of war on the Fort Sill military reservation until 1913.

The Apache prisoners of war were divided into small villages located on generally high ground at different places over the Fort Sill reservation, each under the supervision of a head man appointed from their number. During their first winter they lived temporarily in brush wickiups which they hurriedly erected and covered with pieces of salvaged canvas. The next spring the men were put to work cutting pickets and posts, building houses and fences, and breaking ground for garden plots and small fields. Henceforth, they were engaged in seasonal work under military supervision: cutting and baling prairie hay for sale under contract to the army post, raising and selling melons and vegetables on the local markets, and caring for the cattle purchased for them to be kept in a herd on the open range. This herd became one of the finest in the Southwest, and within a few years brought in a good revenue from annual sales. The Apache were the first to raise kaffir corn for forage in southwestern Oklahoma, from seed brought in by Captain Scott, who worked wholeheartedly for the improvement of his Indian charges during his three-year assignment at Fort Sill.

Soon after their arrival in Oklahoma, a

Geronimo

few of the leaders among the prisoners of war were enlisted as army scouts to encourage their loyalty to the United States. George Wrattan, a friendly Apache who had been with them since their surrender serving as interpreter, remained at Fort Sill in this same capacity. Sometimes, visitors here in these early days passed an Apache on the road, his red head-band, his hard-lined features, and the suspicious look in his hawklike eyes bringing "to mind the pirates of old tales." Naiche as hereditary chief was given more power than the other Apache, a dignified, fine-looking man in military uniform. Geronimo (native name, Goyathlay), medicine man and prophet rather than chief, was always of great interest to the white people. Many stories are still heard about his life at Fort Sill. Contrary to reports, he was not kept in confinement at the military post, although he was sometimes in the guardhouse for drunkenness. Born in 1829, this "Wild Apache" warrior was looked upon as a remarkable character from the Stone Age, proud of his enlistment as a scout. He was given permission by officers in charge, to travel for a few months in 1908 with Pawnee Bill's Wild West Show. He died of pneumonia in a small hut near the Fort Sill hospital on February 17, 1909, and was buried in the Apache cemetery on Cache Creek, where a monument has been erected to mark his grave.

Mission work was first begun among the Apache prisoners of war at Fort Sill in 1899, under the auspices of the Dutch Reformed church through the influence and efforts of the Reverend Frank H. Wright, the noted Choctaw evangelist. During Rev. Wright's first council meeting with the Apache, Geronimo rose and said: "I, Geronimo, and these others are now too old to travel your Jesus road. But our children are young and I and my brothers will be glad to have the children taught about the white man's God." The old warrior himself joined the Apache Mission Church (Dutch Reformed) in 1903, which had been established on Medicine Bluff Creek west of Fort Sill.

Although living conditions were favorable for the Apache after coming to Fort Sill, their numbers slowly diminished with the death of the old people. Geronimo never gave up urging that they be allowed to return to their home country in the West. On account of this deferred hope, Chief Naiche became exasperated, even surly at times, toward the end of the long period under military supervision, altogether twenty-seven years. Apache children born in Florida or in Alabama grew up, were sent to school, and married as "prisoners of war." Finally, in 1913, the people of this Chiricahua band were released as war prisoners through an act of Congress and given their choice of remaining in Oklahoma or going to New Mexico. From their number, 87 remained, and 171 went to make their homes on the Mescalero Reser-

vation in New Mexico. The Apache herd of cattle at Fort Sill was sold, and a pro rata share used for the purchase of lands from the Kiowa and the Comanche, enough to allow an eighty-acre homestead to each of the 87 Apache. They built their homes on their allotments, and the post office of the new town on the Rock Island Railroad in the vicinity was named Apache.

◆ **Government and Organization.** The Chiricahua Apache in Oklahoma have no tribal organization. Of course, they are citizens of the state, and their children attend the local public schools. Many of them have had advantages of vocational training offered in the large schools maintained by the federal government for Indian youth.

In tribal days, the chieftaincy was hereditary in the paternal line. There were many clans within the tribe, some of them recognized in the different sub-tribes through affiliation. Clans were named from the natural features of the country in various localities and never for animals. Marriage was outside the clan, and plurality of wives was the general custom.

◆ **Contemporary Life and Culture.** The Apache are a rural people following modern practices in agriculture and the raising of livestock on their farms. Approximately two-thirds of the Oklahoma group are full blood; the rest are mixed blood by intermarriage with white people and with other Indian tribes, those of one-half white blood predominating. They are a Christianized people, some of them holding membership in the Dutch Reformed church. The old tribal arts and crafts are no longer practiced to any extent, although Apache women were formerly noted for their fine basketry.

Allan Houser, the grand-nephew of Geronimo, born at Fort Sill in 1914, is an outstanding Oklahoma Indian artist. Some of his murals are in the Interior Department building at Washington and at the Fort Sill and Riverside Indian schools. His marble statue "Comrade in Mourning" was recently completed as a memorial to the

Apache Fire Dance in the pageant of the American Indian Exposition, Anadarko

Haskell Indian School students who gave their lives in World War II.

A young woman from the Apache in Oklahoma, Miss Mildred Imach, holds a responsible position as a home counselor to the women among the Oto and other tribes within the Pawnee subagency jurisdiction.

◊ **Ceremonials and Public Dances.** In the interest of their history and former tribal customs, some of the Apache take part in the American Indian Exposition held every year at Anadarko, with programs open to the public. One of the outstanding features usually given is the ancient Apache Fire Dance, in which the main dancers wear masks and special headdresses and costumes, masked clown dancers also having a part. A pictograph of the Fire Dance done in colors on white buckskin by Chief Naiche many years ago is one of the rare objects on exhibit in the Oklahoma Historical Society Museum in the Historical Building at Oklahoma City.

Suggested Readings: Hodge, *Handbook of American Indians;* Barrett, *Geronimo;* Page,*In Camp and Teepee;* Dunn, "Apache Relations in Texas, 1718–1750," in *Texas Hist. Asso. Quart.,* Vol. XIV, No. 3; Reeve, "The Apache in Texas," in *Southwestern Hist. Soc. Quart.,* Vol L, No. 2; Nye, *Carbine and Lance.*

APALACHICOLA

The name Apalachicola has been interpreted from the Muskhogean dialects as signifying "people on the other side" (of a river). The Apalachicola Indians are of the Muskhogean linguistic family. They speak the ancient Hitchiti (q.v.) language, and are both traditionally and historically the "mother" tribe or "town" of the old Creek confederacy. Their original locality was southwestern Georgia; in their later history, they settled upstream and on the west side of the Chattahoochee River, where they became identified with the Lower Creek Division (*see* Creek). The remnant Apalachicola (400 persons) were listed under their tribal name when they came to the Indian Territory with the Creek from Alabama during the Indian removal. They settled in the region south of present Okmulgee. Their "town" ("Tulwa Thlocco" or "Tvlwa-hloko"—"Big Town") was one of the forty-four tribal "towns" comprising the Creek Nation until Oklahoma became a state. The census of the Creek Nation in 1891 gave the population of Tulwa Thlocco as 171. Suggested Readings: Swanton, *Early History of the Creek;* ———, *Indians of Southeastern U. S.;* Debo, *The Road to Disappearance.*

ARAPAHO

The name Arapaho originates in the Pawnee term *tirapihu* (or *larapihu*), "he buys or trades," undoubtedly applied to the tribe from the fact that they were the trading group in the Great Plains region; between the Pawnee, Osage, and others on the north, and the Kiowa, Comanche, and others on the south. The Arapaho call themselves *Inuna-ina,* "our people" or "people of our own kind." They have long been closely associated with the Cheyenne, who call them *Hitäniwo'iv,* "Cloud Men." Their Sioux name *Maq-pi'ăto* has a similar meaning, "Blue-cloud Men."

The Arapaho is one of the westernmost tribes of the Algonquian linguistic family. The tribal group in Oklahoma is the Southern Arapaho, the largest group of the tribe proper. Members of this group are called *Nawathi'neha,* "Southerners," by the Northern Arapaho who live on the Wind River reservation in Wyoming and are considered the parent stem of the original tribe. The lines of kinship have been preserved between the Northern and the Southern groups. They have interchanged visits, and there are occasional intermarriages.

They are known as a friendly, contemplative, and religious people; noted in tribal days as brave warriors in battle, yet they have always been much more tractable than their warlike allies, the Cheyenne (q.v.).

◆ **Present Location.** In Oklahoma, the Arapaho live mostly in rural areas near the towns of Canton, Greenfield, and Geary in Blaine County, and at Colony in Washita County.

◆ **Numbers.** Approximately 1189 Southern Arapaho lived in Oklahoma in 1950. The Indian Office enumeration for 1924 shows 692 members of the tribe in this state. In 1902, they numbered 905. The total population of the tribe reported at different periods after their settlement on their Oklahoma reservation is 1,091 in 1892 when their allotments of lands in severalty were completed; 2,258 in 1881; and 1,664, in 1875.

◆ **History.** The oldest traditions of the Arapaho place their earliest home somewhere east of the headwaters of the Mississippi River as far as the western end of Lake Superior, where they lived in permanent villages and tilled the soil, raising large crops of corn. They eventually crossed the Mississippi and the Red River of the North, and migrated to the headwaters of the Missouri River. Thence, after a long period, they drifted eastwardly out on the Plains, where they said that they "lost the corn," which means that they ceased to plant the seed and till the soil and were henceforth buffalo hunters, becoming a nomadic people who lived in tipi villages.

In these early migrations westward and then eastward, they were generally in company with the Cheyenne, with whom they seem to have been allied far back. About 1835, both tribes divided, the greater portion of each moving south to the Arkansas River region in eastern Colorado. Henceforth, both the Arapaho and the Cheyenne were divided into the Northern and the Southern groups. This division was a matter of choice, and not one of social or factional significance. While the Southern

Arapaho and the Southern Cheyenne have always been closely associated, the Northern Arapaho and the Northern Cheyenne have remained independent, the two latter groups having separate reservations in Wyoming and Montana.

From early times to reservation days, the Arapaho were at war with the Shoshoni, Ute, Navaho, and Pawnee. Since 1840, the Southern Arapaho have been at peace with all other tribes of the Plains. They were sometimes allied with the Comanche and the Kiowa in raids on Spanish settlements far down in Mexico.

The Southern Arapaho have had a common history with the Southern Cheyenne since their treaty with the United States made at Fort Wise, Kansas, on February 18, 1861. At this time, the two tribal groups ceded all their land claims in adjoining portions of Nebraska, Kansas, Colorado, and Wyoming, with the exception of a reservation tract in eastern Colorado lying south from Big Sandy Creek to the Arkansas and the Purgatory rivers. The Southern Arapaho were represented in this treaty

MURIEL H. WRIGHT

Chief Little Raven, who signed the Medicine Lodge Treaty in 1867

by their chief, Little Raven (Hosa) and three other tribal delegates.

The event that led to settlement of the Southern Arapaho in Oklahoma was the great council held by United States commissioners with the chiefs and leaders of the principal tribes of the Southern Plains on the Medicine Lodge River in southern Kansas, in October, 1867. Chief Little Raven, who towered above all the other Indians present in native intelligence and oratorical power, made a speech that would have done credit to an enlightened statesman: He reviewed treaty obligations and the causes of war, scathingly denounced the ill use of the Indians on the Western frontier, and made an impassioned plea for protection and better treatment in the future. Another distinguished Arapaho present during the Medicine Lodge Council was Mrs. Virginia Adams, the tribal interpreter, who knew several Indian languages and English. She was the daughter of the well-known trader Julian Poisol and his Arapaho wife; and her first husband was Major Thomas J. Fitzpatrick (died 1854), who had been prominent in the Rocky Mountain fur trade and was associated with John C. Frémont in some of his early explorations.

A treaty with the Arapaho and the Cheyenne during the Medicine Lodge Council provided the two tribes with a reservation bounded on the north and east by the Kansas state line and the Arkansas River, and on the west and south by the Cimarron River (also called the Red Fork of the Arkansas), a tract lying in the Cherokee Outlet in what is now northern Oklahoma. Opposition and uncertainties among the Western tribes in locating on reservations (and the war on the Plains in 1868 that culminated in the destruction of Chief Black Kettle's Cheyenne village [see Cheyenne] on the Washita River by United States troops under Custer) delayed the settlement of the Plains tribes in western Oklahoma. The Arapaho and Cheyenne did not settle on the reservation assigned

Cheyenne-Arapaho beadworkers about 1900

them, but located their tipi villages south along the North Canadian River. Since they called the latter stream "Red Fork" or "Red River," they thought they were abiding by the terms of the Medicine Lodge treaty. When their chiefs and leaders learned of this mistake, they asked that the government grant their people another reservation, setting forth their objections to the first tract with its poor land, lack of wood and water, and its location—right on the Kansas state line to the north and on the Osage Reservation line to the east—a serious objection, for the Osage were their hereditary tribal enemies.

By Presidential proclamation in August, 1869, the Arapaho and the Cheyenne were jointly assigned a new reservation along the North Canadian and the upper Washita rivers, lying west from the ninety-eighth meridian, bounded on the north by the Cherokee Outlet and on the south by the Kiowa-Apache-Comanche Reservation (*see these tribes*). Most of the Arapaho and Cheyenne encampments at this time were near Camp Supply, the temporary tribal agency in charge of Brinton Darlington, the Quaker who had been appointed their

agent by President Grant. The Cheyenne and Arapaho Agency was established by Darlington in 1870, on the north side of the Canadian River, about two miles northwest of present El Reno in Canadian County. This agency location became known in Indian and Oklahoma history as Darlington. The Arapaho school opened here in 1871 continued as a boarding school for Arapaho children until 1908, when it was consolidated with the Cheyenne Boarding School (*see* Cheyenne) at Caddo Spring about three miles northeast of Darlington. The Cheyenne and Arapaho boarding school was still in operation in 1951 at the Caddo Spring site, which is now called Concho. The Cheyenne and Arapaho Agency, now a subagency of the Anadarko Area Office, is also in operation at Concho, to which place it was moved from Darlington in 1909.

The Arapaho were the first of the tribes of the Southern Plains to recognize the importance and binding force of the treaties made at the Medicine Lodge council. Steadily refusing to join the war factions among the Cheyenne, Kiowa, and Comanche in the uprising on the reservations in western Indian Territory in 1874–75, the Arapaho remained encamped in the vicinity of the agency at Darlington during this difficult period, a peaceable, loyal people in spite of great suffering from their impoverished condition, their buffalo-skin lodges in tatters, their clothing scanty, and near starvation most of the time.

Characteristic of their contemplative, religious disposition as a tribe, they led in the spread of the Ghost Dance religion in 1890. A Southern Arapaho named Sitting Bull, who had lived among the Northern Arapaho for several years, came back to the Indian Territory to spread the word among the reservation tribes of the coming of an Indian messiah and the reunion of all the Indian peoples, living or dead, upon a regenerated earth. The doctrine, professed at different times in early periods among the Indians of Mexico and North America, had recently arisen among the Shoshoni tribes in Utah and Nevada. Ghost Dance ceremonials were instituted during which special songs and dances were given, and individuals were seen in a trance induced by hypnotic practices of the leader or medium, who generally wore regalia newly designed and made. Excitement on the reservations of the Indian Territory reached its height in a great gathering for the Ghost

Dance held about two miles from Darlington, on the Canadian River, in September, 1890, and attended by several thousand Indians, including nearly all the Arapaho and Cheyenne and many other Indians from the tribes of neighboring reservations. Belief in the new religion was given up within a few years under great disappointment, after the Kiowa (q.v.) investigated the source of the doctrine and found it false.

At the height of the Ghost Dance excitement, a United States commission arrived in the Indian Territory seeking an agreement with the Cheyenne and Arapaho for the sale of their reservation, to which many in both tribes were opposed. Chief Left Hand (Nawat, successor to Little Raven) of the Arapaho, after consulting with the religious leader, Sitting Bull, led in making an agreement with the commission members in October, 1890, which was signed by him and 564 other Arapaho and Cheyenne. The terms provided for the sale of the reservation lands to the United States, a total of 3,500,562 acres, for $1,-500,000 to be placed to the credit of the two tribes; and that members of the tribes were also to receive an allotment of 160 acres each. When the allotting of lands was completed through the work of the agency at Darlington, the Cheyenne and

Chiefs of the Cheyenne and Arapaho, 1889

Arapaho country was opened to white settlement on April 19, 1892, by Presidential proclamation, adding six new counties to Oklahoma Territory as well as wide areas to two counties already organized.

◆ **Government and Organization.** The Arapaho have joined with the Cheyenne in the "Cheyenne-Arapaho Tribes of Oklahoma," a constitution and by-laws having been adopted by a vote of the tribal members in September, 1937, under provisions of the Oklahoma Indian Welfare Act of 1936. The governing body of the organization is the Cheyenne-Arapaho Business Committee, consisting of fourteen members, seven of whom are Arapaho, elected every two years by popular vote. Arapaho members of the Business Committee in 1949 were Jesse Rowlodge (chairman), Luther Bringing Good, Thomas Lee, George Levi, William Sutton, Charles Loneman, and Armstrong Spotted Horse.

The Cheyenne-Arapaho Business Committee in its monthly meetings at Concho Subagency transacts business pertaining to the management of tribally owned lands and property, promotes the settlement of tribal claims on the United States, and advises in general welfare matters. The two tribes are still joint owners of the former boarding school lands and property at Red Moon (2,000 acres) in Roger Mills County, at Colony (2,800 acres) in Washita County, and at Cantonment (3,200 acres) in Blaine County. These tracts are divided into farming units leased by the year for cash rent to individual members of the tribes. The large school building at Colony is leased by the year to the local school board and serves as the district public school attended by both white and Indian children.

The Arapaho have retained a nominal tribal government principally for ceremonial and religious purposes, twelve chiefs having been selected in the different communities (near Geary, Canton, Greenfield, Calumet, and Colony) by the old scout and retired Arapaho chief, Ute. The twelve chiefs are Jesse Rowlodge, David Meat, John Hoof, Dan Blackhorse, Ben Spotted Wolf, Bill Williams, Wilbur Tabor, John Sleeper, Annanita Washee, Scott Youngman, Saul Birdshead, and Theodore Haury (deceased). There are also two Cheyenne elected by custom to serve as Arapaho chiefs. They are Ben Buffalo, of Seiling in Dewey County, and Ralph Whitetail, of Thomas in Custer County.

◆ **Contemporary Life and Culture.** Approximately 700 Arapaho are fullblood members of the tribe. The remainder are mixed-blood descendants by intermarriage

Wattan (Carl Sweezey), Arapaho artist, in 1951

with closely associated tribes (fullblood Indians), along with some who have intermarried with white people.

Most of the tribesmen are engaged in farming; about 10 per cent are employed in business and other fields. Carl Sweezey (Wattan), an elderly fullblood Arapaho, has made a name among Indian artists and is classed as a primitive painter, noted for his knowledge of the old tribal ceremonies and costuming.

The Arapaho are generally a Christianized people. Baptist churches are active in several communities, including Swapping Back Church (between Geary and Greenfield) named for the old Indian called "Swapping Back" who gave the ground for the church. There are also Arapaho members of the Mennonite church, Mennonite missionaries having established a mission school at Cantonment about 1881. The American Indian church based on peyotism counts some of the tribe as members.

◆ **Ceremonials and Public Dances.** The Arapaho ceremonials connected with tribal religion, especially that relating to the sacred pipe preserved by the Northern Arapaho, are not open to the public. Visitors are allowed for special celebrations where tribal dances are given, such as the recent Victory celebrations upon the return of the men from service in World War II. Members of the tribe have served at different times as officers in directing the American Indian Exposition held annually in summer at Anadarko, and Arapaho dancers always have a part in its pageantry. Suggested Readings: Grinnell, *The Cheyenne Indians;* Hodge, *Handbook of American Indians;* Mooney, "Ghost Dance Religion," in *14 Ann. Rep.,* Bur. Amer. Ethnol.; Peery, "The Indians' Friend, Seger," in *Chron. of Okla.,* Vols. X and XI; Seger, *Early Days Among the Cheyenne and Arapahoe.*

CADDO

Caddo is a contraction of *Kadohadacho* (Kä'dohädä'cho) signifying "real chiefs," the name of the tribe referred to by ethnologists as the Caddo proper, from which the name of the Caddoan linguistic family is derived. The term Kadohadacho is from *Kaadi* (Kä ädĭ) meaning "chief." The Caddo tribe belongs to the southern division of the Caddoan family and, as known today, includes the remnant of the Anadarko tribe.

When the Caddo were visited by La Salle in 1686, they included approximately twenty-five tribes that formed at least three confederacies: Kadohadacho, Hasinai (*see* Hainai), and Wichita. The Kadohadacho, or Caddo proper, was composed of four tribes, whose dialect became the speech of the people commonly called Caddo today.

At the beginning of the eighteenth century, the principal villages of the Kadohadacho were in the bend of Red River, in southwestern Arkansas and northeastern Texas. Their closely related tribes lived to the south along Red River in Louisiana, where the name Caddo is perpetuated through a parish and a large lake. The name of the Natchitoches tribe, one of the four tribes of the Kadohadacho confederacy, has been perpetuated in the city of Natchitoches, Louisiana, important in the history of the Caddo proper.

Most early writers on the tribes in the Southwest were favorably impressed by the Caddo, describing them as industrious, intelligent, sociable, and lively; courageous and brave in war, and faithful to their plighted word. They were especially known for their friendly welcome to visitors—offering the best accommodations in their houses and food on reed platters, after bathing the face and hands and feet of their visitors. The Caddo were small in stature and were described as "well built and robust, but, at the same time light and strong." The women were considered pretty, having regular features and small hands and feet.

The southern Caddoan tribes were agriculturists. They also manufactured salt, which they traded, along with the wood of the bois d'arc tree, prized in making bows, to other Indian tribes in pre-Columbian days. It was in their trading relations with the tribes on the Western plains that they became proficient in the use of the sign language, by which they conversed with tribes whose speech they did not understand.

The Caddo had secured horses a century before European colonization of the Lower Mississippi region. Although they continued sedentary in their habits, cultivating their fields and raising large crops of corn, in addition to beans and pumpkins, the Caddo engaged more and more in the raising of livestock. While they were primarily a "Woodland tribe," they took on some of the culture of the Plains tribes. The men became fine horsemen and made successful hunting expeditions far west. Trade with other tribes grew, and, by the beginning of the eighteenth century, they were bartering horses in distant regions.

◆ **Present Location.** The Caddo live in Caddo County, their largest settlement in the vicinity of Binger.

◆ **Numbers.** In 1944, the Office of Indian Affairs numbered the Caddo at 1,165, an increase over its 1930 census, which reported 1,005. These population figures include the old tribes of Kadohadacho (Caddo proper) and Anadarko (q.v.), now commonly known under the name "Caddo" in Oklahoma. Their numbers given in the reports of the United States Indian agents at different periods in their history are 497 in 1897, 507 in 1894, 517 in 1889, and 538 in 1880. In 1872, the Kadohadacho and Anadarko together numbered 392; in 1864, 370. On the Lower Reserve in Texas, in 1857, the two tribes totaled 435, of whom 235 were Kadohadacho—this census, however, not including some of their tribal bands north of Red River. An official census in 1851 gives 300 Kadohadahco or Caddo proper in Texas; and a report for 1805 gives a total population of 800. It is estimated by one authority that there were

from 2,000 to 2,400 Kadohadacho in 1700. Since the end of the reservation period in 1901, the census reports for the Caddo show a great increase in population.

◆ **History.** Although archaeological finds in eastern Oklahoma from the Arkansas Valley south to Red River tend to prove a prehistoric mass migration of the Caddoan peoples from the Southwest, the subject is still unsettled in the minds of some ethnologists who have thought that the Caddoan migration in pre-Columbian times was westward from the Mississippi Valley to the Oklahoma region.

Archaeological remains of the so-called "Earth House People," in the form of low mounds along the Arkansas River valley and in southeastern Oklahoma, are said to have been of Caddoan origin, marking the path of a prehistoric migration through this area. The theory that the low mounds in this region and eastward from southern Missouri through Arkansas, Louisiana, and eastern Texas are natural phenomena was apparently disproved by the late Joseph B. Thoburn, pioneer archaeologist in Oklahoma, who reported excavations of some of the mounds in "The Northern Caddoan Peoples of Prehistoric Times and the Human Origin of the Natural Mounds, So Called, of Oklahoma and Neighboring States," a manuscript now in the possession of the Oklahoma Historical Society. Careful excavation of mounds of this type revealed a fireplace at the center and near the bottom of most of them, containing wood ashes, bits of charcoal, fragments of pottery, and flakes of flint and bones.

Some Caddoan villages were found by the first explorers in what is now west central Arkansas, where Caddo Gap in Montgomery County and the Caddo River have perpetuated the name of the tribe.

References to the Caddo appear in the chronicles of the De Soto expedition of 1541. It is also thought that Coronado came in contact with the tribe. Nothing more about them occurs in available records until the middle of the seventeenth century

Pottery from mounds in eastern Oklahoma in the Thoburn Collection

when the Spaniards coming from the southwest into the present state of Texas arrived in a wide territory of a Caddoan people whom they called "Texas" or "Taches" (*see* Hainai).

Following the establishment of the Louisiana colony of Biloxi by D'Iberville in 1699 and the founding of the French post at the Caddoan village of Natchitoches by St. Denis in 1714, the Caddo came under the influence of the French, an influence which continued even after Louisiana was ruled by Spain. In 1719, Bernard de la Harpe was commissioned by the French to make an expedition among the Caddoan tribes along the Red River, during which he established a stockade post among the Kadohadacho, on the south side of Red River not far from the southeastern corner of Oklahoma. In 1770, Athanase de Mézières, in behalf of the Spanish government, held a great council at the Caddo village, called San Luiz de Caddachos by the Spaniards, located about one hundred leagues from Natchitoches, on Red River. Chief Tinhiouen of the Kadohadacho served as spokesman during the council, and a treaty was secured by De Mézières in which the tribe ceded the King of Spain "all proprietorship in the land" which the tribe inhabited.

Caddo encampments and hunting expeditions north of Red River in Oklahoma in this period suffered attacks by the Osage (q.v.) who were waging war against all their neighbors. Before the close of the eighteenth century, bands of different Southeastern tribes from east of the Mississippi, including some of the Choctaw (q. v.), often were at war with the Caddo. Tradition has it that the Caddo were defeated in a hard-fought battle with a Choctaw hunting and war party in the vicinity of a low range of hills known locally as the "Caddo Hills," in present Bryan County, Oklahoma, from which the town of Caddo in that county derived its name.

Soon after the purchase of Louisiana by the United States, Dr. John Sibley, appointed Indian agent for the Territory of Orleans south of the Arkansas River, reported the Caddo people greatly reduced from their original numbers by war and epidemics. He said the Kadohadacho were a brave, industrious people whose main village was located in a flat prairie on Red River about 120 miles northwest of Natchitoches. Sibley succeeded in concluding a peace agreement between the Caddo and the Choctaw, after which a band of Caddo joined a number of Choctaw in an alliance to fight the Osage.

After the purchase of Louisiana, the old alliances and friendships that the Caddo may have had with the French were transferred to the United States, and most of the people of the tribe were henceforth loyal to the federal government. Spanish interests in the Southwest and events in Mexico, however, had a disturbing effect on the tribes south and west of Red River; and small bands of Caddo voluntarily located north of the river in the Indian Territory.

The Nanatscho crossing on Red River southeast of Idabel, in present McCurtain County, later called Harris Ferry, was long the only available crossing for Caddo hunting expeditions from Louisiana to the country north of Red River. In the summer of 1834, a band of thirty-three Caddo arrived at Camp Washita, near the mouth of the Washita River, where they were in readiness to accompany the Leavenworth Expedition to the Plains Indians in southwestern Oklahoma (*see* Wichita).

The settlement of the Indian tribes from southeastern United States in the Indian Territory was now under way. In 1835, the Caddo, who had lived in Louisiana from time immemorial, were also included in the movement. In July of this year they signed a treaty of cession with the United States, giving up all their Louisiana lands and agreeing to move beyond the limits of the United States for the sum of $40,000 in goods, horses, and annuities payable in a five-year period. This treaty vitally affected the Caddo proper, for they were now without a home. Part of them joined the tribes of the Hasinai confederacy in Texas and later established a village with the Hainai and Anadarko (q.v.) on the Brazos River. Another part (estimated at 167 persons) were living in the Choctaw Nation north of Red River in 1842 after receiving the last of their annuity payments from the United States. Two years later, the Choctaw General Council enacted legislation requiring all Indian intruders to leave the nation as soon as practicable,

with the exception of some of the Caddo who had been granted permission to live there by the council in 1843.

The Caddo had already been in possession of firearms for nearly one-hundred years when they began locating farther west in Texas early in the nineteenth century. Some of them joined the Texas Cherokee, Chief Bowl, before his followers were annihilated by the Texans in 1839. These activities brought suspicion on the Caddo who were still living on the Louisiana border, and they were forced to surrender their arms in 1837, when alarm was spread in East Texas that these peaceful bands were going to commit depredations.

An attempt was made in 1842 to bring about some agreement between the Texas Republic and its Indian enemies when the Caddo Chief, Red Bear, asked Robert M. Jones, a prominent Choctaw (q.v.), to act as a mediator. The following year, the Caddo proper (Kadohadacho), Anadarko, and Hainai were among the signers of the peace treaty with the Texas Republic, negotiated at Bird's Fort on Trinity River. These same tribes signed another treaty in 1844 and sent delegations to a peace council with the Texans in 1845.

A few months before the peace council in Texas, a delegation of eight Caddo had attended a great intertribal council that met on the Deep Fork River near present Eufaula, in McIntosh County, Oklahoma, at the call of the Creek Nation. Pierce M. Butler, United States Indian agent, described the Caddo chief, Chowawhana, as a "striking man of great personal beauty and commanding appearance; small in stature, yet beautiful and attractive features; dressed in what would be called Indian magnificence—feathers, turbans, and silver bands." In a speech that was awaited with eager interest and well received, Chowawhana deplored the gloomy past, the worse future prospects, and probable fate of the Red People; he approved the council and advised against hostility among the tribes which "would bring the destruction of their race and ruin of their children."

Intertribal councils called by the Creek and the Cherokee (q.v.) in the Indian Territory paved the way for the treaty negotiated by United States Commissioners Pierce M. Butler and M. G. Lewis at Council Springs on the Brazos River in May, 1846, signed by the chiefs and counselors of the Caddo proper and other tribes of this region in Texas (see Anadarko). The United States was acknowledged as their protector, perpetual peace was to be observed, only licensed traders were to reside among them, and school teachers and preachers of the Gospel were to work in their villages.

Appeals on the part of the Indian agents for a special land tract for the use of the Indian tribes who had signed the treaty at Council Springs were finally heeded by the Texas legislature in 1854. Federal authorities selected a tract along the Brazos River about twelve miles south of Fort Belknap, in Young County, consisting of 37,152 acres, henceforth known as the Lower Reserve, where the villages of the Caddo and their allies were soon located (see Anadarko). By 1858, they had made considerable progress and were living peaceably, having erected comfortable houses and fenced their fields (generally with brush fences), where they raised large crops of corn and vegetables in favorable seasons.

Conditions outside the Brazos Reserve were not favorable; Indian wars in the West, depredations in Texas, and events in the United States fast approaching the cleavage between North and South. Faithful to their word to maintain peace, the Caddo and other tribes under the Brazos Agency furnished warriors to serve as scouts with both federal and Texas troops on their expeditions north against the Comanche and their allies. Hostility on the part of the white settlers toward the Indians increased, rising from the feud between Indian Superintendent Robert S. Neigh-

bors and a former agent who had been dismissed from government service. A band of white men made a sudden attack upon an encampment of seventeen Indians from the Reserve, who were grazing their horses in a bend near the Brazos, early on the morning of December 27, 1858 (see Anadarko). Feeling ran high among both the Indians and the white people, and the situation became so tense that Texas officials and federal agents decided that the removal of the Brazos tribes to the Indian Territory north of Red River would be necessary. A new location was selected in the region known as the Leased District west of the ninety-eighth meridian in the Choctaw domain, set aside by the terms of the Choctaw-Chickasaw treaty of 1855 (see Choctaw and Chickasaw).

Preparations were underway for the removal of the tribes in the summer of 1859 when the word came that a date had been set by the white people to massacre all the Indians on the Reserve. Superintendent Neighbors immediately made every effort to hurry the departure of the 1,430 Indians —men, women, and children. On August 1, 1859, the last of the tribes left the Brazos Reserve, arriving at the end of fifteen days by forced marches in the terrific heat of August, on the Washita River, within present Caddo County, Oklahoma. Exhausted and impoverished, they were placed under the supervision of a new agent and left without military protection from possible attacks by hostile Comanche and Kiowa. A new agency was established, called the Wichita Agency, located north of the Washita on Leeper Creek, about four miles east of the present town of Fort Cobb in Caddo County, near which the new military post of Fort Cobb was established by the War Department in October, 1859.

In the late summer of 1860, the Indian agent reported the tribes on the Washita still threatened and pursued at times by the Texans. Yet the Caddo and their allies, the Anadarko and Hainai, had made efforts to establish their families.

At the beginning of the Civil War, Albert Pike, commissioner of the Confederate States to the Indian nations and tribes, met the leaders of the Caddo and other tribes at the Wichita Agency where they concluded a treaty on August 12, 1861, signed by Principal Chief Quinahiwi and the sub-chiefs of the Caddo. Subsequently, the Caddo were counted with the Five Civilized Tribes in the "United Nations of the Indian Territory" aligned throughout the war with the Confederacy. The "Caddo Battalion" served as scouts and rangers in the Confederate Army, under the command of Showetat, or "Little Boy," better known in Oklahoma history as "Caddo George Washington." Some of the Caddo were said to have had a part with other Indian bands in the destruction of the Wichita Agency in October, 1862, and in the massacre of the Tonkawa (q.v.). The

EUGENE HEFLIN

"Caddo George Washington" (Showetat)

Caddo Battalion was one of the last Confederate Indian forces to surrender at the end of the war, in July, 1865.

A large portion of the Caddo and their allies (the Hainai, q.v.), who remained loyal to the Union, went north to Kansas early in the war, where they remained as refugees until 1867. The next year, the United States agent reported that all the tribes of the old Wichita Agency had returned to their locations near Fort Cobb.

The Caddo began again to build homes and cultivate farms on lands within the Wichita-Caddo Reservation, the boundaries of which were defined by the government in an agreement with the Wichita (q.v.) in 1872. Missionary work was begun on the reservation in the early eighteen seventies by Thomas C. Battey of the Society of Friends and by Baptist missionaries. A government school was opened near the agency for Indian children. The Episcopal church placed a mission on the reservation in 1891, and another was established by the Roman Catholic church in 1891 near present Anadarko.

Caddo leaders during reservation days before Oklahoma statehood included White Deer, sometimes called White Antelope (Caddo delegate to Washington in 1872), Thomas Wisler, Stanley Edge, and George Parton, who was judge of the Caddo Indian court organized under government supervision. Henry Inkinish, who served as an employee in one of the reservation schools, is well known in Caddo County. Every Caddo man, woman, and child received an allotment of 160 acres when the Wichita-Caddo Reservation (*see* Wichita) was allotted in severalty and the surplus lands opened to white settlement in 1901.

◆ **Government and Organization.** The Caddo are organized as the Caddo Indian Tribe of Oklahoma, with a corporate charter issued by the Secretary of the Interior, as provided in the Oklahoma Indian Welfare Act of 1936. The constitution and by-laws of this tribal organization were ratified on January 17, 1938, in an election by tribal members, as certified by the Caddo Tribal Committee composed of Maurice Bedoka, Jesse Adunko, and Stanley Edge. The Caddo Tribal Council, of which in 1951 Lloyd Tounwin, of Hinton, was chairman and Paul W. Edge, of Fort Cobb, was vice-chairman, meets the first Tuesday of every month at the community building near Binger, Oklahoma. Affairs relating to the organization and restricted properties of individual tribal members are under the supervision of the Anadarko Area Office of the Bureau of Indian Affairs. As a tribe, the Caddo do not have a chief as in early days.

◆ **Contemporary Life and Culture.** The Caddo are predominantly of mixed white and Indian descent. About two-fifths of the tribe, or approximately 450 members, are fullblood Indians. They are the descendants of the Caddo proper (Kadohadacho), the Anadarko, and the Hainai. These fullblood Caddo include those of pure blood in each of these tribal groups and those of mixed blood by intermarriage among these tribes that have been grouped under the name "Caddo" since 1880. Mixed-blood families by intermarriage among the Caddo and the early French settlers were usually highly respected and held positions of importance in their communities in Louisiana. Some of their descendants are among the Caddo in Oklahoma today.

The Caddo are an Americanized, rural people, most of them engaged in farming and the raising of livestock. Their children attend the public schools near their homes; some of the orphans attended

EUGENE HEFLIN

Enoch Hoag, the last Caddo chief

Riverside Indian School near Anadarko.

◆ **Ceremonials and Public Dances.** The Caddo form a large group in the pageantry, ceremonials, and dances of the American Indian Exposition held annually in August at Anadarko. In this they are carrying on some of their old traditions and customs.

Suggested Readings: Bolton, *Athanase de Mézières;* Dorsey, *Traditions of the Caddo;* Grant Foreman, *Advancing the Frontier;* Nye, *Carbine and Lance;* Swanton, *Source Material, Caddo.*

CAHOKIA

The Cahokia are listed as a leading tribe of the Illinois Confederacy in the first part of the eighteenth century. They are of the Algonquian linguistic family and were closely associated with the Tamaroa (q.v.).

The two tribes were located in a Jesuit mission settlement about 1698, near the site of present Cahokia, Illinois. The name of the tribe is distinguished by that of the Cahokia Mound, the largest prehistoric artificial earthwork in the United States, still seen in Madison County, Illinois, about six miles east of St. Louis.

Five of the Cahokia chiefs and leaders signed the treaty made at Edwardsville, Illinois, in 1818, by which the tribes of the old Illinois Confederacy ceded half the state of Illinois to the United States. Henceforth the Cahokia were a part of the Kaskaskia and the Peoria (q.v.), whose descendants may be found in Ottawa County, Oklahoma.

Suggested Readings: Grant Foreman, "Illinois and Her Indians," in *Papers in Illinois History,* 1939; ———, *Last Trek of the Indians;* Hodge, *Handbook of American Indians.*

CATAWBA

The name Catawba is said to be from the Yuchi term *kotaba,* "strong people," from the Yuchi words *ko,* "people," and *taba,* "strong."

The Catawba comprise one of the most important Eastern tribes of the Siouan linguistic family. Their original historic home was in South Carolina, where they consisted of two bands, the Catawba and the Iswa, the latter name derived from the Catawba word *iswa,* "river," which was their only tribal name for both the Catawba and Wateree rivers.

Early descriptions of the Catawba vary according to their changing fortune in history. Generally, they were praised for their bravery, courage, and honesty. Their warlike disposition led them into constant wars with the Northern Iroquois and the Shawnee; their advantageous location and their strength as a tribe made them the dominant group that absorbed the weakened remnants of some twenty smaller neighboring tribes in a loose confederacy by 1763. In early tribal days the Catawba were sedentary agriculturists. Their men were good hunters, and the women were noted as makers of pottery and basketry.

◆ **Present Location.** The descendants of some of the Catawba who settled in the Choctaw Nation are now absorbed into Indian population of Haskell and Le Flore counties. The descendants of some of those who settled in the Creek and the Cherokee nations have been reported living southeast of Checotah in McIntosh County. The main portion of the tribe live in the eastern part of York County, South Carolina.

◆ **Numbers.** There are few Catawba in the state, and these are counted in the general Indian population of the state. They were last enumerated as a separate tribe in this region in 1896, their total population in the Indian Territory being given as 132. The largest portion, or 78, lived in the Choctaw Nation, most of them in the region between the present cities of Stigler and Spiro. Seventeen of them gave Checotah, Creek Nation, as their post office, and 15 lived around Texana, in the southwestern part of the Cherokee Nation, now included in McIntosh County. In the same year (1896), there were 125 Catawba living in Arkansas, most of them in and around Greenwood and Barber. Their numbers steadily declined from 4,600 in 1682 to 250 in 1784 through wars and epidemics. Their entire population in 1822 was reported as 450 on their South Carolina reservation; in 1900, in the same location, there were about 100. In 1944, 300 Catawba were reported living in South Carolina, on and around their reservation in York County.

◆ **History.** The traditional history of the Catawba indicates that they migrated from the northwest to their historic abode in western South Carolina where the "Ysa," or Iswa, were first reported by Juan Pardo's Spanish expedition in 1566–67. Although they were one of the tribes allied with the Yamassee against the English in the war that ended in 1715, at all other times the Catawba were loyal to the people of South Carolina.

Their last great tribal chief, Haiglar, described as a man of sterling character and greatly beloved by his people, was murdered by the Shawnee on August 30, 1763. He had offered his services and had been of great assistance to the South Carolina troops in their defeat of the Cherokee in 1759. During the Revolutionary War, the tribe fought on the side of the Colonists against the British. In the twenty-year period before 1840, the tribe was at the lowest ebb of its existence. In March of that year, a treaty was signed with South Carolina by the Catawba chief, Colonel Samuel Scott, a grandson of Chief Haiglar, providing for the cession of more than 100,000 acres of the most fertile lands in the state for a few thousand dollars and the removal of the tribe to North Carolina.

When North Carolina would not provide a location for the Catawba, nearly all of them returned to region of their old homes, a few of them continuing to live on 652 acres in York County, called the "Old Reservation," which was the only tract retained by the tribe in 1840. In October, 1848, William Morrison, chief of a band of Catawba (42 persons) living at Quallatown, Haywood County, North Carolina, addressed a letter to the Commissioner of Indian Affairs asking for the appointment of a superintendent to remove his people to the Indian Territory under the provisions of a Congressional act of July 29, 1848, appropriating $5,000 for the removal of the Catawba living "in the limits of North Carolina." These people expressed their preference for settlement among the Chickasaw, but the Chickasaw Council took no action on the subject.

In December, 1851, a party of nineteen Catawba reached Skullyville, in the Choctaw Nation, six of the twenty-five who had left Carolina having died on the way west. A peaceable, law-abiding people seeking a location for their homes, they asked for admittance into the Choctaw Nation and the right to settle permanently in this part of the Indian Territory. On November 9, 1853, the Choctaw General Council enacted legislation investing William Morrison, Thomas Morrison, Sarah Jane Morrison, and eleven other Catawba bearing the family names of Redhead, Heart Ayers, and Keggo with all the rights and privileges of Choctaw citizens. A further act of the Choctaw Council on November 12, 1856, declared all the fourteen Catawba adopted in 1853 "jointly entitled to a full participation in all funds arising under the treaty of 1855 between the Choctaws and the United States."

The government never assigned a definite location for the Catawba in the Indian Territory, but some of them settled in the Creek Nation. Living in the vicinity of Checotah in the eighteen eighties was Judge LeBlance, a Catawba who married a Creek and became prominent in Creek tribal affairs. He was a prosperous cattleman and merchant and served as judge in the court of the Creek Nation for several years.

In 1944 the South Carolina legislature granted the Catawba all the rights and privileges of citizens of that state, and their children attend the public schools and institutions of higher learning. They are predominantly of mixed white and Indian blood, thoroughly Americanized in speech, dress, and customs. In the public park of Rock Hill, Catawba Township, York County, a handsome monument was erected about 1900 to the memory of seventeen Catawba who served faithfully in the Confederate Army from South Carolina.

Suggested Readings: Bradford, *The Catawba Indians of South Carolina;* 54 Cong., 2 sess., *Sen. Doc. No. 144;* Grant Foreman, *Last Trek of the Indians;* Hodge, *Handbook of American Indians;* Milling, *Red Carolinians;* Swanton, *Indians of Southeastern U. S.*

CAYUGA

The name of the Cayuga is from *Kwĕñio' gwĕⁿᵉ*, "the place where the locusts were taken out." The people of this Indian tribe are of the Iroquoian linguistic family, and they formerly lived on the shores of Cayuga Lake, New York, where they were counted as one of the Five Nations of the Iroquois.

◆ **Present Location.** The Cayuga live in Ottawa County, having been allotted lands in severalty by 1891 among the Seneca in the southern part of the county. Some Cayuga live in New York, and a large number live near the Chippewa in Canada.

◆ **Numbers.** The Cayuga in Oklahoma are counted among the Seneca (q.v.) in Ottawa County. No complete enumeration of the Cayuga in the United States was ever made. They numbered 223 in New York in 1944. Their population was estimated at approximately 1,100 in 1774–75.

◆ **History.** At the start of the American Revolution, a large part of the Cayuga tribe left New York and moved to Canada, where many of their descendants are now living. Other bands of the tribe remained in this country scattered among their neighbors of the Iroquoian Confederacy. Soon after the close of the Revolutionary War, the Cayuga sold their lands in New York, some of the tribal bands moving to Ohio where they joined the remnants of other Iroquoian tribes (Erie, Conestoga, Oneida, Onondaga, and Mohawk) that became known as the Seneca of Sandusky. These people, including the band of Cayuga, moved to the Indian Territory in 1832, soon after concluding a treaty with United States commissioners at Washington (*see* Seneca). In the records of United States Indian affairs, these remnant Iroquoian tribes that formerly lived in New York are referred to as "New York Indians," among whom the Cayuga are generally listed.

It was with the idea of joining their tribal kin among the Seneca in the Indian Territory that a band of Cayuga from Canada and a few from New York, something over 100 persons, came to the Quapaw Agency in 1881. Some of these people were adopted by the Seneca, but the late arrivals were finally forced to return to Canada after suffering many hardships. A part of them set out to return on foot from the Indian Territory, a report later stating that 13 of them died on the way. While the Cayuga are not listed as a separate tribe in the Quapaw Agency records, these people were locally well known and have had a part in the history of the Seneca (q.v.) in the Indian Territory. Their name is incorporated in that of the "Seneca-Cayuga Tribe of Oklahoma," which received a corporate charter in 1937 under the Oklahoma Indian Welfare Act of 1936.

Suggested Readings: Grant Foreman, *The Last Trek of the Indians;* Hodge, *Handbook of American Indians;* Wilson, *Quapaw Agency Indians.*

CHEROKEE

Cherokee is the approved anglicized form of the name rendered *Tsálagĭ'* in the Cherokee language, a name found spelled in nearly fifty different ways in historical records. One authority has suggested that the term was probably applied to the Cherokee from the language of a Muskhogean tribe to signify "people of a different speech." The Choctaw, whose language was long the trade medium in the Southeast, call the Cherokee *Chalakki,* this having been recorded in early Spanish records as the name of the "Province of Chalaque," a part of the historic habitation of the tribe in what is now western North Carolina, which was visited by De Soto in 1540. Since the Cherokee were a mountain people living in the Southern Appalachian highland, the usual interpretation of *Chalaḳḳi* has been "cave people," from the Choctaw word *chuluḳ* or *chiluḳ,* meaning "cave." This theory is substantiated by the fact that in the native languages of tribes to the north the Cherokee were referred to as "cave people" or "people of the cave country." The name is analagous to "Rock People" of the ancient Huron, a related Iroquoian confederacy, among whom the "Tobacco Nation" suggests that the Cherokee term *Tsalagi* might be a mnemonic signifying "Ancient Tobacco People," from their name for wild tobacco *tsal-agayuñ' li* from the Cherokee words *tsâlû,* "tobacco," and *agayûñ' li,* "old" or "ancient." The wild tobacco, called "real tobacco" by the Iroquois, was held sacred and had an important place in the ancient Cherokee deliberative and religious ceremonies. There is an old Cherokee myth about how they lost the tobacco and how a hummingbird brought it back.

The Cherokee refer to themselves in their own language as *Ani'-Yun' wiya',* meaning "principal people," from *ani,* an animate prefix, *yunwi,* "person," and *ya,* a suffix meaning "real" or "principal." In some of the oldest tribal ceremonials, they referred to themselves as *Ani' Kitu' hwagi,* signifying "People of Kituwha." The name *Kitu'wha* was that of the tribal town of refuge in one of the most ancient settlements of the nation, located on the Tuckasegee River in what is now western North Carolina, from which the people spread out into many settlements through a wide region of mountain meadows and river valleys. The *Atali,* or Mountain Cherokee dialect, became the written language and is the language spoken by the Oklahoma Cherokee. The most musical of three Cherokee dialects, it lacks the sound of the English letter *r.*

The Cherokee are well built, are primarily of the "round-head" type, and are medium to tall in height. The fullblood men usually have more of an olive than a dark complexion, and some of the women are fairer, the tribe having been noted for its beautiful girls, especially among the mixed bloods. Though liberal and just, the Cherokee are known for their quick tempers, and some of their friends have said that they are shrewd and crafty in their dealings. They are steady and dignified in their deportment and cheerful in disposition. They have been noted for their bravery and courage in defense of their country and in the maintenance of their rights as a people.

◆ **Present Location.** Thirteen counties and parts of counties in northeastern Oklahoma constitute the area known as Cherokee Nation from its organization in 1839 to its dissolution in 1906. This region does not include the Cherokee Outlet, sometimes (erroneously) called the "Cherokee Strip," which extended across northern Oklahoma west from the ninety-sixth meridian, now included in thirteen counties and parts of counties. Most of the Cherokee today live in the northeastern counties, three of which have the largest Indian population in the state: Adair (6,601), Cherokee (6,298), and Delaware (5,066). Cherokee are found in nearly every large town and city in eastern and central Oklahoma, where they are engaged in business or the professions, or serve in county, state, or federal offices.

The descendants of a small part of the tribe that never moved west are known as the North Carolina or Eastern Cherokee and now live on the Qualla Reservation in western North Carolina.

◆ **Numbers.** Approximately 47,000 Cherokee live in Oklahoma, an increase over the 45,238 reported in the state in 1930. When the rolls of the Five Civilized Tribes were closed on March 4, 1907, the Cherokee Nation reported its citizens as follows: 6,601 full bloods, 29,986 part bloods (including 197 registered Delaware, q.v.), 286 intermarried whites, and 4,925 Negro freedmen, making a total of 41,798 (total corrected to 41,693 in 1914).

The authenticated rolls of the Cherokee Nation in 1881 showed an approximate Indian population in the nation of 19,130, after a very few corrections were made in the published census reports (1880) from the nine districts in the nation. This number included Shawnee (770) and Delaware (985) who had been incorporated in the nation, as well as 170 North Carolina or Eastern Cherokee who had moved to the Indian Territory in 1881.

A census report for the Cherokee Nation in 1867 showed 13,566 members of the tribe in the Indian Territory, which indicated a loss of one-third of their population during the Civil War—it was estimated that the Cherokee numbered 21,000 at the outbreak of the war.

Great loss in population occurred during the final removal of the Cherokee to the Indian Territory in 1838–39 when about one-fourth of the people perished. In 1835, a census report showed a total of 16,542 Cherokee living in Georgia, Tennessee, North Carolina, and Alabama. It was estimated at this time that 6,000 had moved west and settled in the Indian Territory. In 1808–1809, the population of the Cherokee towns was 12,395. At that time, the division of the tribe known as the Western Cherokee (Arkansas Cherokee, or, later, "Old Settler Cherokee") living on the White River in what is now Arkansas probably numbered around 2,000, the total population of the whole tribe being estimated at 15,000 ten years later, with about one-third of the number living in the White River region.

It was said that there were 20,000 Cherokee living in sixty-four towns and villages in their country in the East in 1729. By the middle of the century, they had been greatly reduced in numbers from disease and war. One historian has estimated their number at 22,000 in 1650.

The Eastern Cherokee Agency reported 3,724 members of the tribe living in North Carolina in 1944. A census return in 1895 showed their number to be 1,479; and in 1848, their number was reported at 2,133.

◆ **History.** A Cherokee legend that tells of a prehistoric migration from a land toward the rising sun was lost at a very early period, though it was referred to in one of the ceremonial orations during the annual green corn celebration about 1750. Traditional and historical evidence proves that the tribe once lived on the upper sources of the Ohio River south of the Iroquois, who were their bitter enemies. They subsequently entered the Tennessee region from Virginia along the valleys of the New and the Holston rivers, but were pushed still farther south by their enemies from the North until they came to the Little Tennessee. Their capital or peace town, Itsati, or Echota (Old Chota), was located on the south bank of the Little Tennessee, about nine miles from present Madisonville, Monroe County, Tennessee. In the latter part of the eighteenth century, the capital was moved south to Ustanali, later called New Echota, near the present city of Calhoun, Georgia.

De Soto discovered the province of Chalaque in the spring of 1540 and later reached the town of Guasili or Guaxule, where the chief and leaders of the Indians came out dressed in fine fur robes and feather headdresses to welcome the Spanish expedition. Gold mines in the Cherokee country interested the Spanish colonists in Florida, and there was probably some communication and intercourse between them and the native towns and villages before 1600.

The English first mentioned the tribe as "Cherakae Indians" in 1674. James Moore, secretary of the South Carolina colony, heard of the gold mines in the Cherokee country and headed an expedition into the region in 1690. The year 1700 is the traditional date for the introduction of firearms among the Cherokee, who developed from a mountain tribe of hunters to a warlike people prominent in frontier wars, in which they were generally friendly with the English interests even after the close of the American Revolution.

European colonization of the Atlantic seaboard engendered wars among the native tribes in the eighteenth century. The Cherokee defeated the Tuscarora of Carolina in 1711 and forced them to seek refuge in the North. In 1715, the Cherokee and their allies, the Chickasaw, drove the Shawnee out of the Cumberland River region. The break-up of the powerful Catawba tribe (q.v.) in Carolina was largely due to the warring Cherokee. About 1755, the Cherokee victory over the Creek in the Battle of Taliwa, in the vicinity of present Canton, Georgia, was important in the long struggle between the two tribes for possession of Upper Georgia. War begun with the Chickasaw (q.v.) about 1757 ended in the defeat of the Cherokee in 1768.

The beginning of the French and Indian War between England and France in 1756 saw three forts established in the Cherokee country under terms of treaties made by British officials with the tribal leaders: Fort Prince George near the tribal town of Keowee in the Keowee River region of western South Carolina, Fort Loudon in the vicinity of Echota in eastern Tennessee, and Fort Dobbs about twenty miles west of present Salisbury, North Carolina. Although the tribe sided with the British early in the conflict, arrogance and lawless acts on the part of some British officers—together with an open attack by some white frontiersmen, who killed and scalped a number of Cherokee warriors returning from participation in a British campaign against the Shawnee—brought on war with the Cherokee people, who were led by their war chief, Oconostota (Aganstata). Attakullakulla, the great civil chief of the Cherokee, finally succeeded in stopping the fighting, and a peace treaty was made with the British colonial officers at Charleston in 1761. Two years later when peace was concluded between England and France, Captain John Stuart, superintendent of Indian Affairs, held a great council at Augusta, Georgia, with the chiefs and leaders of the Southern tribes, during which a treaty of mutual friendship and peace was signed. By 1776, the Cherokee had given up large tracts along the eastern and northern boundaries of their tribal lands in so-called treaties with the bordering colonies.

Bitter over the continued cessions of the tribal hunting grounds, Attakullakulla's son, Dragging Canoe, became the implacable foe of the white people who were pushing the frontier farther and farther west. Soon after the Cherokee treaty of 1777, when his towns had been burned by the colonists, Dragging Canoe led a large number of warriors and their families to a location southwest on Chickamauga Creek, where he established a new tribal settlement in the vicinity of Chattanooga, Tennessee. The people of this division came to be known as the Chickamauga, the most hostile and warlike of the Cherokee. Encouraged by British agents, Dragging Canoe's forces continued raids on the white settlements bordering the Cherokee coun-

Tahchee, from McKenney and Hall, *History of the Indian Tribes of North America,* 1838

try after the close of the American Revolution.

Chickamauga leaders and their descendants, celebrated in Cherokee history, included Doublehead, Tahlonteeskee, Young Tassel (better known as John Watts), The Bowl, and Dutch, or Tahchee, noted for his exploits in the early history of the tribe in Oklahoma. Tahlonteeskee became chief of the Western Cherokee in Arkansas, and he in turn was succeeded by his brother, John Jolly, who served as their chief in Indian Territory before the main removal of their tribesmen from east of the Mississippi in the winter of 1838–39. The capital of the Western Cherokee in Indian Territory (1831–39) was called Tahlonteeskee in honor of their former chief, its location being near the Illinois River, about two miles east of the present village of Gore in Sequoyah County.

A bloody encounter between some of the Chickamauga under the leadership of The Bowl and a party of white boatmen traveling down the Tennessee River in 1794 had resulted in the destruction of the Chickamauga towns. Soon afterward, The Bowl brought some of his band and their families west of the Mississippi to the St. Francis River in what is now Arkansas, where they lived and prospered until 1812. They moved in this year to a new location between the White and the Arkansas rivers by arrangement with the United States government. These people became known as the Arkansas Cherokee or Western Cherokee, their numbers increasing from year to year as other bands of the tribe, among them that of Tahchee, or "Dutch," crossed the Mississippi to join them. Their expeditions west during the hunting seasons brought on war with the Osage (q.v.), who rose to defend their tribal claims to the country north of the Arkansas, and notable battles were fought. With the cessation of hostilities between the two tribes, leaders of the Western Cherokee signed a treaty with the United States at Washington in 1828, providing for an exchange of their Arkansas lands for a western tract of seven million acres, including what is now northeastern Oklahoma (except part of Ottawa County). They were also granted "a perpetual outlet west," known in history as the Cherokee Outlet, which extended west from the main tract to the limits of the United States territory. All the Cherokee, west and east, were to settle permanently in this new country. The year after the treaty, the Western Cherokee left their Arkansas homes and moved to their new location. By 1831, they had re-established their written laws and their government, which they continued until the coming of their Eastern tribesmen under the leadership of Chief John Ross in 1839.

Federal relations with the Cherokee had begun with the treaty of Hopewell on the Keowee River, South Carolina, November 25, 1785, signed by thirty-seven chiefs and leaders of the tribe. Large tracts of their tribal lands in Kentucky, Tennessee, and North Carolina were ceded to the United States at this time. From 1785 to 1902, the Cherokee signed twenty-five

MURIEL H. WRIGHT

John Ross

treaties and agreements with the government, eighteen of which provided outright cessions of tribal lands to the United States.

By the middle of the eighteenth century, the Cherokee had advanced in the ways of civilization. Chief Oconostota knew the importance of letters and papers and had placed a number relating to tribal affairs for safekeeping at Echota long before 1750, some of which are now preserved in the Division of Manuscripts in the Library of Congress. The old tribal customs and native dress still prevailed, though the people generally were dependent upon traders' supplies for firearms, hatchets, knives, and some utensils, cloth, and trinkets. Nearly every tribesman owned several head of horses, and hogs and poultry were plentiful throughout the country. A tribal village consisted of a number of native clay dwellings set apart from one another around a centrally located Town House. Extending away from the houses were fields where corn, potatoes, and beans were grown, both men and women sharing in the cultivation of the crops in ordinary times. The native arts of pottery and basketry were carried on by the women. The men were usually successful in hunting expeditions, bringing in furs and pelts which they sold to the traders. Pastimes included the ball game with accompanying dances, wheel and stick game, and a sort of dice game with painted beans played by both men and women.

The years following the first treaty with the United States at Hopewell in 1785 found the Cherokee impoverished and greatly reduced in numbers from continued border warfare, which foreshadowed the formation of new states west of the Allegheny Mountains with demands for more and more of the tribal lands. The government adopted a "civilization" policy to improve conditions in the tribe by furnishing the people with farming implements, spinning wheels, looms, and other necessities for the household.

The annuity payment ($1,000) in goods as provided by a treaty in 1791 was made to the Cherokee in varying amounts during the fifteen-year period from 1791 to 1806. The tribal agent reported in 1801 that the people were industrious in the use of "the wheel, the loom, and the plough," and were generally progressing in farming, home manufactures, and stock raising. The tribal members of the western settlements in Tennessee and Georgia, including the Chickamauga, were more aggressive in taking advantage of the treaty provisions and more enterprising in the use of the articles obtained from the government than some of the isolated, backward mountain people to the east, who complained that they were not securing their fair share. This fact, together with the concern of the whole tribe over continued cessions of their lands to the United States, engendered bad feeling and jealousy that finally culminated in the execution of Doublehead, the Chickamauga chief, ostensibly for having reserved a valuable land tract for his own use by secret agreement with the United States commissioners when negotiating the treaties of 1805. The killing was done in compliance with tribal law, with the consent of the chiefs and by a specially appointed committee commanded by Major Ridge, a prominent fullblood leader of Hiwassee. Out of this startling event arose animosities based on the ancient law of blood revenge that were far reaching in subsequent Cherokee history in Oklahoma.

The remarkable advancement of the Cherokee as a people came about largely through the influence of the mixed-blood families of Irish, German, English, Welsh, or Scottish descent, whose ancestors settled and married in the nation during the eighteenth century. Among them were such names at Adair, Vann, Chisholm, Ward, Hicks, Reese, Wickett, Fields, Ross, Lowry, and Rogers, all well-known tribal families whose descendants were prominent in Cherokee history. Many of them were planters and traders, owners of substantial residences, Negro slaves, and large herds of cattle by 1800.

The first of the great mixed-blood leaders was Charles Hicks, author of the first written law for the Cherokee Nation, adopted by the Council in 1808. A man of fine character and intelligence, with some educational advantages, he was a personal friend and contemporary of Sequoyah (George Guess or Gist), the famous inventor of the Cherokee alphabet.

One-half Cherokee through his mother, who belonged to the Paint Clan, Sequoyah was reared in the old tribal ways and customs without the advantage of any schooling and without knowledge of the English language. After working for many years on his project at his home near Willstown, Alabama, he at last completed his wonderful invention of a syllabary consisting of eighty-five characters representing all the combination consonant and vowel sounds in the Cherokee language. Knowledge of his syllabary quickly spread among his people, and they were writing and reading in the native Cherokee by 1822. Sequoyah subsequently moved west to live among

Sequoyah, from McKenney and Hall, *History of the Indian Tribes of North America,* 1838

the Arkansas Cherokee, and as one of their representatives signed the treaty of 1828, which established the Cherokee domain in Oklahoma. His log-cabin home near Sallisaw, in Sequoyah County, is now preserved as a historic shrine.

It was principally through the interest and influence of Charles Hicks that the Cherokee chiefs gave their consent to the establishment of churches and schools in the nation. The first mission school for the Cherokee was founded by missionaries of the Moravian church at Springplace, Georgia, in 1801. Two mission schools were opened under the auspices of the Presbyterian Assembly in 1803, located in the tribal settlements on the Hiwassee River, near the Tennessee–North Carolina line. Brainerd Mission was established in 1817 at Chickamauga Town, Tennessee, under the auspices of the American Board of Commissioners for Foreign Missions (Presbyterian, Congregational, and Dutch Reformed). This same American Board first established Dwight Mission among the Western Cherokee in 1820 in what is now Pope County, Arkansas. Methodist circuit riders commenced regular preaching in the nation in 1822. Baptist missionary work had begun among the Cherokee in 1817, in which the Valley Towns Mission on the Hiwassee River was noted, the native converts to this faith being counted the largest and the dominant church group in the nation before and after the main removal to the Indian Territory.

The spinning wheel and the loom were said to have been first known in the Cherokee Nation before the American Revolution, and the United States commissioners who returned from Hopewell in 1785 reported the Cherokee women eager to learn weaving of woolen and cotton cloth. Spinning and weaving were major industries in many Cherokee homes by 1820, with the hunting coat or shirt of striped homespun woolen cloth a distinctive part of the native costume.

The first published volume of laws of an

Cherokee Phoenix, June 25, 1828

American Indian government was the *Laws of the Cherokee Nation*, printed by order of the Cherokee National Committee and Council at Knoxville in 1821. The Cherokee government was further organized under a constitution providing regular legislative, executive, and judicial departments, adopted in 1827 at New Echota by a convention of delegates elected from each of the eight districts into which the Cherokee country had previously been divided by law. An appropriation for the establishment of a national press and the printing of a newspaper was voted by the General Council, the first issue of the *Cherokee Phoenix* appearing at New Echota on February 21, 1828, its columns printed both in English and in Cherokee, (using the Sequoyah syllabary). It was the first Indian newspaper in America. The constitution and laws of the Cherokee Nation were also printed on this national press in both English and the native language.

John Ross, one-eighth Cherokee of Scottish descent, was elected under the new constitution by the General Council (legislature) to head the executive department as principal chief in 1828, thus beginning his long and remarkable rule of the affairs of his people. He was the undoubted leader of a large majority, most of whom were fullblood Cherokee. The nation reached the height of its development in the East in 1828, at the time when Georgia was protesting the Indian government within her borders and claiming the right to resort to force, if necessary, in ridding the country of all the Indians. About this time, the discovery of gold in the Cherokee country near present Dahlonega, Georgia, was followed by a clamor for white settlement in the region. The election of the noted Indian fighter of Tennessee, Andrew Jackson, as president of the United States in 1828, gave Georgia a champion in her stand against the Cherokee.

The legislature of Georgia immediately enacted a law annexing the Cherokee country within her borders and placing it under the jurisdiction of state laws, the act to take effect on June 1, 1830. Chief Ross brought suit in the courts to establish the Cherokee property rights. His case, The Cherokee *vs.* Georgia, brought before the United States Supreme Court in January, 1831, was dismissed on the ground that the Cherokee were a "domestic dependent nation" with the United States as guardian, and therefore could not maintain action in the state courts. In its victory, Georgia next indicted the Reverend Samuel A. Worcester, a Vermonter and a missionary of the American Board, for continuing his residence in the Cherokee country without a permit and for refusing to take an oath of allegiance to the state. He was imprisoned and forced to hard labor. His suit, *Worcester* v. *Georgia,* was appealed in March, 1832, to the United States Supreme Court, which handed down a decision in his favor declaring the Georgia laws relating to the

MURIEL H. WRIGHT

Major Ridge

Indians unconstitutional and the law in his indictment null and void.

Continued agitation for a removal treaty on the part of government agents finally brought on a cleavage among the Cherokee, the great majority remaining with Ross, whose educational and cultural advantages and determined fight in their behalf had won respect in the states and at Washington. The opposition was led by Major Ridge's son, John Ridge, also a man of fine personality and educational advantages, who regarded further resistance on the part of the nation as useless and a removal treaty as the only way out of a desperate situation. Rival delegations went to Washington and councils were held in the nation, the question reaching a climax with the signing of a treaty for removal in the presence of United States commissioners on December 29, 1835, at New Echota. Fewer than five hundred Cherokee—men, women, and children—were in attendance during the negotiations out of a population of about seventeen thousand. John Ridge, Major Ridge, and his two nephews, Elias Boudinot and Stand Watie, were the principal signers in behalf of the nation, others among the twenty-two signers including Andrew Ross, Robert and William Rogers, John Gunter, John A. Bell, Charles F. Foreman, George W. Adair, and James Starr.

The main provisions of the New Echota Treaty were these: All Cherokee lands in the East were ceded to the United States, the Eastern Cherokee to have joint interest in the lands ceded to the Western Cherokee in the Indian Territory, for which one patent was to be executed in the name of the Cherokee Nation. An additional smaller tract (800,000 acres) was granted, afterward referred to as the "Neutral Land," in what is now southeastern Kansas. Payment was allowed the individual Cherokee emigrant who left improved property in the East. Every Cherokee was to remove west within two years after the ratification of the treaty, all expenses in the removal and subsistence for one year after arrival in the West to be paid by the United States.

Despite the protests of Chief Ross and his delegation, who were supported by a petition signed by thousands of their followers, the New Echota treaty was ratified by the United States Senate on May 23, 1836. It provided for the cession of approximately 8,000,000 acres of Cherokee land to the United States at about fifty cents an acre, although soon after ratification forty-acre tracts in the gold field were sold for as high as $30,000 by white speculators.

The removal west was to begin on May 26, 1838. The Ridges and their friends, with about two thousand followers, had departed before that date, joining the Western Cherokee or Old Settlers in the Indian Territory. The rest of the people, under the leadership of Chief Ross, remained, hopeful that the treaty would not go into effect. When government agents saw that it would be necessary to remove them by force, General Winfield Scott was placed in command of the situation. He issued an order from his headquarters at New Echota for all the natives to move out immediately. When squads of troops were sent throughout the country, the Cherokee were taken by surprise and driven at the point of the bayonet into stockaded concentration camps. Here families accustomed to refinements and culture were herded in misery and want. A few of the people escaped to a far-off mountain region where they remained in hiding, later forming the nucleus of the Eastern Cherokee division now living on the Qualla Reservation in North Carolina.

With sickness and death in the stockades when the first parties were ready to start for the West in the hot summer weather, the Cherokee Council petitioned General Scott to allow all to remain and move out under the supervision of their own officers after the "sickly season" was over in the fall. The petition granted, the Cherokee Council appointed the special officers, Chief

MURIEL H. WRIGHT

John Ridge

Ross contracting with outside persons to supply the necessary provisions en route. About thirteen thousand Cherokee, including some Negro slaves, were organized into detachments of one thousand persons, each group supervised by their own officers. They set forth late in the fall, thousands traveling on foot along different routes to the Indian Territory. Some detachments were delayed as much as six months on the eight-hundred-mile journey. All endured indescribable suffering from bad roads, storms, blizzards, sickness, and sorrow, more than 4,000 of their number dying before their destination was reached in the early spring of 1839.

Before the emigrating parties had left the East, the General Council meeting at Camp Aquohee on August 1, 1838, adopted a resolution declaring "the inherent sovereignty of the Cherokee Nation," together with its "constitution, laws, and usages," to be in full force and effect and to continue so in perpetuity. The resolution repudiated the treaty of New Echota, referring to it as "the pretended treaty." An act of the Cherokee Council, approved about 1828, imposing the death penalty on any Cherokee who should propose the sale or exchange of the tribal lands, was made effective, though it was not specifically mentioned in the resolution. None of the Ridge party or the Old Settlers (Western Cherokee) had a part in the Aquohee Resolution, nor was it generally known until its publication by the United States War Department more than a year later.

The immigrants were received as friends by the Old Settlers and were soon at work finding locations and making improvements for homes in their new land. On the first Monday in June, 1839, after the arrival of the Ross followers, a convention of all the Cherokee was held at Tukattokah or Double Springs on Fourteen Mile Creek, about ten miles north of Fort Gibson. Officers and leaders of the Eastern division, representing nearly two-thirds of the whole nation, had their meeting place some distance from the Old Settlers, the two groups deliberating separately from each other. The Ross party proposed that a new constitution should be submitted to the vote of the whole nation. The Western chiefs— John Brown, John Looney, and John Rogers—refused on the ground that their own government should remain in force until

the regular October session of their council, during which any necessary changes in the laws could be made legally. They were willing for the newcomers to take part in the voting when the next elections were held. Members of the Ridge party, meeting with the Old Settlers, were in full accord with them. This fact stirred up the old animosity against the Ridges for having signed the treaty of New Echota, and they were bitterly denounced in the throng at Tukattokah by those who had recently endured disaster and suffering in the removal.

On the morning of June 22, 1839, three days after the adjournment of the convention, Major Ridge, John Ridge, and Elias Boudinot were assassinated at almost the same hour in different parts of the country. Stand Watie was also marked for death, but escaped through a timely warning. Friends of these prominent men charged Chief Ross with having instigated the killing, although he vigorously and steadily denied any knowledge of the conspiracy. His assertions were undoubtedly true, yet there were reasons to believe that those who committed the murders were among his followers. The old tradition of blood revenge and the law exacting the death penalty for the sale of any tribal lands were of special significance in the tragedy. It was said that one of the con-

Cherokee Council of 1843, from a painting by John Mix Stanley in the Smithsonian Institution

spirators was the son of Doublehead, the Chickamauga chief who had been executed by a committee under Major Ridge many years before. Feeling ran high after the assassination of the Ridges, and civil war threatened in the Cherokee Nation.

The leaders of the Ross or National party proceeded with plans for organizing the new government by issuing a call for a convention of all the Cherokee to meet on July 1, 1839, at the Illinois Camp Ground, a location on the Illinois River near the home of Chief Ross. Among the two thousand Cherokee in attendance, five were Old Settlers, one of whom was George Guess, or Sequoyah, who served as vice president of the convention. His old friend, George Lowry, second chief of the Eastern Cherokee, served as president, and Elijah Hicks was secretary of the convention.

On July 12, 1839, the convention adopted a formal "Act of Union," by which the Eastern and the Western Cherokee were declared "one body politic, under the style and title of the Cherokee Nation." A national convention was held at Tahlequah in accordance with this act on September 6, 1839, during which a constitution was drafted and adopted. It was also accepted and approved by a convention of Old Settlers meeting at Fort Gibson on June 26, 1840.

About a year before this time, two bands of the Arkansas Cherokee who had migrated to Texas, the first led by The Bowl in the winter of 1819–20 and the second by Tahchee (or "Dutch") in 1831, had been driven out of that country and had come north to live with their kinsmen in the Indian Territory. Henceforth, the history of the Cherokee is that of a reunited people living under the constitution and laws of their own republic where an unusual civilization developed—basically American Indian yet Anglo-American in custom and usage.

The constitution and laws of the Cherokee Nation required that all officers of the legislative, executive, and judicial de-partments be Cherokee by blood. The land was held in common, the individual having the right to establish improvements anywhere under certain limitations. All the country, exclusive of the Cherokee Outlet lying west of the ninety-sixth meridian, was organized into eight districts for governmental purposes, with Tahlequah designated the capital. In 1856, the districts were increased to nine with the organization of the Cooweescoowee District on the northwest, a large tract with the ninety-sixth meridian as its western boundary.

A public school system was established in 1841, with the Reverend Stephen Foreman as national superintendent of schools. The public schools were supported by appropriations of the National Council from the Cherokee educational funds provided in the treaties with the United States. The establishment of mission schools was limited by law. Dwight Mission was moved from Arkansas to the Indian Territory in 1829, remaining the outstanding school of this class among the Cherokee. Teaching was carried on at some of the earlier mission stations for a time, including New Springplace (Moravian mission near the present village of Oaks in Delaware County), Fairfield Mission (near Lyons), and Baptist Mission (near present Westville in Adair County). There were 18 public schools in operation in 1843, the number increasing to more than 120 during the last days of the Cherokee government a half-century later. Two seminaries for higher learning were opened to Cherokee students in May, 1851, with the National Female Seminary located three miles southeast and the National Male Seminary one and one-half miles southwest of Tahlequah.

A national printing press set up at Tahlequah published the *Cherokee Advocate,* the first issue appearing in September, 1844, the first newspaper in Oklahoma, its columns printed in English and in Cherokee. The Park Hill Mission Press at Park Hill, under the superintendency of the Reverend Samuel A. Worcester, rendered great service by printing in Cherokee as well as in the languages of many other tribes in the Indian Territory before 1860. The mission press at Baptist Mission published *The Cherokee Messenger* partly in the Cherokee language. It was the first periodical in Oklahoma, the first issue appearing in August, 1844.

Through the interest of Chief Ross and other native leaders, the Cherokee were active in a number of intertribal councils to promote friendly relations with other tribes, including some from the Plains in the Indian Territory. By 1832, Jesse Chisholm, the noted Cherokee "Pathfinder and Peacemaker" in Oklahoma history, was carrying on trading expeditions among the Plains tribes in western Indian Territory.

The reign of terror that followed the assassination of the Ridges in the summer of 1839 was the beginning of a feud that heightened the old factionalism among the people, often resulting in violence. Nearly every issue of *The Cherokee Advocate* during its first two years carried reports of other assassinations and murders. Political strife arose in attempts to settle the ambiguous terms of the New Echota treaty.

A government commission was appointed, consisting of Colonel Roger Jones, adjutant general of the United States Army, Lieutenant Colonel R. B. Mason, of the United States Dragoons, and Governor Pierce M. Butler, the Cherokee agent, to investigate conditions in the nation and secure some agreement for a settlement among the factions in the nation. When the commission met at Fort Gibson, it was the diplomacy and good sense of Acting Principal Chief George Lowry that guided affairs in the absence of Chief John Ross, who was in the East. Finally, delegations from each of three Cherokee factions met in Washington, where a new treaty was signed on August 6, 1846. It provided for a patent to be issued by the United States to secure all lands in the nation for the common use and benefit of all the Cherokee, a general amnesty for all past offenses in the nation, the adjudication of all Cherokee claims, and the adjustment of other matters that had long awaited settlement.

The cleavage in the old political feud

MURIEL H. WRIGHT

Cherokee Male Seminary, near Tahlequah, 1851–1910

THE
CHEROKEE MESSENGER.

GWY DⱠOꞭⱢℱ.

VOL. I.	AUGUST, 1844.	NO. 1.
ℱＳ.ℐＢꞭ .ℐＳꞝＢＷＯ-Ꭿ 1.	ＳꞬℏ, 1844.	Ｄ4ℐℬᎢ 1.

Translation of Genesis into the Cherokee Language.

.ℐ.ℐℙＷＯ-Ꭿ Aℬℒ .ℐＬꞝℏꞝℰ Ｏℬ ＯꞬℬℬＷＯ-Ꭿ.

ᎥꞬ Ｗℒℐ .ℐＳꞝＢＶ.ℐ Dℏ 6ℏᎫ◮ⰔＱ ＫＴ ＴＥℬℬ ◉ℬＶ◮ .ℐＬꞝℏℰ Ｏℬ ＯꞬℬℬＷＯ-Ꭿ, ℱꞬＷ◮Ｚ Ｔ◮ℐꞬ .ℐℰ.ℐℙＷＯ-Ꭿ Dꞝ .ℐℰℤℒ-ℐℬℬＷＯ-Ꭿ ℏℰℰℱ Dℏ ＧＷＹℬ.

DℬＶ◮Ｔ IV.

1 DᏞＯＺ ＯＳＶᎥ4 Ｔ◉ ＯℬℒＴ; Dꞝ Ｏℐ-ℒＴＴ, Dꞝ Ｏ-◉ＱℐＯ4.ℱℏ,·Dꞝ .ℐℬ.ℐℬ4Ｔ, ℬℱꞬℬＹℏ DＹＯℬ Dℬℱℬℬ.

2 Ｗℒℐℐ Ｏ-◉ＱℐＯ4 ℬᎥＯ-ℰ ℛℱℒ.ℛＴℛＺ DＯ .ℐℐ.ℐℬℬ ℱ4Ｔ,·ℱℏℬℬＹℏ ℱℱＬ.ℐℐℐＯℬℬ-Ꭿℐ ℱ4Ｔ

3 Ｔ-◮.ℐꞬＺ ＴＢꞭ AD ᎡℒℬℬＷℐＴ, ℱℏ Ｏℏℱꞝ ℬℱꞬℬ DℒℬℐℬＷＯ-Ꭿ ℬＶℐ ＯꞬℛ.ℐ.

4 ℛℱℒＺ ◉ℬℬꞝ Ｏℏꞝ Ｏℬℒ ＴＥℬℬ .ℐℏ-ℱＯ-Ꭿ DＯ Dꞝ Ｏℒℛ.ℐꞭ. ℬℱꞬℬ Ｓℬℏ◮Ｖ ℛℱℒ Dꞝ ＯℒℬℬℐꞬＷＯ-Ꭿ.

5 ℱℏℬＹℏ Dꞝ Ｏℒℬℐ◮ꞬＷＯ-Ꭿ Ꭵꞏℬℬℬ-ℏ◮Ｖｔ. ℱℏＺ ＯꞬℐ ＯＷＷℬℬ4Ｔ, Dꞝ Ｇℬ-ＳＺℐℬ ℛＷℐ ◮ℒℬℬＷℐＴ.

6 ℬℱꞬℬ AD Ꭱℬℬ4ꞝ ℱℏ, ℬＶＺ ＴＧℬꞝ-ℬ◮ꞏ? Dꞝ ℬＶＺ ＴＧℬＺ.ℐℬ ℛＷℐℬꞝ ℏＯ-ℬ.ℐ?

7 ＴＧꞝＺ ℬℬ ℬℏℬℱℐℬ, ℱℏＺ ℬＶℬℬ-◉ℏℏℬＹ? ℱℛＺ ℏℱℱ.ℐℬ◮ ℬＹ, Dℬℬ◉ℬＺ

ℬꞬℬℬℐℬℬꞝ ＴＳＯ-ℬ. Dꞝ-Ｚ ℏℐ ℱℬ ＳℐＧＳ-ℬℐ, AℬℬℬＯ-ＴℱℒＳℐꞝ-Ｚ ℱ4ℬℐ.

8 ¶ℱℏℱＺ ＯℒＺℱＷℐ ＯＯ-Ｃ ℛℱℒ: Dꞝ AD ℐℒℬℬＷℐＴ, ℱℱℏℬ DℐＶℬℬＴ, ℱℏ ℬℬℐ-◮4 ＯＯ-Ｃ ℛℱℒ, Dꞝ ＯꞝℬℝＴ.

9 ℬℱꞬℬ AD Ꭱℬℬ4ꞝ ℱℏ, ◉ℱℙ, ℛＧＯ-Ｃ ℛℱℒ? .ℐDＺ Ꭱℬℬ4Ｔ, ℒ ℬℏℬＳＷＯℱ: ℏℐℱ DＢ ᎥＹＯ-Ｃ ℱℬℐℬ?

10 .ℐDＺ Ꭱℬℬ4Ｔ, ℬＶ ＧꞬ.ℐℬ? ℬＶℐ ＴＢꞭ .ℐＹ.ℐＶ ℛＧＯ-Ｃ ＯＹＥ.

11 Dꞝ ℒℬꞝ ℛＧℬ ℛＧℬℬＳℐℬ ℱ4ℬℐ, ◉ℬＹ .ℐＷꞬℬ- ℛＧＯ-Ｃ ＯＹＥ .ℐＫᎫℏ .ℐℰＷＯ-Ꭿ ℱꞝℬＷℬ;

12 ＴＧꞝＺ ℬＶℐ ℬℐꞝＹℬℱꞝℐ,ℐℐ ＴＧ-ℬꞝℰℐ Ꭵℐ ℬℬℐꞝ ℬℱℐ◮4ℱℬℐ; Dꞝ Ｇℱℐ-ꞝℐꞝ Dꞝ Ｏꞝℬ.ℐℐℐꞝ ℱ4ℬℐ ℛＧℬ.

13 ℱℏＺ AD Ꭱℬℬ4ꞝ ℬℱꞬℬ, (ℛꞝ-ℐＧꞝ ℏℬＹℱℱℏℰＴ,) Ꭵꞟ ℱℒ ℬℏℏℬℬℬℬ, ◉ℬＹ ＴＳＴ DＹＹℒℏＴℬℐℬ.

14 ℱℏℬꞝℬ3Ｚ, .ℐℐ Ｔℬ ℬＹℱ◮ℬ ℛＧℬ; Dꞝ ℏℐ .ℐＧℬℬℏℬℬℐℬ Dℰℐℬℬℬℬℐ; Dꞝ Dℰℒℐℱ Dꞝ ℬℬℐℐℬ ℱ4ℬℐ ℛＧℬ; Dꞝ AD Ｏ-ℬℬℒℬℬＷℏ ◉ℏᎥꞝ ℰＹＧ.ℐℬℱℬℐ ℰＹ.ℐℱ-ℬℐ.

15 ℬℱꞬℬ AD Ꭱℬℬ4ꞝＴ, ＴＧꞝＺ ＹＧ ＴD-AᎥℬℐ ℱℏ, ℬℒℬꞝＹ ＴＧꞝℐℐ DℬℒＴℐ ℱ4ℬℐ. Dꞝ ℬℱꞬℬ ＯꞬℬℬＷℐ ℱℏ,◉ℬＹℬＺ ＹＧ ℬℱꞬℬℱꞝℬ ℬℰℬℐℬℐꞝ ℏℱℏ◉ ＴＧℒ-ℬＶ.ℐℬ.

16 ℱℏＺ ℬꞝ Ｏ-ℬꞝℛꞝ ℬℱꞬℬ, Dꞝ Ｚ.ℐℬ ℐ.ℐＷℬＴ,Ｔℬℏ ℱℬ .ℐℬ4ℰ Ｔ.ℐℙ ＯＳꞬℬℱꞝＴ.

MURIEL H. WRIGHT

The Cherokee Messenger, August, 1844

paralleled the divisions that arose among the people at the outbreak of the Civil War. The location of the Cherokee Nation and the influence of its leaders were important in the conflict between the Federal and the Confederate forces on the Southwestern frontier. Negro slavery had been established by law in the Cherokee Nation, although the fullblood people generally did not own slaves and were opposed to the principle of slavery. Chief Ross, as leader of the greater part of the Cherokee, adopted a course of neutrality in view of the impending clash between the North and the South, though he himself was a slaveholder.

Success of Confederate forces in southwestern Missouri in 1861, along with continued pressure from Confederate officers who had brought about the organization of a Cherokee regiment by Stand Watie to co-operate with the Southern armies, finally forced Chief Ross to abandon his position of neutrality. He with other Cherokee leaders signed a treaty at Park Hill on October 7, 1861, with Commissioner Albert Pike, aligning the Cherokee Nation with the Confederacy.

Early in the summer of 1862, the Cherokee troops of Colonel Stand Watie and Colonel John Drew were forced to withdraw in several skirmishes with Federal troops of the so-called "Indian Expedition" ordered south from Kansas. However, this first invasion of the Federal "Indian Expedition" retreated into Kansas, taking Chief Ross and other Cherokee officials with them as prisoners of war. Chief Ross was soon paroled to go to Washington and Philadelphia, where he remained throughout the remainder of the war.

Soon afterward, a meeting of Southern Cherokee was held at Tahlequah, where the constitution and laws of the Cherokee Nation and the treaty with the Confederate States were reaffirmed, and Stand Watie was elected chief. The following February (1863), the Northern Cherokee in the National Council and their friends met at Cowskin Prairie and repudiated the proceedings of the Southern Cherokee, declared the treaty with the Confederate states abrogated and Negro slavery abolished in the nation. Thomas Pegg served as acting principal chief for the Northern Cherokee

in the absence of John Ross. Henceforth to the end of the war, there were two rival governments, each claiming to be the rightful authority in the Cherokee Nation. Cherokee troops were lined up to fight on opposite sides in many bloody skirmishes and battles between Federal and Confederate forces in the Indian Territory and Arkansas.

Three Indian Home Guard regiments were noted for their service within the Federal lines, in which the Second Regiment was mostly Cherokee, and the Third Regiment, all Cherokee "Pins," distinguished by two crossed pins worn on the coat, served as Federal scouts, the terror of the whole countryside. The "Pins" were members of the Keetoowah, a secret society organized in 1859 among the fullblood Cherokee by the Baptist missionaries, Evan Jones and his son, John B. Jones, to promote Cherokee nationalistic aims. The Keetoowah Society, whose name was taken from that of ancient *Kituwha,* was strongly in favor of the abolition of Negro slavery at the outbreak of the Civil War.

Stand Watie was the distinguished lead-

MURIEL H. WRIGHT

Stand Watie

MURIEL H. WRIGHT

Cherokee Female Seminary, near Park Hill, 1852–88

er and officer of the Southern Cherokee, the only Indian officer who attained the rank of brigadier general in the Confederate Army. He was not a military man in the strict sense of the term, but was at his best scouting with a mounted force of two hundred to three hundred men. He surrendered the Southern Cherokee forces and other troops of his command to Federal officers at Doaksville, Choctaw Nation, June 23, 1865, the last Confederate general to surrender at the end of the war. Guerrilla fighting and armies of the opposing sides had swept the Cherokee country, the people living as refugees in and out of the nation, some of them not returning until 1867 to find their settlements in ruins.

The Cherokee treaty signed at Washington on July 19, 1866, with Federal commissioners, began a new era in the Cherokee Nation. Two rival delegations had been in Washington during the long negotiations: the Southern Cherokee represented by such leaders as William P. Adair, Richard Fields, Elias C. Boudinot, and John Rollin Ridge, the Cherokee poet; the Northern Cherokee led by John Ross, their delegation finally succeeding in making and signing the treaty, a victory for the policy of continued nationalism of the Cherokee people furthered by Chief Ross. While the treaty of 1866 was not wholly satisfactory, the Southern Cherokee finally accepted it even though their delegates were not among the signers. The treaty provided for the continuation of the Cherokee government with some stipulated changes in its laws.

At the death of Principal Chief John Ross (August 1, 1866) soon after the signing of the treaty, Colonel Lewis Downing, assistant principal chief, served as the executive until the meeting of the National Council when William P. Ross was selected to fill the unexpired term. He was a nephew of Chief Ross, a graduate of

MURIEL H. WRIGHT

Principal Chief D. W. Bushyhead in 1887

Princeton University, and the former editor of the *Cherokee Advocate*.

A realignment of the old political factions was soon effected through the efforts of Evan Jones and his son, working with their friend, Colonel Lewis Downing, who had formerly served in the Baptist ministry. They succeeded in bringing the full-blood element and the Southern Cherokee together in a new organization, which was afterward known as the Downing party. Chief William P. Ross was the leader of the National party, having broken off his former friendly association with the two Joneses. In the election of 1867, Colonel Downing was chosen principal chief, from which time the old feuds and factions gave way before the common concern of all the Cherokee over their relations with the United States in the increasing pressure for the opening of the Indian Territory to white settlement. When the National party and a new Union party became rivals and dominated Cherokee politics in the

early eighteen eighties, the Downing party was eclipsed for a short period, but was reorganized in 1887 and elected every principal chief from that time until the dissolution of the Cherokee government.

Railroad construction through the Indian Territory, with new towns springing up along the lines, and the growth and progress in adjoining states after the war brought demands in the markets for agricultural products, livestock, timber, stone, and other natural resources. The Cherokee were generally prospering by 1880, in trading, merchandise stores, livestock raising, and farming; some were successful in professional life—law, medicine, and education. Thousands of acres of new land were put under cultivation and fenced, and stock raising increased in the western, organized portion of the country. Tahlequah became well known throughout the Indian Territory and the Western states as the capital and center of cultural and educational life in the Cherokee Nation.

The rich grassland in the Outlet, lying west of the newly organized Indian reservations, became a complicated business for the Cherokee government. In 1879, the National Council passed a law for the collection of fees from outside cattlemen for grazing privileges in the Outlet, hundreds of thousands of cattle driven overland from Texas to shipping points in Kansas having grazed free on the open range for many years. When collection proved difficult and expensive, the Cherokee authorities changed the plan in 1883 by leasing all grazing privileges in the Outlet for five years at $100,000 a year to the Cherokee Strip Live Stock Association, an organization of cattlemen with headquarters at Caldwell, Kansas.

The year that saw the first run for homesteads by white settlers at the opening of the "Oklahoma Country," April 22, 1889, saw the beginning of long-drawn-out negotiations for the purchase of the Cherokee Outlet by the United States, the Congressional act of March 2, 1889, having provided for the appointment of a special government commission to negotiate the purchase. This commission, generally referred to as the Cherokee Commission, finally secured an agreement for the purchase of the Outlet, which was ratified by Congress on March 3, 1893. A deed was executed by the constituted authorities of of the Cherokee Nation on May 17, 1893, relinquishing to the United States the remaining Outlet lands, approximately 6,-574,487 acres, for the sum of $8,595,736.12. This immense tract was opened to white settlement by the most spectacular run for claims in the history of Oklahoma, on September 16, 1893, an area now included in twelve counties and parts of counties extending across the northern part of the state from Osage County to the one-hundredth meridian.

The Cherokee were opposed to any proposal to organize the Indian Territory as a federal territory or state. The Congressional act (March 3, 1893) that ratified the sale of the Outlet to the United States provided also for the appointment of the Commission to the Five Civilized Tribes, commonly called the Dawes Commission, to treat with each of the five tribes to secure agreements for allotment of lands in severalty and the disbanding of their governments preparatory to Oklahoma statehood. For several years the Cherokee steadily refused to enter negotiations with the Dawes Commission, the opposition coming principally from the Keetoowah organizations. After the failure of two agreements between the Dawes Commission and the Cherokee delegation, a third agreement was finally approved by a vote of the Cherokee people on August 7, 1902, in a special election called by Principal Chief T. M. Buffington.

All members of the Cherokee Nation were now duly enrolled. Every man, woman, and child (41,693 reported in 1914) had selected an allotment amounting to 110 acres of average land from the tribal domain by the time the Cherokee rolls were closed in March, 1907. Although the Cherokee government was to have disbanded in March, 1906, it was continued in modified and restricted form under an act of Congress until June 30, 1914, when all business in the division of tribal properties was finished. Principal Chief William C. Rogers, chosen in the last election (1903), continued in his office until 1917 to sign the deeds in the transfer of Cherokee lands.

The dissolution of the Cherokee government left the people of this American Indian nation citizens of the new state of Oklahoma, where their advancement and experience in government gave them prestige and prominence. Among the Cherokee in the Constitutional Convention were the late Clem V. Rogers, of Claremore, and Judge O. H. P. Brewer, now of Muskogee, who is on the bench of District Court No. 15, having been re-elected to this position for many terms. The late Robert Latham Owen, a prominent Cherokee attorney,

MURIEL H. WRIGHT

William C. Rogers, principal chief, 1903–17

MURIEL H. WRIGHT

Cherokee capitol building, Tahlequah,
about 1900

was the first United States senator from Oklahoma, serving continuously in this position from 1907 to 1925. Representatives to the United States Congress from Oklahoma, re-elected for many terms, were the late W. W. Hastings and Charles D. Carter (*see* Chickasaw), both members of prominent Cherokee families. Other prominent leaders include N. B. Johnson, elected justice of the Oklahoma Supreme Court (1948), and the late J. Bartley Milam, president of the Rogers County Bank, both of Claremore. Among leading Cherokee women may be named Isobel Cobb (M.D.), Caroline Eaton, Ellen Howard Miller, Mrs. R. L. Fite, Carlotta Archer, and Minta Foreman. A beautiful memorial building was erected at Claremore by Oklahoma in honor of the world-famous actor, writer, and philosopher, Will Rogers, son of Clem V. Rogers of the Cherokee Nation. One of the state's distinguished high-ranking personnel in the armed forces of the United States in World War II, Rear Admiral Joseph James Clark, is a native Oklahoman of Cherokee descent.

◆ **Government and Organization.** The office of principal chief of the Cherokee Nation is now a nominal one without salary or expense allowance of any kind, although the office is still regarded with honor. Duties include promoting the interest of tribal members in the various government welfare programs in the Office of Indian Affairs and acting in an advisory capacity

in the tribal suits before the Indian Claims Commission. The principal chief in 1948 was J. Bartley Milam (deceased, 1949) of Claremore, who was first appointed to the position on April 16, 1941, by President Franklin D. Roosevelt and reappointed on May 18, 1947, by President Harry S. Truman. W. W. Keeler of Bartlesville succeeded him as chief.

The constitution of the Cherokee Nation (1839–1906) provided for a legislative department called the National Council, composed of a National Committee (upper house or senate) with two elected members for each district (eight districts, later increased to nine), and a Council (lower house) with three elected members from each district. The executive department consisted of a principal chief and an assistant principal chief, elected every four years, with an executive council of five (or three) members appointed by the National Council to serve in an advisory capacity. Supreme, circuit, and lesser courts made up the judicial department. The constitution provided a bill of rights, with trial by jury guaranteed; freedom of religious worship was recognized, but all officers in the government must admit the existence of God and the future state of reward and punishment.

The principal chiefs who served the Cherokee Nation from 1839 to 1906 were John Ross, 1839 to 1866; Lewis Downing, August to October, 1866, and 1867 to 1872 (died in office); William Potter Ross, 1866 to 1867, and 1872 to 1875; Charles Thompson (Oochalata), 1875 to 1879; Dennis Wolf Bushyhead, 1879 to 1887; Joel Bryan Mayes, 1887 to 1891 (died in office); C. Johnson Harris, 1891 to 1895; Samuel Houston Mayes, 1895 to 1899; Thomas Mitchell Buffington, 1899 to 1903; William Charles Rogers, 1903 to 1906 (continuing in office until 1917). Stand Watie was principal chief of the Southern Cherokee in 1863, his recognition as such continuing among his followers until 1866.

The Keetoowah Society, incorporated

Cherokee leaders, about 1896
Standing, left to right: C. V. Rogers, W. W. Hastings, George W. Benge, W. P. Thompson, John E. Gunter; seated: Henry Lowery, Soggy Sanders, R. B. Ross, Percy W. Wyley

with charter by United States court order in 1905, continues today with approximately seven thousand members, nearly two-thirds of whom are fullblood Cherokee. Some make their homes in Muskogee, but most of them live in rural communities in Adair, Cherokee, Sequoyah, Delaware, Mayes, Muskogee, Craig, Nowata, Rogers, Tulsa, Washington, and Osage counties. The Keetoowah members feel a strong mystical relationship with ancient prototypes or tribal patterns and the rest of the natural and supernatural world, although there is no actual historical relationship between the modern society (organized in 1859) and the ancient *Kituwha* (from the Cherokee word for "key"). Members of the Society have always been very conservative, opposed to the breakdown of the old cultural pattern of the Cherokee tribe. When first organized, the Society included persons belonging to the

various Christian church denominations as well as those who worshipped according to the old tribal religion. With the appointment of the United States government commissions to dissolve the Cherokee government, there developed a marked difference between the Christian Keetoowah and the so-called "Ancient Keetoowah."

Soon after the Dawes Commission began its work, the Keetoowah organization split over the question of allotment of lands in severalty. The more conservative group or "Ancient Keetoowah" drew away from the main society under the leadership of Red Bird Smith, whose large following among the fullblood Cherokee became known as the "Nighthawk Keetoowah," the name being applied because they met at night and were vigilant in their activities. This group numbers from 3,000 to 3,500 persons living in rural communities in Sequoyah, Adair, Delaware, Mayes, and Muskogee counties. About 120 full-blood families drew away from the Night-hawk organization in 1932, and formed the "Seven Clans Society" under the leadership of Eli Pumpkin, who has been the chairman of the Society for nineteen years. This Cherokee group has favored the ownership and operation of land as a unit to promote the welfare of its members.

◆ **Contemporary Life and Culture.** The Cherokee are considered one of the most advanced American Indian tribes in Oklahoma. Many citizens of Cherokee descent have gained prominence in business, in the professions, or in political positions. Yet thousands of fullblood Cherokee have remained among the very poorest Indian groups in Oklahoma. Their problems concern health, education, and soil conservation, for they have their cabin homes in the rough, hilly country of northeastern Oklahoma, where the most of the land has always been poor in quality. Many of these people have retained their old tribal integrity of character and energy that makes them want to improve their condition when they have the opportunity.

The development of arts and crafts, especially in weaving and basketry, through the aid of the Indian Arts and Crafts Board of the United States Department of the Interior since 1935, has been successful among the Cherokee in the eastern counties. The Sequoyah Weavers' Association, the oldest of several associations, with headquarters at the Sequoyah Indian Vocational School, Tahlequah, is known for its beautiful homespun woolens, and yearly receives orders for thousands of yards from dealers in the Eastern states. Workers in the Cherokee Basket Association at Jay in Delaware County make a variety of attractive baskets from buckbush, which grows throughout eastern Oklahoma.

The Cherokee, particularly the fullblood people, are practically all members of Protestant denominations. The Baptist and the Methodist churches have the largest membership in the rural communities.

◆ **Ceremonials and Public Dances.** The Nighthawk Keetoowah hold their ceremonials in summer near Gore in Sequoyah County. These are open to the public, dates generally being announced in advance through the press in the state. Old ceremonials and dances are held at an announced time in summer by the Seven Clans Society, about eleven miles north of Proctor in Adair County. Such celebrations have almost disappeared since they are no longer vital in the life of the Cherokee people.

Suggested Readings: Brown, *Old Frontiers;* Dale and Litton, *Cherokee Cavaliers;* Grant Foreman, *Five Civilized Tribes;* Hargrett, *Laws of the American Indians;* Mooney, "Myths of the Cherokee," in *19 Ann. Rep.,* Bur. Amer. Ethnol.; Royce, "The Cherokee Nation of Indians," in *5 Ann. Rep.,* Bur. Amer. Ethnol.; Wardell, *Political History of the Cherokee Nation.*

CHEYENNE

The accepted name of the tribe known as the Cheyenne is from the Sioux language, in which the name *Shahi'yena or Shai-ena* signifies "people of an alien speech," from the word *sha'ia,* "to speak a strange language." The Cheyenne call themselves *Dzi'tsiis-täs* which signifies "people who are alike" or "our people," from their word *ïtsïstau,* "alike," or *ehïsta,* "he is from, or of, the same kind." In the sign language among the Plains Indians, the Cheyenne are indicated by drawing the right index finger across the left several times, a gesture which has sometimes been interpreted to mean "cut fingers," though it really means "striped arrows," alluding to the

MURIEL H. WRIGHT

Little Robe about 1870

preference of the Cheyenne for using turkey feathers to wing their arrows.

The Cheyenne are a most important division of the Algonquian linguistic family and are counted as one of the great tribes of the Plains Indians in Oklahoma. They have long been closely associated with the Arapaho (q.v.). The two tribes are referred to in Oklahoma as the Southern Cheyenne and the Southern Arapaho to distinguish them from their respective northern divisions on reservations in Montana (Tongue River) and Wyoming (Wind River).

The Cheyenne were originally agriculturists and makers of pottery, living in permanent villages in the timbered country of their ancient habitation, now included within the state of Minnesota. In a later period of their history, they became roving buffalo hunters on the Plains. They are characteristically proud, contentious, and brave, and their women uphold high moral standards. During the last century of tribal days when the life of the Cheyenne people was dominated by their warrior society,

called the "Dog Soldiers," the young men of the tribe were trained for and gloried in war.

◆ Present Location. In Oklahoma, the Cheyenne live near Thomas, Clinton, and Weatherford, Custer County; Hammon (Red Moon), Roger Mills County; El Reno and Concho, Canadian County; Kingfisher, Kingfisher County; Watonga and Canton, Blaine County; Seiling, Dewey County.

◆ Numbers. There were approximately 2,100 Southern Cheyenne in Oklahoma in 1950. An enumeration by the Indian Office in 1924 shows 1,228 members of the tribe in the state. In 1902, they numbered 1,903. The total population of the tribe shown in reports at different periods after their settlement on the reservation in Oklahoma are 2,119 in 1892, when allotment of tribal

MURIEL H. WRIGHT

Whirl Wind, head chief, in 1874

lands in severalty was completed; 3,767 in 1880; and 2,055 in 1875, at which time there were 1,727 Southern Cheyenne in Dakota.

◆ **History.** First historical notice of the Cheyenne was recorded in 1680 when a band of the tribe from the Minnesota region visited La Salle's fort on the Illinois River and invited the French to come to their country, which was rich in beaver and other fur-bearing animals. Later the tribe moved west and settled on the Sheyenne (*sic*) River in what is now North Dakota, a region which the Sioux called "the place where the Cheyenne plant," indicating that the immigrants were still an agricultural people. Pushed southwestward by the Sioux, they afterward located in the

Powder Face about 1880

Black Hills near the headwaters of the Cheyenne River in South Dakota. During these migrations, they made war on a number of small tribes that were strangers to them, but united with the *Sutaio* who spoke a language similar to their own. Even after they had come out of the Minnesota river region, they were affiliated in an alliance with the Arapaho, which continued recognition of the two tribes separately. To this day, the Indian subagency at Concho in Canadian County is known as the "Cheyenne-Arapaho Subagency."

During the slowly moving emigration through a period of many years, the Cheyenne lost some of their traditional arts and took up new customs and new ways. An old tradition told by the keepers of their tribal legends recounts how their people "lost the corn." This story undoubtedly refers to a time when, in the course of moving west, the Cheyenne lost the seed corn and could not plant a crop, whereupon they became buffalo hunters. Their medicine-arrow ceremony they claimed was their own from the beginning. The sun dance, which became an annual event, and the buffalo-head medicine ceremonies were adopted from the Sutaio after the alliance with this small tribe. The Cheyenne were known in tribal days for their fine physiques, set off by their colorful costumes of bead-embroidered buckskin, part of their costume and paraphernalia having been adopted from the Sioux, with whom they finally made a friendly alliance.

Modern Cheyenne history began at their meeting with the Lewis and Clark Expedition of 1804 in the Black Hills of South Dakota. Constantly pressed by the hostile Sioux, the tribe moved westward to the upper branches of the Platte River, in turn driving the Kiowa farther south. Four Cheyenne chiefs and a number of warriors signed the first treaty with the United States in behalf of their tribe at a council with government commissioners on the Teton River, Montana, in 1825. The protection of the United States was prom-

Daughters of Little Robe, 1874

ised the tribe in this treaty, thus paving the way for the building of Bent's Fort a few years later on the Arkansas River in what is now southern Colorado. Soon afterward, a large part of the Cheyenne decided to locate permanently on the Arkansas in this vicinity, where they became known as the Southern Cheyenne. The other portion of the tribe roving about the headwaters of the Platte and Yellowstone rivers became known as the Northern Cheyenne. The final separation of the two divisions came in 1851. The Southern Cheyenne have religiously preserved the ancient tribal palladium of four medicine arrows since that time, the public ceremony in connection with these held at intervals and always attended by delegates from the Northern Cheyenne.

Years of warfare between the Southern Cheyenne and the Kiowa reached a climax in a bloody battle fought on Wolf Creek in northwestern Oklahoma, with great loss of warriors on both sides. About two years later, in 1840, the Cheyenne made peace

with the Kiowa, having already made peace with the Sioux. Since that time, the Cheyenne, Arapaho, Kiowa, (q.v.), Kiowa-Apache, and Comanche have been friends and allies.

As has been pointed out, the relations of the Southern Cheyenne with the United States have been in common with those of the Southern Arapaho since their joint treaty with government commissioners at Fort Wise, Kansas, in 1861. Later, under a treaty made at the Medicine Lodge Council in Kansas in 1867, the two tribes were assigned a reservation in Oklahoma (*see* Arapaho).

The fact that they maintained their separate tribal organization, even though closely allied with the Southern Arapaho, meant that the Southern Cheyenne, under the influence of the "Dog Soldier" warrior society, experienced a different history from the Arapaho. They suffered disaster in 1864 when the encampment of Chief Black Kettle and many of his band, on Sand Creek in Colorado, was attacked by

Black Kettle, from a drawing by John Metcalf

MURIEL H. WRIGHT

Cheyenne village in the Washita Valley, 1898

a force of Colorado troops under the command of Colonel J. M. Chivington. Even though Black Kettle and his followers had recently made a friendly agreement with government officers, their village was taken by surprise and destroyed. Many of the Cheyenne were slain, most of them women and children. This event, known as the "Chivington Massacre," or "Sand Creek Massacre," has been referred to as "the foulest and most unjustifiable crime in the annals of America." Although Black Kettle tried to hold his followers in the pathway of peace and sensible conduct, it was many years before the Cheyenne as a tribe had any confidence in or friendly feeling for the white people.

In the summer of 1868, the Cheyenne took part in the general Indian war on the Great Plains, but the war did not end at the close of summer, for United States troops were under command to follow the Indians to their winter encampments in western Indian Territory. The Southern Cheyenne located south of the reservation assigned them by the Medicine Lodge treaty for the same reasons as the Arapaho (q.v.). In the midst of a winter storm on the morning of November 27, 1868, Chief Black Kettle's camp on the Washita River was attacked by United States troops from the Seventh Cavalry under the command of Colonel Custer. Black Kettle and many of his band were killed, their horses slaughtered, and their camp destroyed. From this time, the Southern Cheyenne were bitter and hostile, their warriors taking part in the Indian wars on the Plains and the uprisings on the reservations in Oklahoma until the final surrender of the Quahada Comanche (q.v.) in 1875. The Northern Cheyenne, allied with the Sioux, were among the victorious warriors with Sitting Bull and other Sioux leaders in the Battle of the Little Big Horn in Montana when General Custer and his troops were wiped out.

In the meantime, the reservation for the Cheyenne and Arapaho was finally established by Presidential proclamation, south of the Cherokee Outlet and north of the Washita in what is now western Oklahoma. Camp Supply, Darlington, Fort Reno, Cantonment, Red Moon Agency and school, and Concho Agency are all connected with the history of the Southern

Cheyenne in Oklahoma. The first school for the children in the vicinity of the Cheyenne-Arapaho Agency at Darlington was opened in 1872, with John H. Seger as superintendent.

The people of these two tribes, reared in frontier warfare as roving buffalo hunters proud and free, were expected to begin at once the life of the farmer with rural employment on the reservation. Agent John D. Miles was sanguine in his report for 1879, though he advised that the government program of farming, because of intermittent drought years, be changed to promote stock raising by the Indians. Work found for the Indians included making brick, chopping wood, making hay, hauling wood, splitting and hauling rails, freighting supplies from the railroad in Kansas to the Agency (each Indian to buy his own wagon and use his own wild ponies), with a limited number of Indians employed to serve as police or to carry the daily mail to Fort Elliott, Texas (165 miles away).

Life for the tribes was difficult, however, since the reservation was on the order of a concentration camp with food rations often inferior, scanty, and issued at irregular intervals—sometimes even withheld by orders from Washington for disciplinary measures. In 1880, the Cheyenne Boarding School was established at Caddo Springs (present Concho), about three miles from Darlington. Six years later, the government promoted the plan of Indian colonies for farming and stock raising away from the Agency and Fort Reno, miles west on the reservation.

The Cheyenne, of all the reservation tribes in the Indian Territory, were bitter, resentful, and hard to manage. When the Quahadi Comanche (q.v.) surrendered and the uprising of the Indians around Fort Sill ended in 1875, there were twenty-eight Cheyenne (and two Arapaho) taken as prisoners of war from Fort Reno to St. Augustine, Florida (*see* Kiowa). After the Battle of the Little Big Horn in 1876, the government began bringing bands of the Northern Cheyenne south to settle on the Cheyenne-Arapaho Reservation in the In-

MURIEL H. WRIGHT

Cheyenne captives at Camp Supply, June, 1869
Left to right: Curley Head, Fat Bear, Dull Knife

dian Territory, the largest group (937) arriving from the north at Darlington in August, 1877. They had been opposed to the move and were enervated by the change to the southern climate. Hundreds fell sick with malaria, medical supplies at the Agency gave out, and within a short period many of the Northern Cheyenne died. When their leaders pleaded with the United States Indian Office to allow their people to return north, they were refused.

In the midst of intolerable conditions, Little Wolf and Dull Knife, leading a band of 353 Northern Cheyenne (men, women, and children) left the reservation in the Indian Territory in September, 1878, after sending word to officers at Fort Reno and Darlington that they were going home and did not want to get into any fights on the way. The trouble that followed is known in history as the "Dull Knife Raid." Alarm soon spread in Kansas and Nebraska that the Indians were on the warpath. Several fights occurred in which both Indians and white people were killed. United States troops at western military posts had already been ordered out to bring in the runaway Cheyenne, but Little Wolf and Dull

Knife managed to elude their pursuers and finally led most of their band through to the North, where they surrendered and remained with government approval. In 1883, the last of the Northern Cheyenne bands in the Indian Territory left for the reservation established for them by the government on the Tongue River in Montana, where their descendants are now located.

The Southern Cheyenne were assigned allotments of land in severalty on their Indian Territory domain along with the Arapaho (q.v.). Their surplus reservation lands (3,500,562 acres now included in nine western counties) were organized as a part of Oklahoma Territory and opened to white settlement on April 19, 1892. The tribal agency and the Cheyenne-Arapaho Indian School are maintained at Concho, a few miles north and west of El Reno, in Canadian County.

◊ **Government and Organization.** The Southern Cheyenne are organized with the Southern Arapaho (q.v.) as the "Cheyenne-Arapaho Tribes of Oklahoma," a constitution and by-laws having been adopted by a vote of the tribe in 1937, under pro-

MURIEL H. WRIGHT

Cheyenne women and children at Camp Supply about 1870

MURIEL H. WRIGHT

Cheyenne lodge with willow windbreak in the 1890's

visions of the Oklahoma Indian Welfare Act of 1936. The Business Committee and Council of this organization have charge of all matters relating to their tribally owned lands (*see* Arapaho) in western Oklahoma and their tribal claims now before the Indian Claims Commission. Cheyenne who have served as members on the tribal council are Albert Hamilton, second vice president, Joseph Washa, secretary, Ben Osage, Fred Bushyhead, Woodson Shortman, Ralph Goodman, and Fred Standingwater.

The Cheyenne have retained a nominal tribal government, principally for ceremonial and religious purposes. Before the division into the Northern and Southern groups, there was a council of forty-four elected chiefs, four of whom constituted a higher body with the power to elect one of their own number as head chief of the tribe. The council of forty-four was symbolized by a bundle of forty-four invitation sticks which were kept with the four

sacred medicine arrows and sent around when it was necessary to convene the council. Today, by custom in their association with the Arapaho, four Arapaho are elected to serve as Cheyenne chiefs; in turn, two Cheyenne are elected to serve as chiefs of the Arapaho (q.v.).

◆ **Contemporary Life and Culture.** Approximately 1,700 members of the Cheyenne are fullblood Indians. These include the fullblood Cheyenne and the mixed-blood descendants (fullblood Indians) by intermarriage with closely associated tribes, among whom are some of Sioux descent. Among the comparatively few mixed-bloods by intermarriage with white people, some of French descent are found.

Most of the Cheyenne are engaged in farming and stock raising, with a small percentage employed in business and other fields besides day labor. Living conditions among them are generally above the average. The fact that Cheyenne women in tribal days were rulers of the camp and had an important place in tribal society gave a certain strength of character that is still retained. In the old days, the "good family" was the one that reared "good brave men and sensible women."

The Cheyenne are generally Christianized, with membership found principally in the Baptist, Dutch Reformed, or Mennonite churches. The American Indian church based on peyotism has a strong following in the tribe.

◆ **Ceremonials and Public Dances.** Ceremonials connected with the four medicine arrows are not generally open to the public, although an ethnographical motion picture of the sacred arrow ceremony has been made by Forrest E. Clements, an ethnologist. Members of the tribe are prominent participants in the American Indian Exposition held annually in summer at Anadarko in Caddo County.

Suggested Readings: Grinnell, *The Cheyenne Indians*; ———, *The Fighting Cheyenne;* Llewellyn and Hoebel, *The Cheyenne Way;* Mooney, "Ghost Dance Religion," in *14 Ann. Rep.,* Bur. Amer. Ethnol.; Seger, *Early Days Among the Cheyenne and Arapahoe.*

CHICKASAW

This is the approved anglicized form of *Chikasha,* the Choctaw name for the tribe. The term is a mnemonic, *chik'asha* (chĭk'äshä), from the original phrase *chikkih ashachi,* meaning "they left as a tribe not a very great while ago," from the old Choctaw expression *chikkih,* "not a very great while ago," and *ashachi,* "to leave," used in the plural sense with reference to a group or tribe. Both legend and tradition point to the separation of the Chickasaw from the Choctaw some time before their discovery by De Soto in 1540. The name *Chikasha* or *Chickasaw* has also been said to signify "rebellion."

The Chickasaw are of the Muskhogean linguistic family and are one of the Five Civilized Tribes of Oklahoma. Their native written language is the same as that of the Choctaw; their speech is also identical except for some dialectal expressions. The two tribes are closely related and have been associated in their history, although with the coming of the European traders and colonists to the native habitation east of the Mississippi River during the eighteenth century, they were sometimes at war with each other.

The country of the Chickasaw in historic times was in northeastern Mississippi, their original land claims extending east into what is now Alabama and north through western Tennessee and western Kentucky to the Ohio River. On the frontiers of this region, they were confronted on the east, north, and west by Indian peoples of alien tribal cultures: on the east and southeast by the Iroquoian; on the east and northeast by the Algonquian; on the north by the Southern Siouan; and on the west by the Caddoan. The Chickasaw were always a comparatively small tribe but were courageous in the defense of their homes and territory. They became noted for their warlike disposition which brought them into frequent conflict with neighboring tribes in the eighteenth century. The fullblood Chickasaw are generally of medium height, having small hands and feet and regular features. Some of the mixed-blood members of the tribe, both men and women, have been noted for their beauty. As citizens of Oklahoma, they are successful in business, and many of them have been signally honored in professional life.

◆ **Present Location.** Twelve counties and parts of counties east of the ninety-eighth meridian, lying between the Canadian and the Red rivers in southern Oklahoma, comprise the region included in the

OKLAHOMA HISTORICAL SOCIETY

Old Chickasaw capitol, now the courthouse at Tishomingo, from a photograph taken about 1923

Chickasaw Nation from 1855 to 1907. Families of Chickasaw descent are living in this region, the largest fullblood settlements being found in Pontotoc, Johnston, and Love counties. Many of the Chickasaw make their homes in the large cities and towns in the state, including Oklahoma City, Tulsa, McAlester, Durant, Ardmore, and Pauls Valley.

◊ **Numbers.** The United States Office of Indian Affairs reported 5,350 Chickasaw in Oklahoma (census of 1944), of whom approximately 700 were fullblood members of the tribe. These numbers represent persons identified with the Chickasaw tribal interests under the administration of the Five Civilized Tribes Agency at Muskogee, but do not include all persons of Chickasaw descent in Oklahoma, since many are not officially under agency administration.

When the Chickasaw rolls were closed on March 4, 1907, they showed 6,319 members of the tribe, of whom 1,538 were classed as full blood, 4,146 as part blood, and 635 as intermarried white.

The census report of the United States Indian Office for 1890–91 gave a total of 6,400 Chickasaw. At the close of the Civil War in 1865, their numbers were reported at 4,500, showing a decrease of 500 since the beginning of the war, those who had gone north during the conflict not yet having returned and settled in their homes in the Indian Territory.

Frontier wars and epidemics which decimated all Indian tribes during the eighteenth century reduced the numbers of the Chickasaw, their estimated population of between 3,000 and 3,500 in 1700 decreasing to 2,290 in 1780.

◊ **History.** Chickasaw legend and tradition tell of the ancient migration from the Far West and their settlement on the east side of the Mississippi River. These myths, like those of the Choctaw relate the travels of the Chickasaw from a home in the West over a long period of time, following their leader, who carried a mystic pole that leaned toward the east until some time after crossing the Mississippi. The oldest location of the Chickasaw in what is now Mississippi was long known as "Chickasaw Old Fields," a beautiful prairie extending about ten or twelve miles from north to south and lying east of Tupelo, in Lee County.

In this region, near a river, probably the Tombigbee, the tribe was discovered by the Spanish explorer De Soto and his men, who arrived there late in 1540. In the narratives of this expedition, the Chickasaw have the distinction of being one of the Five Civilized Tribes mentioned by the name that they still bear, the spelling given as *Chicaca* or *Chicaza*. During the winter of 1540–41, the Spaniards encamped near the Chickasaw villages, on one occasion Chief "Miculasa" visiting the encampment and bringing many presents of deerskins and other materials.

In his preparations to leave the country toward spring, De Soto demanded that the Chickasaw send him two hundred men to serve as burden carriers. Incensed by the order and by previous cruel acts on the part of the Spaniards, the brave Chickasaw warriors made a skillful attack on the encampment during the night of March 4,

1541. De Soto's men were put to rout, and most of their horses and their large herd of hogs were lost. In winning this battle, the Chickasaw made the greatest stroke for freedom in the early history of the Southeast and justified their later reputation as a fighting people.

Only scattered references to the tribe occur in the Spanish records for the next 150 years. In 1698, the English made their first contacts with the Chickasaw leaders, and by 1700, English traders reached the Mississippi River, soon establishing their trading operations in the Chickasaw country, which served as the base for British trade and power. Henceforth, the Chickasaw were the loyal allies of the English until the American Revolution, when they became attached to the American colonies, some of their warriors and leaders serving with distinction in the Colonial armies.

Throughout the eighteenth century, they were often at war and won a number of decisive victories over the neighboring tribes: the Shawnee, in 1715 and 1745; the Yatasi (Caddoan) west of the Mississippi, in 1717; the Cherokee, in a battle fought at the Chickasaw Old Fields, in 1768; and the Creek, who invaded the Chickasaw country, in 1793–95. The Chickasaw, in alliance with English traders, were blamed for the uprising of the Natchez in 1729, which brought the annihilation of the Natchez by the French two years later.

Rivalry between the English and the French for the trade and the control of the Mississippi region was the main cause of the Indian frontier wars in the eighteenth century. As allies of the English, the Chickasaw were harassed by the Choctaw and their neighbors who were aligned with the French. In the midst of this trouble, the Chickasaw inflicted two decisive defeats on the French and their Indian allies; the first, on D'Artaguette's army and bands of Illinois tribes; the second, on the French commander Bienville, with the Choctaw, in the famous Battle of Ackia on May 26, 1736. Powder and lead captured in the first

engagement served the Chickasaw well in the second when they made their stand in their strong stockaded village of Ackia, over which it was reported the English flag was seen during the fighting. This battle was fought about five miles northwest of Tupelo, in Lee County, Mississippi, and was important historically in that it indicated the power of the English and foreshadowed their final defeat of the French in America.

The Chickasaw settlements centered in what is now Pontotoc County, Mississippi, in the eighteenth century, extending generally eastward toward the Chickasaw Old Fields in Lee County, on the upper sources of the Tombigbee River. In 1720, there were four of these settlements situated like the sides of a square, some distance apart, each extending from four to ten miles in length. Toward the close of the century, the tribe had been greatly reduced in population, and nearly all the Chickasaw had settled in a rich tract about three miles in extent, which formed the northern angle of their ancient settlements in the vicinity of the Old Fields. Each settlement had consisted of several villages or "towns," of which there were seven listed in a report in 1771, one called Hashuk Homma (*Ashuck* hooma), "Red Grass," strongly fortified with a high surrounding stockade.

A number of houses in one locality made up a village, some winter houses and others summer houses, each with a "hot house" or "sweat house," corn crib, potato house, and sometimes a chicken house near at hand. The winter house was circular in shape with an earthen floor about three feet below the surface of the ground, and was constructed of a heavy framework of pine timber covered with poles lashed together with split saplings, plastered with a thick coating of clay, and thatched on the outside with long dry grass. The summer house was rectangular in shape with a gable roof and was less compactly built than the winter house, the clay-plastered walls whitewashed inside and outside the dwelling. The peculiarity of the Chickasaw summer house was the central partition dividing it into two rooms, a plan which is said to have been the origin of the double log cabin that became popular on the western frontier.

From about 1700, the Chickasaw engaged extensively in English trading operations in the Southwest. A Chickasaw representing the English interests was seen at the Tawakoni (q.v.) village on the Arkansas River in Oklahoma when the French officer La Harpe first visited this region in 1719. Trading activities and war expeditions were long the principal occupations in the tribe, little attention being given to agriculture other than the raising of vegetables and the cultivation of small fields, tended mostly by the women. Large supplies of corn were purchased from the Choctaw.

White traders and employees settled and married among the Chickasaw and were the progenitors of a number of mixed-blood families prominent in the history of Oklahoma. Among the names of white men in the Chickasaw country listed by the British Colonial Office at London in 1766–67 were James Calbert (Colbert?), James Adair, Alexander McIntosh, William Kemp, William James, Martin Cheadle, and Benjamin Sealy. Others identified with the Chickasaw about the time of the American Revolution included James Gunn, John McLish (or McCleish), Malcomb McGee, James Allen, E. (?) Pickens, John Bynum, Bernard McLaughlin, and Thomas Love, some of whom were reported British loyalists. The sons of Thomas Love—Henry, Benjamin, Isaac, Slone, William, and Robert—were prominent in Chickasaw history. Much of James Adair's *History of the American Indians,* published in London in 1775, was devoted to descriptions of life and customs among the Chickasaw. The Colbert family has long been notable: William, George, Levi, and James Colbert were all prominent tribal leaders in their day, the sons of a Scot who married a Chickasaw sometime before the Revolution.

In their tribal government, the Chickasaw were ruled by a head chief or mi^nko, which means "chief" but is usually found translated as "king" in the historical records concerning the Chickasaw, in accordance with the translation used by the early English traders and officers. The mi^nko or "king" was selected from the highest-ranking clan in the tribe and was chosen by the tribal council to serve in the office for life. Originally, each clan was ruled by a subchief, descent in the clan being reckoned in the female line. Next to the Chickasaw "king" was the war chief or $tishu\ mi^nko$, signifying an "assistant to the chief," an old title which was also used in the Choctaw tribal government.

The last Chickasaw war chief was the noted Chief Tishomingo, who was awarded a pension for life from the national Chickasaw funds for "his long and valuable services" by the terms of the treaty of Pontotoc in 1832. He was reported to have died on the Trail of Tears and to have been buried near Little Rock, Arkansas, about 1838, at the age of 102 years. The old and revered "queen" of the Chickasaw, named $Paka^nli$ ("Puc-caun-la") also died about the same time on the journey west. She, too, was awarded a life pension by the treaty of Pontotoc and was undoubtedly of a high-ranking clan and accorded the title of "queen" in her own right, probably as the mother or aunt of the last Chickasaw "king," Ishtehotopa, in the old tribal government in Oklahoma. Ishtehotopa was chosen "king" in 1820, and died in the Chickasaw District in the late eighteen forties.

Official relations between the tribe and the United States began in 1786, when the first Chickasaw treaty was signed at Hopewell on the Keowee River, South Carolina, by their representatives under the leadership of the noted chief Piamingo. This treaty established the Ohio River as the northern boundary of the Chickasaw country, stipulated that all trade in the tribe be regulated by Congress, and provided for the cession to the United States of a tract five miles square at the Muscle Shoals, on the Tennessee River, for a trading post. Up to 1902 there were a total of fourteen Chickasaw treaties and agreements with the United States, not including two special ones with the Choctaw (q.v.)—one, in 1837, providing for the settlement of the Chickasaw in the Choctaw Nation; the other, in 1854, establishing the boundary line between the two nations. In 1818, all Chickasaw lands north of the southern boundary of Tennessee were ceded to the United States by treaty.

The plan for the removal of the tribe from Mississippi was first projected in the treaty of 1832, which was signed at the tribal council house on Pontotoc Creek, in present-day Pontotoc County, Mississippi, and provided for the cession to the United States of all Chickasaw lands east of the Mississippi River. These lands were to be surveyed and sold by the government, the net proceeds to be paid to the Chickasaw Nation. Every Chickasaw family could select from one to five sections of their Mississippi lands, upon certain conditions, to be held as an allotment until a new country was found west of the river, the proceeds from the sale of all allotments to be placed in the national funds.

Dissatisfaction among the leaders and their people led to two supplemental treaties, on October 22, 1832, and May 24, 1834, which resulted in the granting of land allotments in fee simple, the proceeds from all sales to be placed in the national funds for the benefit of the individual allottees. Furthermore, a Chickasaw commission was created—composed of Ishtehotopa, Levi Colbert, George Colbert, Martin Colbert, Isaac Alberson, Henry Love, and Benjamin Love—to have supervisory control over the national funds, with the power of certifying the competency of the individual Chickasaw allottee in the management of his affairs and the money derived from the sale of his allotment. The Chickasaw treaty of 1834 marks the first use on record of the term "competent," with the implication of "incompetent" in regard to members of an Indian tribe.

No suitable country had been found for the settlement of the Chickasaw as late as 1836. The government's removal of the Indians was reaching a crisis, and there was insistent demand in the Southeastern states that all the tribes be moved out from their boundaries.

At the urging of government agents, a meeting was arranged between representatives of the Chickasaw and the Choctaw at Doaksville, where an agreement was finally signed on January 17, 1837, concerning the settlement of the Chickasaw in the Choctaw Nation, with all the rights and privileges of Choctaw citizens, a district to be set aside and organized as the Chickasaw District, the land within its boundaries to be held in common by the

Cyrus Harris, first governor of the Chickasaw Nation, 1857

two nations. The people of the Chickasaw District were to have equal representation in the Choctaw General Council with the citizens of other districts organized under the Choctaw (q.v.) government. Each Choctaw and Chickasaw had the right to choose a location and make a home in any district in the country. For the rights and privileges secured in the Doaksville treaty, the Chickasaw were to pay $530,000 out of their national funds to the Choctaw Nation. It was further stipulated that all financial affairs of the two nations should be kept entirely separate and under the control of their respective officers.

The Chickasaw, who were advanced in civilization, educated their children and generally lived in comfortable circumstances according to Mississippi frontier standards, although they still held to many of their old tribal customs and beliefs. Missionary efforts had been begun among the people in 1819 by the Reverend Robert Bell, under the auspices of Elk Presbytery of the Cumberland Presbyterian church.

They were the wealthiest of any of the Indian nations or tribes when they emigrated from Mississippi in the winter of 1837–38. A large national fund from the sale of their lands (approximately 6,283,-804 acres) had been invested under government auspices to bring in an income to be paid out in annuities or for the benefit of all the Chickasaw. All families had disposed of their allotments to advantage and invested some of the proceeds in Negro slaves. The influential mixed-blood families were wealthy in slaves and other property. Pitman Colbert, an enterprising trader, had six mules and a special wagon to haul his money (in gold loaded in kegs) from Mississippi to Doaksville, where he later operated a trader's store.

Although the Chickasaw traveled west to the Indian Territory in comfort by comparison with other Indian tribes during the removal, they too, endured many hardships. They had been practically forced to leave their old homes and the country that

their people had fought for and cherished through many generations. They suffered deprivations and epidemics in the emigration, and some of their people died and were buried on the way.

The Chickasaw arrived in the Indian Territory at two points: at Fort Coffee near the Choctaw Agency by way of steamboats up the Arkansas River, and at Doaksville near Fort Towson by way of the military trail west from the Arkansas boundary and on beyond the Mountain Fork River. The people first made their homes in Choctaw districts that had already been organized for several years. Since the Chickasaw District had been recently organized, it lay west, extending to the western boundaries of the Choctaw Nation in the region where the Comanche and other Plains tribes had their villages, the hostile bands sometimes raiding herds of stock as far east as the mouth of the Washita River and threatening trouble to any newcomer who might settle here. The United States established Fort Washita, in present Bryan County, in 1842, for the protection of the Chickasaw, but another decade passed before there was any extended permanent settlement in their district.

When the Chickasaw came to the Indian Territory in the winter of 1837–38, they were listed in four companies—Tishomingo's, McGilbery's, Isaac Alberson's, and Thomas Sealy's—which had been organized for expediting tribal business and payment of annuities. These four companies continued the listing of those living in four districts that had been originally organized in 1815 under the supervision of the United States agent for the payment of annuities.

The power of Ishtehotopa as "king" was nominal for many years, especially with the creation of the Chickasaw Commission in 1834, when that body virtually took over the rule of the nation. Soon after the treaty of 1834, the death of Levi Colbert, who had served with the United States troops under General Jackson in the battle of New Orleans and had long been recognized as a councilor by his people, left the leadership in the hands of George Colbert, who was the recognized chief of the Chickasaw at the time of the removal until his death in 1839. George Colbert was buried at Fort Towson with honors, for he was a veteran of the American Revolution, having served under General Washington and been commissioned a major in the army and awarded a sword. He had also served under General Wayne and under General Jackson, by whom he had been commissioned colonel in the Seminole wars. Colonel Colbert has been described as physically and mentally a great man, with an erect carriage even in his last years before his death at the age of ninety-five.

The Chickasaw were unreconciled to their new situation, their leaders complaining that they were outnumbered in the General Council and had little power in their government relations with the Choctaw. Moreover, they were fearful that the Choctaw would eventually control their finances. With the establishment of Fort Washita, tribal settlements increased along the Texas Road and were prospering in the vicinity of Perryville, Boggy Depot, Fort Washita, and on south to the Red River valley, where some of the Loves and the Colberts had large plantations. The disposition and control of their national funds led to feuds among the Chickasaw that in time resulted in lawlessness and, in some instances, murders in the neighborhood of Fort Washita.

Two factions arose. Isaac Alberson, who had been elected and was serving as chief of the Chickasaw District in 1844, advocated the settlement of all the people in the Chickasaw District with their own laws, officers, and schools. His opponents, led by Pitman Colbert, objected to the appropriation of money from the national funds for the establishment of schools and advocated the observance of the old tribal customs. When the time came for the annuity payments, Agent William Armstrong would not turn the funds over to the members of the Chickasaw Commission, but paid out the money direct to the individual members of the tribe.

Finally a meeting of the Chickasaw Council was held in 1845 at Boiling Spring, a short distance west of Fort Washita, where members and other leaders voiced their views of the tribal controversies before a throng of tribesmen and visitors. Pitman Colbert controlled the council proceedings and dominated the scene—an event long remembered—his son-in-law, Sampson Folsom, furnishing thirty-two beeves to feed the crowd.

While dissatisfaction and contentions continued over finances, tribal affairs took on a semblance of unity with the election of Edmund Pickens as the chief under the formal written constitution (their first) adopted by the Chickasaw in 1848. Provisions aimed at the settlement of the problem concerning the national funds were secured in a treaty made at Washington in 1852, signed by Edmund Pickens, Benjamin S. Love, and Sampson Folsom, the certified commissioners in behalf of the "Chickasaw tribe of Indians."

The most important event in their history after their removal to the Indian Territory was the conclusion of the treaty of 1855 at Washington, signed by George W. Manypenny, commissioner for the United States; Peter P. Pitchlynn, Israel Folsom, Samuel Garland, and Dixon W. Lewis, commissioners for the Choctaw; and Edmund Pickens and Sampson Folsom, commissioners for the Chickasaw. This treaty defined the boundaries of a district wherein the Chickasaw were secured "the unrestricted right of self-government and full jurisdiction, over persons and property." This district comprised approximately 4,-707,903 acres lying between the Canadian and the Red rivers as far west as the ninety-eighth meridian, the eastern boundary of the large tract beginning on Red River at the mouth of Island Bayou, thence running northwesterly to the source of the eastern prong of the bayou, and thence due north to the Canadian River. Furthermore, all lands under the Choctaw patent from the Arkansas boundary to the one-hundredth meridian were open to settlement anywhere by the Choctaw and the Chickasaw.

Since the Chickasaw numbered approximately one-fourth the population of the Choctaw, the sum of $800,000 paid by the government under the terms of the same treaty for the perpetual lease of the lands west of the ninety-eighth meridian (see Choctaw, "Leased District") was divided on the basis of one-fourth to the Chickasaw and three-fourths to the Choctaw. This ratio has been observed by the government in the division and payment to the respective tribes of the income from royalties and sales of tribal property (coal, asphalt, timber, stone, etc.).

The new treaty was proclaimed at Washington on March 4, 1856, and the following August a mass convention of the Chickasaw was held at Good Spring on Pennington Creek. This place had been established as the tribal council grounds and a hewn-log council house erected here in 1853. Jackson Kemp served as president of the convention, a constitution drafted by Holmes Colbert and Sampson Folsom was adopted, and the new government of the Chickasaw Nation organized with legislative, executive, and judicial departments. Members of the bicameral legislature were elected by the people, the executive authority was vested in the "Governor of the Chickasaw Nation" elected by the people, and members of the supreme court were elected by the legislature. Cyrus Harris was elected the first governor, and Holmes Colbert, national secretary. The capital of the nation was established at Good Spring and named "Tishomingo City," in honor of Chief Tishomingo.

Unfortunately, the manuscript of the constitution and laws was lost on the way to Texas to be printed. This was cause for alarm, for no one knew the new laws, and the tribal officials seemed unable to enforce the Choctaw laws which were to re-

MURIEL H. WRIGHT

Bloomfield Academy—old building near Achille, Bryan County, burned January, 1914

main in effect until the new Chickasaw government was established by stipulation in the treaty of 1855. A special session of the council in August, 1857, succeeded in establishing the new order with a redraft of the constitution and laws, which were published soon afterward at Tishomingo City. A brick capitol completed there the following year was the meeting place for the Chickasaw legislature until a handsome stone capitol was erected near the same location, through an appropriation of tribal funds in 1896. This stone building has served as the county courthouse at Tishomingo, the county seat of Johnston County.

The first written law of the Chickasaw in 1844 provided for an appropriation to establish a tribal academy. At a cost of nearly $12,000, a large stone building was completed about three miles southeast of Tishomingo, and the institution was opened in 1851 as the Chickasaw Manual Labor School for boys. The Reverend J. C. Robinson, missionary preacher of the Methodist Episcopal church, served as superintendent. Four other boarding schools were subsequently opened: Wapanucka Institute for girls, 1852; Bloomfield Academy for girls, 1852; Collins Institute (later called Colbert Institute), 1854; Burney Institute for girls, 1859.

At the outbreak of the Civil War, a treaty with the Confederate States was signed jointly by the Chickasaw and the Choctaw. Nevertheless, a strong element among the Chickasaw remained loyal to the Union, including several prominent leaders; and nearly 250 members of the tribe went north to Kansas, where they remained as refugees until after 1865. Chickasaw troops served in the Confederate Army and were the last Confederate forces in the Indian Territory when they surrendered under the order of Governor Winchester Colbert on July 14, 1865.

In 1866 a treaty with the United States signed jointly by the Chickasaw and the Choctaw (q.v.) re-established the governments of both nations. A new constitution was adopted for the Chickasaw Nation in a convention held at Camp Harris in 1867, Cyrus Harris having been chosen governor in the elections held the preceding year. The four counties that had been organized by a resolution of the Chickasaw Senate in 1859 were continued under their old names: Panola, Tishomingo, Pontotoc, and Pickens.

The most important task in the reorganization of the government was the reopening of the schools in the nation, all having been closed since the beginning of the war. The interest on the Chickasaw national fund and a special annuity for schools, payment of which had been suspended by the federal government during the war along with all other compensation, were re-established by the treaty of 1866, the total paid over to the Chickasaw treasury for the fiscal year of 1866–67 amounting to $65,735.98. From 1867 on, a large part of this income was used to maintain the public school system, twelve neighborhood schools being in operation by 1869. Because of insufficient funds, the old Chickasaw academies, all of them in a bad state of repair, were not reopened as national boarding schools until after 1876. From that time each was supervised by a superintendent under contract with the

Chickasaw school trustees, thus divorced from the work and interests of any church —in contrast to the plan followed before the war.

With the opening of the neighborhood schools, sessions were held in the available buildings at the five academies and in log buildings erected for that purpose in the various communities. Teachers, some of them natives who had attended the national academies before the war, were paid three dollars a month for each pupil in attendance, the child to be furnished books and school supplies out of this sum, although a separate amount was allowed for fuel to heat the buildings. Children living over two and one-half miles from a school were each allowed $7.50 a month for board in the vicinity, a plan that soon developed into the novel system of payment of this sum direct to parents of every child of school age.

The care of the large number of orphans after the war was another problem, and some years later many of them were provided a home at old Burney Institute, henceforth known as the Chickasaw Orphan School, near the village of Lebanon in present Marshall County.

A special section devoted to "public education" in the constitution adopted in 1867 created the office of Superintendent of Public Instruction, the superintendent to be elected every four years by members of the legislature. The superintendent and the school trustees, one appointed for each school in the nation, were paid annual salaries commensurate with their duties. School expenses increased annually, the Chickasaw government disbursing large sums through the years in the maintenance of the educational system, with practically every Chickasaw personally interested and the best-paying teaching positions distributed through political patronage and favoritism.

After the end of the war, the Chickasaw was the first nation in the Indian Territory to promote "the manufacture, refinement,

Chickasaw capitol, Tishomingo City, erected in 1858

and exporting of petroleum" in their country, under an act of their legislature in November, 1865, granting to the Petroleum and Railroad Company a charter which gave the directors or agents of the corporation the "right to grant, convey and lease real estate." Since the Choctaw were the joint owners of the tribal domain, this clause made the act invalid, especially since the act itself had been passed before the treaty of 1866 was signed. In 1872, the Chickasaw Oil Company, by granting a franchise to a Missouri company for the development of petroleum, became the first oil company organized within the present state of Oklahoma. Since the franchise involved the leasing of tribal lands—rights to which were not clarified and approved by the Secretary of the Interior for many years—no development was undertaken by this first company. A half-century later, however, the lands named in this franchise were a part of the Fitts oil field near Ada, Oklahoma. Oil springs in the Chickasaw district west of Good Spring, later Tishomingo, had attracted attention before 1854.

Travel to Texas through the Indian Territory called for the building of bridges across the larger streams by a number of enterprising Chickasaw, who secured the privilege of operating them as toll bridges from their legislature. With the growth of ranching in the Indian Territory and

Texas, cattle raising became the leading industry among the Chickasaw, many prominent mixed-blood families establishing ranch headquarters in the western part of the nation, where their herds fed on the open range on the prairies and in the valleys of the Washita and the Canadian rivers.

The thirty-eighth article of the treaty of 1866 established white persons who married among the Chickasaw as full citizens of the nation, with all rights and privileges and protection under the Chickasaw laws. Since extraordinary opportunities were apparent in this country, many white men married and settled among the Chickasaw, for after the construction of the Missouri, Kansas and Texas Railway (M. K. and T.) through eastern Indian Territory in 1872, the white population increased from year to year in the towns and the adjacent countryside. In the struggle for political supremacy, the conservative Chickasaw, mostly full bloods with a few mixed-blood leaders, made up the National party, the members of which viewed conditions with misgivings and were opposed to any innovation in their land holdings and to any more railroad building through the nation. Most of the mixed blood of the old well-to-do families, some enterprising full bloods, and the intermarried whites made up the Progressive party, whose membership steadily increased.

When railroad building was begun again following the Congressional act of 1886, the matter of granting a charter to the Gulf, Colorado & Santa Fe Railway for a right-of-way and contracts for timber and stone for construction purposes in the western part of the Chickasaw Nation gave rise to bitter political strife. The legislature refused to make any provisions in railroad matters, thus handicapping Governor William M. Guy in his official duties, even though it had chosen him governor at the beginning of the session. He had been the Progressive candidate in the campaign for that office in 1886, but, when none of the three candidates in the field received a majority of votes cast, the selection of the governor had devolved upon the legislature. Upon the order of the Secretary of the Interior, Governor Guy personally made contracts with the Santa Fe for necessary construction materials in building its road. When the company paid for these materials, the legislature refused to accept the money in behalf of the nation.

The campaign in 1888 was the most bitter in Chickasaw history, partisan feeling running high on the rights of citizens by blood and on the collection of a high cattle tax that was unfavorable to the white people (non-citizens) who had poured into the country along the new Santa Fe railroad. Governor Guy was re-elected to his position as the Progressive candidate, but the legislature threw out some of the votes in the Guy precincts and declared William L. Byrd, the National party candidate, the new governor. When armed conflict threatened under the leadership of Senator Sam Paul, there was a recount of the votes, and the Speaker of the House declared Governor Guy re-elected. But the Governor failed in his attempt to convene the legislature, for there was not a quorum present. Shortly afterward, Byrd quietly called his supporters together in a legislative session and carried on the government. He was later sustained in this step by the Secretary of the Interior.

Governor Byrd's administration succeeded in securing legislation in 1889 which disfranchised the intermarried white citizens in the nation. The primary purpose of this legislation was to protect the citizens by blood in their land and property rights; its effect was the annihilation of the Progressive party. In the campaign of 1890, only the votes of citizens by blood were counted, and Governor Byrd was re-elected by an overwhelming vote over the Progressive candidate, Sam Paul. Partisan feeling during these years led to personal feuds that resulted in more than one murder in the Chickasaw Nation. In the early eight-

een nineties, the troubles among the Chickasaw were cited in relating the need of laws to protect the non-citizens in the nation, and undoubtedly strengthened the demand of the thousands of white people who had come to live in the towns along the Santa Fe for Congressional action to disband the Chickasaw government along with other Indian governments in the Indian Territory. After the Dawes Commission began its work with that end in view, Chickasaw affairs were closely identified with those of the Choctaw (q.v.), and their tribal interests usually lined up on the conservative side in the steps that culminated in the organization of Oklahoma in 1907.

In proportion to their numbers among the Five Civilized Tribes, the Chickasaw have probably had more men and women of influence and prominence in their home communities and in Oklahoma than any other of these tribes. They include the late Charles D. Carter who served for twenty years as congressman from the Third District of Oklahoma; Earl Welch, justice of the Oklahoma Supreme Court, Reford Bond, member of the Corporation Commission, and the late Homer Paul, state senator from Pauls Valley. A descendant of the Love family in the Chickasaw Nation, Mrs. Jessie R. Moore, has served as clerk of the Oklahoma Supreme Court (1928–32), the only Oklahoma woman honored with statewide election to this office (1928–32). The late Alice Hearrell Murray, the wife of former Governor William H. Murray, was proud of her Chickasaw lineage. The governor of Oklahoma elected in 1950 was Johnston Murray, son of former Governor and Mrs. Murray. Among young women of Chickasaw descent nationally known in the entertainment and dramatic field are Te Ata (Mary Thompson) of New York, Ataloa (Mary Stone) of Los Angeles, Laurie Douglas (Douglas Johnston Smith) of New York and Hollywood, and Mobley Lushanya (opera star) of Chicago.

◆ **Government and Organization.** The

offices of governor and national attorney to represent the interests of the Chickasaw in property held jointly with the Choctaw (q.v.) have been continued under provisions of the Congressional act of April 26, 1906. The governor of the Chickasaw in 1951 was Floyd E. Maytubby, of Oklahoma City, who was appointed to the position by President Franklin D. Roosevelt in October, 1939. The Chickasaw Tribal Protective Association, organized at the old capitol building at Tishomingo on November 11, 1929, has continued to meet at irregular intervals upon call of the governor or the association secretary, serving in lieu of an advisory council and giving the Chickasaw assembled an opportunity to express their desires in matters of tribal interest that remain under the supervision of the Five Civilized Tribes Agency at Muskogee.

When the governments of the Five Tribes were dissolved in 1906, the incumbent governor of the Chickasaw, Douglas H. Johnston, continued in this office. Governor Johnston held the same position until his death, with the distinction of serving longer than any executive of an Indian nation in the history of Oklahoma.

The constitution of the Chickasaw Nation provided that the governor should be elected every two years to hold office until his successor was qualified, but not to hold the same office "for more than four years in any term of six years." The governors of the Chickasaw Nation and their terms of office were Cyrus Harris, 1856–58; Dougherty (or Winchester) Colbert, 1858–60; Cyrus Harris, 1860–62; Dougherty Colbert, 1862–66 (Horace Pratt, acting governor 1864, and Jackson Kemp, governor pro tem, 1866); Cyrus Harris, 1866–70; W. P. Brown, 1870–71; Thomas J. Parker, 1871–72; Cyrus Harris, 1872–74; B. F. Overton, 1874–78; B. C. Burney, 1878–80; B. F. Overton, 1880–84 (Hickeyubbee, acting governor, 1881); Jonas Wolf, 1884–86; William M. Guy, 1886–88; William L. Byrd, 1888–92; Jonas Wolf, 1892–94 (T.

A. McClure, acting governor, June to October, 1894); Palmer S. Mosely, 1894–96; Robert M. Harris, 1896–98; Douglas H. Johnston, 1898–1902; Palmer S. Mosely, 1902–1904; Douglas H. Johnston, 1904–1906. In the last tribal election in 1906, Peter Maytubby, well-known leader and legislator, was elected governor, though he did not serve in this position, for Congress, on April 26, 1906, provided for the continuance of the "present tribal governments" and Governor Douglas H. Johnston continued in office.

The Chickasaw had no written laws before their settlement in the Indian Territory. A form of written constitution was reported to have been adopted by them in 1846, but the document has not been discovered in the historical records. The first formal constitution, titled "Constitution of the Chickasaws," which is in manuscript, was adopted at Boiling Springs in 1848, and another was adopted in 1851 "by the

Floyd E. Maytubby, appointed governor of the Chickasaw in 1939

Chickasaw people at Post Oak Grove" (present Emet in Johnston County). The Chickasaw Council, serving as a legislative body, met annually, its members elected by the people. The chief and a supreme court judge were elected by the council every two years.

Though Ishtehotopa was the "king" of the Chickashaw until his death in the late eighteen forties, the treaty of Doaksville was signed by the Chickasaw chief, George Colbert, who served as such until his death in 1839. Under provisions of this treaty, Chickasaw district chiefs were elected, but were not always in regular attendance at the annual sessions of the Choctaw General Council. The following men served as Chickasaw chief from 1844 to the establishment of their nation under a separate government: Isaac Alberson, 1844–46; James McLaughlin, 1846–48; Edmund Pickens, 1848–50; Dougherty Colbert, 1850–56, who signed his name over the title "financial chief" after about 1852. Cyrus Harris served as acting chief in 1851, and Jackson Frazier served as Chickasaw district chief in 1855.

◆ **Contemporary Life and Culture.** The Chickasaw have exerted marked influence on and have achieved recognition in the development of Oklahoma. Many of them are successful in the professions and business, and are serving in positions of trust in state and county administrations. Since the latter part of the eighteenth century, the majority of the members of the tribe have been of mixed white and Indian descent. The highest percentage of intermarriage with other Indian tribes has been with the Choctaw. In reporting Indian tribal census records in 1919, the Office of Indian Affairs gave 5,659 Chickasaw by blood, 645 intermarried whites, and 4,652 Chickasaw freedmen (former Negro slaves and their descendants). Although there were a large number of their former slaves in their midst after the Civil War, the Chickasaw never granted the Negroes rights of citizenship in the nation.

While Christian church denominations had the loyal support of many Chickasaw members, the work and influence of mission churches and schools were never predominant in the nation, especially after the Civil War. However, all the Chickasaw are Christianized and the majority are church members today. Their children attend the public schools. Underprivileged children from families with a high percentage of Chickasaw blood attend Indian schools, including Carter Seminary at Ardmore, Jones Academy for boys in Pittsburg County and Goodland Indian Orphanage in Choctaw County. Carter Seminary is the former Bloomfield Academy which was opened in 1852 near Achille in present Bryan County.

The ancient Chickasaw clans and social organization in general were broken up with the removal to the Indian Territory, and few families know their clan relationship today. The tribe was formerly divided into three associations. The highest or first was a dual division, called the *Koi* and the *Ishpanee,* the "kings" being chosen from the latter, each division having different interests and religious ceremonials. These two were subdivided into a number of totemic groups or clans having animal names, Wildcat, Deer, and so on. The third association consisted of a great number of local family or "house" groups having "house names," such as *Inchuka chaha* ("tall house"), *Inchuka ahli* ("his own house"). Marriage was outside the clan, and descent was reckoned through the female line.

◆ **Ceremonials and Public Dances.** Old tribal ceremonials and dances are only a matter of historical interest among the Chickasaw today. The Pishofa ceremony was a special tribal institution or practice in the cure of the sick. The family of the sick person called in the "doctor," who performed certain rites four times for three successive days, during which a fire was kept burning in the clean-swept yard a short distance in front of the door of the house, which nearly always faced the east. Special objects, usually wands painted different colors and decorated with ribbons or feathers at the top, were placed between the door and the fire and were said to be of great assistance to the "doctor" in effecting a cure. He also administered herbs from where he stood behind the patient, who was placed inside the house facing the door. Only the patient's kinfolk (house group) were allowed to attend the ceremonials, during which the men and women danced at night near the fire—the corn dance, the snake dance, the bean dance, and the bison dance. In the afternoon of the third day, all feasted on *pishofa* (boiled hominy and pork), as they sat in two lines from the door of the house to the ceremon-

ial fire, the men in one line facing the women in the other. To this day, pishofa is the national dish of the Chickasaw often served at "big" meetings, although the last Pishofa ceremony with its "doctor," ceremonial fire, and dances was held seventy-five years ago.

The Chickasaw are usually, represented in the pageantry of the American Indian Exposition at Anadarko by a "princess" selected from the Chickasaw girls.

Suggested Readings: Grant Foreman, *Five Civilized Tribes;* Malone, *The Chickasaw Nation;* Swanton, *Indians of Southeastern U. S.;* ———, "Social and Religious Beliefs, Chickasaw," in *44 Ann. Rep.,* Bur. Amer. Ethnol.; S. C. Williams (ed.), *Adair's History.*

CHIPPEWA

Chippewa is the popular, adapted form of the name of the tribe correctly called *Ojibway,* the tribal expression meaning "to roast till puckered up." This name has reference to the puckered seam on the Ojibway or Chippewa moccasins and is derived from their words *ojib,* "to pucker up," and *ub-way,* "to roast."

The Chippewa are of the Algonquian linguistic family and comprise one of the largest tribes in North America. In their traditional and early historic life, they lived along the shores of Lake Huron and Lake Superior and westward to the Turtle Mountains of North Dakota. Large groups of the Chippewa, many of whom are mixed-blood Indian and white (French and English), are living in Canada and in the northern United States, including Min-

nesota, Wisconsin, and Michigan. Bands of the Chippewa were allied and united with some of the Ottawa (q.v.) before the French and Indian War, and their descendants now live in Ottawa County, Oklahoma. In 1859, two bands of Chippewa confederated with the Munsee (q.v.) or "Christian Indians" in Kansas, who settled in the Cherokee Nation by contract with the Cherokee in 1867. Still another group of Chippewa were identified with the Potawatomi (q.v.) in Kansas, whose descendants now live in Pottawatomie County, Oklahoma.

Suggested Readings: Connelly, *History of Kansas;* Grant Foreman, *Last Trek of the Indians;* Hodge, *Handbook of American Indians.*

CHOCTAW

Choctaw is the approved, anglicized form of the tribal name *Chahta (Chäh'ta).* It seems to have been first applied to the tribe

about the beginning of the eighteenth century and is found spelled in a number of different ways in historical records. The origin is undoubtedly from the Creek word *cate* (pronounced *cha'te*), meaning "red," a significant term among the native Muscogee (*see* Creek) tribes that once lived in the southeastern United States. The red towns were the "war towns," and the white towns, the "peace towns," a distinction which began disappearing soon after the European colonists settled in this region. Old tribal names among the Choctaw and old place names are often highly abbreviated phrases or mnemonics of the original terms. It has been suggested that the name Choctaw is from the Spanish word *chato,* meaning "flat," descriptive of the ancient tribal custom of flattening the forehead of male infants.

The Choctaw are of the Muskhogean linguistic family and formerly included a number of sub-tribal groups in the southeastern United States. At the beginning of the historic period, the tribe was found in central and southern Mississippi and southern Alabama. Their language was the trade medium throughout the lower Mississippi region after the coming of the Europeans. Many place names in the Southeast all the way to the Atlantic Coast are undoubtedly of Choctaw origin. In Oklahoma, the Choctaw are one of the Five Civilized Tribes and have been associated in history with the Chickasaw, a closely related tribe.

While the physique of the Choctaw varies according to regional groups, they are generally well proportioned and medium in height, tending to be heavy-set in maturity. Because of their mild ways, they have been accused of being corruptible by some critics; because of their reticence and tenacity of purpose, they have also been adjudged selfish. They are generally intelligent and able and have proved themselves receptive to education, modern advancement, and culture. Their tribal characteristics were patience, diplomacy, and great strength in defensive warfare; they seldom engaged in expeditions of aggression outside their own country. They were the preeminent agriculturists among the southeastern tribes.

◆ **Present Location.** Thirteen counties and parts of counties in southeastern Oklahoma, between the Arkansas and Canadian rivers on the north and the Red River on the south, comprise the country included within the boundaries of the Choctaw Nation from 1866 to 1907. Families of Choctaw descent are found throughout this region, the largest fullblood settlements being located in McCurtain, Pitts-

MURIEL H. WRIGHT

Armstrong Academy for Boys, Bokchito, Bryan County, 1843–1921

burg, Le Flore, Pushmataha, and Choctaw counties. Many persons of Choctaw descent make their homes in cities and towns, including Oklahoma City, Tulsa, Muskogee, McAlester, Poteau, and Durant. The descendants of one portion of the Choctaw who did not migrate to the Indian Territory still remain in Mississippi, on a reserved tract some miles east of Philadelphia in Neshoba County.

◆ **Numbers.** The office of Indian Affairs reports a total of 19,000 Choctaw in Oklahoma (census of 1944), of whom approximately 5,000 are fullblood members of the tribe. These numbers represent the members identified, in one way or another, with the administrative affairs of the Five Civilized Tribes Agency at Muskogee, and does not include persons of Choctaw descent who were born since the tribal rolls were closed and have had no contacts with the agency. The Choctaw tribal rolls, when closed on March 4, 1907, listed 8,319 full bloods and 10,717 Choctaw by blood (i.e., mixed bloods), making a total of 19,036 members of the tribe, not including 1,585 intermarried white persons who were also enrolled and allotted lands in severalty.

A house to house census taken in Mississippi in 1831 just before the removal of the tribe to the Indian Territory shows 19,554 Choctaw, the large majority of whom were full blood. At the close of the removal in 1834–37, approximately 12,500 Choctaw had arrived in their new country, more than 2,500 having died since the emigration from Mississippi had begun. The numbers reported by the United States Indian Office at different periods were 18,-500 in 1843, 12,760 in 1850, 16,000 in 1855, 18,000 in 1861, 12,500 in 1865, 16,000 in 1878, and 18,000 in 1889. In 1904, a census of the Choctaw made by the Indian Office shows 15,550 members of the tribe who were descendants of the early immigrants to the Indian Territory, and 2,225 "Mississippi Choctaws," persons who had emigrated recently (after 1866) from Mississippi and had been enrolled and alloted

lands in severalty in the country west. It was estimated that approximately 9,500 enrolled members of the tribe were living in 1950; that is, persons whose names appeared on the rolls when they were closed in 1907.

The descendants of members of the tribe (from 1,000 to 2,000) who remained in Mississippi after the removal in the eighteen thirties, now number 2,232 (census of 1944). In 1910, they numbered 1,162. These Mississippi Choctaw are under the jurisdiction of a separate agency and have no property rights with the enrolled Choctaw in Oklahoma.

In a journey among the Choctaw in the region of the lower Mississippi River in 1730, Joseph Christophe de Lusser, a captain of the French garrison at Mobile, counted the strength of their villages visited at 3,010 men bearing arms. This indicates a total population of between 15,000 and 16,000 at that time. Other estimates of the Choctaw in the eighteenth century numbered them at about 20,000 members; throughout this period they were one of the largest southern tribes.

◆ **History.** Choctaw legend tells of the origin of the *chahta,* or "red people," on a mountain or hill called *Nanih Waya,* a name that signifies "productive mountain," from *nanih* (pronounced *nu nih*), "mountain," and *waya,* "to produce." (This name is frequently found as an entirely different term in historical records, spelled *Nanih Waiya,* which means "leaning" or "bending mountain," the word *waiya* meaning "to bend" or "to lean," the appropriateness of which is difficult to explain, if it is not unexplainable.) The legend says that in the beginning a great "red man" came down from above and built up Nanih Waya in the midst of a vast muddy plain or quagmire; when the hill was completed, he called for the "red people" from its midst.

The Choctaw also have a national legend which tells of their ancient migration, following a sacred pole carried by an ap-

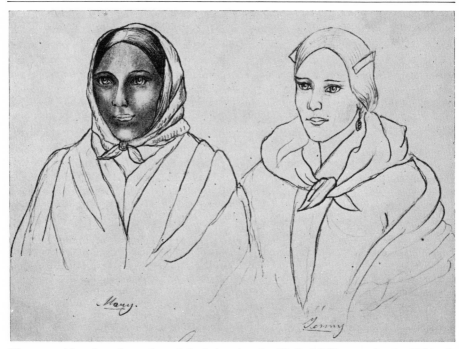

Choctaw girls, 1853, from the original drawing by H. B. Möllhausen in the Whipple
Collection, Oklahoma Historical Society

pointed leader, from a distant country in
the West (*hvshi aiokatula,* "place where
the sun falls into the water") to the country
in Mississippi where Nanih Waya was
located. Here the tribe settled and, under
the direction of their chief or "miko" (pronounced nearly *minko*), established their
government. Throughout the historic period, the great mound located about ten
miles southeast of Noxapater, in Winston
County, Mississippi, was always known as
Nanih Waya, the sacred center of the Choctaw country before the removal to the Indian Territory. The last great national
council of the Choctaw was held at Nanih
Waya in Mississippi in 1828.

The large number of Choctaw place
names on the lower courses of the Mobile
and the Alabama rivers in southern Alabama indicates that this region was once a
part of a Choctaw tribal confederacy referred to in historical records as *Mauilla,* or
Mowill, from which the name Mobile origi-

nated. Choctaw warriors from the villages
in this region fought to the finish in defense of their great chief, Tuskalusa, when
the stockade town which the Spaniards referred to as "Maubila" was attacked by
De Soto and his men on October 18, 1540.
The Spaniards reported that thousands of
natives lay dead and the town was in black-
ened ruins at the end of this desperate conflict, after which there was little mention
of the Choctaw in the records for nearly
two hundred years.

Reports by the French, English, and
Spaniards listed a total of 115 Choctaw vil-
lages known by name in the eighteenth
century. These tribal settlements extended
in a southerly direction from the Nanih
Waya mound. Those to the west in present
Neshoba County, Mississippi, were known
as the Western Division or *Okla falaya*
("Tall People"), also referred to as the
"Big Party"; those to the east in Kemper
County, as the Eastern Division or *Okla*

tannap ("People of the Other Side"), referred to as the "Little Party." The Okla tannap were at a later time called the *Haiyip tuklo* ("Two Lakes"), or more correctly the *Ahe pat okla* ("Potato-eating People"). There was also a smaller Central Division, called Kunsha, in southeastern Kemper County, Mississippi, on the uppercourse of the Chickaswhay River. About 1800, government officials and agents referred to these three large divisions according to their territorial locations as districts, the Kunsha being the leading group in the Southern or Southeastern District. The noted Choctaw chief Pushmataha (1764–1824) and his nephew Nitakechi, who came west as a chief in 1832, belonged to the Kunsha. Another well-known portion of the tribe lived south of the Kunsha in the Southern District, forming a settlement of six villages called the *Okla hannali* ("Six Town People").

With the beginning of French settlement in Louisiana in 1699, the Choctaw became prominent in intertribal wars and politics as allies of the French in the colonies of Biloxi, Mobile, and New Orleans. By 1700, the English interests were pushing into the Mississippi Valley, English traders soon being found among the Natchez and the Chickasaw (q.v.), who remained firm allies of the English and generally enemies of the French throughout the century. The rivalries in the Indian trade between the English and the French brought on a series of wars in the Mississippi region which culminated in the uprising of the Natchez (q.v.) and the massacre of the French garrison at Fort Rosalie (Natchez Bluff) on the Mississippi River in 1729. In these struggles the Choctaw had a conspicuous part as allies of the French and were lined up against the Chickasaw, who came to the assistance of the Natchez. During the bloody battle that took place at Ackia (*see* Chickasaw) in 1736, the English flag was flying over the stockade where the Chickasaw made their stand and defeated the French together with their Choctaw allies. This event was momentous in that it brought on civil strife among the Choctaw themselves and prolonged their enmity with the Chickasaw.

Shulush Homma (Red Shoes) of the Western Division, who had been advocating peace, rose as the Choctaw leader of the pro-English faction, joined by a part of the Okla hannali. The Okla tannap (Eastern Division) remained aligned with the French under Governor Bienville of Louisiana. A year after he was succeeded by the Marquis de Vaudreuil, twelve hundred Choctaw met the new governor at Mobile, though Shulush Homma refused to take any part in this meeting. Throughout the Mississippi region from north to south, English and French intrigue was rife in the Indian trade. Before the council with the Choctaw at Mobile in 1744, De Vaudreuil had refused to see a delegation of Chickasaw who called upon him at New Orleans without the presence of the Choctaw. This incident, along with Shulush Homma's action and the further fact that the French home government did not wholeheartedly support the Louisiana governor in his administrative and commercial policies, meant prolongation of trouble among the Choctaw. In the bloody civil war that followed, Shulush Homma was executed for having taken the life of a French officer in revenge for a personal insult. The chief's death weakened English influence among the people of the Western Division, the English party among the Okla falaya and the Okla hannali finally receiving a crushing blow in 1750 at the hands of the French officer Grand-Pré and his Choctaw allies. Strict measures were now instituted by the so-called "treaty of Grand-Pré" that brought all the Choctaw under the complete control of the French, any individual henceforth to suffer the death penalty for introducing an Englishman to his village, the whole Choctaw Nation to continue the war of extermination against the Chickasaw.

The southern tribes knew well that their

interests had been played upon by the Europeans. The terms of the Grand-Pré treaty had the effect of uniting the Choctaw. From their experience in the long period of bitter strife and bloodshed, they became skilled as diplomats, a reputation that they have held in Oklahoma. Governor Kerlerec, who succeeded De Vaudreuil in 1753, stated after meeting their leaders, "They are men who reflect, and who have more logic and precision in their reasoning than is commonly thought." A year later he again remarked with some heat that they were "covetuous, lying and treacherous."

On the Southwestern frontier, far from the battlegrounds in the struggle between the English and the French known in American history as the French and Indian

Mosholatubbe in 1834, from the Catlin painting in the Smithsonian Institution

War, the Choctaw took little part in this conflict. After the defeat of the French and the signing of the peace treaty at Paris, the Mississippi tribes were under British rule. In 1765, the English authorities at Mobile negotiated a treaty with the Chickasaw and the Choctaw, establishing the eastern boundary lines and determining trading relations for the two tribes. Yet French influence remained among the Choctaw with the marriages, before and during this period, of a number of Frenchmen with Choctaw women, whose descendants are well known in the history of the tribe, among them the Juzon, Cravat, LeFlore, and Durant families.

During the American Revolution, Choctaw warrors served on the side of the Americans under the command of Generals Washington, Morgan, Wayne, and Sullivan. In 1830 twenty of the old warriors who had served with General Anthony Wayne were pensioned for their military service by the United States, under the provisions of the treaty signed at Dancing Rabbit Creek. Among them was Captain Tishomingo (not to be confused with the Chickasaw Chief Tishomingo), who signed the treaty of 1830, moved to Oklahoma, and died in 1841 near Eagletown in present McCurtain County. He was reported also to have served with the Choctaw troops under the command of General Andrew Jackson in the War of 1812, altogether having taken part in nine different battles on the side of the United States.

The war record of the Choctaw has continued notable. Joseph Oklahombi, a full blood from McCurtain County, saw service with the American forces in France in World War I. He was awarded the *Croix de guerre* and cited for exceptional bravery by the French government, one of his many brave exploits consisting in his having rushed machine-gun nests and taken prisoner 171 Germans at one time. Enlisted men and officers of Choctaw descent were among those who gave gallant and distinguished service in the American forces in World War II.

In 1783, the same year that the United States established independence by the Treaty of Paris, England was also forced to give up to Spain all claims in the province of Florida, a large part of the Choctaw country lying within the Spanish area. From that time, Spain made every effort to establish the southeastern tribes as a barrier against the United States. Among treaties made with several tribes by the Spanish officials at Pensacola in 1784, that with the Choctaw acknowledged the protection of Spain and agreed that trade should be carried on only with persons holding Spanish licenses. Choctaw affairs were henceforth more or less involved with Spanish policies and land claims on the Southwestern frontier, even to the Spanish treaty with the United States in 1819.

In the meantime, friendly trading relations with the Choctaw were important to the new American Republic, especially since they held rich lands in the lower Mississippi Valley. The tribal chiefs and captains made the long journey overland in 1786 to Hopewell, on the Keowee River in South Carolina, where they signed the first treaty between the Choctaw Nation and the United States. It defined the boundaries of the Choctaw hunting lands, acknowledged the protection of the United States, and provided for the establishment of trading posts and trading relations within the Choctaw domain.

Through the years to Oklahoma statehood in 1907, the Choctaw Nation was a party to a total of sixteen treaties and agreements with the United States government, each one of which either made large concessions or outright cessions of land, or both, to the United States. Each usually provided nominal payment to the tribal members named in the treaty for services rendered to or for claims due from the tribe.

Choctaw tribal life and customs centered around the growing of corn, which was often produced in abundance and traded to the Chickasaw and neighboring tribes. Melons, pumpkins, and sunflower seed were also grown and used for food, along with certain wild fruits, nuts, and berries. After French colonization, garden vegetables, poultry, and hogs were raised and sold at the trading posts. The Choctaw also brought other articles, including bear's oil, honey, tobacco in kegs, nuts, and peltries and skins of all kinds, to trade for cloth, iron tools, arms and ammunition, and plows.

Scarcity of game and meat supplies at home, even with the enforcement of strict hunting laws, necessitated periodic or seasonal "big hunts" in the Mississippi bottoms and west of that river. Choctaw hunting parties came west up Red River into Oklahoma long before 1800, and fights with bands of hunters and warriors from other tribes sometimes took place. Tradition says that one of the notable encounters

MURIEL H. WRIGHT

Peter P. Pytchlynn in 1850

was with the Caddo in the region of the Caddo Hills in present Bryan County, where the bleached bones of those who fell in the conflict could be found down to modern days. Chief Pushmataha, the famed Choctaw hunter, warrior, and leader, was with a party of his tribesmen on an expedition west to fight the Osage, during which he engaged in a fight with the French-Canadian trader, Joseph Bougie (or Bogy) and his men near the mouth of the Verdigris River in 1807.

Hardly had the Spanish treaty of 1819 been signed than United States officials began pressing for the removal of the Choctaw and their settlement in the West. They were the first among the southeastern tribes ceded land in Oklahoma, in the treaty signed with the United States in 1820 at Doak's Stand, Mississippi, by the three chiefs Pushmataha, Apuckshenubbee, and Mosholatubbee. Pushmataha was the tribal spokesman and General Andrew Jackson headed the government commissioners. The treaty assigned the Choctaw a vast domain including southwestern Arkansas, the southern part of Oklahoma, and a part of eastern New Mexico. (Pushmataha, who was opposed to the removal west, called General Jackson's attention to the fact that his people were giving up a large tract of their richest lands in Mississippi for the western country, part of which was already settled by white people and another part owned by a foreign nation [Mexico]. To meet the chief's objections, a special commission was to be appointed to examine and define the boundaries of the western land.) The treaty further provided that fifty-four sections of good land in Mississippi be set aside and sold, the proceeds to be used as a special fund for the education of Choctaw children. A part of this fund made possible the establishment of the famous Choctaw Academy at Blue Springs, Kentucky, in 1824, under the auspices of the Baptist Mission Association, where for nearly a quarter of a century Choctaw boys were educated, some of whom afterward

were outstanding leaders among their people in Oklahoma.

The final removal of the whole Choctaw Nation to the West was provided for in the treaty signed on September 28, 1830, at the council grounds on Dancing Rabbit Creek, Mississippi, by 171 Choctaw leaders —among them were Greenwood LeFlore, chief of the Western District (Okla falaya); Mosholatubbee, chief of the Northeastern District (Ahepat' Okla); and Nitakechi, chief of the Southern District (Ku^{n}sha), the nephew of Pushmataha, who had died in Washington and had been buried in the Congressional cemetery in 1824. The Choctaw were the first of the five great southern tribes to move as a nation to the Indian Territory, the first time in its history that the United States had undertaken mass removal of an entire tribe.

The removal continued through the fall and winter seasons for three years (1831–34), the emigrants traveling (mostly on foot) in parties of 500 to 1,000 persons each, under the supervision of United States agents and officers. Many hundreds died on the way through the wilderness every season, and there was terrible suffering from blizzards in winter, epidemics of cholera and other diseases, lack of supplies, and accidents. Government agents and officers themselves were hard pressed and could do little to alleviate conditions, lacking experience, knowledge of the country, proper organization, and funds. For several years in the new country, the death rate was high, and there were instances where whole communities of Choctaw were practically wiped out as a result of the hardships endured during the journey.

The treaty of Dancing Rabbit Creek provided for the cession of all Choctaw lands (approximately ten million acres) in Mississippi to the United States; in turn, all the country in southern Oklahoma from east to west, assigned by the terms of the treaty of Doak's Stand (with certain readjustments by the treaty of 1825) was granted in fee simple to the Choctaw Nation. The treaty of 1830 secured to the "Choctaw Nation of Red People the jurisdiction and government of all the persons and property that may be within their limits west, so that no Territory or State shall ever have a right to pass laws for the government of the Choctaw Nation of Red People and their descendants; and that no part of the land granted them shall ever be embraced in any Territory or State." The treaty also stated that "Congress may consider of, and decide the application" of the Choctaw for a delegate in the Congress of the United States, but Congress never granted such representation. Certain sums were to be paid by the United States, some in the form of annuities, to be used for maintaining the Choctaw government, for educating Choctaw youths, and for building a national council house and dwellings for the three district chiefs at convenient locations in the new country. A stipulated number of acres was to be selected from the tribal cession in Mississippi and allotted to eighty-four individuals named in the treaty, to all orphans in the tribe, and to a limited number of heads of families who wished to remain and become citizens of Mississippi. The last-named provisions later were involved in trafficking and frauds in Mississippi lands by white people that necessitated federal government investigation.

The first permanent Choctaw settlements in the Indian Territory were in three general regions: northeast, extending along the Poteau River in present Le Flore County and along the Arkansas River into present Haskell County; southeast, on the tributaries of Little River and on Red River in present McCurtain County; and west, extending west from the Kiamichi River in present Choctaw County. These settlements were organized into three politico-geographic districts, with designated boundaries, under the constitution of the Choctaw Nation, on June 3, 1834, the first constitution written and adopted within the limits of Oklahoma. The first meeting of

the tribal council in this region was held at this time at the crossing of the military road from Fort Smith to Horse Prairie, on the Jacks Fork, where a commodious log council house was erected in 1837. This was the first capital of the Choctaw Nation in the West, located about one and one-half miles west of the town of Tuskahoma in present Pushmataha County. The new capital was named *Nanih Waiya* (correctly "Nunih Waya") in memory of the sacred mound back in Mississippi. Subsequently, Doaksville, Boggy Depot, and Chahta Tamaha (Armstrong Academy) were each designated for a time as the national capital. In 1883, the General Council

MURIEL H. WRIGHT

Last Choctaw Council House, Tuskahoma, in 1884

made an appropriation for the erection of a substantial brick capitol, the Tuskahoma Council House, located about two miles northeast of the site of the old Nanih Wayah Council House. Through the efforts of the Choctaw Advisory Council, the Tuskahoma Council House was repaired in 1936.

The Choctaw were noted for their educational system and schools, which became the pattern for similar institutions established by the Creek, Chickasaw, and Seminole nations. Twelve neighborhood schools were in operation in the Choctaw Nation in 1838, the teachers paid from the educational funds accumulated under treaty stipulation and the children supported by the parents. Some of these schools

OKLAHOMA HISTORICAL SOCIETY

Wheelock Mission Church erected in 1846

were operated at mission stations founded by the various church organizations—Presbyterian, Baptist, and Methodist. In addition, five mission schools were operated as part of church work at Wheelock, Providence, Shawneetown on Red River, Lukfata, and Pine Ridge.

Missionaries of the American Board of Commissioners for Foreign Missions (Congregational and Presbyterian) had carried on work among the Choctaw in Mississippi and moved west with the tribe to begin their labors in the field of education in this region. Among the well-known missionaries were Cyrus Kingsbury, Alfred Wright, Cyrus Byington, and Ebenezer Hotchkin. The Reverend Kingsbury, who in 1818 had established Elliot Mission, the first mission station among the Choctaw in Mississippi, and who died in Oklahoma in 1870, was called the "Father of the Choctaw Mission." As early as 1801, the Choctaw chiefs had asked that teachers be sent

to instruct their women in weaving, and in 1819 all the tribal annuities had been given over to schools.

In 1841, the Choctaw General Council provided for the erection of buildings for Spencer Academy for boys, about nine miles north of Doaksville on the military road to Fort Smith. After the first year, this famous school was operated by principals and teachers from the Presbyterian church.

In 1842, the General Council established a system of boarding schools for boys and for girls, to be maintained from the tribal school fund originating under the treaty of Doak's Stand (1820). Within three years, Spencer, Fort Coffee, and Armstrong academies were in operation for boys; Kunsha (Goodwater), Ianubbi, Chuwahla (Pine Ridge), Wheelock, and New Hope seminaries for girls. Besides regular elementary and academic subjects, boys were trained in farm work and girls in household arts and sewing. Wheelock Academy (first founded as a mission in 1832) for Choctaw girls was still in operation in 1950, one of Oklahoma's most interesting and beautiful historic institutions, located near Millerton in McCurtain County.

Eagletown, Doaksville, Skullyville (Choctaw Agency), Boggy Depot, Tamaha (on the Arkansas River), Perryville, and Mayhew were well-known trading centers in the nation before 1850. Some citizens of the nation (members of prominent mixed-blood families—Folsom, Walker, McKinney, Perry, Jones, McCurtain, Turnbull, and Wall) conducted businesses or trading establishments at these places, generally in partnership with licensed white traders from the states, or operated farms and plantations in the vicinity with Negro slave labor. Robert M. Jones, who had attended the Choctaw Academy in Kentucky, the leading trader and wealthiest planter, before the Civil War was the owner of nearly 500 Negroes, five plantations, and steamboats plying Red River to New Orleans. Newspapers were published in the native language and English at Doaksville and Boggy Depot. The establishment and operation of the Butterfield Overland Mail through the Choctaw Nation in 1858–62, the first transcontinental United States mail route from Missouri to San Francisco, was a notable event, Choctaw citizens maintaining stage stands, ferries, and some turn-pike roads along the route by permission of the Choctaw General Council. For the most part, however, life in the nation was rural, the fullblood people living in isolated communities, operating small farms, and raising livestock.

An important event in the decade before the Civil War was the separation of the Chickasaw from the Choctaw in 1855, although through the terms of this treaty the Choctaw and the Chickasaw have held joint interest in the lands within their respective domains. The Chickasaw (q.v.) had purchased the right of settlement in the Choctaw Nation by the payment of $530,000 as provided by the treaty of Doaksville in 1837. A fourth politico-geographic district had been organized in the nation, known as the Chickasaw District, any Chickasaw or Choctaw having the right of settlement in any one of the four districts. This right was continued after 1855 with the establishment of the Chickasaw Nation, which included all the country west of the head of Island Bayou, between the Red and the Canadian rivers to the ninety-eighth meridian. The Chickasaw now made their own laws and organized their own government within this area; but each tribe was enjoined not to sell any part of either nation without the consent of the other.

The country lying west of the ninety-eighth meridian became known as the

MURIEL H. WRIGHT

New Hope Academy for Girls about 1890

Leased District and was organized under the laws of the Choctaw Nation as Hotubbee District, the new fourth district of the nation, although no Choctaw (or Chickasaw) settled permanently within the area. The Leased District acquired its name from the leasing of this great tract of land to the United States for the settlement of other Indian tribes; and the Caddo, Hainai, and other small tribes known as the Reserve Indians of Texas (*see* Caddo *and* Anadarko) were brought there by the government in 1859.

The outbreak of the Civil War saw the Choctaw siding with the Confederacy, their ties of kinship, church, and trade having been with the South. A treaty with the Confederacy was negotiated by Albert Pike, Confederate commissioner, and signed jointly by delegates of the Choctaw and Chickasaw nations on July 12, 1861. Choctaw troops were organized and served throughout the war in the Confederate Army, participating in major battles in

MURIEL H. WRIGHT

Allen Wright, who named Oklahoma, about 1880

OKLAHOMA HISTORICAL SOCIETY

Robert M. Jones

Arkansas and Indian Territory. The Choctaw capital, Chahta Tamaha (Armstrong Academy), sometimes referred to as the Confederate capital of the Indian Territory, was the meeting place from 1863 of the Grand Council of the "United Nations of the Indian Territory," of which the Choctaw were one of the six member tribes. At the close of the war, federal commissioners negotiated the joint Choctaw-Chickasaw treaty of 1866, which re-established the Choctaw Nation. This document, in addition to providing for Choctaw tribal matters, gave detailed plans for the organization of all Indian tribes and nations living within the present boundaries of the state into a territorial government to be called "Oklahoma," the name being suggested by Allen Wright, a Choctaw delegate. While the plan for an Indian territorial government was never carried out, the name Oklahoma became widely known and was adopted for Oklahoma

Territory in 1890, and for the forty-sixth state of the Union seventeen years later.

After the Civil War, increased white immigration along the overland trails to the Southwest and the building of the first railroad through the Choctaw Nation (right-of-way having been granted for railroad construction in the treaty of 1866) brought drastic changes in the life of the Choctaw. The effects of the great westward expansion of the United States—together with the need to reopen tribal schools and churches, to control trading activities, and to develop the natural resources in the nation—meant that the early tribal laws written for a simple pastoral society had to be changed to deal with the rising industrial organization. Meetings of the General Council were important, the members elected from the counties in the nation convening in annual and special sessions at the call of the Principal Chief, and business was carried on as in a session of a state legislature, with the exception that relations with the federal government were conducted through the Office of Indian Affairs in the Department of the Interior.

All the Choctaw domain was held in common, any citizen of the nation having the right to make his home anywhere in the country and to fence the surrounding land for fields and pastures so long as he did not trespass on the already fenced lands and claims of another Choctaw. Any citizen could sell his improvements—houses, barns, fences—to another citizen, but he could not sell the land. The railroad (Missouri, Kansas, and Texas) opened the way for shipping coal, stone, timber, livestock, and agricultural products to markets in the states. Coal mining, begun in the McAlester field in 1872 and later extended to the vicinity of Lehigh, grew into one of the big industries of the time in the whole Southwest under the operation of mining companies from the Eastern states.

After the construction of the M. K. and T. Railway through the Choctaw Nation in 1872 and three other railroads within the next twenty years, small towns grew up along the tracks, generally in the vicinity of the coal mines or near the old settlements. Some of the enterprising mixed-blood Choctaw and some of the intermar-

MURIEL H. WRIGHT

Tuskahoma Academy for Girls in 1892

ried white men brought their families to live in these towns, erected substantial residences, and engaged in various businesses—trading stores, coal land, timber or stone-quarry leasing, and farming and ranching. The employing of tenants to farm lands increased, bringing more white people from the neighboring states into the country.

The fullblood Choctaw lived off in the country or in remote communities in the eastern part of the nation, where they cultivated small fields near their homes and looked after their livestock that fed upon the open ranges. Many prominent full bloods had good homes and were well-to-do, operating extensive farms and owning large herds of livestock. Practically every Choctaw citizen took an interest in tribal politics and elections in the nation, districts, and counties. The full bloods held the balance of power and were generally conservative on party lines, with large representation in the General Council. In their communities the native language was used almost exclusively and English was rarely ever heard. Although laws of the General Council restricted the playing of tribal ball, especially on Sunday, games were matched in the summer time between counties or districts in the nation and large crowds gathered to witness these exciting events.

When the Allotment Act of 1887 was passed by Congress, foreshadowing the later creation of the Commission to the Five Civilized Tribes, or Dawes Commission, the Choctaw were opposed to allotment of lands in severalty, the fullblood people being particularly bitter in their opposition. Shortly after the creation of the Dawes Commission in 1894, the conservatives in the Choctaw Council sought the passage of a tribal law exacting the death penalty for any citizen who advocated change in the status of land ownership in the nation. The law failed to pass in the Council, but was indicative of the feeling against the proposed work of the Commission. In fact, the Commission

MURIEL H. WRIGHT

Edmund McCurtain

made little headway in treating with the Choctaw until the signing of an agreement at Atoka with representatives of the nation on April 23, 1897. This instrument, henceforth known as the Atoka Agreement, provided for allotment, every enrolled Choctaw and Chickasaw (q.v.)—man, woman, and child—to receive a fair and equitable share of land, the character, fertility, and location of the land to be taken into consideration and such allotments to remain untaxable for twenty-one years. Where coal and asphalt were found in commercial quantities, the land was segregated and reserved from allotment to be sold on the public market for the benefit of all enrolled members of the two nations.

When Congress sought to enact arbitrary legislation and assume full control of all the Five Civilized Tribes preparatory to clearing the way for complete domination by white settlers in the Indian Territory, delegations from the Choctaw and others of the Five Tribes went to Washington to protest. After strenuous opposition, the measure, including the Atoka Agreement and other provisions relating to the Five Civilized Tribes, was passed by Congress and approved on June 28, 1898. This law, henceforth known as the Curtis Act, went into effect within two days; but it was many months before some of its provisions could be carried out, since the Atoka Agreement required the approval of the majority of the Choctaw and the Chickasaw in elections to be held before December 1, 1898. The elections were held on August 24, and the votes were counted in the presence of the three members of the Dawes Commission on August 30, when it was found that the Atoka Agreement had been ratified by a majority of 798 votes. Immediately, Green McCurtain, principal chief of the Choctaw Nation, and Robert M. Harris, governor of the Chickasaw Nation, issued proclamations declaring the Atoka Agreement in amended form as incorporated into the Curtis Act in full force and effect in the two nations.

The Choctaw and the Chickasaw, holding their national domains jointly, were the largest propertyholders of any of the Five Civilized Tribes at the beginning of allotment. The total area of the two nations amounted to 11,660,951 acres, of which 6,953,048 acres were in the Choctaw Nation in southeastern Oklahoma. When the survey of these lands had been completed by the United States Geological Survey, additional surveys of each forty-acre tract in the populated sections of the country had to be made to apportion and equalize the individual allotments. All Choctaw and Chickasaw lands, appraised by the Dawes Commission, were valued at from $6.50 an acre for natural open bottom land to 25 cents per acre for rough mountain land. The basis of an individual Indian allotment was $1,041.28, or the value of 320 acres of average allottable land; the basis of allotment for a freedman (former Negro slave or his descendant) was $130.16, or the value of 40 acres of average allottable land. The Indian allottee could choose a homestead at one place and one or more additional tracts to complete the total value apportioned elsewhere in the tribal domain.

The Dawes Commission soon found that the affairs of the two nations could not be satisfactorily administered and settled under the Atoka Agreement. Therefore, another agreement, known as the Supplemental Agreement, was negotiated with representatives from the Choctaw and the Chickasaw, ratified by Congress, approved by the President on July 1, 1902, and in special elections held by the two nations on September 22, 1902. The Supplemental Agreement set forth the method of determining the citizenship rolls, the status of the Chickasaw freedmen, and the rights of persons to be enrolled as Mississippi Choctaw. When the rolls were completed, there were 19,097 Choctaw by blood and intermarriage, and 5,994 Choctaw freedmen as finally approved by the Secretary of the Interior in 1907 and subsequently corrected in 1914.

The Supplemental Agreement made special provisions for the coal and asphalt lands reserved from allotment and the sale of this property to outside interests, directing that the proceeds be divided equally among the enrolled Choctaw and Chickasaw (excepting freedmen) in the ratio of three-fourths to the Choctaw Nation and one-fourth to the Chickasaw Nation (based on the comparative population of the two peoples). Several large tracts of coal and asphalt lands amounting to 433,950 acres, lying in what are now Haskell, Le Flore, Latimer, Atoka, and Pittsburg counties, were segregated. The surface of these lands was sold under provisions of the Congressional act of February 12, 1912, with the coal and asphalt reserved in the joint ownership of the Choctaw and Chickasaw nations. Part of the coal was sold, and part leased to mining companies operating in Oklahoma.

Another valuable property was the 1,-373,324 acres of rich timber land in the Choctaw country, containing some of the most valuable forests in southwestern United States, which were reserved from allotment by the Indian Office under instructions from the Department of the Interior in 1906–1907. These timber lands were sold and are now owned by large lumber companies operating in southeastern Oklahoma.

The Curtis Act provided that the Choc-

taw government (along with the governments of all the other Five Civilized Tribes) continue for eight years, or until March 6, 1906. A few days before this date, a joint resolution was introduced in the United States Senate (February 27, 1906) to extend the Choctaw government until March 27, 1907. This resolution was signed by the President twenty-four hours before the tribal government was to have been dissolved. Congress subsequently included the subject in an act of April 26, 1906, which provided "for the final disposition of the affairs of the Five Civilized Tribes and for other purposes." This important legislation continued the Choctaw government under certain limitations until completion of tribal affairs, by interpretation provid-

MURIEL H. WRIGHT

Choctaw leaders in 1910
Left to right: Principal Chief Green McCurtain; Victor M. Locke, Jr., secretary to the Principal Chief; Peter J. Hudson, delegate; Dr. E. N. Wright, resident delegate at *Washington*

ing for the appointment of the Choctaw principal chief by the President of the United States.

The offices of principal chief, national attorney, and mining trustee, with regular salaries paid out of the tribal income from coal royalties, were retained until 1948, thus continuing the tribal government in limited form, the officials serving under the supervision of the United States Office of Indian Affairs. These officials represented the interests of the Choctaw in the tribal estate, and the signature of the principal chief was necessary to make legal all deeds in the sale of property on behalf of the tribe. The last elected members of the General Council before the dissolution of the Choctaw government in 1906 continued to meet at irregular intervals until about 1916.

In July, 1922, a large number of Choctaw, many of them fullbloods, met in a convention at Albion, in Le Flore County, to review tribal affairs and particularly to protest the long delays by the Indian Office in making the settlements due the tribe in accordance with the Atoka and Supplemental agreements. Besides drafting the usual protests and memorials to Congress and the Indian Office in Washington such as Choctaw meetings and councils had been presenting for nearly fifty years, the Albion Convention unanimously adopted a special resolution to appoint a committee of five Choctaw to work out ways and means to urge and secure a settlement of all tribal affairs with the government. To give more emphasis to tribal matters, the Choctaw Committee openly declared itself in politics and showed enough strength in the Congressional elections in Oklahoma in 1926 and 1928 to exert considerable influence on the administration of the Office of Indian Affairs. As a result of a study of conditions among the Indians over the United States made in 1928 by the Institute of Government Research, the Indian Bureau set up a new program consistent with the conclusions and recommendations of the Institute's report. The new administration in 1933 made radical departures in the management of Indian affairs throughout the country by introducing and securing the passage by Congress of the Wheeler-Howard Bill that became a law on June 18, 1934.

In the spring of 1934, before the passage of this bill, the Choctaw organized for concerted action in tribal affairs. Conventions were publicized and held throughout the counties that had comprised the Choctaw and Chickasaw domain in 1906 (held originally under the Choctaw patent) and also in Oklahoma, Tulsa, and Muskogee counties, where many Choctaw families made their homes. A total of 168 delegates elected in these meetings attended an important convention at Goodland Indian School near Hugo, June 5–8, 1934. This Goodland Convention, conducted under regular parliamentary law and order, devoted three full day and evening sessions to a review of Choctaw interests. Following open discussions, resolutions were passed that included approval of the Wheeler-Howard Bill with certain amendments, organization of an advisory council of eleven Choctaw, election by the delegates present of the principal chief recently appointed by the President, recommendation for the purchase of taxable Choctaw lands for landless members of the tribe, and suggestions that historic spots be marked and the old Council House near Tuskahoma be repaired as a monument in Choctaw history.

The Choctaw Advisory Council was organized immediately and thereafter met in annual and special sessions from October, 1934, to 1946. Although it had no legislative power, yet its recommendations received consideration by the Indian Office and in Congress; thus it has promoted the welfare and honor of the Choctaw in Oklahoma. Among its achievements were the establishment and erection of the Indian Hospital (general) at Talihina, the repair of the Choctaw Council House and the purchase of adjoining land for use in a tribal educational and welfare program, the study of and recommendations in the preparation of the Oklahoma Indian Welfare Act of 1936, the unanimous approval of the Choctaw attorney's moves against any Congressional action to reopen the tribal rolls, and consistent effort in furthering the disposition of the tribal coal and asphalt properties still held in common.

Under recent Congressional legislation, a contract between the Secretary of the Interior and the representatives of the joint ownership of the common tribal property —the Principal Chief of the Choctaw and the Governor of the Chickasaw (q.v.)— was made in May, 1947, wherein it was agreed that the United States would purchase the residue of the coal and asphalt, the sale of which was a foremost issue in tribal affairs. The United States agreed to pay $8,500,000 for approximately 370,000 acres of coal (estimated at 1,600,000,000 tons) and asphalt. Of the total amount paid, $3,500,000 represented the purchase price and $5,000,000 was in lieu of estimated losses sustained by the tribal owners in the management of the coal and asphalt under the supervision of the Indian Office during a period of forty-six years. This extra sum would offset the possibility of tribal suits against the government in the Indian Court of Claims to recover such losses. The sale contract was approved by a majority of the Choctaw and Chickasaw in a special election early in the spring of 1948, and was approved by Congress on June 14, 1948, the money for the purchase of the coal and the asphalt under this contract being appropriated by Congress in the spring of 1949. Per capita payments to the enrolled Choctaw and Chickasaw or their descendants were completed in 1949–50, bringing toward a close the federal government's relations with the Choctaw and Chickasaw nations as separate governments within the boundaries of Oklahoma.

The establishment and the just settlement of Choctaw property in Oklahoma, involving the education, welfare, and ad-

vancement of this people, have been the concern of many brilliant Choctaw during a period of 150 years, as well as of high officials in government departments and the Office of Indian Affairs and of nationally known attorneys. Among the outstanding Choctaw leaders in this period were Pushmataha, Mosholatubbee, Apuckshenubbee, Nitakechi, Captain Tishomingo (United States Army veteran, named in the treaty of Dancing Rabbit Creek, 1830), David Folsom, Israel Folsom, Robert M. Jones, Peter P. Pitchlynn, Tandy Walker, Cornelius McCurtain and his three sons (Jackson, Edmund, and Green), Forbis LeFlore, McKee King, Allen Wright, Cole Nelson, Coleman Cole, Jonathan Dwight, Joseph Dukes, and Jane Austin McCurtain.

Choctaw prominent in the history of the Indian Territory and Oklahoma since 1898 include Benjamin F. Harrison, member of the Oklahoma Constitutional Convention, legislator, and state budget officer, 1923–35; Victor M. Locke, Jr., legislator and superintendent of the Five Civilized Tribes Agency; Henry J. Bond, treasurer of Atoka County; Eliphalet N. Wright, M.D., president of the Indian Territory Medical Association and chairman of the Choctaw Committee, 1922–29; Frank H. Wright, D.D. (Presbyterian, U. S.), evangelist and singer; Thomas J. Hunter legislator and county judge, Choctaw County; Gabe E. Parker, member of the Oklahoma Constitutional Convention and of the committee to design the Great Seal of the state; William A. Durant, sergeant-at-arms in the Constitutional Convention, legislator, and speaker of the House in its third session; James Dyer, legislator; Edgar A. Moore, legislator; Lyman Moore, banker; Todd Downing, novelist; Thomas P. Howell, M.D., physician and rancher; Wendell Long, M.D. and LeRoy D. Long, M.D., physicians and surgeons; Czarina C. Conlan, on the staff of the Oklahoma Historical Society for twenty years; Mary Mc-Alester, prominent philanthropist and club woman of McAlester; and William G. Stigler, former Choctaw national attorney and a member of the United States Congress from the Second District of Oklahoma (elected to his fourth term in 1950). ◇ **Government and Organization.** Choctaw tribal officials as of July 1, 1948, were William A. Durant, principal chief; Hampton Tucker, mining trustee; and Ben Dwight, national attorney. These officials were recommended and appointed through the United States Indian Office with the approval of the President of the United States. The Choctaw Advisory Council of eleven members subject to call by the Principal Chief held its session in this year at the Choctaw House near Tuskahoma in Pushmataha County.

In a convention held at Doaksville, Choctaw Nation, in 1860, the conservative and progressive elements in the nation drew up a new constitution, referred to thereafter as the Doaksville Constitution, providing for legislative, executive, and judicial departments, which remained in force until the dissolution of the Choctaw government in 1906. Under the Doaksville Constitution, the executive power consisted of one "principal chief" (limited to two successive terms) and three district chiefs to serve in an advisory capacity, although the latter offices were soon only nominal. Principal chiefs of the Choctaw Nation

have been George Hudson, 1860–62; Samuel Garland, 1862–64; Peter P. Pitchlynn, 1864–66; Allen Wright, 1866–70; William Bryant, 1870–74; Coleman Cole, 1874–78; Isaac Garvin, 1878–80; Jackson McCurtain, 1880–84; Edmund McCurtain, 1884–86; Thompson McKinney, 1886–88; Ben F. Smallwood, 1888–90; Wilson N. Jones, 1890–94; Jefferson Gardner, 1894–96; Green McCurtain, 1896–1900; Gilbert Dukes, 1900–1902; Green McCurtain, 1902–1906.

Wesley Anderson was elected principal chief in August, 1906, but did not serve since the Congressional act of April 26 continued the Choctaw government with the incumbent officials, Green McCurtain serving as principal chief until his death in 1910. Through the work of the Choctaw Committee, an election of principal chief was held in August, 1926, when Dr. Eliphalet N. Wright was elected by an overwhelming majority. This election was not sanctioned by the Indian Office. On June 12, 1948, an election was held under order of the Indian Office and Harry J. H. Belvin was elected. Choctaw chiefs appointed by the President of the United States have been Green McCurtain, 1906–10; Victor M. Locke, Jr., 1911–18; William F. Semple, 1918–22; William H. Harrison, 1922–29; Ben Dwight, 1930–37; William A. Durant, 1937–48.

Choctaw Senate in 1898
Green McCurtain, principal chief, is at the center

The first written constitution of the Choctaw Nation was adopted in 1826 and provided for the election of members to the tribal council by the people and for the election of three district chiefs. David Folsom of the Northeastern District (in Mississippi) was the first elected district chief under this constitution. At the beginning of the main removal to the Indian Territory, the chiefs of the three Choctaw districts in Mississippi were Greenwood LeFlore, Western District; Mosholatubbee, Northeastern District; Nitakechi, Southeastern or Southern District, all of whom signed the treaty of Dancing Rabbit Creek on September 27, 1830. Chiefs Mosholatubbee and Nitakechi came west with their people, but Greenwood LeFlore remained in Mississippi where he was later prominent in state affairs.

In 1834, the Choctaw Nation was organized and the country divided into three districts: Mosholatubbee, Okla falaya (renamed Apuck shunnubbee later), and Pushmataha. A new written constitution adopted by the people in this year provided for a "Declaration of Rights" and three departments of government—legislative, executive, and judicial. Each district was served by elected members in the Council, a district chief, and four judges on the Supreme Court of the nation. With the admission of the Chickasaw in 1837, a fourth district, called the Chickasaw District of the Choctaw Nation, was organized by law. Trial by jury was guaranteed by the constitution, and the laws in the nation were carried out with a fair degree of efficiency, lighthorsemen appointed by the district chiefs serving as a police force. Punishment for law breakers consisted of fines, whipping, and death. The Choctaw were noted for their stoicism in meeting the death sentence. After trial, the convicted person was allowed his freedom, for there were no jails in the country for many years. On the day set by court order, he returned punctually to meet his sentence of death from the rifle in the hands of the

executioner, usually a squad of several lighthorsemen appointed by the court.

Laws of the Choctaw Nation were printed in both the native language and in English. The Choctaw have left more original official documents and published laws in their native language than any of the Five Civilized Tribes. These are now on file in the Oklahoma historical archives.

In 1857, a convention of Choctaw at Skullyville adopted a new constitution patterned closely after state constitutions, the chief executive officer titled "governor of the Choctaw Nation." A large majority of the people opposed these innovations, and civil war threatened the nation. As a result, a special election was held which resulted in calling another convention which adopted the Doaksville Constitution in 1860. Men who served as governor of the Choctaw Nation under the Skullyville Constitution were Alfred Wade, 1857–58; Tandy Walker, 1858–59; and Basil Le Flore, 1859–60. In subsequent Choctaw history under the Doaksville Constitution, the executive always officially signed himself "principal chief of the Choctaw Nation," but in general conversation, he was addressed as "governor" as a courtesy title.

◆ **Contemporary Life and Culture.** The Choctaw have many leaders in Oklahoma, a large number engaged in the professions—law, medicine, and teaching —and in business. Many are also serving in federal, state, and county offices, and in the United States Indian Service—agencies, schools, and hospitals. Most of these groups are of mixed Indian and white descent, though the fullblood Choctaw are also represented. The highest percentage of intermarriage with other Indian tribes has been with the Chickasaw. World War II changed general population trends, yet the great majority of the fullblood Choctaw live in rural communities in the southeastern counties. Most of these people are poor, engaging in farming and stock raising, small-business enterprises, clerking, lumbering, or day labor. The women of some of these communities, as members of the Choctaw Spinners' Association, have won a reputation for their fine spinning in the wool-weaving projects in eastern Oklahoma, promoted by the Choctaw Advisory Council in co-operation with the Arts and Crafts Division of the United States Indian Office. This work, as well as a revival of basket-making from cane and buckbush gathered locally, has proved valuable to the rural home and has tended to raise the standard of living.

Children of these Choctaw rural families attend the local public schools. Orphans and underprivileged children are sent, through the work of the Education Division of the Indian Office, to one or another of the several Indian schools in eastern Oklahoma—Wheelock Academy for girls, Jones Academy for boys, Seneca Boarding School, Sequoyah Training School, or Goodland Orphanage (Presbyterian U. S., Mission). When prepared in their studies, some boys and girls go on to Chilocco Indian Agricultural School, Bacone College, and later to the state colleges and the university.

Christian missionary efforts among the Choctaw, begun in 1818, have borne fruit, for practically all members of the tribe are identified with church denominations to-day, principally the Protestant churches—Presbyterian, Baptist, and Methodist. The Methodist Episcopal church probably has the largest membership.

Few Choctaw families today know their line of descent according to the ancient tribal clans or *iksa.* One of the weakening forces of the removal to the Indian Territory was the breaking up of the old tribal clan system which had been strictly observed for countless generations. Formerly, the Choctaw comprised two great divisions without respect to their geographical location: the *Okla i^n hulata* or *Hatak i^n hulata,* signifying "beloved people" or "friends"; and the *Kashapa okla,* "part of the people." Marriage within these divisions was forbidden and descent was reckoned in the female line, the child belonging to the

Allen Wright's home, built in 1860 at Old Boggy Depot, as it looked in 1940

mother's clan. In making up the Choctaw tribal rolls in 1902, even though the old clan system had been forgotten, the line of descent was reckoned through the mother. In addition to the two great divisions, some authorities who made an early study of the Choctaw clan system listed six subclans; Okla falaya, Haiyip tuklo (or Ahe pat okla), Okla hannali, Kunsha, Chickasha, and Apela.

◆ **Ceremonials and Public Dances.** Choctaw tribal dances are no longer held in Oklahoma. Choctaw ball games and some old customs are now seen only as a part of educational and entertainment programs given by the Choctaw schools to present tribal history. Within recent years, such programs have been given during the meetings of the Choctaw Advisory Council at the old Council House near Tuskahoma, in Pushmataha County, often with several thousand visitors in attendance.

Suggested Readings: Benson, *Life Among the Choctaw Indians;* Debo, *Rise and Fall of the Choctaw Republic;* Grant Foreman, *Five Civilized Tribes;* ———, *Indian Removal;* Hargrett, *Laws of the American Indians;* Swanton, *Indians of Southeastern U. S.;* ———, *Source Material, Choctaw;* articles in various issues of *Chronicles of Oklahoma,* Vol. I– (1921–).

COMANCHE

The origin of the name Comanche has not been positively established, though it has been said that it is a contraction of the Spanish term *camino ancho,* which means literally "the broad trail" and refers to the wide range traveled by the warriors of this tribe on their trading and war expeditions. The name was first applied to the tribe soon after 1700 and is found spelled in a number of different ways, such as *Camanche, Commanche,* or *Cumanche.* These Indians call themselves *Nerm,* also written *Neum* or *Nimenim,* meaning "people of people." Some early writers referred to the tribe as Padouca, from Padonka, the name by which they were known among the Osage.

The Comanche are of the Shoshonean linguistic family, which also includes the Shoshoni, Bannock, Ute, and Paiute, that developed in the Shoshoni and Snake River regions of Wyoming and Idaho. This linguistic stock is said to have been of Nahuatl origin in Mexico and therefore is remotely related to the Aztec. The Comanche are the only division of the Shoshonean family who left their Rocky Mountain haunts and established themselves on the Plains as one of the great tribes of this region. Later, they became divided into as many as twelve different bands, of which the most prominent in the history of Oklahoma are the Penateka (from *Penateka,* meaning "honey eaters"), and the Quahadi (from *Kwahari,* meaning "antelopes").

The Comanche were the most skillful horsemen of all the American Indians and ranked as the most powerful nomadic tribe on the Plains of the Southwest. Their language became, as it were, the court language of this region, resorted to by the Caddoan tribes whenever the sign language was inadequate in an intertribal council.

The fullblood Comanche has a bright copper-colored complexion, acquiline nose, and thin lips; he is medium in height and generally heavy-set. Certain tribal leaders became famous in early days on account of their huge size.

The Comanche were hospitable and generous and generally rated higher morally than other nomadic tribes in the region. They were noted for their courage and gave no quarter and asked none in war.

These characteristics generally prevail among the Comanche to this day. A good number are leaders in their communities in Oklahoma, and some hold positions of trust in the state; others, with educational advantages and opportunities, have made their mark in professional life.

◆ **Present Location.** The Comanche live in or near the cities of Anadarko, Fort Cobb, Carnegie, and Apache in Caddo County; Mountain View, Gotebo, and Hobart in Kiowa County; Lawton, Cache, and Indiahoma in Comanche County; and near Walters in Cotton County. Their tribal interests and any restricted properties of individual tribal members are under the supervision of the Kiowa-Comanche-Apache Agency of the Anadarko Area Office at Anadarko.

◆ **Numbers.** The approximate total population of the Comanche in Oklahoma in 1950 was 2,700. Their numbers according to annual reports at different periods were 1,718 in 1924, 1,476 in 1910, 1,553 in 1898, 1,399 in 1880, and 2,538 in 1869. In 1851, Texas reports estimated the Comanche population at 20,000, an exaggerated number according to United States Indian Agent Jesse Stem. He estimated the southern Comanche bands (Penateka) living below the Brazos River, under Chiefs Katemsie, Buffalo Hump, and Yellow Wolf, at 600; and two friendly northern bands under Chiefs Pahayuka and Shanico, who usually came south to winter in the upper Cross Timbers, at 1,300—making a total of 1,900 Comanche in Texas. Stem commented that besides these bands large numbers of the tribe, about whom little was known, were constantly on the move—some wintering in the upper parts of Texas, hunting buffalo on the "great northern prairies" in summer and again mixing with the Indian tribes of New Mexico. Before 1850, their total numbers were generally exaggerated.

◆ **History.** In their traditional history, the Comanche were hunters who lived on fish and large game in the Rocky Mountains, supplementing their diet of meat with wild berries, fruits, and edible roots. At intervals, the different bands would make expeditions to the Plains to hunt buffalo. In time, when they had secured horses after the Spanish colonization of Mexico, the Comanche hunters did not return to their Rocky Mountain country. Their habits in life changed, and they became a truly nomadic people. When they moved out toward the east, their early locations were on the North Platte River, which as late as 1805 was still known as the Padoucah Fork. Under pressure of their enemies, the Sioux to the north, they began migrating southward, moving their tipi villages to new locations. Yet they kept up their friendship with the Shoshoni, and occasionally went back to visit them in the Rocky Mountains. When horses became their most prized possessions, bands of Co-

MURIEL H. WRIGHT

Quanah Parker's home near Cache, Oklahoma, about 1909

REV. F. H. WRIGHT

Comanche women erecting a tipi in 1898

REV. F. H. WRIGHT

The finished tipi

manche sometimes engaged in long expeditions, traveling more than one thousand miles, even as far away as the Bolson de Mapimí of Chihuahua in Mexico, to replenish their herds either in trade or in attacks on the Spanish settlements, from which they often carried away women and children into capitvity.

As the Comanche migrated southward, they attacked and displaced other Plains tribes with which they came in contact. The first driven out were the Quiviran peoples of the great Caddoan family (see Wichita) who were living in what is now central Kansas. The first meeting of the Comanche with white men in this region was with Du Bourgmont, who visited their village in 1724. He reported that they owned horses and were skillful riders, indicating that they had already had contact with the Spaniards to the southwest. The French succeeded in securing a peace alliance between the Comanche and the Caddoan people (Jumano) in 1746 from which time these tribes were generally allies in war (see Wichita). At this period, the Comanche range was between the Platte and the Red rivers, but later extended to the Río Grande.

South from central Kansas along the Cimarron and the North Canadian rivers, the Comanche found the Plains Apache, who were likewise driven out of the region. They also fought the Kiowa (q.v.), who had come out of the far Northwest to the Plains about 1700. After many years, the Comanche and the Kiowa held a council during which a peace agreement was made (about 1790) that has never been broken by either of the two tribes. The Penateka Comanche were not present and were not a party to this agreement, since they had located south of Red River where they later were known as the Southern Comanche.

As the years passed, the Comanche had increased to such an extent that the tribe virtually had become a loose confederation of bands, each of which acted on its own initiative. The northern bands that were counted among the nomadic tribes on the Plains north of Red River became notorious for their raids on the Southwestern settlements, actions which brought them into conflict with the Spanish military forces. They were even dreaded by other tribes and were continually at war with the Apache. In the spring of 1758, the Apache (Lipan) mission, founded by Catholic missionaries on the San Saba River in Texas, was wiped out by a large force of Comanche and their Caddoan allies. In this period, some Spanish officials secured peace treaties with certain groups of the Comanche, but members of other bands did not feel obligated to honor these pacts.

About 1815, the tribal bands made their first acquaintance with English-speaking traders in their early Western ventures from the states. The first of these traders in Oklahoma was General Thomas James of Illinois, who in 1822 established a profitable trade with the Comanche, whom he erroneously called the "Pawnee," at his stockade post near the Canadian River somewhere within present Blaine or Dewey County.

The tribe first met with official representatives of the United States in 1834 when the Dragoon Expedition, under the command of Colonel Henry Dodge, held a council with the Plains tribes at the Wichita village on the North Fork of Red River, in present Kiowa County (see Wichita). Among the throng of Indians present was the Comanche head chief, Ee-shah-ko-nee, or Ishacoly, "Traveling Wolf," and the second chief, Tabequena, "Sun Eagle," the latter a huge man weighing over three hundred pounds. As a result of this council and a later one the following September with other Indian delegations at Fort Gibson, the Comanche signed their first treaty with the United States at Camp Holmes on the Canadian River, in August, 1835. The nineteen chiefs and leaders whose names appear on this treaty, including Ishacoly and Tabaquena, represented the

Northern Comanche bands. Leaders of some of the Northern Comanche also signed the treaty between the Kiowa (q.v.) and United States commissioners at Fort Gibson in 1837.

Although the Penateka band were not a party to the Camp Holmes treaty, the names of their chiefs appear along with those representing the Caddoan (*see* Anadarko) and other Texas tribes who signed the treaty made at Council Springs on the Brazos River in 1846. By an act of the Texas legislature in 1854 and through continued efforts of United States agents, two reservations for the tribes represented in this treaty were selected and surveyed by Captain Randolph B. Marcy the following year. One on the Brazos River, known as the Lower Reserve, was assigned the Caddo (q.v.) and their allied tribes; the other, known as the Upper Reserve (18,576 acres), located forty-five miles west on the Clear Fork, was assigned the Comanche. Most of the Penateka settled peaceably on the Upper Reserve. In 1858, they were reported by the United States agent as advancing in civilization: raising crops, building good houses, and sending their children to school on the reservation.

The annexation of Texas in 1845 and the gold rush to California in 1849 found the Northern Comanche among the most hostile of the western tribes, for new hazards and precarious living as hunters on the Plains had roused their fears and hatred against the white traders and emigrants along the Santa Fé Trail and other highways to the Southwest and the Far West. A peace treaty was signed by some of the Comanche chiefs with the United States at Fort Atkinson (near present Dodge City, Kansas) in July, 1853; but only one of the tribal bands seems to have been represented. This was the Yamparika band, whose chiefs—Shaved Head, White Bear, and Ten Bears—were well known as promoters of peace. Conflicting interests arising out of the terms of the treaty soon

REV. F. H. WRIGHT

Comanche women skinning a beef, 1898

brought on war between the Comanche and the Osage that endangered the Western frontier.

Increase of Indian depredations brought widespread alarm among the settlers of the Southwest in 1857. When the hostile Texans resumed a war of extermination against the Indians, especially the Northern Comanche and their allies the Kiowa, detachments of Texas Rangers, as well as United States troops accompanied by friendly Indian scouts employed from the reservations on the Brazos, brought the war north across Red River into western Indian Territory.

In the spring of 1858, a Comanche village near the mouth of Little Robe Creek in what is now southwestern Ellis County, Oklahoma, was attacked by a detachment of Texas Rangers and Indian scouts from the Brazos under the command of Captain John S. Ford. In the fight, the Comanche chief, Pohebits Quasho, or "Iron Jacket," who had bravely tried to ward off the attack on the village, was killed. The Texans were soon forced to retreat when they found themselves outnumbered by angry Comanche warriors who, warned of the impending attack, had precipitately returned from a hunting expedition.

Several months later, a Comanche encampment at the Wichita village on Rush Creek, near present Rush Springs in Grady County, was attacked by four companies of the Second United States Cavalry, accompanied from Texas by Indian scouts (Caddo and Tonkawa) from the Brazos Reserve, under the command of Major Earl Van Dorn. Unknown to Major Van Dorn, this band of Comanche had just come from a friendly meeting with United States officers at Fort Arbuckle and had stopped on their way west to visit with the Wichita (q.v.) In the battle at the Wichita village, Major Van Dorn was among the wounded, Lieutenant Van Camp was killed, and Indian losses in life and property were heavy. This unfortunate event was not soon forgotten among

MURIEL H. WRIGHT

Horseback in 1875

the Comanche, for they were more suspicious and hostile than ever, especially toward the Texans.

Early in the summer of 1859, Chief Katemsie represented the Penateka band among the delegations from nine tribes in a council with United States officials at Fort Arbuckle, planning the settlement of these tribes in the Leased District in the Indian Territory (*see* Choctaw). A few weeks afterward, when the Texans threatened a massacre of the Indians of the Brazos reserves, under military escort 380 members of the Penateka left the Upper Reserve for the Leased District, along with the Caddo (q.v.) and their allies, as exiles from Texas. They settled along the Washita River under the supervision of federal agents of the Wichita Agency near Fort Cobb, but suffered heavy losses in livestock and property by the forced removal.

During the Civil War, attempts to keep the friendship of the great Comanche tribe were made by both the Federal and the Confederate governments through several agreements and treaties with the different bands. Soon after the fall of the Wichita Agency and Fort Cobb into the hands of the Confederate forces, Commissioner Albert Pike secured two peace treaties with the Indians at the Wichita Agency in behalf of the Confederate States, in August, 1861, in which all the leading Comanche bands were represented with the exception of the Quahadi. The effects of the war and the uncertainties concerning the tribal treaties with the two contending governments led the Comanche and other tribes into widespread disturbances and depredations along the Santa Fé Trail and elsewhere in the West in 1864. A campaign against the Indians was immediately begun by Federal forces from New Mexico led by Kit Carson, in which the Comanche came out undefeated because of their strategy and quick movement. This action incited the Comanche's hostile spirit and

MURIEL H. WRIGHT

Toshaway in 1871

led to fighting in the Indian Territory and Texas at a later period in their history.

The year 1865 saw the Comanche and Kiowa (q.v.) in attendance at two peace councils. The first was held at Camp Napoleon, near the present site of Verden in Grady County, in May, 1865, before news of the fall of the Confederacy had reached this area. More than five thousand Indians from over the Indian Territory were in attendance to meet with Confederate officials from Texas and representatives of the Mexican government. Terms for a confederation or league for peace were set forth in the Camp Napoleon Compact, with the motto, "An Indian shall not spill an Indian's blood," which was signed by delegations from twelve great tribes of the Indian Territory, six leading bands representing the Comanche.

The second council was held at the mouth of the Little Arkansas River (in Kansas) in October, 1865, where a peace treaty was drawn by United States commissioners, among whom was Kit Carson, and signed by the Kiowa (q.v.) and the Comanche, the latter represented by such leaders as Ten Bears, Iron Mountain, Horseback, Toshaway (or Tosawi), and Mowway. The two tribes were granted "undisturbed use and occupation" of the country extending east from the eastern boundary of New Mexico to the ninety-eighth meridian, covering present western Oklahoma from the Red River north to the Cimarron.

Failure of the government to carry out the terms of the treaty of the Little Arkansas and an intensive military campaign against the Cheyenne and the Sioux incited the Plains tribes to another period of bloody warfare, in which the Comanche and their allies had a conspicuous part. When the autumn of 1867 came, the Indians were still undefeated. A movement for peace promoted by federal officials friendly toward the Indians resulted in the creation of a government peace commission, and a call was sent out to the tribes of the southern Plains to meet in council in October, 1867.

This council on Medicine Lodge Creek in Kansas, a few miles north of the Oklahoma line, was one of the most memorable and colorful gatherings of Indians in this region under the auspices of the government. It was attended by high-ranking United States officials, army officers, press representatives, Indian scouts and interpreters, and thousands of tribesmen who accompanied their leaders.

At the close of lengthy conferences, the chiefs present were persuaded to sign treaties which provided, among many other things, that their tribes should settle on reservations assigned them by the United States in the Indian Territory. Settlement within the boundaries of any reserved tract had been bitterly opposed by the Indian delegations during the council, Chief Ten Bears of the Comanche voicing his views in an oration that stands out as one of the finest delivered by an Indian in the history of America. He referred indirectly to the fact that the Comanche had already been granted the free and unmolested use of a wide region (by the treaty of the Little Arkansas in 1865), saying in part: "The Comanches are not weak and blind. . . . They are strong and far-sighted, like grown horses. . . . I was born upon the prairie where the wind blew free and there was nothing to break the light of the sun. . . . I want no blood upon my land to stain the grass. I want it clear and pure, and I wish it so that all who go through among my people may find peace when they come in and leave it when they go out."

The treaty of the Medicine Lodge did not solve the Indian problem, for white settlement on the buffalo ranges and the presence of soldiers at the Western military posts, ready for action at the least sign of trouble, made the tribes wary and more hostile than ever. It was not until after the Battle of the Washita (see Cheyenne) in November, 1868, that the Comanche began setting up their tipi villages

on their reservation in the vicinity of Fort Sill. Their reserved lands (see also Kiowa) assigned at the Medicine Lodge council consisted of a tract of 2,968,893 acres now included in eight counties and parts of counties south of the Washita in Oklahoma, extending west from the ninety-eighth meridian to the North Fork and the western boundary of the state.

New and difficult conditions of reservation life along with the disappearance of the buffalo herds throughout the West roused the tribal bands to old hatreds and wild action against the white people and a rebellious attitude against government agents. Detachments of the United States Army were sent out from Fort Sill and other Western posts to force the surrender of the recalcitrant bands. Comanche took part in the attack on the Wichita Agency at Anadarko and threatened ranchmen in the western part of the Chickasaw Nation during the dry, hot summer of 1874; they were in the attacking parties in the Adobe Walls (July, 1874) and the Buffalo Wal-

MURIEL H. WRIGHT

Mow-way in 1871

low (September, 1874) fights in Texas. Military force, however, brought about the final capitulation of the hostile Indians.

The last of the Comanche who came to the reservation were the Quahadi; this band had remained on the Staked Plains of Texas for many years, away from United States treaty-making and agencies, often taunting other tribal bands for their acceptance of reservation life. A Quahadi band of four hundred men, women, and children under the leadership of Quanah (Quanah Parker), having finally accepted the terms offered by military scouts, set out in orderly line from the Staked Plains, with all their belongings and a herd of nine hundred ponies, for Fort Sill, where they surrendered on June 24, 1875.

This move marked the end of the old customs and habits of living on the Plains and the beginning of the reservation period in the Kiowa-Comanche country. Before many years had passed, on the open prairie the tipi gave way to the two-room frame house, government built, for the Indian family. Children and young people were sent away from their relatives to boarding schools under government orders. After the last big hunt for buffalo in 1878, the Comanche engaged more and more in the raising of cattle on the reservation, which, along with the leasing of grass lands to outside cattlemen, became the principal source of income for members of the tribe. Comparatively few Comanche engaged successfully in farming. There was some temporary and seasonal employment at Fort Sill in making posts and building fences, cutting and storing hay in summer, and freighting government supplies to the fort and the Indian agency. In 1878, soon after the consolidation of the Kiowa-Comanche Agency with the Wichita Agency at Anadarko, the Indian police had been organized by the Indian Office, and the Comanche contributed signally to the success of this local guard on the reservation. About this time, the old tribal bands were broken up, and for the first time the Co-

manche were looked upon as one tribe. The Comanche did not find it easy to adjust themselves to great changes in their habits and customs, but with time and patience, they achieved a measure of contentment and tranquillity under difficult conditions.

Quanah Parker, the best-known Comanche of the reservation period, is one of the romantic Indian characters in the history of Oklahoma. Born about 1845, he was the eldest son of Nokoni, leader of the Quahadi band, and his wife, Cynthia Ann Parker, who as a child had been taken captive by the Comanche from her white parents in Texas and had grown up among the Quahadi. Quanah led his band in the Battle of Adobe Walls, and after the surrender at Fort Sill, he was the first recognized chief of all the Comanche. Upon his return from a visit to his mother's white relatives in Texas about this time, he advocated and promoted the adoption of much of the white man's civilization among his people. He served as a member

MURIEL H. WRIGHT

Chief Quanah Parker

of the Indian police, went as a delegate from his people to the Capitol at Washington many times, and was appointed one of the three Indian judges on the Court of Indian Offenses, which was established by the United States in 1888 to mete out justice in cases involving the prohibition of tribal dances and polygamy, as well as in those of theft and crime on the reservation. (This court carried on its work in the Indian way and was highly commended for efficiency, fairness, and dispatch in making decisions.) Quanah Parker died in 1911 at his home near Cache, which is now considered a historical shrine. His son, White Parker, in 1950 was a minister of the Methodist Episcopal church, with a pastorate in Oklahoma City.

Under the terms of an agreement with United States commissioners (members of the Cherokee or Jerome Commission) in October, 1892, the Comanche, together with the Kiowa and Apache (q.v.), were allotted land in severalty (160 acres each), and the surplus of their reservation lands sold to the United States. Allotment to the Indians was completed and the surplus lands on the Kiowa-Comanche-Apache Reservation opened to white settlement on August 6, 1901. The approximately half-million-acre tract known as the "Big Pasture," reserved from the reservation and leased to cattlemen for revenue for these tribes, was opened to white settlement in 1906, the last Indian land opening in western Oklahoma.

◆ **Government and Organization.** The Comanche as a tribe are represented by their elected members on the Kiowa-Comanche-Apache Intertribal Business Committee, Lee Motah (Comanche of Anadarko) serving as chairman in 1950. Other Comanche members at this time included Wiley Yellowfish, Robert Coffey, Lawrence Tomah, Shannon Wahnee, and Ben Chistine. The Business Committee meets once a month at the Federal Building in Anadarko to consider business relating to the three tribes that come under the provisions of the Oklahoma Indian Welfare Act of 1936, and to decide and make recommendations on some matters under the jurisdiction of the Kiowa-Comanche-Apache Agency at Anadarko.

◆ **Contemporary Life and Culture.** The Comanche are largely of mixed-blood Indian and Spanish descent. The custom of adopting into the tribe women and children seized in raids on the Spanish settlements had prevailed so long by the end of the raiding in their tribal history that it was stated that there was not a member of the tribe of unmixed blood, practically all of them being of Spanish descent in varying degrees.

Most of the Comanche live in rural communities and are members of various church denominations, Christian missionary work having begun early in the reservation period in Oklahoma. Comparatively few Comanche belong to the peyote cult, for which Quanah Parker had leanings (he never became a member of a Christian church). The Dutch Reformed church operates the Comanche Mission near Lawton, in which the Reverend Robert Paul Chaat (Comanche) is pastor and leader.

Young men of the tribe served with distinction in the armed forces of the United States in both world wars. The first American Indian to be commissioned in the Army Corps of Chaplains in World War II was First Lieutenant James Collins Ottipoby, a Comanche and formerly a Home Missions leader in the Dutch Reformed church.

◆ **Ceremonials and Public Dances.** The Comanche are an outstanding group in the pageantry and ceremonials of the American Indian Exposition held every summer at Anadarko. Albert Atocknie, one of the old Comanche leaders, has served as assistant director of the pageant in the Exposition during several seasons; Edgar Monetahchi (Comanche) was president of the Exposition board of directors (all Indian) in 1950.

Suggested Readings: Hebard, *Sacajawea;* James, *Three Years Among the Indians and Mexicans;* Nye, *Carbine and Lance;* Richardson, *The Comanche Barrier to South Plains Settlement;* Thoburn and Wright, *Oklahoma,* I.

CONESTOGA

The Conestoga, once an important Iroquoian tribe that lived along the Susquehanna River and near the Chesapeake Bay, were annihilated in the Indian and colonial wars of the seventeenth century. A remnant of the tribe joined their neighbors, the Erie (q.v.), in Ohio, and by 1830 became known as the Seneca of Sandusky. Their descendants are among the Seneca (q.v.) in Ottawa County, Oklahoma. The name Conestoga is from *Kanastoge,* "at the place of the immersed pole." The great Conestoga freight wagons used in the western trade over the old Santa Fé Trail that crossed what is now Cimarron County, Oklahoma, were manufactured at the village of Conestoga, which perpetuates the name of this once-powerful Indian tribe in Lancaster County, Pennsylvania.

Suggested Reading: Hodge, *Handbook of American Indians.*

CREEK

The name Creek is from "Ochese Creek Indians," the title given the first group of the tribe in Carolina government relations as reported by the British agents for the Indian tribes in 1720. Ochese Creek was an old name for the Ocmulgee River, Georgia, along the upper course of which the easternmost part of the tribe lived when English trade began. As time passed, the name for this tribal group was shortened to "Creek Indians" or "Creeks," and finally "Creek" became the popular designation for the whole tribe. The terms Upper Creek (for the western part of the tribe) and Lower Creek (for the eastern part) later became stereotyped names used by the commissioners and agents in Colonial government service. In the latter part of the eighteenth century, these terms referred to the geographical position of the two tribal divisions that occupied the greater part of the country now included in the states of Alabama and Georgia—the Upper Creek living on the Coosa and Tallapoosa, the main branches of the Alabama River; and the Lower Creek, on the Chattahoochee and Flint rivers near the present Alabama-Georgia border.

Another name for the tribe was accepted by the Creek themselves sometime after 1700. In the native language it is rendered *Musko'ke* or *Masko'ge.* By adding the native suffix *algi,* "people," the collective plural *Maskokal'gi,* "Maskoke people," is formed. The English spelling of the name is *Muscogee* or *Muskogee.* Neither the origin nor an explanation of this name has yet been found in the Creek language. Some ethnologists have thought that the name *Maskoke* may have originated from an Algonquian word *Maskek* or *Maskeg,* "swamp" or "marsh." The Delaware, of the Algonquian family, call the Creek *Masquachki,* "swamp land," and the Shawnee, who are also Algonquian, call them *Humaskogi,* "they are masko," though the word *masko* and its meaning have not been traced to the Shawnee language.

The name *Maskoke* (sometimes spelled *Muskoki* or *Muskoke*) is more likely to have had its origin in the Choctaw language, which was the medium used in trading relations in the southeastern United States from the sixteenth century almost to the close of tribal occupation in that region. The Choctaw term *im-uski,* literally "their cane," abbreviated, like many old Choctaw names, to *'m-uski,* with the addition of the Creek suffix *algi,* "people," would form *'m-uski-algi,* meaning "their cane people." Likewise, the term *humaskogi,* signifying "red cane people," may be from the Choctaw word *humma,* "red," combined with *uski,* "cane," and the Creek suffix *algi,* "people." The term "red cane people" is analogous to "Red Sticks," the well-known popular name given the Creek war group. (The word "stick" was also applied for "tribe.") It has reference to the old tribal method of keeping count of the days in beginning a war. When a time was designated for the Creek warriors to assemble, small sticks or pieces of split cane painted red were tied up in a bundle and one stick discarded every day until the last stick indicated the appointed day. The Creek war in 1813–14 was called the "Red Stick War" among the Creek people. In the eighteenth century the French called the Muskoke or Creek proper *Kanchak,* the Choctaw name for a species of hard cane (*see* Koasati).

The Muskoke or Creek belong to the Muskhogean linguistic family, the name of this great linguistic stock coming from the name of this tribe. The Creek are one of the Five Civilized Tribes in Oklahoma. They have always been noted for their conservatism and for dramatic color in their tribal ceremonials. The Creek men are generally tall and lithe; the women are shorter in stature and well formed. The individuality and independence of the women were duly recognized in tribal life. The Creek people are characteristically proud, sometimes arrogant, and have always been brave and courageous in war. Many of them are numbered among the brilliant characters and leaders in the history of Oklahoma.

◇ **Present Location.** Seven counties and parts of counties in Oklahoma were organized under the state constitution from the country that comprised the Creek Nation from 1866 to 1907. These counties are in the general region north of the Canadian River (South Canadian), lying east from the eastern boundary of Seminole County to the eastern boundary of McIntosh County, thence extending north to a line drawn east from the city of Tulsa. The largest Creek settlements today are in McIntosh County in the vicinities of Eufaula, Checotah, and west; in Hughes County in the vicinities of Weleetka and Okemah; and in Okmulgee County. Many Creek people make their homes in the cities and towns of this region, including Tulsa, Sapulpa, Henryetta, Holdenville, Eufaula, Broken Arrow, and Coweta.

The first party (McIntosh party) of immigrant Creek were from the Lower Creek, arriving in the Indian Territory in 1828 and settling in the northern part of the new country, north of the Arkansas River and west of the Verdigris. The town of Coweta in Wagoner County takes its name from the ancient Coweta tribe of the Lower Creek. The Upper Creek came with the main migration beginning in 1836, settling in the region between the Canadian and the North Fork rivers, west to the mouth of Little River, and up the valley of the Deep Fork. As the years passed, some of the Creek families moved from one part of the country to another, confusing their alignment in the two divisions by the interchange of their locations. Thus the old organization lines were gradually weakened, making it difficult to distinguish the members of the Upper and Lower Creek today.

◇ **Numbers.** A census by the Five Civilized Tribes Agency at Muskogee in 1944 reported 9,900 Creek. This did not include persons of Creek descent outside the agency rolls, a group known to be increasing in numbers. In 1915, the Indian Office reported 11,967 Creek in the state, of which 6,873 were full blood, 1,698 were half blood or more, and 3,396 less than half blood. A census of the Creek Nation made by order of the National Council in 1890 numbered 9,139 Indian citizens by blood, not including the Yuchi, who were also citizens of the Nation. A Creek census taken by the Indian Office in 1857 gave 14,888 members of the tribe. Census figures in the twenty-year period before that varied from 20,000 to 25,000, the total number shown in the census taken in 1832, just before the removal to the Indian Territory, being 21,-733. In the decade before 1800, their numbers were estimated from 25,000 to 30,000. It should be noted that census figures in the eighteenth century and early nineteenth century represented the combined population of all the towns of the Creek confederacy, which included the remnants of a number of other tribes.

◆ **History.** The origin of the Maskoke people is given in several versions of a legend about their ancient tribal migration from a far western country and their settlement in what is now southeastern United States. The earliest of these legends was told in 1735 to Governor Oglethorpe at Savannah, Georgia, in a speech made by Chekilli, who was referred to as the "Head-Chief of the Upper and Lower Creeks." The legend was said to have been written in curious red and black characters on a buffalo skin which was then framed and hung in the Georgia Office in Westminster, England, but was afterwards lost. An English translation was also made at the time of Chekilli's speech, but it, too, disappeared. A German translation from the English version was published in 1741 for the German emigrants from Salzburg to Georgia. Over one hundred years later, Albert S. Gatschet discovered the German text, and through his efforts the legend was translated again into English and also into the Maskoke language. Chekilli's story is remarkable in that many place-names in the tribal migration can be identified with those known in historic times in the Gulf Coast region. The origin of four tribes of

the Maskoke proper is given in the legend: the Kasihta (Cusseta), Coweta, Abihki, and Coosa.

The Kasihta were visited in 1540 by De Soto after his Spanish expeditionary force had wandered for days over rough waste country in what is now southeastern Georgia. De Soto's advance guard came to a river where they were met with pomp and ceremony by the chieftainness of the region, who, in behalf of her people, received them into the tribal town on the opposite bank of the river. This was the town called Cofitachequi, of the Kasihta, who headed the peace group of the Maskoke people. The town was located some miles below the present city of Augusta, Georgia, on the opposite side of the Savannah River, in South Carolina, near the border of Barnwell and Hampton counties. The native inhabitants of the country were described as "brown of skin, well formed and proportioned." They were said to have been more civilized than any of the peoples of the "Florida" provinces. They wore clothes and shoes and had some objects of European manufacture, probably secured from earlier Spanish expeditions that had visited the coast of South Carolina in 1521–26. The country was reported to have been quite populous until decimated by a pestilence a short time before De Soto's visit.

Prior to discovery of them by the Spaniards, some of the Maskoke tribes were leagued together for mutual protection; for example, the Kasihta and the Coweta who became the nucleus of the Lower Creek (or Lower Towns), and the Abihka and the Coosa who thus formed the beginning of the Upper Creek (or Upper Towns). This trend in uniting for a common purpose resulted in the great Creek Confederacy, in which the Maskoke-speaking peoples were dominant. The Maskoke proper comprised approximately twelve separate tribal groups, including the Kasihta, Coweta, Coosa, Abihka, Wakokai, Eufaula, Hilabia, Atasi, Kolomi, Tukabahchee, Pakana, and Okchai.

In the Lower Creek division, the Kasihta were the "white" or "peace" group, and the Coweta, the "red" or "war" group. Though the Kasihta were described as having first place among the four Maskoke tribes in the migration legend, the Coweta became the leaders of the Lower Creek and, for a long period, were considered the leaders of the whole nation. Both Spanish and French writers as early as 1700 spoke of the chief of the Coweta as the "emperor of the Creeks."

At the time they were visited by De Soto in July, 1540, the Coosa were the most powerful of the group of allied tribes afterwards known as the Upper Creek. Their principal town was called Coosa, also spelled *Coca* or *Coza* in early Spanish records, known as the ancient city of refuge where anyone accused of crime found asylum until judged by the tribal council. Although it had declined in prestige and grandeur, Coosa was still the name of a town noted in 1799 in a beautiful location on the left bank of the Coosa River, in what is now Talladega County, Alabama. Tulsa, Oklahoma, now referred to as the "Oil Capital of the World," takes its name from the Coosa tribal town known as "Big Tulsa," probably the same place mentioned in the De Soto narratives as *Tallise,* which was originally located somewhere in Lowndes County, Alabama.

The Tukabahchee were one of the four foundation "sticks" (tribes) of the Creek Confederacy and the leading "town" of the Upper Creek division. From their traditions, they seem to have been originally a distinct tribe who were associated at an early period with the Shawnee and who migrated from a northerly direction to the Southeast after the arrival of the Maskoke tribes of Chekilli's legend. Their principal "town" was known as Tukabatchee, located on the right bank of the Tallapoosa River opposite Big Tulsa, in present Elmore County, Alabama, as reported in 1799. This was the leading town among the Upper Creek settlements and was said to have long been considered the capital of the Creek Nation, East. The Tukahbachee were the most populous tribal group in the confederacy (1,287 in the census of 1832), and to this day their settlement north of Holdenville, in Hughes County, is the largest of the old Creek "towns."

In the early historic period, the Creek claimed all the country from the Savannah River south to the St. Johns River, including the islands along the Atlantic Coast, thence west to Apalachee Bay, and from this north to the Appalachian Highland. After the defeat of the allied Indian tribes by the English of South Carolina in what was known as the Yamassee War in 1715, the Lower Creek living on the streams in east central Georgia (the Ocmulgee, Oconee, Ogeechee rivers) moved west to the Chattahoochee and Flint Rivers. The tribe soon gave up a wide strip of country along the coast and all the islands to the British by treaty. From this time, the Creek were in treaty alliance with the English of South Carolina and Georgia and generally in conflict with the Spanish colonists in Florida.

About the year 1700, some unrelated tribes of the southeastern region, weakened by war and pressure from the advance of European settlements, began joining the Creek Confederacy. Among these allied tribes were the Alabama, Koasati, Hitchiti, Natchez, Yuchi, and even a band of Shawnee. Each of these tribes had its own language and customs and lived in "towns" or settlements in the Creek country, the location of each determining the alignment of the tribal members with either the Upper or the Lower Creek divisions. William Bartram in his travel through the country in 1777 reported a total of fifty-five towns in the whole Creek Nation, each town including several villages.

The history of the Creek during the eighteenth and nineteenth centuries is largely revealed in the lives of their chiefs and leaders. Alexander McGillivray—born in 1740 (in some records 1759), the son of Lachlan McGillivray, a Scot, and his beautiful French-Creek wife, Sehoy Marchand —attained international fame in his career as "Emperor" of the Creek Nation, 1783–93. He was commissioned a colonel in the British Army, and it was through his shrewd leadership that the Creek people remained loyal to England during the Revolutionary War. Through his mother, he was a member of the ruling Wind Clan of Otciapofa Town, commonly called "Hickory Ground," of the Coosa tribal group, Upper Creek division, and was eligible to a chieftaincy. He made his home at Little Tallassie (Little Tulsa) on the Coosa River and, after the Revolution, became wealthy through his friend and partner, William Panton, a Scottish royalist and member of the trading company of Leslie and Panton of Pensacola, Florida. Proud, ambitious, with keen insight and talent as a writer, Alexander McGillivray was a diplomat and political leader rather than a warrior on the actual field of battle. At the close of the Revolutionary War, the friendship and the trade of the powerful Creek Nation were sought by the United States and by Spain through its officials in Florida and Louisiana. In advancing the interests of his people as well as his own personal affairs, McGillivray was brilliantly successful and remarkable in that he was recognized by and in alliance with both governments at the same time. His great work was the unification of the Creek Nation. He knew full well the value of the Creek country, and his efforts to hold its boundaries as they had stood before the Revolutionary War remained in principle the land policy of the Creek people. On the other hand, McGillivray's contempt for United States citizens, especially the people of the adjoining states, did not promote the pathway of peace.

Members of the McIntosh (MacIntosh) family, the descendants of Captain William McIntosh, a Scot who married two wives from the Coweta, Lower Creek, were prominent chiefs and leaders in the nation. The Captain's eldest son, William McIntosh, was born at Coweta, in Georgia, in 1778, and served as chief of the Lower Creek from about 1800 to his tragic death in 1825. Roley (or Roderick), his half-brother, was born at Coweta in about 1790, and served as chief of the Lower Creek from 1828 to his retirement in 1859. Another celebrated leader was William Weatherford, born about 1780, the son of a British trader and his Creek wife, a half-sister of Alexander McGillivray. Two who bore native names were Menawa (Big Warrior), born about 1765, a second chief of the Upper Creek, who came to the Indian Territory in 1836; and Opothleyahola (Hupuihilth Yahola), born about 1798, who lived at Tukabatchee Town where he became the principal speaker in the Upper Creek council.

Carrying out an agreement with Georgia to extinguish the Indian title to all lands within the borders of the state, the United States had secured the relinquishment of millions of acres from the Creek Nation by 1805. The chiefs and leaders became alarmed at the prospect of losing all their country at the hands of the clamoring, land-hungry Anglo-Americans. During a council of the Creek Nation in 1811, Chief William McIntosh secured approval of a law forbidding the sale of any more tribal land under penalty of death. This same year, Tecumseh, the Shawnee chief, visited Tukabatchee, where he sought the co-operation of the Creek Nation in building up a great confederacy of all Indian tribes to check the advancing frontier of the United States. His cult of doing away with everything learned from the white people was adopted by a group of Creek "prophets" who opposed the Anglo-American civilization and secretly promoted a return to the old tribal ways and beliefs. These moves were in the background when at the beginning of the War of 1812 the Creek national council decided to remain neutral. The following year, some Creek war parties were implicated in troubles with white settlers on the frontier, which together with the activities of the Anglo-Americans in eastern Florida brought a cleavage among the Creek people. Of the two hostile factions, that friendly to the United States included, such leaders as Menawa, Chief William McIntosh of the Coweta, Little Prince, who was the principal chief of the whole nation, Tustennuggee Hopaie, speaker of the Lower Creek, and others. The members of the opposition, called "Red Sticks," took up the cult of the prophets and were in the majority when joined by most of the Upper Creek towns. Their leaders included William Weatherford, Hillis Hadjo (or Francis), the venerable chief Hoboithle Micco of Tallasie (Big Tulsa), and Peter McQueen, a mixed-blood leader of the same town.

The war that followed was called the Red Stick War among the Creek, the Red Stick faction striking Tukabatchee Town and destroying crops and property in some of the opposing Upper Creek villages. When the news came that 1,000 Red Sticks had attacked Fort Mims and raided white settlements in the vicinity in August, 1813, the people of Georgia, Tennessee, and Mississippi Territory sprang to arms for fighting in the Creek country. The power of the hostiles was finally broken with the slaughter of nearly 1,000 warriors in the terrible Battle of the Horseshoe on the Tallapoosa River, March 27, 1814, by 2,-000 American and allied Indian troops commanded by Andrew Jackson. The Americans pursued a scorched-earth policy throughout the Upper Creek country, and by August, 1814, a total of 8,200 members of the tribe were dependent upon the United States for rations. William Weatherford surrendered to Jackson, and the Creek people were forced to cede all their country in southern Georgia to the United States.

The Creek treaty of 1814 forced the nation to "abandon all communication, and cease to hold any intercourse with any British or Spanish post, garrison, or town." The ceded lands were opened to white settlers, and thus the new settlements came nearer the towns of the Lower Creek, who laid the blame for the recent war on the Red Sticks and their leaders. William McIntosh, head chief of the Coweta, who had a prominent part in the Battle of the Horseshoe as an ally to the American forces, was thenceforth aligned with the progressive element and generally opposed by the conservative group within the nation. Further cessions of land to meet the demands of Georgia, signed by McIntosh and town chiefs of the minority party, reached their climax in a treaty negotiated with United States commissioners on February 12, 1825, at Indian Springs, Georgia. The year before, the Creek national council had reenacted the death penalty for any Creek who ceded any more of the tribal lands. A Creek uprising seemed certain after the signing of the treaty, but was forestalled in a meeting of the council when the sentence of death under the tribal law was passed on Chief McIntosh. A party of warriors from the Okfuskee towns (descendants of the Coosa) led by Menawa of Tukabatchee, was designated to carry out the sentence, and surrounded and fired the house of Chief McIntosh on May 1, 1825. He was shot to death when he tried to escape. His son, Chilly McIntosh, escaped and sought refuge among the white people in Georgia, though others among the Chief's followers were assassinated at the time of the trouble.

The protest of a great majority of the Creek chiefs and warriors against the Indian Springs treaty resulted in another treaty negotiated at Washington, D. C., in January, 1826, signed by Opothleyahola, Menawa, and ten other Creek leaders. This document declared the recent treaty of Indian Springs null and void and ceded all the Creek lands in Georgia to the United States. Furthermore, the friends and followers of the late Chief McIntosh had the privilege of moving to a new location west of the Mississippi, where the United States agreed to purchase a country for them. This was the first step toward formation of the Creek Nation in the Indian Territory. An exploring party of five Creek leaders came west in 1827 and selected a location for settlement west of the Verdigris and the Grand rivers and north of the Arkansas, in what is now Wagoner County.

A favorable report on the western country was made to the Creek national council, and the first of the "McIntosh party" (733 men, women, and children) under the leadership of Chilly McIntosh set out for the West in the midst of difficulties and deprivations. The first members of the group reached Fort Gibson in February, 1828, on board the steamboat *Facility,* the rest traveling overland and joining them the following November. These people were from the Lower Creek towns, with Roley McIntosh as chief. By 1830, there were 3,000 Creek living on the Arkansas in the Indian Territory, with the arrival of about 2,400 men, women, and children, although the later immigrants were not of the McIntosh following. While some of the wealthy members of the tribe soon settled themselves in comfortable log houses surrounded by fenced fields, the great majority of the immigrants were poor and wretched, suffering from want and disease, for the government delayed for a long period in furnishing promised supplies, including implements, seed for planting, and other necessities. Added to these hardships were the depredations on their livestock and growing crops by bands of the Delaware and by the Osage, who resented the arrival of the newcomers in the country long claimed by the Osage tribe (q.v.).

Another treaty signed at Washington on March 24, 1832, by a Creek delegation of seven members, including Opothleyahola, William McGillivray, and Benjamin Marshall, ceded all the tribal lands east of the Mississippi to the United States. The Creek people were to leave Alabama as fast as they were ready to emigrate, the United States to pay all expense for their removal

and subsistence for one year after arrival in the West, the treaty stating that no Creek was compelled to emigrate, "but they shall be free to go or stay, as they please." Furthermore, ninety Creek chiefs and the head of "every other Creek family" had the right to remain in Alabama and were allowed to select a certain allotment of the tribal domain to be patented to each in fee simple by the United States, all land selections and other tribal matters to be resolved within five years.

Opotheyahola, the great Creek leader. From McKenney and Hall, *History of the Indian Tribes of North America,* 1838

Before the end of the period, the Creek people were in the midst of chaos. The old tribal rule for law and order was disrupted in the Creek settlements; promises on the part of the United States to keep the white people out of the tribal lands were not observed. Some of the tribal groups were ready to move west, others were opposed, and still others wanted to settle in Texas instead of the Indian Territory. Fraudulent sales of Creek land tracts promoted by unscrupulous white men left many of the tribe destitute. There were murders and killings among the Creek themselves; and, in a few instances, marauding parties robbed and threatened some of the white settlers—all of which was beyond the control of the tribal chiefs and authorities. Open clashes occurred when white men attacked some old tribal members working at their crops and, jealous of some of the well-to-do Indians, forced them out of their homes, beat them, and drove them away from their property. Eneah Emathla, chief of the Lower Creek, led forth a company of warriors to retaliate. At the outbreak of the second Seminole War (q.v.) in Florida in 1835, some of the Creek leaders joined the Seminole in the hostilities. The jealousy and enmity of the land-hungry white people on the borders of the Indian country in Alabama soon forced the opening of the Indian lands to settlement, the unprincipled and lawless actions of the whites sustained as a matter of political expediency by officials at Washington.

In the early part of 1836, General Winfield Scott, in command of several thousand United States troops, state volunteers, and small bands of warriors representing the tribal authorities (among them Opothleyahola), set out to put an end to the "Creek War." The chiefs and leaders who had protested conditions were finally taken captive and shackled and their people captured. In the midst of starvation and misery, 14,609 Creek, of whom 2,495 were enrolled as hostiles with their proud chiefs chained and handcuffed, were forcibly removed, most of them walking overland under military escort, to the Indian Territory. Hundreds died and were hurriedly buried on the way. In the spring of 1837, officers and removal agents reported 15,045 Creek had arrived and were receiving subsistence in the vicinity of Fort Gibson. Within a short period, fully 3,500 of the immigrants died as the result of exposure or from the fevers prevalent in the new country.

In the meantime, those who had been living in the West for nearly a decade, referred to as the Western Creek, were beginning to prosper. They had established a form of tribal government and had secured a treaty with the United States in 1833 that defined the boundaries of their new country in the Indian Territory, where all the Creek people should have a home, extending west and south of the Cherokee country and north of the Canadian River to the one-hundredth meridian. Viewing with alarm the coming of the hostile element from the East, most of whom were enemies of the McIntosh party, Chief Roley McIntosh urged that a parley be arranged with the newly arrived chiefs and leaders. The meeting was held by authorization of General Matthew Arbuckle, commandant of Fort Gibson, and Captain Francis Armstrong, superintendent of Indian removal, during which Eneah Emathla and others of the old-line chiefs and leaders resigned their tribal offices and surrendered to the government of the Western Creek with Chief Roley McIntosh at the head.

The Upper and the Lower Creek divisions were nominally reunited in the government of the Creek Nation, West, in 1839 (or 1840), though they remained aloof from each other until after the Civil War, except for meetings of the General Council. There was a principal and a second chief for each of the two divisions, and every one of the towns had a principal chief and a second chief. The principal chiefs of the towns, referred to in English as "kings," together with the two principal chiefs of the nation, were elected for life and composed the annual General Council, in which the two chiefs sat side by side, though Roley McIntosh was the admitted leader by seniority while he held office. Each of the two divisions also had a council. The Lower Creek had two lighthorsemen who served in the capacity of sheriffs. The Upper Creek elected four councilors, one of whom was the principal chief. A group of officers, called "lawyers," in each of the towns and numbering from four to forty-five according to population, administered the laws made by the General Council and approved by the two principal chiefs. Written laws of the nation, compiled before the removal in 1826, the earliest of which was dated 1817, were approved by the General Council, West, in 1840. Some of the old towns had been wiped out by the death of their inhabitants before the emigration from the East. Others that had grown weak were consolidated with those that were re-established in the Indian Territory. The present village of Council Hill, in Muskogee County, is east of the site of the first capital or council ground of the Creek Nation, West. It was called "High Spring" because of a beautiful spring on a wooded hill (Sec. 31, T.13 N., R.15 E., Okmulgee County) that marked the location in the middle of a wide prairie which separated the Upper Creek from the Lower Creek settlements.

The Upper Creek settlements extended west on the North Fork, the Deep Fork, and the Canadian about eighty miles to Little River, with Little Doctor serving as the principal chief in the early eighteen forties. The people of this division were conservative in observing the old ways and customs and native dress, and continued cultivating their crops in communal fields for some years. All were industrious, and there were few cases of extreme poverty among them. After the removal, Tukabah-chee Miko was often referred to as the chief of the Upper Creek, though he was in reality the "principal medicine maker." The people of Tukabatchee Town cultivated his fields for him and he was allowed an annual salary of $500 out of the national treasury. Tukabatchee Town was located on the Canadian River near the present village of Melette, about ten miles southwest of Eufaula, and was the only one of the towns that constructed in the Indian Territory the great tcokofa, or "round house," in connection with the square-ground and its four ceremonial buildings. Opothleyahola, the speaker of the Upper Creek before the removal, remained one of the most influential citizens of this division and was reputed the wealthiest citizen of the whole nation just before the Civil War.

The Lower Creek settlements were located on both sides of the Arkansas River west about eighty miles, from the Verdi-

MURIEL H. WRIGHT

Main building at Eufaula Boarding School

gris to the Red Fork River. These people were generally classed as the progressive element in the nation, having done away with much of the former town organization and the cultivation of communal town fields. Some of them owned Negro slaves and herds of livestock and operated well-fenced plantations, where they had erected commodious log dwellings furnished comfortably with good furniture, silverware, and other luxuries purchased in the markets in the states. Among the wealthy citizens were Benjamin Marshall, Benjamin Perryman, and several members of the McIntosh family.

In the twenty-five-year period before the Civil War, the Creek people were remarkable for their adaptation to new conditions and for their general progress, as well as for the maintenance of their own national government which had been all but disrupted by war and the removal west. When they had come to the Indian Territory during the main removal, thousands were forced to travel empty handed with only the ragged clothing they wore. They had to become acclimated to this western country and to learn about the new soil and the natural resources. Food, clothing, implements, and other necessary supplies promised by the United States government were long delayed after their arrival, and frauds in government contracts were notorious. Even a common woodsman's axe was not seen among thousands who for generations had known comfortable houses and had cultivated fields in their old homeland. Most of the people had to resort to primitive methods in erecting shelter and providing utensils, and in clearing and breaking new land for growing their crops.

Trading posts licensed by the government were established at convenient locations near the large settlements. Among these were trading houses at the Creek Agency south of the Arkansas River and just west of present Muskogee, at North Fork Town northeast of present Eufaula in the forks of the Canadian and the North

Canadian rivers, and at Edwards Trading Post near the mouth of Little River. Smuggling and sale of intoxicating liquors from the border states flourished, and drinking and drunken orgies were frequent occurrences at tribal ball games, ceremonials, and council meetings, although these conditions violated the United States Intercourse Act of 1834, which prohibited the introduction and sale of liquor in the Indian Territory.

The missions and schools operated by Protestant denominations opposed these evils and promoted the standard for Christian living that eventually brought results.

The Baptists began missionary efforts among the Lower Creek on the Arkansas and Verdigris rivers in 1829, but Christian preaching and church services were generally not allowed by the chiefs and did not receive the full approval of the Creek Council until 1848, native converts in some instances being severely punished for taking up the new religion. The first book published for the Creek people in Oklahoma was a primer, called *The Child's Book,* printed on the Union Mission Press in 1835. Koweta Mission (Presbyterian) was founded by the Reverend Robert M. Loughridge in 1842, at Coweta Town near present Coweta in Wagoner County. The mission school was opened in 1843 and later was enlarged and operated as Koweta Manual Labor School for boys and girls. The Reverend Loughridge was also the founder and first superintendent of Tullahassee Mission (Presbyterian), which was opened as a boarding school in 1850, attended by boys and girls. Worthwhile work was accomplished at Tullahassee in the education of the Creek people by the Reverend William S. and Mrs. (Ann Eliza Worcester) Robertson. In the same year Asbury Mission (Methodist) was opened near North Fork Town.

During this period, the old principle of the Creek Confederacy was continued in the admission and incorporation of remnant tribal groups that came west at the time of the removal, among them being the Appalachicola, Alabama, Koasati, Hitchiti, and Natchez. The Yuchi (q.v.) were a comparatively large group that had been merged with the Creek for more than a century. The admission of the Seminole people from Florida gave rise to dissension and controversies which were not settled until 1856, when the United States purchased a tract of the Creek country for the exclusive use of the Seminole (q.v.). Bands of Shawnee, Delaware, Quapaw, Kickapoo, and Piankashaw, living in small settlements but not subject to the Creek government, were left undisturbed in the west central part of the Creek country. The spirit of international co-operation in the Indian Territory was fostered through the years by the General Council, and the Creek country was the meeting place of a number of intertribal councils attended by delegations from the Plains tribes as well as the Five Civilized Tribes.

The beginning of the Civil War found the Creek people divided in their sympathies, the greater part of the Lower Creek siding with the Confederate States. Chief Motey Canard, Chilly McIntosh, Daniel N. McIntosh, Benjamin Marshall, Timothy Barnard (or Barnett), George Stidham, Samuel Checote, and John G. Smith were active in the organization of the pro-Confederate "United Nations of the Indian Territory" (Choctaw, Chickasaw, Creek, Seminole, Cherokee, and Caddo) at North Fork Town in June, 1861. On July 12, 1861, Albert Pike, Confederate commissioner, succeeded in negotiating a treaty with the Creek Nation in behalf of the Confederacy. Opposition in the nation was led by Opothleyahola, who with more than 5,000 men, women, and children—some on foot, some on horseback, and others in wagons loaded with household goods—left the Creek country for Kansas in November, 1861, seeking refuge within the Union Army lines. On the way north, these "Loyal Creek" were overtaken by Confederate troops and three battles were fought, in

the last of which Opothleyahola's brave warriors were defeated. Scattered in the midst of a blizzard, the survivors finally reached Kansas, where some of them remained until 1865. In 1866, a new treaty was signed with the United States at Washington, providing for the cession of the western part of the Creek country to the United States, the "eastern half" to be "forever set apart as a home" for the Creek Nation.

Soon after the close of the war, the Creek people, generally disorganized and weakened, began moving back to their country, for even the "Confederate Creek" had been compelled to flee from their homes during the four-year conflict. Houses had to be rebuilt, the fields cleared and fenced, and what was left of once great herds of livestock rounded up and located again on the open ranges. The people of the tribal towns came together again, but the ancient ceremonials never regained their former prestige. The building of the first railroads in the Indian Territory brought many changes. With demands for coal, timber, stone, livestock, agricultural products, came, above all, insistence from border states, chiefly Kansas, for the opening of the country to white settlement. The Creek people met the conditions by uniting under a written constitution (*see* Government Organization) in 1867, designating Okmulgee the capital of the Creek Nation. In keeping with the spirit of internationalism fostered by the old Creek Confederacy, Okmulgee was the meeting place of the General Council of the Indian Territory beginning in 1870, with delegations representing the nations and tribes of the Territory in attendance. This General Council, with Enoch Hoag, superintendent of Indian Affairs, presiding, wrote and adopted the so-called "Okmulgee Constitution," the plan for the eventual creation of an Indian state within the boundaries of the Indian Territory which had been promoted by government officials at Washington. While never officially approved by Congress, the annual meetings of the General Council for nearly a decade fostered a spirit of solidarity and co-operation among the Indian tribes in the Territory.

The Creek treaty of 1866 provided funds for rebuilding Tullahassee and Asbury mission schools. The work of the Christian churches was revived, Creek leaders prominent in the last years of the tribal government being members of the different denominations. Among them were Samuel Checote, Methodist preacher, lieutenant colonel of the First Indian Cavalry Brigade of the Confederate Army, elected principal chief of the Creek Nation in 1867 and for several succeeding terms; Joseph M. Perryman, Baptist minister, elected principal chief of the Creek Nation in 1883; Pleasant Porter, Presbyterian, superintendent of Creek schools, delegate to Washington, last elected chief of the Creek Nation in 1903. A number of boarding schools were established by the Creek government before 1890, and neighborhood schools in-

Pleasant Porter, last elected chief of the Creek

creased through the years, separate schools being maintained for Negro children. Qualified students were sent to seminaries or colleges in the states at the expense of the Creek Nation, most of them being young men, though a few older girls were selected from time to time. In the eighteen eighties a limited number of Negro students were also sent to schools outside the Creek country. In 1896, there were seventy neighborhood schools in operation, besides the Levering Mission, the Creek Orphans Home near Okmulgee, and six boarding schools—Eufaula High School (outgrowth of Asbury), Wealaka, Nuyaka, Wetumka, Euchee, and Coweta. The Pecan Creek Colored Boarding School and the Colored Creek Orphans Home were also maintained by the Creek government as separate schools, in addition to a number of the neighborhood schools for Negroes.

The old lines of cleavage between the Upper and Lower Creek, intensified during the Civil War, carried over into the political life of the nation in the postwar period. There was often bitter partisanship in the elections, the council meetings, and the administration of public affairs. The "Green Peach War" (so called because it began when the peaches were green) a bloody affair in 1881, with skirmishes a year later near Wewoka and Okemah, was the outgrowth of a feud between a Northern fullblood faction led by Isparhecher (Ispahitca) and the followers of Chief Checote, a Southern faction. The election of Isparhecher as principal chief of the Creek Nation in 1895 indicated the opposition of the people to allotment of lands. An agreement concluded with the Dawes Commission at Muskogee on September 27, 1897, was opposed by the Chief and rejected by the National Council. This agreement was later amended and included as Section 30 of the Curtis Act in 1898.

Authorized members of the Creek delegation—Pleasant Porter, George A. Alexander, David M. Hodge, Isparchecher, Albert P. McKellop, and Cub McIntosh—entered into a new agreement with members of the Dawes Commission at Washington on March 8, 1900, which was proclaimed in effect on June 25, 1901. It provided that every man, woman, and child, including Negro freedmen, should select 160 acres as an allotment from the Creek domain (3,072,813 total acres surveyed) and that the tribal government should be dissolved on or before March 4, 1906.

Among the prominent citizens of the Creek Nation in its last days before statehood were Alexander Posey, beloved poet of the nation and editor of the *Indian Journal,* remembered for his "Fus Fixico Letters" in English-Indian dialect; Roly McIntosh of Tuskegee (namesake of the late Chief Roley McIntosh), Creek orator and statesman; and Chitto Harjo, a member of the House of Kings and leader of a full-blood faction opposed to any changes in the Creek government and the ownership of lands, who made the last attempt to reestablish and continue the old tribal laws.

◆ **Government and Organization.**   The Creek have continued a nominal organiza-

MURIEL H. WRIGHT

Chitto Harjo (Crazy Snake) in 1904

tion, with a written constitution and by-laws, under the title of the "Creek Tribe of Oklahoma." The council meets every two months in the old Council House at Okmulgee to review matters of interest to the tribe and make recommendations for the education and public welfare of the Creek people to the United States Indian Office through the Five Civilized Tribes Agency at Muskogee. The council employs attorneys to appear before the Indian Claims Commission to present all unsettled claims arising from former treaties with the United States. Representatives to the council are elected by the present tribal "town" members—one representative for every one hundred members, no town to have more than two representatives—living in seven counties that were formerly included in the Creek Nation: Hughes, Okfuskee, Creek, Tulsa, Wagoner, Muskogee, and McIntosh. Although Seminole County comprised the Seminole Nation (q.v.) from 1866 on, the many Creek people living in the area today are represented in the Creek tribal organization.

The 1951 "Principal Chief of the Creek Nation" was John Davis, Okemah, who succeeded the late Roly Canard of Wetumka, appointed by the President of the United States under the provisions of the Congressional act of April 26, 1906. Officers of the Creek Council have included Niffey Grant, chairman; Canuky Lowe, assistant chairman; Turner Bear, secretary, Thompson King, treasurer; and Roman Harjo, interpreter. There is also a special Business Committee, members of which in 1950 were Roly Canard, chairman, Turner Bear, Roman Harjo, Thompson King, Ben Porter, Jacob Alexander, and Clem Robinson.

Three Creek tribal groups are organized with constitutions as credit associations under the Thomas-Rogers Bill (Oklahoma Indian Welfare Act), the corporate titles and meeting places of which are as follows: "Thlopthlocco Tribal Town of the Creek Indian Nation," meeting of the

Principal Chief Roly Canard in 1938

town members held annually at Thlopth-locco Methodist Episcopal Church, about eight miles south of Okemah in Okfuskee County; "Alabama-Quassarte Tribal Town," meeting of town members held on the last Thursday bi-monthly in northeastern Hughes County, in the vicinity of Wetumka; "Kialegee Tribal Town," meeting of town membership held annually on the second Thursday in June, at an appointed place near Wetumka.

The constitutions of each of these associations provide organization along the lines of the Creek town, with a chief and council members, and a special business committee meeting at regular intervals.

Changes in the Creek government had been first carried out in elections during the meeting of the General Council in June, 1859. At this time, Roley McIntosh of the Lower Creek and Tukabahchee Miko of the Upper Creek retired from public life. Motey Canard, former second chief, was elected principal chief of the Lower Creek, and Jacob Derrisaw, second chief; Echo Harjo, former second chief, was elected principal chief of the Upper Creek, and Oktarharsars Harjo (or "Sands"), second

chief. A form of written constitution was adopted, but none of these changes in the tribal government were fully effective because of the outbreak of the Civil War.

In 1867, all parties united in establishing the "Muskogee Nation," with a written constitution and code of laws that remained in force until the dissolution of the Creek government forty years later. The constitution provided for the election of a principal chief and a second chief every four years by the vote of the people. The legislative body, called the National Council, consisted of a House of Kings (Senate) and a House of Warriors (House of Representatives) that met annually in regular session at the national capital. The House of Kings was composed of one representative from each tribal town, elected by the people of the town. The House of Warriors consisted of one representative elected from each town and one additional representative for every two hundred persons belonging to the town. A Supreme Court consisted of five "competent, recognized citizens of the Muskogee Nation" chosen by the National Council for a four-year term. A judge, prosecuting attorney, and a company of lighthorsemen (captain and four privates) were chosen for each one of the six districts in the nation, serving for designated terms. The laws passed by the National Council and approved by the Principal Chief were published in book form both in the native language and in English.

Okmulgee was established as the capital, and a permanent Council House of stone was built there in 1878. The six judicial districts were Coweta, north of the Arkansas (northeast); Muskogee, south of the Arkansas (formerly Arkansas District, east central); Eufaula, between the North Fork and the Canadian (formerly North Fork District, southeast); Wewoka, between the North Fork and the Canadian (southwest); Deep Fork, between the North Fork and the Deep Fork (west central); and Okmulgee, north of the Deep Fork (Muskogee District, northwest). After the

MURIEL H. WRIGHT

Moty Tiger, appointed principal chief in
1907

Civil War there were forty-four towns
among the Creek proper. Late census records approved by the National Council
listed three additional towns inhabited exclusively by Negroes.

The principal chiefs of the Creek Na-
tion from 1867 to the dissolution of the
tribal government were Samuel Checote,
Locher Harjo (Lotca Hadjo), Ward
Coachman, Joseph M. Perryman, Legus
Perryman, Isparhecher (Ispahihtca), and
Pleasant Porter. Since the death of Chief
Porter in 1907, the appointed chiefs have
included Moty Tiger, G. W. Grayson,
Washington Grayson, and George Hill.
The second chiefs from 1867 to the close
of the tribal government included Micco
Hutke (Miko Hatki), Ward Coachman,
Hotulke Emarthla (Hotalgi Imathla or
Edward Bullet), Roly McIntosh of Tuske-
gee, and Moty Tiger of Tukabatchee.

◊ **Contemporary Life and Culture.** Numerous persons of Creek Indian descent live
in the towns and cities in the eastern part of
Oklahoma, where they are engaged in the
professions (law, medicine, education, the
ministry), in the oil industry, and in other
businesses. This class of people is largely
composed of the mixed-bloods (white and
Indian). There are also fullblood Creek
families who have gained wealth from the
discovery of oil on their allotments, some
of them living in well-provided rural
homes.

Most of the fullblood Creek, however,
live in rural communities and make their
livings by their daily labor and from farming and the raising of livestock. They are
practically all members of some church
(usually Baptist, Methodist, or Presbyterian), and their children attend the public schools. The Eufaula Boarding School
for girls is the only one of the old Creek
tribal schools now in operation.

About 50 per cent of the present Creek
population are of mixed white and Indian
blood. There was some admixture with the
Negroes, beginning as early as 1700, but
the Negro strain is not as common among
the Creek proper as has been generally reported. The Creek country within the present boundaries of Georgia, even for some
time after the organization of the colony
of Georgia, was considered free territory,
to which Negro slaves escaped from their
masters in South Carolina and from Spanish slaveholders in Florida. The incorporation of the Negro fugitives was a matter of
much concern to the Creek chiefs and council members long before the American
Revolution. Some of these Negroes or their
descendants fought on the side of the tribe
in the Creek wars and made themselves
useful in the nation, thus paving the way
for their gradual acceptance and assimila-
tion. Some of their descendants were good
citizens in the Creek Nation, West, individuals of more than half Indian blood
being considered a part of the native population as time passed. It should be noted
that these persons were not of the Negro
slave class. Laws made by the Creek Council before the Civil War forbade intermarriage with Negroes. After the war, persons of predominantly Negro descent were
classed as Negroes. Creek freedmen (former slaves and their descendants) are Ne-

groes who were granted rights of citizenship in the Creek Nation in August, 1865, through the influence of the United States Agent J. W. Dunn. When the tribal rolls were closed in 1906, a separate roll listed 6,807 Creek freedmen who received allotments of land in severalty.

Some groups among the fullblood people, even though they are members of a Christian church, still observe the tribal Green Corn Dance or "busk" at an appointed time in summer. The old arts of making pottery and basketry and the grinding of corn for hominy with the wooden mortar and pestle have disappeared. Hominy is called "sofky" (*safke*) in the native language and is occasionally made in the homes. Sometimes ball teams are organized, and old-time tribal ball games are played on special occasions. In the Creek ball game, a goal is set up at either end of a long field, something like a modern football goal, each goal consisting of two poles set up about six feet apart, between which the small ball (about the size of a golf ball) must be thrown in making a score. Every player carries a pair of ball sticks (each about thirty inches long with a cuplike device on the end), the object of the game being to catch and throw the ball with the sticks against interference from the opposing players.

The Creek tribal social organization was quite complicated and closely integrated with political life in the days of the Creek Confederacy. Old-time customs and classifications have small place in Creek life today and are seldom recalled except for their historical significance. Seven different units or groups within the tribal social organization included, among others, the family, the clan, and the town.

Women in the family owned their own property and the houses, only moving away as new homes were built for them.

Families having a traditionally common ancestor made up the clan. There were formerly more than fifty clans in the tribe, among which the Bear, Wind, Bird, and

Beaver clans were of high rank. Clan membership was determined in the female line. The clans were grouped into two divisions: white clans having to do with peace councils and ceremonials, red clans ("bearers of the red sticks") with war.

The town or *talwa* was a settlement made up of several villages (usually families of a clan) located around a square-ground where the town ceremonials were held and the political life of the community centered. The office of town chief was hereditary. The chief and the principal officers at the time of the busk or Green Corn Dance were each attended by a com-

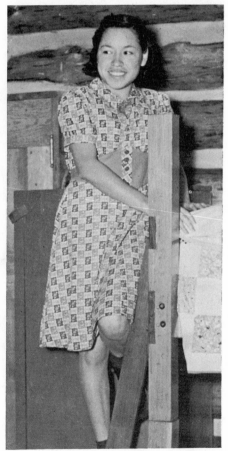

U. S. INDIAN SERVICE

Minnie Tiger, at Haskell Institute, Lawrence, Kansas, in 1940

panion or lieutenant called *heniha*. The highest officer among the war officials was called *tustengugee* (*tastanagi thlako*), a great honor only attained by warriors of real ability and long and successful service.

◆ **Ceremonials and Public Dances.** Some old Creek towns still maintain square-grounds within the boundaries of the former Creek Nation where their ceremonials in the Green Corn Dance are held at a selected time in summer. The names and locations of these square-grounds (not including the Yuchi, q.v.) are: Pakan tallahassee, about four miles southwest of Hanna, McIntosh County; Wiogufki, four miles west of Hanna, McIntosh County; Okchai, about two miles southwest of Hanna, McIntosh County; Eufaula Canadian, about six miles southwest of Eufaula, McIntosh County; Hickory Ground, about six miles southeast of Henryetta, on Wolf Creek in McIntosh County; Okfuskee, about five miles northwest of Castle, Okfuskee County; Tallahasutci, about seven miles southeast of Wewoka, Seminole County; Little River Tulsa (or New Tulsa Town), about six miles southeast of Holdenville, Hughes County; Greenleaf, about four miles southwest of Okemah, Okfuskee County; Chiaha, fifteen miles north of Coweta, on the Verdigris River in Wagoner County; Hatchee tcaba, about four miles southwest of Henryetta, Okmulgee County; Abihka, about five miles southeast of Henryetta, Okmulgee County; Nuyaka, about seven miles northeast of Okemah, Okfuskee County. (The Creek names of towns are given in the original spelling. Mileage directions are approximate airline distances.)

Town members come from their homes to camp in the woods near the square-ground during the time of the busk. Good order is maintained under definite rules and regulations. Visitors are allowed to witness the ceremonial dances from outside the square-ground, and they may be impressed with the monotonous repetition unless they know something about the symbolism and the traditions in the busk. Members of Little River Tulsa claim that they still have the sacred fire brought from Alabama over a century ago, kept lighted through the years by a special officer. They are sometimes joined by the old Tukabatchee Town members in celebrating the Green Corn Dance at the square-ground of Little River Tulsa.

The busk is in the nature of a thanksgiving celebration, originally held after the corn had matured in summer and lasting through eight days. In tribal times, it was a period of amnesty and forgiveness for injury and crime. The ritual dances and ceremonials are now carried on for two days and nights, following the old forms and pattern within the square-ground, which extends for about seventy-five feet on each side, with the earth tramped down hard and kept clear of vegetation. Arbors erected on each of three sides (now sometimes four sides) face the center of the square where the sacred fire is kept burning during the two-day celebration. The chiefs are seated in the west arbor, where they are regularly consulted by the messenger in the ceremonials. The "warriors" are seated in the north arbor. Leaders seated in the south arbor keep time during the dances with a continuous chant to the rattle of a small gourd.

Women are important in the dances, though they have no special costuming except perhaps varicolored ribbons worn as streamers in their hair and on their dresses. Leaders among the women dancers wear heavy clusters of terrapin shells above their ankles as rattles, which they use expertly in keeping the dance rhythm. The women's Ribbon Dance is especially interesting. The period of fasting ends on the second day when both men and women partake of the "black drink," an emetic formerly made by boiling the leaves of the *Ilex cassine*. In Oklahoma today, the Creek use a native plant called "red root" for their ceremonial potion. The so-called black drink is really a "white drink" since it has an important place in the peace ritual. Late in the afternoon on the second day, a feast is held for everyone, after which the young men and women play a ball game around a tall goal post off to one side of the square-ground. The playing is followed by dances, in which young and old—men, women, and children—take part.

Suggested Readings: Debo, *The Road to Disappearance;* Grant Foreman, *Five Civilized Tribes;* ————, *Indian Removal;* Swanton, *Early History of the Creek;* ————, *Indians of Southeastern U. S.;* "Social Organization, Creek," *42 Ann. Rep.,* Bur. Amer. Ethnol.

DELAWARE

The Delaware call themselves *Lenape,* meaning "our man," or *Leni-lenape,* signifying "men of our nation." The English name Delaware was given the tribe from the river named for Lord de la Warr, the valley of which was the tribal center in earliest Colonial times, extending from what is now southeastern New York into eastern Pennsylvania and through New Jersey and Delaware.

At the beginning of the historic period, the Delaware or Lenape proper constituted a powerful and formidable confederacy of the Algonquian linguistic family, referred to by the French as *Loupe,* meaning "wolves." Among the Algonquian tribes to the west, the Lenape and many small kindred tribes on the Atlantic Coast as far north as New England were known as *Wapanachki* meaning "easterners" or "eastern land people." All the Algonquian and others of the eastern Woodland peoples called the tribe "Grandfather" in token of respect and reverence, thus recognizing the high political position of the Delaware in the central homeland as the parent from which many tribes had sprung.

The Delaware have been generally notable for their light complexion and well-proportioned physique. Early missionaries and historians who lived among them described them as discreet and modest and unassuming in their relations with others. Tribal chiefs and leaders were commended for their intelligence, good sense, and justice. The women were looked upon with

respect by their own people, and the men were well known for their ability and trustworthiness as scouts and guides. Many Delaware served on important exploring expeditions in early days of the West and Southwest, including those of John F. Frémont to the Pacific Coast and Captain Randolph B. Marcy through Oklahoma.

In the van of all the Indian tribes moving westward for a period of two hundred years, during which they contributed to the history of ten different states, the Delaware won the reputation of being wild and implacable in the frontier wars and in their determined opposition to Anglo-American settlement. At the end of nearly every one of their many different moves from the Atlantic Coast to Oklahoma, United States agents and others pointed out the debasing effects of such moves and the miserable condition of the tribal members through dissipation and shiftless habits. Yet, wherever the Delaware remained for a time, their settlements were remarkable for their well-cultivated fields and good crops and in the industry of the people.

◆ **Present Location.** Two groups of Delaware live in Oklahoma. The main part of the tribe, known as "Registered Delaware," came from their reservation in Kansas and settled by contract in the Cherokee Nation in 1867. Their descendants live in Washington, Nowata, Craig, and Delaware counties, at or near Bartlesville, Dewey, Copan, Wann, Alluwe, and in a number of rural communities.

A band of Delaware who associated early in the nineteenth century with the Caddo and the Wichita on the Brazos Reservation in Texas came to the Washita River in the Indian Territory in 1859, where they remained under the jurisdiction of the Wichita Agency, now the Wichita-Caddo Agency of the Anadarko Area Office, at Anadarko. Descendants of this Delaware band live in Caddo County, principally in or near Anadarko and Carnegie.

Early in the nineteenth century, some of the Delaware migrated to the Pacific Northwest where they were employed as trappers, hunters, and scouts by the Hudson's Bay Company. Their descendants are living in Idaho, Montana, and Oregon, affiliated with various tribes, including the Crow, Nez Percé, and Blackfeet. There are some Delaware living in Wisconsin among the Stockbridge (Mahican); in Minnesota among the Chippewa; and in Ontario, Canada, where three groups are known: "Moravians of the Thames," "Munsees of the Thames," and another with the Six Nations on Grand River. Descendants of Delaware who became United States citizens and remained in Kansas are living in that state and in Wisconsin near Lake Winnebago. A few members of the tribe are said to be living in Mexico.

◊ **Numbers.** There were approximately 1,250 descendants of Registered Delaware in 1950, about 750 of whom live in eastern Oklahoma, mostly in Washington, Nowata, and Craig counties. There were also 162 Delaware living in Caddo County, within the jurisdiction of the Anadarko Area Office.

In 1867, a total of 985 Delaware registered for tribal membership in Kansas and came to the Cherokee Nation. The number reported in the Cherokee Nation in 1875 was 1,000. A specially published census for the Indian Territory in 1890 reported 286 heads of Delaware families and 754 members of the tribe in the Cherokee Nation.

The Dawes Commission reported 1,079 Delaware interviewed for enrollment in the Cherokee Nation in 1902, of whom 1,036 were fully enrolled at the time and 43 subject to further review. A separate

MURIEL H. WRIGHT

Payment of the Delaware at Alluwe in 1896. The old gentleman in the center on the porch is Chief Journeycake

roll in 1907 listed 197 Registered Delaware living in the Cherokee Nation, which did not include the Delaware whose names were regularly entered on the Cherokee rolls. In the same year, the Delaware Business Committee approved a special roll of 1,100 persons who were entitled to a tribal per capita payment made to the Registered Delaware and the descendants of Registered Delaware, payments being first made at Bartlesville on April 23, 1906.

In 1818, the part of the tribe living on the White Water River in Indiana numbered 800, and another band lived in Ohio. Within five years, it was said that 2,400 had left their locations north of the Ohio River and had come west of the Mississippi. In 1839, ten years after the assignment of their reservation in Kansas, they numbered 921 in this new location. In the next decade, their number here was estimated at 1,500, other small bands having joined them. A census taken at the Delaware Agency in Kansas in the spring of 1862 gave a total of 1,085 members of the tribe living on the reservation.

In 1820, the Delaware living in Texas were estimated at 700. All of them, or their descendants, moved north eventually, the group remaining on the Brazos Reserve coming with the Wichita and the Caddo to the Washita River, Indian Territory, in 1859. In 1874, a band of 61 Delaware formally united with the Caddo under one chief and the following year were living on the Wichita-Caddo Reservation. At the same time, 30 were living on the Kiowa and Comanche Reservation. There were 95 Delaware living on the Wichita Reservation in 1890. The Kiowa agent reported 102 Delaware allotted lands in severalty among the Wichita and Affiliated Bands in 1902.

During the nineteenth century, general estimates of the number of Delaware gave from 2,400 to 3,000. The tribe was reported decreasing in 1906, available figures for that year totaling about 2,200 living in the United States, Canada, and Mexico. From the best estimates in 1950, there are probably 2,500 Delaware living in America.

◆ **History.** The *Walum Olum,* "Red Tally," a pictograph record of the national legend of the Lenape, told of the prehistoric migration of the tribe from a generally northern and western direction to the Atlantic Coast. It was upon their traditional history that they made claims to territory in the Ohio Valley and were closely allied with other tribes in this region during the eighteenth and the early part of the nineteenth centuries.

When the Dutch first sailed up the Hudson River in 1609, the Lenape occupied the Delaware River Valley and included three main tribal divisions: the *Minsi* (or *Munsee*), signifying "mountaineers," who lived in the mountain country near the source of the river, with hunting grounds in present New Jersey, Pennsylvania, and New York; the *Unami,* signifying "people down the river," who lived on the right bank of the Delaware from the Lehigh Valley southward; and the *Unalachitigo,* signifying "people who live near the ocean," who occupied what is now Delaware. The three divisions considered themselves a unit in organization, but often acted separately.

William Penn bought land from the Delaware in establishing the province of Pennsylvania, concluding a treaty of peace and purchasing a large tract from Chief Tamenend of the Unami and the leaders of the Unalachitigo in a meeting on the tribal council ground at Shakamaxon near present Germantown in 1683. Chief Tamenend was famous in his time and long remembered among the colonists, some of his admirers during the Revolution perpetuating his name as "Saint Tammany, the Patron Saint of America" in the ceremonials of the Tammany societies. The influence and advice of the Friends (Quakers) were important in the subsequent history of the Delaware in Pennsylvania, the tribe always remembering Penn as their personal friend and benefactor.

Conflicting claims arose over the land

purchased by Penn within fifty years after the signing of the "Great Treaty," and his heirs sought confirmation of their title. Pennsylvania officials accomplished this in the notorious "Walking Purchase" on September 19–20, 1737, the Delaware having agreed that the tract confirmed should cover all the land that could be walked over in a day and a half. The tribe also retained the right to remain within the tract which, at the end of the Walk, was found to include their settlements at the Forks of the Delaware River.

Early in the seventeen twenties, the Iroquois Confederacy in New York, better known from this time on as the Six Nations, finding themselves threatened on the north by their enemies, the French and their Indian allies, set out to strengthen the confederacy by inviting the Delaware to take the middle or neutral position as peacemaker in the organization. The Delaware accepted and were firm in keeping the position. Some years later, they refused to take part in the fighting over some intertribal land claims and in troubles with

Black Beaver

white squatters on Indian-owned lands. This angered a part of the Iroquois, who retaliated by calling the Delaware "women." The intertribal feud that arose from this insult was important in the later history of the Pennsylvania and the Ohio frontiers.

In 1751, the Delaware began settling in eastern Ohio with the Huron (*see* Wyandot). Within another decade, most of the tribe were living on the Muskingum and other streams in Ohio. Early in the French and Indian War, they declared their independence from the Iroquois, most of the Delaware in Ohio siding with the French.

The first treaty made by the United States with an Indian tribe was with the Delaware at Fort Pitt in 1778. At the beginning of the Revolution, Captain White Eyes of the Unami and his followers had declared themselves in favor of the American colonists; Captain Pipe of the Minsi and his followers had remained friendly with the British. Both leaders were signers of the treaty at Fort Pitt, in which the first official statement appeared for the organization of an Indian state, Article VI providing that, with the approval of Congress, an Indian state should be formed with the "Delaware nation" at the head and should have representation in Congress. This plan had been promoted by the Reverend Davis Zeisberger, the zealous Moravian missionary who, though he favored the Iroquois, would thus placate the powerful and hostile Delaware on the frontier and make them the leader of all the tribes.

Missionary efforts of the Moravian church had been carried on among the Delaware since early in the seventeen forties, one of the earliest missions having been planted in the Wyoming Valley. The massacre of the peaceful, Christian Delaware at the Moravian mission of Gnadenhutten, Ohio, in March, 1782, was an atrocity perpetrated by frontiersmen that made the tribe a determined foe to the advance of the Anglo-American settlements. To escape the murderous war in Ohio, a band of Delaware crossed the Mississippi in 1789 and settled in Spanish territory in what is now the state of Missouri in 1793 by permission of Governor Carondelet. Two years before this, another band had gone to live in Canada, where Zeisberger founded the Moravian mission of Fairfield.

On August 20, 1794, United States forces under the command of General Anthony Wayne gained a decisive victory over the Delaware and their allies in the Battle of the Fallen Timbers, near the present location of Toledo, Ohio. Some months later, the Mohawk chief, Joseph Brant, of the Six Nations then living in Canada, urged the tribes to further resistance. To settle the old score on the part of the Iroquois, he made a dramatic appearance and officially placed the war club in the hands of the Delaware, declaring that they were no longer "women but men."

The chiefs and leaders of twelve tribes, including the Delaware, met General Wayne on August 3, 1795, at Greenville in western Ohio (present Darke County), where a treaty was signed granting them the rights of hunting, planting, and dwelling within all the region included in what is now northern Ohio, Indiana, Illinois, Michigan, and Wisconsin, with the exception of certain tracts reserved by the United States. Within thirty-five years after the treaty of Greenville, the Delaware signed twelve treaties with the United States: That signed at St. Mary's in Ohio, in 1817, ceded all tribal lands in Indiana to the United States and guaranteed the tribe a country west of the Mississippi River; another, signed on August 3, 1829, ceded the last of the Delaware lands in Ohio; and that signed September 24, 1829, provided for the removal of the tribe from Missouri to the country selected at the forks of the Kansas and Missouri rivers (eastern Kansas), which was "conveyed and secured by the United States, to the said Delaware Nation, as their permanent residence." This treaty was signed by twelve of the leading

Delaware, headed by William Anderson, the venerated principal chief of the tribe. Chief Anderson moved west to the new location on the Kansas River with a band of one hundred Delaware in 1830. Before his death a year later, he spoke of his satisfaction and pleasure in "seeing his people settled in their own country, where they were to remain." His four sons—Captains Shounack, Secondyan, Pushkies, and Sarcoxie—were well known as trustworthy scouts and guides on the Western frontier for many years.

The Delaware reservation embraced 924,160 acres in a triangular tract between the Kansas and Missouri rivers, extending west forty miles from the Missouri boundary and thence north forty miles. Beyond this tract, a hunting outlet ten miles wide extended from the western boundary indefinitely west.

When Independence, Missouri, and later Westport became ports of trade on the Santa Fé Trail, some of the Delaware were employed as trappers, hunters, drivers, and guides by Western fur companies, including the American Fur Company and the Bent and St. Vrain. Many members of the tribe were energetic and enterprising as farmers, settling in the eastern part of the reservation on the military trail to Fort Leavenworth.

The Methodist Episcopal church established mission work on the Delaware reservation in 1832, and later operated the Manual Labor School attended by Delaware children. The Baptist General Missionary Convention began work on the reservation in the same year, with mission headquarters at Shawnee, on the Shawnee reservation, where books were printed in the Delaware language, including religious works, hymnals, and elementary readers. The Moravians opened a mission on the reservation near Westport. Early reports had stated that the Delaware were acquiring bad habits—drinking whiskey, gambling, and racing horses—from living near Fort Leavenworth. This accusation, however, did not apply to all the tribe, for the Delaware as a whole were dependable and upright and prominent in the later history of Oklahoma.

Timber depredations and cattle stealing by marauding whites on the Kansas reservation, attempts of territorial officials to collect taxes from the Indians, and lack of protection under Kansas territorial law to their property and persons forced the chiefs and councilors of the Delaware to sign a new treaty at Washington on May 6, 1854. It left the Delaware an approximate tract ten miles wide, extending along the Kansas River for forty miles and lying west of land (thirty-six sections) formerly sold the Wyandot (q.v.). This treaty was never approved by the Delaware Council. Though exasperated and outraged by the unjust terms, the tribal members accepted them in the hope of securing undisturbed possession of their remaining lands.

Another treaty with the United States, signed at Sarcoxieville on the Delaware reservation in 1860, provided for the allotment of tribal lands in severalty, share and share alike, to be inalienable except to the United States, and for the purchase of their surplus lands (223,966.78 acres) by the Leavenworth, Pawnee and Western Railroad Company (later the Union Pacific). The company gave security on another 100,000 acres, thereafter called the "Delaware Diminished Reserve," which was later appraised by the Secretary of the Interior at $2.50 per acre and bought by the Union Pacific Railroad Company, the date of transfer being January 7, 1868.

Certificates to allotments of eighty acres each were issued by the United States to members of the tribe in 1861 amidst great excitement. In that year, more than 2,000 white people who were refugees from the bitter border strife between Missouri and Kansas were living on the Diminished Reserve and some of the Delaware allotted lands. Guerilla raids demoralized this section of Kansas in the early years of the Civil War, and the Delaware, surrounded

by intolerable conditions, sought permission from the government to select a country in the Rocky Mountains where they could settle and live under their own tribal government. The request was not granted, but the Commissioner of Indian Affairs replied that he greatly desired the removal of the Delaware from Kansas if they could find a country to the south in the Indian Territory.

Bands of Delaware had penetrated into Oklahoma as early as 1812. They were allies of the Western Cherokee (q.v.) in war against the Osage (q.v.), who rose to arms when the eastern tribes began settling west of the Mississippi and encroaching on the Osage hunting grounds in Oklahoma. A number of Delaware were among the Cherokee in the attack on and massacre of the Osage near Claremore Mound in 1817; others joined forces with Captain Dutch, or Tahchee, the Cherokee leader, in border fights and troubles during the next decade, for a time living in a Cherokee settlement near the mouth of the Kiamichi River in the Choctaw country. There were fields and cabins occupied by the Delaware in the eastern part of the Cherokee country before 1828, a region that was organized and named Delaware District by the Cherokee in honor of their allies when the Cherokee founded their national government in the Indian Territory in 1839. Delaware County in the present state of Oklahoma includes a part of the former district and continues the name that has been known in this section of the Southwest for more than a century. Early in the eighteen forties some of the tribe were living on Wapanucka Creek, now called Delaware Creek, in Johnston County, Oklahoma. The name of this creek and that of the town of Wapanucka in the vicinity stem from the name *Wapanachki,* by which the Lenape and their kindred tribes were known on the Atlantic Coast three hundred years ago. A law of the Choctaw Council in 1844 granted a number of Delaware families permission to live in the Choctaw Nation, which then included what is now Johnston County.

A new treaty with the United States, signed on July 4, 1866, by the Delaware chiefs, provided for the removal of the tribe to the Indian Territory. It was agreed that any tribal member who desired to become a citizen of the United States and re-

OKLAHOMA HISTORICAL SOCIETY

Charles Journeycake about 1890

main in Kansas could do so; he would also receive an allotment of land in Kansas and a proportionate share of the tribal invested funds. Members wishing to retain their tribal affiliation were duly enrolled and were henceforth known as Registered Delaware, a total of 985 members. This group was to remove to the Indian Territory, where a tract of land sufficient to give each registered member 160 acres was to be purchased by the United States out of Delaware tribal money, the land to be selected by a special tribal delegation.

The tract explored and recommended was on the Caney River (Little Verdigris) just south of the Kansas border in the Cherokee Nation, extending from the state line south on the ninety-sixth meridian thirty miles, thence east ten miles, north to the state line, and west to the point of beginning—an area which now comprises the greater part of Washington County, Oklahoma. A formal agreement was approved by President Andrew Johnson, having been signed on April 8, 1867, at Washington, by William P. Ross, principal chief, and Riley Keys, delegate, of the Cherokee Nation; and by John Conner, principal chief, and Charles Journeycake, Isaac Journeycake, and John Sarcoxie, delegates, of the Delaware. The agreement provided for the purchase by the Delaware of a tract of 157,000 acres from the Cherokee, at $1.00 an acre, allowing 160 acres for each Registered Delaware; and further payment of $121,824.28 (allowing $123.00 for each Registered Delaware) for equal rights and equal participation in the Cherokee national government and in its property and funds. Since some of the Cherokee were living within the region selected by the Delaware, the 157,000-acre tract was not definitely designated, but left for future determination.

The Registered Delaware began moving from Kansas to the Indian Territory in the fall of 1867 at their own expense. Some families in fortunate circumstances made the journey easily, their household goods loaded in wagons and driving their flocks and herds with them, arriving in time to begin improvements on their new locations before the planting season in spring. A large number in the tribe, however, were in an impoverished condition at the end of the war, and some of their wagons had to make several trips back and forth from Kansas in the cold and damp of winter conveying their aged, sick, and dying to the new country.

Arriving in the Indian Territory, the Delaware settled along the Caney River and neighboring streams where there was good land. Members of the tribe were now citizens of the Cherokee Nation, and their children attended the Cherokee schools.

Yet complete and harmonious adjustment to the new environment was slow. Owing to errors made in early land surveys, some found that they had begun improvements and were working land across the line in the Osage country or had settled on tracts previously claimed by others in the Cherokee Nation. This caused trouble with the local Cherokee and forced hundreds of Delaware to shift around until they could find permanent locations.

Years later, as a minority group in the Cherokee Nation, the Delaware complained of discriminations against them by some Cherokee officials. When per capita payments were made from the national funds received for cattle-ranch leases in the Cherokee Outlet, the Delaware were denied their share. Since these conditions were not corrected by officials, the Delaware chief and councilors were given authority by Congress to bring suit against the Cherokee Nation in the Court of Claims to determine the status of the Delaware rights purchased in 1867. On May 22, 1893, the court sustained the contention of the Delaware, holding that the tribal members had equal rights with the Cherokee in all lands of the Cherokee Nation and in the proceeds therefrom. The Delaware then received their share of Cherokee funds and participated in the per capita payment made citizens of the nation in the sale of the Cherokee Outlet.

Early in the eighteen seventies, the government resumed payments from the interest on the Delaware tribal invested funds, amounting in different years from $28.00 to $60.00 per capita semiannually. The principal of tribal invested funds was finally paid out, the last sum amounting to $459,664, or $527.72 per capita, paid by the United States agent on August 17, 1893. Times of the various payments were memorable occasions at the Delaware payhouse on Lightning Creek near Alluwe.

In 1890, the Delaware were living in two compact communities in the Cooseweecoowee and the Delaware districts, notable in the Indian Territory for their well-built residences and churches, good farms, orchards, mills, and trading establishments, and the general thrift and intelligence of the people. The 286 heads of Delaware families owned property (crops in the field, farm machinery, and livestock) valued at $625,693, with more than 27,878 acres of improved land. Some of the tribe had been elected from time to time to represent their districts in the Cherokee National Council.

Many of the leaders in the last period of Delaware tribal history had influential and constructive roles in the development of the Indian Territory and Oklahoma. Among them and their descendants were Charles Journeycake, the principal chief of the tribe and founder of the Delaware Baptist church at Alluwe; William Adams, Baptist minister in Kansas and Indian Territory; John Sarcoxie, who served in the Baptist church at Alluwe; James Ketchum, ordained minister of the Methodist church and one of the most eloquent Indian orators; Richard C. Adams, who resided at Alluwe and Washington, D. C., well known for his writings on the history and folklore of the Delaware; Nannie Journeycake (Pratt) Bartles, daughter of Chief Journeycake, founder of the Baptist church at Dewey, and wife of Jacob B. Bartles, early-day merchant and businessman at Silver Lake, for whom Bartlesville was named; Roberta Campbell Lawson, granddaughter of Chief Journeycake, civic leader in Tulsa, lecturer on Indian music and folklore, clubwoman who was elected and served as national president of the General Federation of Women's Clubs from 1935 to 1939; and John W. McCracken of Nowata, county treasurer of Nowata County. The most prominent man in the history of the Caddo County Delaware was Black Beaver, famous guide and scout. Among his descendants are John R. Osborne, Charles Beaver Pruner, Frank Osborne, and Mattie Pruner Sturm, all of Caddo County. A. A. Exendine, nationally known

Reunion at Anadarko

Kiowa Jack Hokeah (far right) welcomes the Beaver family at the American Indian Exposition in 1944. Left to right: Mrs. Beaver, WAVE Delores, Jones, Mr. Beaver, WAVE Beulah

football coach, is a member of the Delaware tribe of Caddo County.

◆ **Government and Organization.** A Delaware Business Committee continues in an advisory capacity in matters relating to Registered Delaware tribal claims against the United States and in the appointment of attorneys to represent them. Officers and members of the Business Committee in 1948 were D. W. Frenchman of Copan, chairman; Mary L. K. Townsend of Bartlesville, secretary; Joe Bartles of Dewey; John W. McCracken of Nowata; and E. T. Miller of Tulsa.

The Delaware of Caddo County who were merged with the Caddo under the supervision of the Indian agency at Anadarko call themselves the "Lost Delaware Tribe." They claim that they are representative of the Delaware proper since they received none of the tribal payments the government made to the "Registered Delaware in the Cherokee Nation." Billy and Jack Thomas were sons of Chief Bill Thomas of Caddo County, who died just after statehood in 1907. He was succeeded by Chief Jim Bob, and at his death Jack Thomas became chief. Since Chief Thomas's death, his brother, Billy has served as chief of the Caddo County Delaware; Frank Exendine, William Exendine, Stella Ellis, and Jimmie Bobb were members of the tribal council in 1950.

The three Lenape sub-tribes or geographical subdivisions of the early Delaware Confederation each claimed mystical descent from a totemic animal: the Minsi from the Wolf; the Unami from the Turtle; and the Unalachitgo from the Turkey. Originally, these three sub-tribes were divided into thirty-six gens or families (twelve gens each) bearing female names and indicating a basic matriarchal rule. Descent was through the female line, the child belonging to the gens of his mother.

Desire for orderly living among their people on the reservation in the midst of demoralized conditions in Kansas led the chiefs and councilors to adopt a series of laws written by a Delaware on December 18, 1862. These first written laws of the tribe provided for a national organization administered by the hereditary chiefs and councilors, and the appointment of a clerk, sheriff, treasurer, and jailer; it regulated probate matters and marriage, and set punishments for misdemeanors and crimes by fines, jail sentences, or death. The same code of laws was amended and adopted by the chiefs and councilors on July 21, 1866, at the tribal council house in Kansas.

After their settlement in the Indian Territory, the Delaware kept their tribal organization in limited form, though it was without authority since they were subject to the laws of the Cherokee Nation of which they were citizens. However, the tribal organization served in an advisory capacity in promoting the general welfare of the people.

Some months after the death of the last principal chief, Charles Journeycake, on January 3, 1894, a special committee was appointed to supervise the election of a new chief. After consideration, no election was held since the Delaware were citizens of the Cherokee Nation. Early in 1895, Dew Wisdom, United States agent at Muskogee, called a meeting during which a Delaware Business Committee of five members was elected to have charge of affairs relating to the tribe. Acting in a supervisory capacity, the Business Committee approved and assisted in making the final tribal rolls of the Registered Delaware and

their descendants. In the final reports of the Dawes Commission, the 197 living Registered Delaware were carried on a special roll, all other tribal members being counted on the Cherokee rolls for allotment of lands in severalty.

◆ **Contemporary Life and Culture.** Fifty years ago, it was said that there were not more than three fullblood Delaware living in the Cherokee Nation. Today, tribal descendants are largely an admixture of Anglo-American and various Indian stocks with which they have been associated during the three hundred years since leaving the Atlantic Seaboard. They are for the most part members of Christian churches, with the Baptist the strongest denomination. A few tribal members have joined the American Indian church which recognizes peyotism. The Delaware are now citizens of the United States and merged with the general population.

◆ **Ceremonials and Public Dances.** The tribal religious ceremonials have practically disappeared. During World War I, a meeting was held by Delaware tribal members and prayer offered to the "Great Spirit" for the return of all the young men who had gone to war. It is said that all returned after the Armistice.

The tribal "temple," called the "Big House" or the "Long House," in which old tribal religious rites were conducted was located about five or six miles east of Lawrence, Kansas, in reservation days. In the Indian Territory, the Big House was on the Little Caney River west of Copan in present Washington County. The house itself was about fifty-two by twenty-seven feet in size, built of logs set up stockade fashion, with the door facing the east. It later was moved three or four hundred yards from its original site and erected on an acre set aside by the Dawes Commission. The house was remodeled in 1913, but has now fallen in ruins, the carved wooden masks hanging on the center post inside having been recently taken away and placed on exhibition in Philbrook Museum in Tulsa. The Big House ceremonials were reorganized in the Indian Territory by men of the Yellow Tree or Poplar band, three men of the Wolf Clan carrying on the worship. After the Delaware left Pennsylvania, the names of the three sub-tribes (Minsi, Unami, Unalachtigo) gradually disappeared, members of the tribe being known respectively by the corresponding totemic or clan names of Wolf, Turtle, and Turkey.

Suggested Readings: Adams, *Brief History, Delaware;* Boyd, *Indian Treaties Printed by Benjamin Franklin;* Brinton, *The Lenape;* Carolyn T. Foreman, "Black Beaver," *Chron. of Okla.,* Vol. XXIV, No. 3; Grant Foreman, *Last Trek of the Indians;* Speck, *Oklahoma Delaware Ceremonies;* ———, *Study of Big House Ceremony.*

EEL RIVER INDIANS

An Algonquian tribe who sold their reservation in Boone County, Indiana, in 1828 and merged with the Miami (q.v.), among whom their descendants may be found in Ottawa County, Oklahoma.

Suggested Reading: Grant Foreman, *Last Trek of the Indians;* Hodge, *Handbook of American Indians.*

ERIE

The last of the Erie, an Iroquian tribe that lived near Lake Erie in the seventeenth century, joined the remnant of their neighbors, the Conestoga (q.v.), and became known by 1830 as the Seneca of Sandusky, Ohio. Their descendants are among the Seneca (q.v.) living in Ottawa County, Oklahoma. The name Erie signifies "at the place of the panther," and is said to be the French form of the Tuscarora word *kĕn'raks* "lion," a modern rendering of the old Huron term *yĕnresh,* "it is long tailed," referring to the eastern puma or panther. Suggested Reading: Hodge, *Handbook of American Indians.*

HAINAI

The Hainai are known in Oklahoma history as Ioni or Inie, which is also misspelled "Ironeyes" or "Ironies." Historians have generally discounted the origin of the name *Hainai* from the Caddo word *ayano* or *hayano,* meaning "people," yet the term was probably first applied to the tribe by the French in the Lower Mississippi region who thought this general term from the Caddo language the definite name of this important tribe. The so-called Hainai are referred to in early historical records by several other names, including *Animay, Cachae,* and *Hasinai.* Their descendants, and sometimes the Caddo, call themselves *Hasinai,* "our own people." Ethnologists and historians in recent years have employed the name *Hasinai* for the Hasinai Confederacy, a southern group of tribes of the Caddoan linguistic family who formerly lived in what is now southeastern Texas. Strictly speaking, the name *Hasinai* was another general term in the native language and not the name of a single tribe. However, both Spanish and French writers in Colonial days used it interchangeably to designate the Hainai, the leading tribe from which the *chenesi* or head chief of the Hasinai Confederacy was chosen. Still another name, *Texas* or *Taches,* meaning "allies" or "friends," was applied to the Hainai, or Hasinai, as well as the Caddo by early Spaniards.

Early writers acquainted with the Hainai described them as industrious, intelligent, friendly, and moral people, "always ready for war expeditions and of good courage." They were commended for these general characteristics and their advanced civilization at the Wichita Agency near Anadarko in 1875. The Hainai were an agricultural people who lived in fixed villages, with customs and habits similar to the Caddo. They were especially friendly to the Spaniards and well disposed toward the French in early Colonial days.

◆ **Present Location.** The Hainai are a part of the Wichita living in Caddo County, Oklahoma.

◆ **Numbers.** The present population of Hainai is estimated at about 100 in Oklahoma. In 1877, available figures show that there were approximately 90 Hainai (or Ioni) under the supervision of the Wichita Agency. Their last separate enumeration as a tribe, made in 1876, showed 30 members, not including a group living among the Shawnee in this region. In 1864, there were 150 Hainai counted among the refugee Caddo in Kansas. A tabulated population estimate by John Swanton of the Hasinai or Hainai in fifteen periods of their history gives their numbers at 2,400 to 2,800 in 1699 and 30 in 1876.

◆ **History.** The tribe was first noted by the De Soto expedition in 1541–42. The narrative of the La Salle expedition of 1687 refers to an Indian tribe encountered on the Colorado or Brazos rivers as the "great nation called the Ayano, or Cannohatinno" —the latter name from *Kanohatino,* the Caddo name for Red River, along which the Caddoan tribes lived and with which

they were identified. Three centuries after De Soto's expedition, the Hainai lived near the Brazos River in Texas as allies of the Kadohadacho or Caddo proper (q.v.), having left earlier locations on the Angelina and Neches rivers.

As the leader of the eight tribes that composed the Hasinai Confederacy, the Hainai were important in early Spanish and French relations with the Indians of East Texas. Their village on the Angelina River, in present Nacogdoches County, had long been the center of the tribal religious ceremonials, and the great chief who lived here promoted peace among the Caddoan tribes. This village was the site of one of the four missions founded by the Quereteran Catholic missionaries in July, 1716.

In their tribal history in the Indian Territory and in the Republic and the state of Texas, the Hainai, called Inie, were closely associated with the Caddo (q.v.). In 1859, Chief Kutchaw of the Hainai represented his people among the nine tribes in council with government officials at Fort Arbuckle preparatory to the settlement of these tribes in Indian Territory. Soon afterward the Hainai were under the supervision of the Wichita Agency in the Washita River region.

With the outbreak of the Civil War, the Confederate treaty made by Commissioner Albert Pike at the Wichita Agency on August 12, 1861, was signed by "Ca-shao, Principal Chief of the Ai-onais" (i.e., Chief Kutchaw). Subsequently, most of the tribe went north to Kansas where they remained as refugees in the Union lines during the war. Upon their return to the Indian Territory, they located on the Wichita-Caddo Reservation, where they received individual allotments of land in 1901 as one of the Wichita and Affiliated Tribes (*see* Wichita).

Suggested Readings: Bolton, *Athanase de Mézières;* ———, "Native Tribes, E. Texas Missions," Texas State Hist. Assoc. *Quarterly* (1908); Swanton, *Source Material, Caddo.*

HITCHITI

The Creek term *ahit'chita,* "to look up" (the stream), has been generally given as the origin of the name *Hitchiti.* The Hitchiti are classed in the Muskhogean linguistic family, but they were traditionally an ancient tribal group living in what is now southern Georgia and northern Florida before the arrival of the Muskoke or Creek proper in that region. The Hitchiti were looked upon as the "mother" town or tribe of the Lower Creek people in the Creek Confederacy (*see* Creek). Their language or dialect is different from that of the Muskoke proper. In 1832, the population of the nine "towns," including the Apalachicola (q.v.) and the Okmulgee who spoke Hitchiti language, numbered 2,036. When they came west to the Indian Territory during the Creek removal from Alabama, they settled in the region southeast from present Okmulgee to the village of Hitchita in McIntosh County. The Creek census of 1891 gave the population of this tribal town as 182.

Some of the most prominent leaders in the Creek Nation were from the Hitchiti-speaking towns. The Perrymans were an outstanding family, members of the Mc-Intosh faction in tribal affairs: Benjamin Perryman, a chief in Alabama, had his portrait painted by Catlin at Fort Gibson in 1834; two of this family—Joseph M. and Legus Perryman—were elected to the office of principal chief of the Creek Nation; and Thomas Ward Perryman, a prominent minister and translator of the Gospel, was Creek delegate to the General Assembly of the Presbyterian Church at New York City in 1889. Samuel Checote, Southern leader and minister in the Methodist church, was elected principal chief of the Creek Nation for three terms. Roly McIntosh of Tuskegee Town (*see* Taskigi), the orator, was elected second chief of the Creek Nation (1895–99). Pleasant Porter, one of the most prominent and able Indian leaders in the Indian Territory at the time of allotment of lands in severalty and the last elected principal chief of the Creek Nation, was from the Hitchiti-speaking group.

Suggested Readings: Debo, *The Road to Disappearance;* Meserve, "Chief Pleasant Porter," "The Perrymans," "Chief Samuel Checote," in *Chron. of Okla.,* Vols. IX, XV, XVI; Swanton, *Early History of the Creek;* ——, "Social Organization, Creek," 42 *Ann. Rep.,* Bur. Amer. Ethnol.

ILLINOIS

The name of the Illinois Indians is from the tribal term *ilinewek,* signifying "they are men," from *ilini,* "man"; *iw,* "is"; and *ek,* the plural ending which has changed by the French to *ois.* The Illinois were a confederacy of Algonquian tribes, comprising the Kaskaskia, Peoria, Michigamea, Moingwena. Cahokia, and Tamaroa, the separate histories of which are given under their respective names elsewhere in this volume. The remnants of these tribes were incorporated with the Confederated Peoria (q.v.) now located in Ottawa County, Oklahoma.

The historic period of the Illinois began when the Jesuit missionary Claude Jean Allouez, met a tribal band in 1670. Their tribal home was in southern Wisconsin, northern Illinois, and along the west bank of the Mississippi River as far south as the Des Moines River, Iowa. The remnants of the Illinois settled in Kansas in 1832 and subsequently (1867) in the Indian Territory (*see* Peoria).

Suggested Readings: Alvord, *Kaskaskia Records, 1778–79;* Grant Foreman, "Illinois and Her Indians," in *Papers in Illinois History, 1939;* Hodge, *Handbook of American Indians;* Wilson, *Quapaw Agency Indians.*

IOWA

The name *Iowa,* pronounced "Ioway," is from the tribal term *Ai'yuwe,* which is said to mean, or have some connection with, "marrow." This seems to discount the translation "sleepy ones," an interpretation formerly given the name. The Iowa call themselves *Pahodje,* "snow covered" ("gray snow" or "dusty ones'). They belong to the Siouan linguistic family and are closely related to the Oto and the Missouri (q.v.).

When the first reports were given about them at the beginning of the eighteenth century, the Iowa were primarily agriculturists. They were known for their manufacture of pipes from the red pipestone quarries in Minnesota and excelled in dressing buffalo skins and other pelts. Trading these articles with other Indian tribes gave them a background that made them of some importance in the later trading relations with the French. Thus they began assimilating European civilization at an early period. In 1811 they joined the Sauk and Fox (q.v.) in the recovery of lead from the mines belonging to the Fox west of the Mississippi in what is now Iowa. Years before the Iowa settled in Oklahoma, they were living in comfortable houses and operating good farms on their Kansas reservation. Yet they were clannish in their tribal relations. When they met difficulties as an Indian group in Kansas, they were ready to seek a new location where they might have a chance to build and live as a happy and contented people.

◆ **Present Location.** Iowa in Oklahoma live south of Perkins in Payne County, near the Payne-Lincoln county line. A large band of Iowa live in northeastern Kansas near the Kansas-Nebraska boundary.

◆ **Numbers.** There were 118 Iowa in Oklahoma in 1950. In 1891, allotments from their Oklahoma reservation lands had been completed for 109 members of the tribe. In 1901, 88 Iowa were enumerated at the Sac and Fox Agency. In 1874, before the Iowa began coming to the Indian Territory, they totaled 226 at the Great Nemaha Agency, then in southeastern Nebraska. The report of the United States Indian Office in 1843 gave their total number at 470.

◆ **History.** The Iowa were located at the mouth of Blue Earth River, Minnesota, when first reported by the French explorer Le Sueur in 1701. According to tribal tradition, they left their original country north of the Great Lakes with their relatives, the Winnebago, traveling southwestward; during the migration, the Iowa separated from their ally and located at the mouth of the Rock River in what is now Illinois. Thence, migrating again over a period of years, their stopping places at different times included the Des Moines River region, present Iowa, and the red pipestone quarry in Minnesota.

Their treaty relations with the United States began in 1815, several of their subsequent treaties also including terms with the Sioux and the Sauk and Fox. The Iowa ceded all their lands in Missouri to the United States in 1824. They, together with the Sauk and Fox of the Missouri (q.v.), in 1836 were assigned a reservation of four hundred sections south of the Missouri River and along the Great Nemaha River, the Iowa to have the upper half of this reserve. In 1885, those Iowa who were living on the "diminished reserve" of these lands in Kansas were granted allotments in severalty.

When the question of allotment was discussed in 1876, about one-half of the 224 Iowa under the supervision of the Great Nemaha Agency (Nohart, Nebraska) were bitterly opposed to the plan. These Iowa soon began moving away in small bands seeking homes in the Indian Territory, making their encampment on the reservation of the Sauk and Fox (q.v.). In 1880, there were 46 of them at the Sac and Fox Agency in a destitute condition and without a permanent location to build their homes; the following year, they were joined by 47 more of their kinsmen from Kansas. In answer to their plea to Government officials, they were assigned a reservation in the Indian Territory by executive order in 1883. This tract of 225,000 acres, well supplied with timber, water, and grass land, extended west from the Sauk and Fox line to the Indian Meridian, lying between the Cimarron and the Deep Fork rivers, a region now included in adjoining portions of Payne, Logan, Oklahoma, and Lincoln counties. By an agreement made with United States commissioners in May, 1890, the Iowa were allotted lands in severalty (109 individuals, 80 acres each). Most of the Iowa allotments were located in the Cimarron Valley south of Perkins; a few were near the "Old Iowa Village," a well-known settlement on the reservation near the present village of Fallis, in Lincoln County. Surplus Iowa lands (about 216,-000 acres) were opened to white settlement by Presidential proclamation, with a run starting at twelve o'clock noon, September 22, 1891.

◆ **Government and Organization.** The Iowa here are organized as the Iowa Tribe of Oklahoma, under a charter from the Department of the Interior, and have a constitution and by-laws. The charter was ratified by a majority vote of the adult Iowa in an election held on February 5, 1938, as certified by Jack Lincoln, chairman, and Marie Roubidoux, secretary of the Iowa tribe. Tribal members who have served on the Business Committee of their organization include Solomon Kent (chairman), F. Roubidoux, Edward Small, Robert Small, Jacob Dole, A. Springer, and Phoebe Small.

◆ **Contemporary Life and Culture.** Full-blood Iowa constitute 73 per cent of their tribe in Oklahoma. The mixed-bloods are descendants by intermarriage with associated tribes (Fox, Sauk, and Oto) and whites, some of French blood. Solomon Kent, chief of the Iowa, is the grandson of Chief Frank Mannaway Kent (a fullblood, one of the first of the tribe to come to the Indian Territory from Kansas) and his wife, Emma Tohee Kent, a daughter of Chief Tohee, who came to Oklahoma in 1876. The Tohee and the Whitecloud families ranked high among the Iowa and were distinguished by a small circle tattooed on the forehead.

Unsettled conditions concerning their reservation and lack of funds delayed the Iowa in the improvement of their farms until after 1891. Nearly all the tribal members could speak and read and write English at the time of the opening of their reservation, though bark houses were still seen in the Iowa settlements. The old tribal customs were fast disappearing, yet some of the tribesmen had continued the old funeral rites, placing their dead, wrapped in blankets and bark, on the branches of trees in the woods. The Iowa are Christians, missionaries of the Friends, the Baptist, and the Methodist churches having worked among them before the opening of their reservation. They are a rural people making their living by farming and stock raising.

Suggested Readings: Chapman, "Dissolution of the Iowa Reservation," *Chron. of Okla.*, Vol. XIV, No. 4; ——, "Establishment of the Iowa Reservation," *Chron. of Okla.*, Vol. XXI, No. 4; Grant Foreman, "Illinois and Her Indians," in *Papers in Illinois History*, 1939; Hodge, *Handbook of American Indians;* Miner, *The Iowa;* Skinner, *The Ioway Indians.*

KASKASKIA

The name of the Kaskaskia is probably from the tribal term *kaskaskahamwa,* "he scrapes it off by means of a tool," referring to the method of dressing hides and pelts for clothing and other articles. The Kaskaskia were the leading tribe of the Illinois Confederacy (q.v.) of the Algonquian linguistic family.

◊ **Present Location.** Descendants of the Kaskaskia, an important tribe of the Confederated Peoria (q.v.), are located in Ottawa County, Oklahoma.

◊ **Numbers.** The United States Indian Office census for the Peoria (q.v.) includes the present number of the Kaskaskia. The tribe was greatly reduced in power and strength by attacks of enemy tribes from the north after the close of the French and Indian War, 600 members being reported in 1764 and 210 in 1778.

◊ **History.** Marquette visited the principal village of the Kaskaskia near the present site of Utica, La Salle County, Illinois, in 1673, and the following year founded the Mission of the Immaculate Conception among them. With the location of other Illinois tribes in the vicinity, this became a large settlement. In 1700, when the Kaskaskia decided to leave the country and join the French in Louisiana, Father Gravier induced them to locate instead at the mouth of the Kaskaskia River near the present site of Kaskaskia, Randolph County, Illinois. When a Kaskaskia Indian murdered the great Ottawa (q.v.) chief, Pontiac, at Cahokia, Illinois, in 1769, tribes from the north, including the Sauk, Fox, Kickapoo, and Potawatomi vowed vengeance and began a war of extermination against the Illinois (q.v.).

Fifteen Indian treaties with the United States either refer to the Kaskaskia or bear the names of their chiefs, one of the most prominent of whom was James Baptiste Ducoigne, whose daughter Ellen many years later was assigned the last tribal tract of 350 acres near the town of Kaskaskia. Under the terms of the treaty made at Vincennes on August 30, 1803, by Governor William Henry Harrison, superintendent of Indian Affairs, the Kaskaskia with whom the remnants of the Michigamea, the Cahokia, and the Tamaroa had long been consolidated ceded all lands claimed by them in the "Illinois territory," to the United States. The government in turn promised its immediate care and patronage to afford the Kaskaskia "a protection as effectual against other Indian tribes, and against all other persons whatever, as is enjoyed by their own citizens." President Jefferson in his message to Congress in October, 1803, mentioned the recent acquisition of the valuable Illinois territory, referring to the Kaskaskia as the friendly tribe "with which we have never had any difference." Some years later, they confederated with the Peoria, the two tribes being assigned a reserve of 150 sections in Kansas under a treaty with the United States in 1832, since which time the history of the Kaskaskia has been identical with the Confederated Peoria both in Kansas and in the Indian Territory.

Suggested Readings: Grant Foreman, "Illinois and Her Indians," in *Papers in Illinois History,* 1939; ———, *Last Trek of the Indians;* Hodge, *Handbook of American Indians;* Illinois State Hist. Soc. *Journal,* 1908—; Wilson, *Quapaw Agency Indians.*

KANSA

The Kansa are one of the five tribes in the Dhegiha group of the Siouan linguistic family. They have the same language as another of the Dhegiha, the Osage (q.v.), with whom they were often allied in war during early tribal days. The name *Kansa* signifies "Wind People" or "South Wind People." In the tribal organization of the Omaha, also one of the Dhegiha, the Kansa led in a war ceremonial in recognition of the power of the wind to aid warriors setting forth to war. They also had the office of starting the ball games between the two great divisions of the Omaha, in which the Kansa were significant in imparting to the ball the power and swiftness of the wind. The Osage call the Kansa people *Ko^nçe,* probably an abbreviation of *ko^nça-gi,* "fleet" or "swift." Among the numerous variations of the name Kansa found in historical records is *Kansas,* which became the name of the Kansas or Kaw River near which the tribe formerly lived, the name of the river afterward being chosen for the state of Kansas. In Oklahoma history, the Kansa are generally referred to as the Kaw. *Kaw* is doubtless an abbreviation of *ak'a,* from the Siouan dialects, "south wind," the abbreviation having been written *Kau* or *Kaw* by early French traders.

The Kansa have always been known for their conservativeness and long resisted changing from their old tribal customs. They were a warlike people living principally by hunting the buffalo, though they grew small crops to some extent near their semipermanent villages. They were hostile to the Pawnee, from whom, however, they seemed to have learned to erect timber-framed, dome-shaped, earth-covered lodges for dwellings.

◆ **Present Location.** The Kansa or Kaw live in Kay County, Oklahoma. Those who live on their allotments are located in northeastern Kay County, the former Kaw reservation area that lies east of the Arkansas River to the Osage County line.

◆ **Numbers.** There are approximately 580 Kansa in Oklahoma. The United States Indian Agency reported 544 members of the tribe in 1945, an increase of 8 over the previous year. An enumeration in 1924 shows a total population of 420. The Indian Office Report for 1906 shows that

their reservation lands had been allotted to 247 members of the tribe. Their population had diminished from about 1,700 in 1850.

◆ **History.** There is a tribal tradition that during an ancient migration of the Siouan Dhegiha the Kansa ascended the south side of the Missouri River to the mouth of the Kansas River. Their settlement farther north was blocked by the hostile Cheyenne. Marquette heard of the Kansa living in this region in 1673. Subsequently, their villages were located farther west on the Big Blue River.

In 1846, the United States secured the cession of two million acres that had been previously assigned the Kansa, a tract thirty miles wide extending west from a line located a few miles west of present Topeka, Kansas. The tribe soon moved and established their villages at Council Grove on the Neosho River, where a reservation about twenty miles square was assigned them. Here, in 1850, the Methodist Episcopal church built the best mission ever erected in Kansas. However, few of the Kansa and their children ever joined the church or attended the school which was one of the first in Kansas to admit children of white settlers and employees in the trade over the Santa Fé Trail that crossed this region.

A treaty made in 1859 ceded to the United States about half the Kansa reservation. The remaining tribal tract (nine by fourteen miles) was subsequently sold by acts of Congress (1872, 1874, 1876, 1880) and the money used to purchase a new reservation in the Indian Territory. This new tract covered 100,000 acres in the northwestern corner of the Osage reservation, the location determined and purchase arranged for in a meeting of special United States commissioners and delegations of the Osage and the Kansa at the new Osage agency, now Pawhuska, in the Indian Territory.

The Kansa left Kansas early in June, 1873, arriving in the Indian Territory after

Nos-kah-noie, assistant chief, and Wash-shun-gah, chief of the Kansa, in Washington in 1902

an overland journey of seventeen days. Their new agency was known as the Kaw Agency (a subagency of the Osage Agency) and was located on the present site of Washunga in Kay County. Near Beaver Creek, buildings were erected to house the Kaw Boarding School, which was operated under government auspices for many years. The Kansa were slow in making progress in their new country since they had first to recover from the deplorable conditions under which they had lived during their last years in Kansas, when they had suffered near starvation and severe loss of population. Their population of 533 upon their arrival in the Indian Territory in 1873 diminished to 194 in 1889.

Tribal members on the reservation opposed allotment of lands in severalty, although in 1892 some of the mixed-bloods favored the assignment of a homestead of 160 acres to each member. When the Cherokee Commission sought to acquire Indian reservation lands for the government in 1893, no sale agreement was made with the Kansa. It was about this time that the leasing of Kaw reservation lands to outside cattlemen for grazing purposes began. Surplus lands—those acres not cultivated or otherwise used by members of the tribe—were divided into fourteen pastures of from 500 to 10,500 acres each and leased annually to cattlemen by the tribal council, the income being credited to the tribe.

The Curtis Act of June 28, 1898, which provided for sweeping changes in the conduct of the affairs of the Five Civilized Tribes, gave impetus to allotment in severalty of all Indian lands in Oklahoma Territory and Indian Territory, thus paving the way for statehood. By 1900, the Kansa were all in accord about securing a settlement with the government on their tribal lands and money interests. In doing so, they had the friendly interest and aid of the most prominent Indian in recent American history, their fellow tribesman Charles Curtis, who represented his native Kansas for many years in the United States Congress, both as representative and as senator, and who later, in 1929, became vice-president of the United States.

An agreement regarding the Kansa or Kaw tribal lands and funds was signed at Washington on February 2, 1902, by seven authorized representatives of the tribe: Chief Wash-shun-gah, Forrest Chouteau, Wah-noh-oeke, William Hardy, Mitchell Fronkier, Akan Pappan, and W. E. Hardy. In accordance with this agreement, the Kaw reservation lands were divided equally among the members of the tribe, each enrolled allottee receiving 405 acres (160 acres homestead and 245 acres surplus), a total of 260 acres being reserved for cemetery, townsite, and school purposes. When allotments were completed, the former reservation area was attached to Kay County, Oklahoma, by a Congressional act in 1904. Some of these allotments later brought the Indian owners wealth through the discovery of oil and gas. Most of the former Kaw reservation area has been sold by the original owners, leaving only about 13,000 acres of Indian-owned lands in the tract today.

◆ **Government and Organization.** Nominal tribal organization was retained by the Kansa until about 1935 to promote and secure the settlement of certain tribal claims before the United States Court of Claims. The last chief of the Kansa in this organization was the late Emmet Thompson, a respected citizen of Ponca City.

◆ **Contemporary Life and Culture.** The admixture of French blood among the Kansa is large; many of the old mixed-blood families bearing French names show their descent from their intermarriages with early French traders. The fullblood Kansa comprise about 18 per cent of the total tribal population. Most of these members of the tribe live in rural communities and are engaged in farming and stock raising. The mixed-bloods as a class have been well educated and for the most part are engaged in business in Kay County.

Suggested Readings: Chapman, "Charles

Curtis and the Kaw Reservation," *Kansas Hist. Quarterly,* Vol. XV (1947); Connelly, *History of Kansas;* J. O. Dorsey, "Siouan Cults," *11 Ann. Rep.,* Bur. Amer. Ethnol.; Fletcher and LaFlesche, "The Omaha Tribe," *27 Ann. Rep.,* Bur. Amer. Ethnol.; Hodge, *Handbook of American Indians.*

KICHAI

The Kichai are called *Kitsash* in the Wichita language. They spell their own tribal name *Kĕ'chä.* It is found in most historical records spelled phonetically *Keechi.* The name is said to signify "red shield."

The Kichai belong to the Caddoan linguistic family and were one of the member tribes of the early Caddoan Confederacy (*see* Caddo), but later were identified with the Wichita Confederacy in the Red River region of Louisiana, Texas, and Oklahoma. The Kichai language is nearer that of the Pawnee than the Caddo proper.

Like the Kadohadacho or Caddo proper, the Kichai are shorter and have a darker complexion than the people of other tribes who have long been their neighbors on the Plains. Their dominant characteristic seems to have been that they seldom, if ever, operated separately, but were allied with one or more of their neighboring tribes. In friendly alliances they were reported loyal and courageous. They have retained their tribal solidarity and native language to this day.

◆ **Present Location.** Most of the Kichai live between Gracemont and Anadarko in Caddo County, which was a part of the Wichita-Caddo reservation where they were allotted lands in severalty in 1901 under the supervision of the Indian Agency at Anadarko. The tribal members are identified with the Wichita in this region.

◆ **Numbers.** A recent enumeration (1950) reports 190 Kichai in Oklahoma, 47 full bloods and 143 mixed-bloods. In 1905 the Indian Office reported 30 members of the tribe under the supervision of the agency at Anadarko. An official enumeration of the tribe in 1894 listed 52 Kichai on the Wichita-Caddo reservation. In 1857 there were 300 members of that part of the tribe associated with the Wichita in the Leased District of the Choctaw Nation (*see* Choctaw), a region now included in southwestern Oklahoma. In 1849, approximately 300 Kichai were reported living in the vicinity of Torrey's Trading House near the present site of Waco, Texas. In 1778 there were an estimated 500 members of the tribe in two settlements on the Trinity River, in the vicinity of present Palestine, Texas.

◆ **History.** In 1701 the Kichai lived on the upper Trinity River in Texas and on the upper waters of the Red River in what is now Louisiana, where they were visited by a French expedition. They were already in possession of horses and were allied with the western tribes of the Caddoan Confederacy. Some years later their tribal villages were found on the Trinity River as far south as present Leon County, Texas, where two creeks and a town are called Keechi.

When the French commandant and explorer, La Harpe, made his first expedition to the Oklahoma country in the summer of 1719, two Kichai (Quidehais) served as his guides. The expedition traveled through southeastern Oklahoma and on north to the Tawakoni village on the Arkansas River, near the present site of Haskell in Muskogee County, where, during a council with the Tawakoni (q.v.) and eight other neighboring tribes, an alliance was made in behalf of the King of France, the first peace council between a European nation and any of the Oklahoma Indian tribes. The two guides had been selected for their important mission by their tribal chiefs living on the upper Red River in Texas. The French at this time referred to the Kichai, along with the Waco and Tonkawa, as the "roving nation," reported on the warpath against the Apache (*see* Lipan). From La Harpe's time on, the Kichai were faithful in their pledges to the French.

The Kichai were frequently mentioned in the history of western Oklahoma in the first half of the nineteenth century. In 1837 some of the tribal bands were living with the Wichita in several villages in southwestern Oklahoma where they raised large crops of corn and traded with the Kiowa. Soon afterward, a band of Kichai was living in the abandoned buildings of the Chouteau Trading Post located on Chouteau Creek in the Creek Nation, between the present sites of Norman and Lexington in Cleveland County. In 1842, General Zachary Taylor attended a grand council of Indian tribes called by the Creek Nation on the Deep Fork River, near present Eufaula, where the Kichai were one of fifteen tribes represented.

In 1843 Kichai chiefs and warriors were present at the intertribal council with government agents at Warren's Trading Post near the mouth of Cache Creek, in present Cotton County. About this time, a band of Kichai had a village in the Wichita Mountain region of Oklahoma. As a tribe they were faithful in their friendship with the United States; tribal bands in Texas were often at war with the Mexicans.

In 1857 a part of the people of the Wichita village on Rush Creek were Kichai who were "following the Wichita road" in raising corn, pumpkins, and watermelons. After the battle of the Wichita village (*see* Wichita) in the summer of 1858, when United States troops attacked a Comanche camp in the vicinity, the Wichita and Kichai fled to Fort Arbuckle for protection from the hostile Comanche. During a council there between nine tribes and government officers in 1859, Chief Tawahkassee represented the Kichai. In that same year the Kichai living among the Indians on the Brazos Reservation in Texas were brought north by government agents to the Washita River in the Indian Territory, where the tribe was henceforth listed among those of the Wichita Agency.

After the outbreak of the Civil War, a part of the Kichai were in alliance with the Confederacy, the name of their second chief, Ki-is-qua, appearing among the signers of the treaty made on July 12, 1861, with the Penateka Comanche and other tribes at the Wichita Agency by Albert Pike, commissioner for the Confederate States. Later, the main part of the tribe and the Wichita (q.v.) loyal to the Federal government left the Washita River and went north to Kansas, where they remained as refugees until the end of the war. Many of these Indian refugees died during an epidemic of cholera that swept through Kansas in 1867, just before they set out to return to their former location on the Washita. Afterward, the remnant of the Kichai were a part of the Wichita and Affiliated Tribes on the Wichita-Caddo reservation.

◆ **Government and Organization.** Kichai who have served in the Wichita Tribal Council, which is organized to promote the welfare and business interests of the Wichita and Affiliated Tribes, are John Haddon, Frank Miller, and Rose Collins, all of Gracemont, and George Bates, Ned Greeley, and Emma Leonard, all of Anadarko.

The Kichai tribal government was formerly like that of the Wichita, with a hereditary chief approved for the position by the tribal council. So-Ko-No, who served as chief after the Civil War for nearly forty years, was the last of the old tribal line of chiefs. After his death, another member of the tribe, John Tatum, served as chief and made several trips to Washington as delegate for the Wichita and the Kichai.

◆ **Contemporary Life and Culture.** The Kichai have intermarried with the Wichita and other tribes in southwestern Oklahoma, including the Kiowa and the Caddo proper. Like the Wichita with whom they have been associated in Oklahoma for 125 years, they have been primarily farmers. Their old tribal customs were similar to the Wichita (q.v.). Today most of the Kichai are engaged in farming, although some are employed as carpenters.

The Kichai are a Christianized people; many of them are members of the "Keechi Mission Church" near Gracemont, maintained by the Southern Baptist Association. This church began with the work of Jove Kah (or "Keechi Joe"), a Seminole who learned the Kichai language and married a Kichai woman in the early eighteen seventies. When the Baptist missionary John McIntosh (a Seminole Indian) came from eastern Oklahoma to work among the Wichita and the Kichai, Jove Kah served as his interpreter, translating the Seminole language into the Kichai. Then,

in turn, the Kichai was interpreted into the Wichita language by a Kichai man known as "Keechi John," who had married a Wichita woman. A number of the Kichai and the Wichita were converted and became members of the "Keechi Mission Church," which is still in charge of the Seminole Baptists.

◆ **Ceremonials and Public Dances.** As one of the southwestern Oklahoma tribes, the Kichai among the Wichita are represented in the pageantry in the American Indian Exposition held at Anadarko, Oklahoma, each August.

Suggested Readings: Grant Foreman, *Advancing the Frontier;* Hodge, *Handbook of American Indians;* Lewis, "La Harpe's First Expedition in Oklahoma," *Chron. of Okla.,* Vol. II, No. 4; Swanton, *Source Material, Caddo.*

KICKAPOO

The name Kickapoo is from *Kiwigapawa,* "he stands about," or "he moves about, standing now here, now there." The people of this tribe belong to the Algonquian linguistic family, and have a close ethnic connection with the Sauk (or Sac) and Fox (q.v.).

The Kickapoo have always been remarkably independent and clannish, especially in retaining their tribal religious beliefs and ceremonies. Even in the last years of the reservation period they lived in their traditional bark-covered houses neatly arranged in fixed villages. They have always been primarily an agricultural people. They were one of the first tribes from the Illinois country to learn about horses while on buffalo hunts in the West, where they became well acquainted with the Plains tribes. The expeditions of some of the Kickapoo bands for stock in the Southwest gave the tribe the reputation of being thieves and renegades. Yet Captain R. B.

Marcy, who met some Kickapoo hunters near Fort Arbuckle in 1852, stated: "They were fine-looking, well dressed young men with open, frank countenances and seemed to scorn the idea of begging." The commanding officer at Fort Smith about this time wrote that many of the Kickapoo "are well educated, and speak and write the English language fluently." Those who were allotted lands in Kansas in 1862 have generally been thrifty farmers who have improved their property. The Mexican Kickapoo, so called from their long sojourn in Mexico, were described as a "sarcastic, haughty, yet peaceable people" when they began moving to the Indian Territory in 1871. They resisted any attempts at coercion by government officials and opposed allotment of lands in severalty on their reservation. Their United States agent from 1895 to 1901 stated that the Kickapoo would respond only to respect and persuasion; that they were a people who "are imbued with pure American spirit and stand upon it."

◆ **Present Location.** The largest settlement of the Kickapoo in Oklahoma is near McLoud in Pottawatomie County.

◆ **Numbers.** Approximately 314 Kickapoo live in Oklahoma. An enumeration of the tribe taken at the Shawnee Agency in 1920 gives 194, practically all full bloods bearing individual Indian names. In 1905, 283 Mexican Kickapoo were finally allotted lands on their Oklahoma reservation. In 1876, there were 312 members of the tribe on this reservation and 252 in Kansas, a band of about 100 still remaining in Mexico. In 1825, the total number of the whole tribe was estimated at 2,200, before any of them settled in the Southwest. In 1950, the Kickapoo tribe totaled about 800 in the United States (Oklahoma and Kansas), with a group still living in the state of Coahuila, Mexico.

◆ **History.** The Kickapoo were found by the Catholic missionary, Father Allouez, between the Fox and the Wisconsin rivers in southern Wisconsin about 1667. After the break-up of the Illinois (q.v.) following the French and Indian War, the Kickapoo moved into southern Illinois and, later, eastward to the Wabash River. They were included in the great Indian confederacy of Tecumseh, the Shawnee (q.v.), in 1811–13, and many of them rallied to the support of Black Hawk, the Sauk and Fox leader, in the Indian uprising twenty years later. In 1837, one hundred Kickapoo warriors were enlisted by the United States Army to fight the Seminole in Florida.

Treaty relations between the United States and the Kickapoo began with General Anthony Wayne's treaty of Greenville in 1795. A treaty in 1819 provided for the cession of all Kickapoo lands in Illinois (nearly half that state) and the assignment of a tribal reservation in Missouri, which in turn was relinquished by treaty in 1832 when a second reservation (twelve miles square) was assigned along the Missouri River in what is now northeastern Kansas. This Kickapoo reservation was reduced and opened to white settlement by treaties in 1854 and 1862. The latter treaty provided the Kansas Kickapoo allotments of land in severalty, the surplus lands (about 123,000 acres) of their reservation later being sold to a railroad company at a low price, the proceeds to be used for the benefit of the tribe in Kansas. The Kickapoo were the followers of Kanakuk, their chief until his death about 1852. He was known as the Kickapoo prophet and had established a tribal religion in Illinois, teaching virtuous and abstemious living, which he said was based upon direct word from the Great Spirit. Some of his followers later settled among the Mexican Kickapoo in the Indian Territory.

A large band of Kickapoo who objected to the cession of their Illinois lands in 1819 and to settlement in Missouri soon went to Texas, where they became allies of the Texas Cherokee (*see* Cherokee). When the latter were defeated in battle by the Texans in 1839 and forced to retreat to the Indian Territory north of Red River, the Kickapoo came to the Choctaw Nation. Part of them established a village on Wild Horse Creek, in present Garvin County, where they lived until they went to Mexico in 1850–51 with Wild Cat, the Seminole (q.v.). They were known as the Mexican Kickapoo from that time on. Their village site on Wild Horse Creek became the location of Fort Arbuckle, which was established by Captain R. B. Marcy in 1851. Another band of Kickapoo from Texas settled by permission of the Creek people on the Canadian River, about fifteen miles above the mouth of Little River, their efficient fighting men serving as a vanguard on the western border of the Creek settlements against possible incursions of Comanche and other tribes from the Plains. At the outbreak of the Civil War the Canadian River Kickapoo went to Mexico, losing some of their number as well as nearly all their property and livestock in an attack and defeat by the Texans on the way. These tribesmen were impoverished, yet rendered good service to the Mexican people against Comanche and Apache raids from the north. After the war, bands of Mexican Kickapoo were charged with stealing horses and cattle across the international boundary in Texas.

In 1870, attempts of United States agents to persuade the Kickapoo to leave Mexico were unsuccessful. Three years later, after an illegal raid on them by United States troops in the mountains of Mexico, a specially appointed United States commission finally induced them to return to the Indian Territory. As a rule, they were energetic, built neat bark houses to live in, and religiously observed their tribal ceremonies; yet they were poor and dissatisfied for many years and violently opposed sending their children to school—these attitudes and conditions resulting in part from the long delay by the government in carrying out promises to locate them permanently in their farming and stock raising. A reservation was first assigned them in 1883 by Executive order. This tract of about 100,000 acres extended west from the Sauk and Fox reservation line to the Indian meridian, between the Deep Fork and the North Canadian rivers, a rich country already coveted by white settlers. Well-known places on the reservation were the Kickapoo village at Horseshoe Lake northeast of Harrah, in Oklahoma County, and Kickapoo Station near present Dale, in Pottawatomie County, and Kickapoo Trading Post, operated by a white trader, near the present site of Wellston in Lincoln County.

An agreement made by United States commissioners with the Kickapoo in 1891, provided for the cession of the reservation to the United States and allotments of land to the tribal members. They protested the allotment provision under the leadership of their chief, Ocquenahkose, asking for a diminished reservation to be held in common by the tribe. The agreement was approved by Congress in 1893, and allotment of eighty acres to each member of the tribe

was completed the next year. Fully two-thirds of the tribe, referred to as the "Kicking Kickapoo," refused to acknowledge their allotments or accept any per capita money due under the terms of the agreement. The Kickapoo reservation was organized as a part of Oklahoma Territory and the surplus lands opened to white settlement by run on May 23, 1895, under a cloud of political intrigue and "sooner" claimants.

It was not until 1901 that the Mexican Kickapoo were getting established on their allotments with some semblance of order in their tribal affairs. In this period, the tribe had two chiefs, one of them a woman named Wah-Poho-ko-wah, who ruled with good judgment yet whose word was law. She was the last chief by right of inheritance under the old tribal regime. Some of the Kickapoo were members of the Friends church which resulted from the mission school founded among them by the Society of Friends in 1892. The Kickapoo school operated by the government about two miles from McLoud had good attendance in 1901, and fifteen older boys and girls from the tribe were in Carlisle Indian School in Pennsylvania.

◆ **Government and Organization.** Kickapoo organized as the "Kickapoo Tribe of Oklahoma," under provisions of the Oklahoma Indian Welfare Act of 1936, with a charter from the Department of Interior ratified by a vote of the adult members of the tribe on January 18, 1938, as certified by Francis Allen, chairman, and Dwight Kishketon, secretary-treasurer of the Kickapoo tribe. Members of the tribal Business Committee have included Ernest Murdock, William Murdock, James Stevens, Jim Wahweah, and Sweeny Stevens. Monthly meetings are held in the community house near McLoud.

◆ **Contemporary Life and Culture.** The Kickapoo are a notable fullblood Indian group in Oklahoma, with only fourteen of their number listed as mixed-blood Indian and white. They are, of course, citizens of the state, and their children attend the public schools. They make their living mostly by farming and stock raising. Any restricted property interests are under the supervision of the Shawnee Subagency at Shawnee. In view of their numbers and their finances, they were liberal in their purchase of government bonds in World War I. Their young men were enlisted and made good records in the United States armed forces in World War II.

Suggested Readings: Buntin, "The Mexican Kickapoos," *Chron. of Okla.,* Vol. XI, Nos. 1 and 2; Chapman, "The Cherokee Commission at the Kickapoo Village," *Chron, of Okla.,* Vol. XVII, No. 2; Grant Foreman, *Last Trek of the Indians;* Hodge, *Handbook of American Indians.*

KIOWA

The name Kiowa, by which the people of this tribe are commonly known, is from their own name *Gá'igwu* (or *Ká'i-gwu*), signifying "principal people." Seventy-five years ago some of their oldest men said that this was not originally their tribal name; it was of foreign origin and not translatable in their own language. It was also the name of one of the six divisions that made up the tribal camp circle when they came eastward to the Plains from their original home in the Rocky Mountains. The tribe is the only one classed in the Kiowan linguistic family.

The Kiowa are one of the great tribes of the Plains, reputed the bravest and most courageous, yet the most warlike and defiant, of the tribes in the Southwest. In their raids, which ended seventy-five years ago, they were said to have killed more white men than any other tribe. Today they are considered one of the most progressive Indian groups in southwestern Oklahoma. In appearance, they are dark and heavily built.

◊ **Present Location.** The largest settlement of Kiowa is near Carnegie, in Caddo County. They are a rural people, but their homes are usually modern, for many families have gained considerable wealth from the discovery of oil in their communities.

◊ **Numbers.** Approximately 2,800 Kiowa proper live in Oklahoma. (Total numbers in census reports usually include all the Kiowa-Apache, q.v.) There was a total of 1,699 members of the Kiowa proper in 1924. Their numbers in official reports of the Indian Office in preceding periods are 1,195 in 1905, 1,037 in 1895, 1,169 in 1885, and 1,070 in 1875. No accurate population count of the Kiowa was ever made before their final surrender at Fort Sill in 1875, but a conservative estimate of their numbers before that time indicates that the tribe never exceeded more than 1,400 members. An epidemic of measles in 1892 resulted in the death of nearly 15 per cent of the population, mostly children, and in great losses of tribal property (thousands of dollars' worth) through the destruction of ponies and horses and valuable blankets and other personal belongings at the graves of the deceased, in accordance with old tribal custom.

◊ **History.** The Traditional history of the Kiowa locates them in the mountain region at the sources of the Yellowstone and Missouri rivers in what is now western Montana. According to legend, a dispute arose between two rival chiefs that grew into an angry quarrel, and one chief withdrew with his band to the northwest; the other with the rest of the tribe (the Kiowa of today) moved southeast until they met the Crow, with whom they made a friendly alliance. They settled east of the Crow, where they first procured horses, but about 1700 drifted out on the Plains and soon were in possession of the Black Hills (western South Dakota) as well as the region westward

MURIEL H. WRIGHT

Kiowa village with shelters, Kiowa-Comanche-Apache Reservation, 1892

toward the Yellowstone River. They left this country about 1805, moving south to the Arkansas River, after many years of war with the Cheyenne and Dakota tribes that had pushed into the Black Hills region from the north. Thence they moved over to the headwaters of the Cimarron River in what is now western Kansas and eastern Colorado, where they established their council fire and subsequently gained control of the country south to the Wichita Mountains and the headwaters of Red River, a region that included most of western Oklahoma.

In the period during which the Kiowa developed as a formidable tribe of the Plains, their relations with neighboring tribes of the region were important not only in their own history but in the history of the settlement of these tribes on reservations in Oklahoma. Even before the Kiowa had left their early mountain home, they were associated with the Kiowa-Apache, a small Athapascan group that had become a component part of the tribal circle by the time the Kiowa established their council fire on the Cimarron River. The alliance of these two tribes continues to this day in Oklahoma. About 1790 the Kiowa made permanent peace with the Comanche (q.v.) after a long period of warfare. This

alliance was the basis for the Kiowa-Comanche reservation in Oklahoma when the two tribes were settled here by the United States three quarters of a century later. In 1840 the Kiowa made permanent peace with the Cheyenne and their allies the Arapaho.

They were on friendly terms with the Wichita and their allies—the Tawakoni, Kichai, and Waco—in the region of the Wichita Mountains; but they were enemies of the Caddo and the Tonkawa, as well as of the Navaho, the Ute, and some of the western Apache groups. The end of many years of war with the Osage, in 1834, marked the beginning of Kiowa relations in Oklahoma with the United States government.

The Kiowa are notable among the Indian tribes north of Mexico for their pictograph records in the form of calendar histories. In these unique calendars, a specific event of tribal importance is recorded for each summer and each winter from 1832–33 through 1892 by paintings made on skins. (George Poolaw, a Kiowa, continued the record from 1893 until he died in 1939.) Four of the calendar histories had been brought to light by 1893 and made available to the reading public by James Mooney. The pictographs are most interesting. The summer of 1833, for example, is recorded as the "summer that they cut off their heads," the pictograph commemorating the massacre of the Kiowa by the Osage, who cut off the heads of their Kiowa enemies, placed them in copper kettles, and left them at the scene of the massacre—on the headwaters of Otter Creek about twenty-five miles northwest of the site of Old Fort Sill. The following summer is marked by the return of *Gunpä´ ñdamä* ("Medicine-tied-to-tipi-pole woman"—a Kiowa girl who had been captured by the Osage in the massacre) by the Dragoon Expedition under Colonel Henry Dodge.

Colonel Dodge was in the area to hold a peace council with the Southern Plains tribes at the Wichita village on the North Fork of Red River (*see* Wichita). A number of Kiowa bands (comprising about ninety persons in all) attended this council, which was the first meeting of the tribe with United States officials within the boundaries of Oklahoma. The Kiowa were described at this time as "tall and erect, with an easy graceful gait, long hair reaching often nearly to the ground, with a fine Roman outline of head." At the meeting the head chief, Takatacouche ("Black Bird"), spoke of their friendship for the whites; and again, later, he headed a delegation of his people at a special conference called at Fort Gibson in September, 1835, by Colonel Dodge with representatives of various tribes in the Indian Territory. Two years later, in 1837, the names of Takatacouche and Dohasan ("Little Bluff," chief of the tribe for more than thirty years) appear among those of ten Kiowa chiefs and leaders who signed the first treaty between the Kiowa and the United States, establishing peace with the Osage and the Creek. All the tribes concerned in this treaty were

OKLAHOMA HISTORICAL SOCIETY

Hummingbird and family, 1894

MURIEL H. WRIGHT

Millie Oytant in a dress trimmed with elk
teeth valued at $1,000 (1900)

to have equal hunting rights on the Southern Plains as far west as the limits of the
United States; but citizens of the United
States were to be allowed free access
through the Plains region in travel to and
from Mexico and Texas.

The Kiowa were located at this time on
the upper waters of the Arkansas, Canadian, and Red rivers, their friends the Comanche and the Wichita living in the same
region, though ranging to the east and
south. Soon after the 1837 treaty, Colonel
A. P. Chouteau established the first American trading post in the Kiowa country, on
Cache Creek, about three miles south of
the present site of Fort Sill.

Their alliance with the Comanche and
their subsequent settlement at the headwaters of the Cimarron found the Kiowa
hostile toward the Spanish settlements and,
later, the Texans, periodic raids continuing

to the end of the Indian wars in the Southwest when General Phil Sheridan's cam-
paigns from 1868 to 1876 finally met with
success. The alliance between the Kiowa
and the Cheyenne (q.v.) in 1840 strengthened the resistance of the Indians of the
Southern Plains to white emigration to the
West along the overland trails. That the
existence of this Indian barrier was fully
recognized by the United States is seen in
the provisions for peace contained in a
treaty made at Fort Atkinson on July 27,
1853, with the Kiowa, Kiowa-Apache, and
Comanche. Despite such efforts on the part
of government commissioners, however,
the Kiowa rose to their greatest height as
an independent war tribe during the next
decade under the leadership of Chief
Dohasan.

Widespread depredations on the Plains
in the summer of 1864 brought detachments of the United States Army out after
the hostiles. Government officials who had
favored negotiation with, rather than war
on, these tribes succeeded in concluding a
treaty with the Kiowa and Comanche in a
council held on the Little Arkansas near
present Wichita, Kansas, on August 15,
1865. As a result, the two tribes agreed to
settle on a reservation to be assigned them
south of the Arkansas River in what is
now western Texas and Oklahoma. Although Dohasan was bitterly opposed to
the plans offered by the government during the council, his name appears as a
signer of the treaty along with the names
of other prominent Kiowa, including Satanta (or Set-t'aiñte, "White Bear") and
T"ené-ango'pte ("Kicking Bird"), both of
whom were prominent in the early history
of Fort Sill. With the death of Chief Dohasan in 1866, the day of the Kiowa as a great
war tribe was coming to a close. Lone Wolf
now became the chief and the war leader,
the last of the old-line chiefs who experienced the change from tribal to reservation
life.

In the following year, in October, 1867,
came the treaty of the Medicine Lodge (*see*

Comanche) when the names of ten Kiowa leaders appeared as signers, among them Satank ("Sitting Bear") and Satanta, who was acknowledged the greatest Indian orator present. At this time the Kiowa-Apache (q.v.) were officially recognized as a confederated part of the Kiowa and the Comanche. Article 2 of the treaty set forth the boundaries of the reservation, henceforth known as the Kiowa-Comanche reservation, lying west from the ninety-eighth meridian, between the Washita on the north and the Red River and its North Fork on the south.

Immediately after the massacre of Chief Black Kettle's Cheyenne (q.v.) band in the Battle of the Washita in November, 1868, the Kiowa were forced to go to their reservation in the vicinity of Fort Sill, where they acquired the reputation of being the most defiant of the Plains tribes. Satanta, uncompromisingly embittered and dis-

MURIEL H. WRIGHT

Kicking Bird in 1874

trustful after his arrest and imprisonment by Colonel Custer following the fight with the Cheyenne, was a leader in the revolt against any authority on the reservation.

Despite all efforts to control them, the Kiowa continued crossing Red River to carry out raids in Texas, destroying property, driving away horses and mules, killing whites, and carrying off captives. After a bloody raid in 1871, Satanta, Satank, and Big Tree were arrested by military order and sent to Texas for trial and punishment; Satank resisted and was killed on the road shortly after leaving Fort Sill. Then the Kiowa importuned government authorities for the release of Satanta and Big Tree, who were finally allowed to return to the reservation in 1873. Suspected of hostile influence, if not actual participation, with the Comanche, Kiowa, and Cheyenne in the fight at Adobe Walls, Texas, in 1874, Satanta was rearrested and taken back to

MURIEL H. WRIGHT

Big Tree about 1871

MURIEL H. WRIGHT

Lone Wolf in 1878

prison in Texas, where he committed sui-
cide four years later. Bands of the Kiowa
were also involved in a number of outbreaks on the reservation, including the
attack on the Wichita Agency at Anadarko
in 1874, the beginning of a cleavage with
the Wichita which is only now being
mended.

Following the surrender of the hostile
Comanche at Fort Sill and the Cheyenne
on their reservation near Darlington in the
spring of 1875, seventy Indians who had
had a part in the recent outbreaks (Comanche, Kiowa, Cheyenne, and Arapaho)
were taken into custody by military authorities to be sent as prisoners of war to
Florida. Selection of the twenty-six Kiowa
was attended by tragedy in the mysterious
death of the Kiowa chief, Kicking Bird,
supposedly from poisoning by an enemy
tribesman. Respected for his fine character,
Kicking Bird had been appointed by government officials for the difficult task of
naming the Kiowa who were to be taken to
Florida. During their three-year stay there,

a number of the prisoners died of tuberculosis or other diseases. Some of the younger
men were eventually sent to Carlisle Indian School in Pennsylvania, and the old
men were allowed to return to the reservation in 1878. Among the latter was Chief
Lone Wolf, who had lost his only son and
a favorite nephew during the Indian wars
in Texas.

The first Kiowa-Comanche agent from
the Indian Office was a Quaker, Lawrie
Tatum, who began his duties with a staff
of Quaker assistants at the Kiowa-Comanche Agency at Fort Sill in 1869. The first
teacher of the Kiowa was Thomas C.
Battey, also a Quaker, who won the confidence of and had influence with Kicking
Bird and his associates, and who began his
school in 1873. Missionary work on the
reservation was begun by the Episcopal
church about 1881, other denominations
entering the field in 1887—Methodist,
Presbyterian, Baptist, and Catholic. In
1879, the Kiowa-Comanche Agency was
moved from Fort Sill and consolidated
with the Wichita Agency at Anadarko. In
1888, the Indian agency promoted the organization of an Indian court to have
charge of Indian offenses on the reservation,
with Chief Lone Wolf (II) of the Kiowa
appointed one of the three judges (*see*
Comanche).

The Kiowa calendar records important
happenings on the reservation: In 1877, an
epidemic of measles and fever caused many
deaths; ten houses built under government
auspices, the first on the reservation, had
been completed and one each assigned to
two Kiowa chiefs. The people, however,
generally preferred to live in the old-time
tipi and did so for many years. The year
1879 saw the disappearance of the buffalo,
a great tragedy for the Kiowa, who were
reduced to killing their ponies for meat
to keep from starving. In 1890–91, the
craze of the "Ghost Dance" religion spread
among the Kiowa, raising hope for re-
newal as a tribe. A'piatan, a nephew of
the old Chief Lone Wolf, sent by tribal

leaders to investigate the truth of the reports about it from the northern tribes, returned to brand as false accounts of the coming of an Indian messiah to lead the tribes.

An agreement made with the "Cherokee" or "Jerome" Commission, signed by 456 adult male Kiowa, Comanche, and Kiowa-Apache on September 28, 1892, cleared the way for the opening of the country to white settlement. The agreement—providing for an allotment of 160 acres to every individual in the tribes and for the sale of the reservation lands 2,488,-893 acres) to the United States—was to go into effect immediately upon ratification by Congress, even though the Medicine Lodge treaty of 1867 had guaranteed Indian possession of the reservation until 1898. When the Indian signers of the agreement were apprised of this fact, they demanded that their names be stricken from the document, thus repudiating its provisions as misrepresentation by government officials to the tribal council. Furthermore, a delegation representing the three tribes, with A'piatan as the leader, journeyed to Washington in the spring of 1894 to protest the agreement. As a result, it was not ratified by Congress until June 6, 1900. Chief Lone Wolf immediately filed proceedings against the act in the Supreme Court, but the Court decided against him on June 26, 1901. The President issued a proclamation on July 4, 1901, for opening the Kiowa-Comanche-Apache reservation on the following August 6.

A total of 443,338 acres of land had been allotted to 2,759 tribal members, and 2,033,583 acres (purchased by the United States for $2,000,000) were opened to white settlement. Pasture lands totaling 480,000 acres of the original reservation, reserved for the use of the Indians under the agreement of 1892, were also finally opened on September 19, 1906, to the highest bidders among the white people. The former Kiowa-Comanche reservation lands are now included in Tillman, Cotton, Comanche, Stephens, and Jefferson counties, and parts of Caddo and Grady counties (west of the ninety-eighth meridian).

The transition from the old tribal customs to reservation life and the white man's civilization was attended by suffering and difficulty for the Kiowa. Yet they proved their talents and ability as a virile people in accepting much that was offered in the way of education. In 1906 there were three reservation boarding schools—Riverside, near Anadarko (in operation in 1950); Rainy Mountain, southeast of Gotebo; and Kiowa, near Fort Sill (in operation in 1950); and four mission schools—St. Pat-

MURIEL H. WRIGHT

Gotebo, Kiowa subchief, about 1898

rick's, near Anadarko (Roman Catholic, in operation in 1950); Methvin, at Anadarko (Methodist); Mary Gregory Memorial, east of Anadarko (Presbyterian, established by Rev. S. V. Fait); and Cache Creek, twenty miles from Anadarko (Dutch Reformed). The Kiowa Hospital, one of the first hospitals in the Indian Service in Oklahoma (established about 1917) has accomplished much in promoting

Kiowa mother and child, 1946

health in the Anadarko Agency jurisdiction.

◆ **Government and Organization.** Official recognition by the United States of confederated Kiowa, Kiowa-Apache, and Comanche at the time of the Medicine Lodge treaty in 1867 practically ended the power and prestige of the three tribes as separate governments. The Kiowa continued a nominal tribal organization (formerly consisting of a head chief, the chiefs of several bands, and the war chiefs) that amounted to a despotism. While various factions struggled to control the position of head chief after the death of Dohasan, nevertheless the solidarity of the Kiowa in their social and religious life has gained for them acknowledgment as a people even to modern times. Lone Wolf (II), better known as Delos K. Lone Wolf, was officially recognized as chief for many years from the fact that he bore the name of his foster father, Chief Lone Wolf, who died in 1879, although A'piatan, called Ahpeahtone ("Wooden Lance"), who died on August 8, 1931, had been chosen by his people as the last chief of the Kiowa and was highly respected by both the Indians and the whites for his ability, integrity, and quiet dignity.

Five Kiowa are among the twelve members of the Kiowa-Comanche-Apache Intertribal Business Committee, whose recommendations influence the Indian Office in its decisions on matters relating to these tribes. Under its constitution, this committee holds monthly meetings at the Anadarko Area Office. Members are elected every four years, the Kiowa generally holding their elections at Carnegie. Among the Kiowa who have served on the committee are Robert Goombi, Louis Toyebo, Guy Queotone, Gus Bosin, Frank Kauahquo, Jasper Saunkeah, and Scott Tonemah.

◆ **Contemporary Life and Culture.** Approximately one-half of the Kiowa are full-blood members of the tribe. Before allotment of lands in severalty, one-fourth of the tribe were mixed Kiowa descendants of captives taken in war—Mexicans, Mexican Indians, Indians from other tribes, and some whites from Texas. The mixed-blood Kiowa today include fullblood Indians from intermarriage with members of other tribes from the reservations in southwestern Oklahoma.

Five artists—Stephen Mopope, Monroe Tsatoke, James Auchiah, Jack Hokeah, and Spencer Asah—have made the name of the Kiowa famous both in America and abroad. In 1927 the five young men became protégés of the Art Department of the University of Oklahoma and soon were the leaders in a revival of Indian art in this country. Other Kiowa artists have received recognition in recent years, notable among them Lois Smokey and Woody Big Bow.

Most of the Kiowa are Christians, the Methodist and the Baptist churches claiming the largest membership. In their tribal religion, the Kiowa deified the powers of nature, with the sun as their greatest god. The last Kiowa Sun Dance, a folk drama without the tortures and savage rites practiced by some other tribes, was held in the summer of 1891.

◆ **Ceremonials and Public Dances.** Colorful Kiowa ceremonials and dances no longer have a vital place in the life of the people, except for recreation and training

U. S. INDIAN SERVICE

Private Amos Toahty, Company B, 179th Infantry, Oklahoma National Guard, in Third Army maneuvers in Louisiana during World War II

for public exhibitions. In the annual American Indian Exposition held at Anadarko, the Kiowa take an important and leading part, large groups of them presenting various traditional dances of the tribe. Many of the directors of the Exposition have been drawn from their numbers, and they are exceedingly interested in promoting the festival.

Suggested Readings: Grant Foreman, *History of Oklahoma;* Marriott, *The Ten Grandmothers;* Mooney, "Calendar History of the Kiowa," *17 Ann. Rep.,* Bur. Amer. Ethnol.; Nye, *Carbine and Lance;* Rister, *Border Command.*

KIOWA-APACHE

The Kiowa-Apache are also called the Prairie Apache. The name Apache was applied to them many years ago through the error of thinking, says Hodge, that they were the same as the Apache peoples of Arizona. They are of the Athapascan linguistic family, but never had any political connection with the Apache tribes of the Southwest, for they came from the north as a component part of the Kiowa, he adds. However, more recent authorities believe that the Apache divided, probably somewhere in Montana, the main body going southward on the west side of the mountains and the smaller body going northward with the Kiowa on the east side of the mountains. Whichever theory of their origin is correct, the Kiowa-Apache have a distinct language and call themselves *Nadi'ish-dena,* "our people." The Pawnee and the early French explorers and settlers called them *Ga'ta'ka,* the form *Kataka* appearing as their name in the first treaty they signed with the United States. In tribal days, their customs and characteristics were like those of the Kiowa, though they were reported to be much more agreeable and reliable than their companions.

◆ **Present Location.** The Kiowa-Apache live in the vicinity of Fort Cobb and Apache, in Caddo County.

◆ **Numbers.** Approximately 400 of the Kiowa-Apache live in Oklahoma. The Indian Office census reported only 194 in 1924, probably including only those directly connected with the Anadarko Agency. Official reports give their numbers in preceding years at 208 in 1896; 349 in 1889; 344 in 1875; and 378 in 1871. The Lewis and Clark report made in 1805 included the first estimate of the population of tribe recorded—300.

◆ **History.** According to their traditional history, the Kiowa-Apache were associated with the Kiowa proper before the latter left the Rocky Mountains. In 1682, La Salle, referring to them as the "Gattacka," said that they had horses, which they sold to the Pawnee who lived on a western tributary of the Mississippi River northeast of them. Following his visit to Oklahoma in 1719, La Harpe mentioned the tribe as the "Quataquois" living on the Arkansas River as neighbors of the Tawakoni (q.v.). Lewis and Clark in their 1805 account reported the "Catacka" living between the forks of the Cheyenne River in the Black Hills region of northeastern Wyoming. In 1837, the Kiowa-Apache signed their first treaty with the United States, under the name Kataka, at Fort Gibson. Since that time, they have been identified with the Kiowa and the two tribes for the most part have had a common history (*see* Kiowa).

In 1865, at their own request, the Kiowa-Apache were officially attached to the Cheyenne as a result of the treaty of the Little Arkansas, but were reunited with the Kiowa two years later by the treaty of the Medicine Lodge. Their principal chief, Pacer, was friendly to the white people and used his influence to promote peace among the tribes on the Kiowa-Comanche reservation until his death in 1875. The year before, A. J. Standing, a Quaker (or Friend) schoolteacher, had established the first school among the Kiowa-Apache at their request.

The group had settled peaceably on the reservation and were highly commended by the authorities for their industry and their efforts to make their own living. In 1894, Apache John (*Goñkoñ*, "Stays-in-tipi"), a conscientious leader, represented them in the delegation to Washington with A'piatan in protesting the agreement of 1892. Most of the Kiowa-Apache were living in the vicinity of present Apache, in Caddo County, under the leadership of their chief Tsáyădítl-ti, or "White Man," just before allotment in severalty and the opening of the reservation lands to white settlement in 1901.

◆ **Government and Organization.** The Kiowa-Apache have two members on the twelve-member Kiowa-Comanche-Apache Business Committee. Fort Cobb is usually the scene of the four-year elections of the Kiowa-Apache members of the committee. Kiowa-Apache who have served include Tennyson Berry of Fort Cobb and Alfred Chalpeah of Apache. Tennyson Berry has also been prominent in assisting in directing the historical pageant which is an important part of the annual American Indian Exposition at Anadarko.

Suggested Readings: Hodge, *Handbook of American Indians;* Mooney, "Calendar History of the Kiowa," *17 Ann. Rep., Bur. Amer. Ethnol.;* Nye, *Carbine and Lance.*

KOASATI

The name of the Koasati tribe is spelled in a number of different ways in historical records. In Oklahoma today the corrupt spelling "Quassarte" is employed by the Indian Office, adapted from the form used in the Creek Nation, of which the Koasati have been a part since their removal west in 1836. An early ethnological study of the Koasati suggested that the name may signify "white cane," from the Choctaw words *kanshak,* a species of hard cane, and *hata,* "white." Knives made from this cane were called "kanshak" and were widely used by the southeastern tribes of the Gulf Coast region. Early French writers also referred to the Muskoke or Creek proper as "Kanshak."

The Koasati are of the Muskhogean linguistic family and are closely related to the Alabama (q.v.), with whom they are now associated in Oklahoma. The Koasati language is almost identical with the Alabama, but nearer the Chickasaw and the Choctaw than the Creek. Although they were not Maskoke, or Creek proper, the Koasati (Coo-sau-dee) living in the compact town on the right bank of the Alabama River, three miles below the junction of the Coosa and Tallapoosa, in the latter part of the eighteenth century belonged to the Creek Confederacy and took part in the Creek tribal ceremonies.

Early writers reported the Koasati to be an industrious people. They grew large crops of corn in fenced fields, both men and women sharing in the labor. The men were fine hunters, bringing in quantities of deerskins and bear oil for sale to traders. They were wise in the ways of the river and many of them were said to be good oarsmen. In their later tribal history in Oklahoma, they were known for their baskets made from dogwood.

◊ **Present Location.** Most of the Koasati in Oklahoma live southeast of Weleetka, in rural communities in southeastern Okfuskee County and northeastern Hughes County. A large group of the tribe live in Allen and Jefferson parishes, Louisiana; and another part are on the Alabama-Coushatti reservation in Polk County, Texas (*see* Alabama).

◊ **Numbers.** There are an estimated 150 Koasati in Oklahoma. In 1944, the Indian Office reported the population of "Alabama Quassarte Tribal Town," recently organized under the Oklahoma Indian Welfare Act (*see* Alabama), at 152, of which a possible 50 were from the remnant Koasati in the state. A census of the tribal towns in the Creek Nation, Indian Territory, made by the Creek officials in 1890, gave a total population of 127 in the two Koasati towns—Quassadi No. 1 and Quassadi No. 2. The total Indian population in Allen and Jefferson parishes, Louisiana, the greater portion of whom were Koasati, numbered 274 in the census figures for 1930. The Indian Office in 1944 reported a total Indian population of 368 on the reservation in Polk County, Texas, of which approximately 120 were Koasati. According to an enumeration made in 1792, before a large portion of the tribe emigrated to Louisiana, there were approximately 650 Koasati living in the Creek country east of the Mississippi.

◊ **History.** De Soto visited the Koasati in 1541, when they were living on an island, probably Pine Island, in the Tennessee River, which was later sometimes referred to as the "River of the Cussatees." By 1684, a part of the tribe had settled west of the forks of the Coosa and Tallapoosa rivers. Within another hundred years, two large villages of the Koasati had settled in this same region and greatly strengthened the Creek Confederacy. The van of voluntary tribal emigration westward included a large portion of the Koasati who settled on Red River in Louisiana between 1793 and 1795. Part of these people subsequently moved west to the Sabine, Neches, and Trinity rivers in Texas, and within recent years their descendants have joined the Alabama in Polk County.

Those of the Koasati who remained among the Creek came with the main body of this nation to the Indian Territory in 1836 and thereafter were counted as a part of the Creek Nation, West. By 1900, they abandoned their two original towns, Quassadi No. 1, a few miles west of present Eufaula, and Quassadi No. 2, near old Hilabi in McIntosh County, and were al-lotted lands in severalty in a number of localities reaching as far west as Hughes County. Their more recent history has been in association with the Alabama (q. v.). Most of the Koasati in Oklahoma and Texas are members of the Baptist church.

Suggested Readings: Hodge, *Handbook of American Indians;* Swanton, *Early History of the Creek;* ———, *Indians of South-eastern U. S.;* ———, "Social Organiza-tion, Creek," *42 Ann. Rep.* Bur. Amer. Ethnol.

LIPAN

The Lipan call themselves *Tcicihi,* "people of the forest." Their common name *Lipan* is an adaptation of *Ipandes,* from the Apache term *n'de* for "people," *Ipa,* a per-sonal name, probably of some early tribal chief.

The Lipan belong to the Athapascan lin-guistic family. They were originally an off-shoot of the Jicarilla Apache, though they were enemies of the Jicarilla in the historic period and have been identified with the Mescalero Apache in New Mexico in re-cent reservation days. The Lipan lived farthest east of the Apache (q.v.) sub-tribes on the plains of Texas and in western Oklahoma, but were pushed from this early home south to the Gulf of Mexico and southwest to Old Mexico by the Coman-che and other enemies. During a period of nearly three hundred years they developed as a separate tribe and were generally listed as such in Texas and other areas of the Southwest.

Naturally industrious and clannish, the Lipan became notorious for their raiding expeditions for supplies and livestock dur-ing their long struggle for existence against their enemies in Texas. Records show, how-ever, that the Lipan were usually on hand and ready for any council to promote peaceful settlement.

◊ **Present Location.** The Lipan are num-bered among the Kiowa-Apache (q.v.) now under the Kiowa-Comanche-Apache Agen-cy of the Anadarko Area Office. There are some among the Tonkawa (q.v.) in the vicinity of the town of Tonkawa in Kay County, under the jurisdiction of the Paw-nee subagency at Pawnee, Oklahoma.

◊ **Numbers.** An estimated 30 Lipan live in Oklahoma. In 1905, out of an estimated total of 35 members of the tribe living in the United States, 10 were reported in Oklahoma and 25 on the Mescalero reser-vation in New Mexico. In 1872, a total of 315 Lipan were on the reservation in New Mexico. In 1880, there were 17 Lipan among the Tonkawa (q.v.) at Fort Griffin, Texas. These few Texas Lipan were counted as a part of the Tonkawa after their removal to the Indian Territory in 1885. The ranks of the 900 Lipan reported living in Texas in 1836 were greatly dim-inished during the wars to exterminate the Indians in Texas during the early eighteen fifties, and many moved into Coahuila, Mexico. One hundred years before this, they were reported one of the strongest tribes in the Southwest, able to muster 2,-000 fighting men, which indicates a pos-sible population of 8,000 at that time.

◊ **History.** Lipan legendary history places the origin of the tribe in the north and west. About the year 1600 they seem to have separated from the Jicarillo Apache of the Arizona–New Mexico region and gradually migrated eastward to the plains of Texas and on into Oklahoma. Before 1700 the Lipan were fighting the Comanche from the northwest, beginning a long period of hostility between the two tribes.

The French commandant, La Harpe, reporting on his expedition to visit the Tawakoni (q.v.) on the Arkansas River in 1719, left one of the earliest records about the Lipan in Oklahoma. The French called this tribe the *Cancy,* the French form of the Caddo name, *Kantsi,* for the Apache. En route through eastern Oklahoma, La Harpe passed a Cancy or Lipan encampment in the vicinity of present Wilburton in Latimer County.

The friendship between the Spanish government in Mexico and the Apache sub-tribes was broken in 1736. The Lipan, however, continued aid to the Spanish forces from time to time against enemy tribes, including hostile bands of the Mescalero Apache. The hope of the Lipan in the Roman Catholic mission of San Saba near the present town of Menard, Menard County, Texas, was short lived with the destruction of the mission in 1758 by the Comanche (q.v.), one year after its founding.

A treaty negotiated in 1787 by Spanish officials provided for the settlement of the Apache sub-tribes near Santa Rosa on the Sabinas River in Old Mexico. The governor of Coahuila, Juan de Ugalde, soon appointed Picax-Ande, the great chief of the Lipan (sometimes loosely called *Llaneros*), head chief of the tribes near Santa Rosa, his commission from the Spanish government being granted on March 6, 1788. Noted for his soldierly bearing, character, and truthfulness, as well as his great prestige among the Apache sub-tribes, Picax-Ande made this classic remark upon meeting Governor Ugalde in council: "There are only three great chieftains, the Great One above, you, and I. The first one is looking down upon us and listening to

what we say so that we shall see who is lacking in truth."

The Lipan were represented among the ten tribes who signed their first treaty with the United States on May 15, 1846, at Council Springs on the Brazos River, Commissioners Pierce M. Butler and M. G. Lewis representing the federal government. When the Indians of the Brazos Reserve (*see* Anadarko *and* Caddo) were brought to the Washita River in 1859, some of the Lipan also sought refuge in the Indian Territory. When commissioners for the Confederate States held a great council with the Plains tribes and others at Camp Napoleon, near present Verden in Grady County, in May, 1865, Chief Woodercarnervesta, as delegate for his people the Lipan, signed the Camp Napoleon Compact, which had for its motto, "An Indian shall not spill an Indian's blood." It was part of this band of Lipan who later merged with the Kiowa-Apache near Fort Sill in 1895.

Reports from Captain J. B. Irvine, acting Indian agent at Fort Griffin, Texas, in 1879–80, stated that the 17 Lipan among the destitute Tonkawa at that place were industrious and provident and wanted land of their own. Under a special appropriation made by Congress in 1884, these Lipan came with the Tonkawa to the Indian Territory in June, 1885, and were settled on the former Nez Percé reservation under the jurisdiction of the Indian agency at Oakland, near present Tonkawa (*see* Tonkawa). While for some time it was thought that the Tonkawa and the Lipan were on the way to extinction, yet reports within recent years show them on the increase.

Suggested Readings: Hodge, *Handbook of American Indians;* Lewis, "La Harpe's First Expedition in Oklahoma," *Chron. of Okla.,* Vol. II, No. 4; Nelson, "Juan de Ugalde and Picax-Ande Ins-Tinsle," *Southwestern Hist. Soc. Quart.* Vol. XLIII, No. 4; Opler, *Myths and Legends, Lipan;* Reeve, "The Apache in Texas," *Southwestern Hist. Soc. Quart.,* Vol. L, No. 2.

MIAMI

The name Miami is from the Chippewa term *Omaumeg,* "people who live on the peninsula." The Miami call themselves in their own language *Twaⁿh twaⁿh,* "the cry of the crane," from which was adapted the name "Twightwees" used by early English writers in referring to this tribe of the Algonquian linguistic family. They were discovered by the Jesuits about the middle of the seventeenth century in the general region of Green Bay, Wisconsin.

The Miami men were described in early times as swift runners fond of racing. They were well built, medium in height, of the round-head type, and had agreeable countenances. The French explorers reported them notable for their polite manners and their ready response and obedience to their chiefs. Unlike most tribes of the Great Lakes region, the Miami traveled by land rather than in canoes.

◆ **Present Location.** The Miami tribe live in Ottawa County as a part of the Confederated Peoria (q.v.), the town of Miami perpetuating the name of the tribe.

◆ **Numbers.** Approximately 320 Miami are connected with the Quapaw Subagency in Oklahoma. The Indian Office census for 1944 gives 307 members of the tribe, of whom 143 were living in Ottawa County and 164 elsewhere in the state. There were 124 members of the tribe living in the Indian Territory in 1905. In 1900, there were also 243 Miami in Indiana, who were mostly mixed-blood white and Indian, some of whose descendants may still be found in that state. In 1885, only 57 Miami were officially listed at the Quapaw Agency, Indian Territory. A total of 1,100 Miami moved from Indiana to Kansas in 1846–47, although nearly half returned to Indiana the following year. The ranks of those who remained were decimated by disease and dissipation, leaving only about 300 in Kansas within a short time. Earlier estimates of their numbers

indicate that the Miami probably never exceeded 1,500.

◆ **History.** By 1700 the Miami were migrating from their original home to northeastern Illinois, northern Indiana, and western Ohio, where three rivers have been named for them. They had a prominent part in the Indian wars in the Ohio Valley, and in their early relations with the United States were considered the owners of the Wabash River region in Indiana and of a large part of western Ohio.

Their first treaty with the government, the treaty of Greenville made by General Anthony Wayne in 1795, was signed by the chiefs of four Miami bands, including the "Eel River Tribe" whose reservation in Boone County, Indiana, was sold to the United States in 1828, at which time members of this band joined the rest of the Miami and thereafter shared their fortunes.

By the terms of a treaty in 1840, the Miami ceded the last of their tribal lands in Indiana to the United States and agreed to move within five years to a reservation assigned them in the West. This was a 500,000-acre tract of the finest lands in Kansas, a part of which is now included in Miami County. Disease and epidemics were suffered by the tribal members upon their arrival in Kansas in 1846–47; furthermore, the rich annuities paid them by the government for their eastern lands largely in the form of cash, and their fine lands made them a prey for unprincipled white people. Finally these conditions broke up the tribe. The 300 Miami left in Kansas in 1848 established their village on the east bank of the Marais des Cygnes River, in the southern part of present Miami County. Both the Roman Catholic and the Baptist churches established missions near this village.

The organization of Kansas Territory in 1854, with the demand for opening the rich lands of the reservation to white settlement, saw a treaty concluded at Washington between George W. Manypenny, the United States commissioner, and delegates of the Miami, providing for allotment of lands in severalty (200 acres each) to the tribal members living on the Kansas reservation, a reserved tract of 70,000 acres to be held in common by the tribe and the surplus lands to be sold to the United States.

By the terms of their last treaty, on February 23, 1867, those Miami who wished to become citizens of Kansas were to remain there; the rest were to move to the Indian Territory to be confederated with the Peoria, Kaskaskia, Wea, and Piankashaw. This arrangement was delayed by the slowness of the Indian Office in carrying out the terms of the treaties. Finally 72 of these long-suffering Indians were settled in the Indian Territory, where they were henceforth known as the "United Peorias and Miamis," by provisions of a Congressional act of March 3, 1873. The history of the Miami in the Indian Territory since that time has been that of the Peoria (q.v.).

Suggested Readings: Connelly, *History of Kansas;* Grant Foreman, "Illinois and Her Indians," in *Papers in Illinois History,* 1939; Hodge, *Handbook of American Indians;* Wilson, *Quapaw Agency Indians.*

MICHIGAMEA

The name Michigamea, from which that of Lake Michigan is derived, is said to be properly *Mishigamaw,* "the great water" or "big lake," from the Algonquian words *michi,* "great," and *guma,* "water."

The Michigamea, formerly one of the tribes of the Illinois Confederacy, are of the Algonquian linguistic family. In the historic period, their original home was near the headwaters of the Sangamon River in Illinois. They were an agricultural people, skilled in the use of the bow, and used the lance and the club in war. The crane was their totem.

◆ **Present Location.** Descendants of the Michigamea may be found among the mixed-blood Indians of the confederated Peoria in Ottawa County, Oklahoma.

◆ **Numbers.** No separate census of Michigamea was ever made by the Office of Indian Affairs. In 1736, they were counted as the largest tribe of the Illinois Confederacy (*see* Illinois). In 1803 it was supposed that there was only one man living of the Michigamea, an erroneous report since a delegation of three Michigamea in 1818 signed the United States treaty with the Peoria and Kaskaskia in behalf of their tribe.

◆ **History.** Under pressure of enemies from the north, including the Sioux, the Michigamea migrated at an early date from Illinois to a large lake in what is now northeastern Arkansas, where they were found by Marquette in 1673. About 1700 they were driven from this region by their enemies, among whom were the Chickasaw, and returned to Illinois. They soon joined the Kaskaskia (q.v.) with whom they were afterward identified in their history.

Suggested Readings: Grant Foreman, "Illinois and Her Indians," in *Papers in Illinois History,* 1939; ———, *Last Trek of the Indians;* Hodge, *Handbook of American Indians;* Swanton, *Indians of Southeastern U. S.*

MODOC

In their own language, the Modoc call themselves *Maḳlaḳs,* "people." The name Modoc is from *Moadokkni* (or Moatokni), "southerners," their kindred tribe, the Klamath, referring to them as *Moadok Maḳlaḳs,* "people of the south."

The Modoc and Klamath are classed as the two branches of the Lutuamian linguistic family, whose original home was in the Klamath Lake and the Tule Lake regions of south central Oregon and northern California. The two tribes have the same language, usually referred to as Klamath, with slight dialectic differences in speech.

The fullblood Modoc were described as superior fighting men in tribal days. They were slow to action, but remarkable for their independence and perseverance. Wherever they have been allowed to remain undisturbed on the land, they have been peaceable, temperate, and industrious.

◆ **Present Location.** The Modoc in Oklahoma are living in Ottawa County, having been allotted lands in the Eastern Shawnee reservation (*see* Shawnee). Most of the tribe, however, live on the Klamath reservation in Oregon.

◆ **Numbers.** About 50 Modoc are living in Oklahoma. According to a separate listing of the tribe by the Quapaw Agency, there were 40 in the state in 1923. The Modoc have always been a small tribe, their numbers estimated at about one-half that of the Klamath during the historic period. The combined population of the two tribes at discovery has been estimated at 2,000. In 1861, there were 310 Modoc reported on the Klamath reservation in California. In 1864 the number of Modoc attending the treaty negotiations at Fort Klamath. Oregon, was 339. In the next year, their total number in California and Oregon was 700.

At the end of the Modoc War, the tribe was divided. Those who had had a part in the conflict were brought to the Indian Territory, 153 arriving at the Quapaw Agency in November, 1873; the rest, numbering about 100, remained on the Klamath reservation in Oregon, where they finally settled and increased. In 1890, there were 84 reported in the Indian Territory and 151 on the Klamath Reservation; in 1905, 223 on the Klamath Reservation and 56 in the Indian Territory. The official census of the Indian Office in 1944 listed 334 Modoc living on the Klamath Reservation in Oregon.

◆ **History.** Modoc were first noticed in the latter part of the eighteenth century by Spanish missionaries of the Roman Catholic church in California. The introduction of the horse among the Indian tribes of the Pacific Northwest in the early eighteen thirties resulted in changes in tribal life, and within twenty years the Klamath and the Modoc established trading relations with inhabitants of the Pacific Coast region to the northwest and came into closer contact with the tribes to the north and the east from the region of the Plains.

The Klamath reservation in northwestern California along the Klamath River was first opened in 1855. Then, by the terms of a treaty signed by the Modoc and the Klamath on October 14, 1854, at Fort Klamath, Oregon, this tract was given up and another of 1,056,000 acres in southern Oregon was set aside as the permanent Klamath reservation. Under this treaty, the two tribes ceded to the United States the country east of the Cascade Mountains in northeastern California, the Modoc agreeing to move to the new Klamath reservation in Oregon. But the United States agent refused to protect the Modoc from the Klamath, who, greatly outnumbering them, were hostile and interfered with their peaceable settlement on the reservation.

Restless and discontented, a band of

Modoc led by their chief, Kintpuash, called "Captain Jack," set out in 1870 for his home country on the Lost River, where they remained, demanding that a separate reservation be assigned the tribe. Attempts to return them to the Klamath reservation brought on the Modoc War of 1872–73, during which Captain Jack and about eighty warriors, with their families, retreated to the rocks and caves in the impenetrable lava beds south of Tule Lake.

Fighting at first was desultory, but after the killing in April, 1873, of General E. R. S. Canby and another of the commissioners who had come to discuss peace terms with Captain Jack and his band, pursuit of the Modoc was stepped up. A full-scale military campaign was launched against them by seasoned, well-equipped troops, at one time numbering 1,000 regulars, 78 Indian scouts, and a company of Oregon volunteers. The knowledge that annihilation was certain if resistance was

Yellowhammer (Modoc) about 1890

continued, coupled with the desertion of some of his own men, finally compelled the surrender of Captain Jack. He and three other warriors were condemned in a court-martial at Fort Klamath for the murder of the commissioners, for which crime they were hanged on October 3, 1873.

The remainder of the band set out on October 24, under military escort, by train to Fort McPherson, Nebraska, whence they were taken to the Quapaw Agency in the Indian Territory. During the journey, members of the band were praised for their good behavior and willing co-operation with the authorities. On June 23, 1874, the government purchased a tract of land two and one-half miles square (4,040 acres) in the northeastern corner of the Eastern Shawnee reservation for the permanent settlement of the Modoc (*see* Shawnee).

The Quapaw Agency in Indian Territory reported the Modoc, almost without exception through the years, to be loyal, peaceable, and industrious, generally living on the products of their own farm labor, although members of the tribe never ceased to long for their old homes in the Northwest.

Many were active members of the mission church of the Society of Friends. Frank Modoc (also called "Steamboat Frank"), one of the warriors, was the first fullblood American Indian ever recorded as a minister of the Society of Friends, his ministry being acknowledged by the Spring River quarterly meeting of ministry and oversight and his appointment made by the Grand River monthly meeting on June 28, 1884.

In 1890 it was reported that every Modoc child of school age could read and write in English, and the children took great pride in attending the day school erected on the reservation near the Agency.

Allotment of lands in severalty on the Modoc reservation was begun before 1890, seventeen families living on and cultivating their own lands in that year. A total of 3,976 acres out of the surveyed 4,040 acres was finally allotted to sixty-eight Modoc before statehood, small plots being reserved for the timber and for church, cemetery, and school purposes.

An act of Congress, approved March 3, 1909, provided that the remnant of Captain Jack's band should be restored to the Modoc tribal rolls at the Klamath Agency, Oregon, and accorded all the rights and privileges of other Indians living there. Tribal members allotted lands in Oklahoma were granted the right to sell or lease (for a period not to exceed five years) their allotments and return to Oregon. The last one of the original Modoc warriors, Johnny Ball, left Oklahoma and returned to the Klamath Reservation in 1913. Among the Modoc who remained in Oklahoma, in 1948 Mrs. Cora P. Hayman, of Tulsa was the last full blood and the only survivor of the band brought to the Indian Territory. Her son, Claude Hayman, is an employee at Chilocco Indian School.

◆ **Government and Organization.** Government relations with the Modoc in Oklahoma were closed by 1924. During the agency period, each member of the tribe had been dealt with individually by the Quapaw agent. The band had only a nominal tribal organization in the Indian Territory, military authorities having appointed Charley Jackson, better known as "Scarface Charley," as chief of the band on the way from Oregon. He had been one of Captain Jack's leading warriors and was reputed to be the first who fired a shot in the Modoc War. He proved a good, thrifty man and was respected and loved by his followers. A Christian convert, he was a member of the Society of Friends.

◆ **Contemporary Life and Culture.** The Modoc who reside in Oklahoma are, of course, counted in the general Indian population as citizens of the state. There has been some admixture by intermarriage with white people and with members of other tribes in Ottawa County since allotment of lands in severalty. For many years after the Modoc War, there was little admixture with other races, and the tribe was slow in overcoming their retarded condition. Their friendly relations with other tribes in the Quapaw Agency jurisdiction and with the white people were always commendable. The old tribal culture, however, was practically nonexistent in the Indian Territory.

Suggested Readings: Curtin, *Myths of the Modoc;* Kroeber, *Handbook of Indians of California;* Meacham, *Wi-ne-ma and Her People;* Riddle, *Indian History of the Modoc War;* Spier, *Klamath Ethnography.*

MOINGWENA

The name Moingwena, sometimes given as Moins, was applied to this tribe by the French from the name of their tribal village Moingona (or Monin-guinas) which is said to be a corruption of the Algonquian word *mikouag,* signifying "at the road." The name apparently had reference to the well-known Indian trail or road leading from the head of the lower rapids to the village of Moingona at the mouth of the Des Moines River, in the vicinity of the present town of Montrose, Lee County, Iowa.

The Moingwena are of the Algonquian linguistic family. They were living on the west side of the Mississippi River near the Peoria, in the Des Moines River region, as reported by Marquette in 1673. Afterward the Moingwena lost their tribal identity and became a part of the Confederated Peoria (q.v.) whose descendants now live in Ottawa County, Oklahoma.

Suggested Readings: Gue, *History of Iowa;* Hodge, *Handbook of American Indians.*

MOHAWK

The name *Mohawk* is from the Narraganset term *Mohowauuck* which signifies "man-eaters." The Mohawk were a leading tribe, one of the "Three Elder Brothers," in the organization of the Six Nations or Iroquois Confederation in what is now New York. They were located farthest east of the Iroquoian linguistic family at the time of their discovery about 1600, living along the Hudson River westward up the valley of the Mohawk River and north to the St. Lawrence River. The introduction of firearms by the Dutch when they settled in the Hudson River Valley increased the power and strength of the Mohawk, who thereafter became notorious among both their Indian and their white neighbors for their insolence and warlike character.

◆ **Present Location.** Descendants of the Mohawk are located and counted among the Seneca (q.v.) in Ottawa County, Oklahoma. The largest groups of the Mohawk live in Ontario, Canada.

◆ **History.** With their power broken and their numbers decimated by the wars in the eighteenth century, the Mohawk sold the last of their tribal lands to the state of New York by treaty in 1797. A band of the tribe settled among the Seneca of Sandusky in Ohio, with whom they moved to the Indian Territory in 1832 (*see* Seneca). A report in 1837 gives 50 Mohawk living on the Seneca lands here in the territory, with Isaac White, principal chief, and George Heron, second chief. The majority could read the gospels in the Mohawk language. They held public services in their Episcopal church organization, in the vicinity of the Seneca Agency, reading the Book of Common Prayer, singing hymns, and carrying on religious exercises. They were an industrious people whose general condition was similar to that of the Seneca.

Suggested Reading: Hodge, *Handbook of American Indians.*

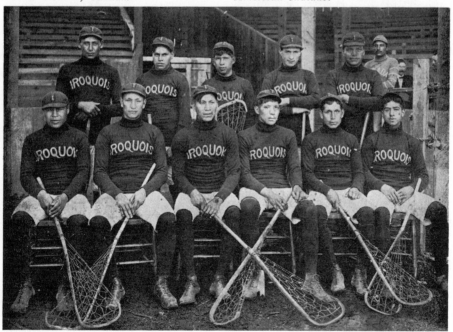

LAURENCE SNOW

Lacrosse team of New York Iroquois at Columbian Exposition, St. Louis, 1904

MUNSEE

Munsee is an adaptation of *Minsi,* the name of one of the three principal divisions of the Delaware (q.v.), from the tribal place-name *Min-asin-ink,* "at the place where stones are gathered together." During a period of over one hundred years when they were gradually migrating westward from their original home on the headwaters of the Delaware River in New York, Delaware, and Pennsylvania, this division of the Leni-lenape, or Delaware, became recognized as a separate tribe under the name Munsee, sometimes spelled "Muncie." They are of the Algonquian linguistic family.

◆ **Present Location.** Descendants of the Munsee are in the former Cherokee Nation, probably within the limits of Washington and Nowata counties.

◆ **Numbers.** No separate census has ever been made for the Munsee in Oklahoma. It is estimated that there are less than 100 living in the state. The largest group of Munsee live in Canada among the Chippewa (in 1906 enumeration of two Munsee bands showed 486).

◆ **History.** During the War of 1812, part of the Munsee went to Canada where they became affiliated with the Chippewa. Under terms of the treaty between the United States and the Menominee in 1832, a band of Munsee joined the Stockbridge (q.v.) in the purchase of a reservation tract on Winnebago Lake, Wisconsin. These confederated tribes were thereafter known under the name Munsee, in their later history referred to as "Christian Indians" from a band of Munsee that were identified with the Moravian missions since the early work of that church in Pennsylvania.

Under the terms of a treaty with the Stockbridge (q.v.) and the Munsee in 1839, a band of 169 of these confederated tribes out of a total of 342 emigrated to Kansas and located on the Delaware reservation. When objections arose to their remaining in this location, the "Munsee or Christian Indians" were confederated with the Chippewa (Swan Creek and Black River bands) on a small reservation assigned them (by treaty in 1859) in present Franklin County, Kansas. When Kansas wanted to rid its borders of all Indian reservations after the Civil War, these Munsee in 1867 entered into a compact with the Cherokee whereby they became citizens of the Cherokee Nation, and located near the Delaware in northern Indian Territory.

Suggested Readings: Grant Foreman, *Last Trek of the Indians;* Hodge, *Handbook of American Indians.*

NATCHEZ

The name *Natchez* is undoubtedly a mnemonic that has its origin in the Choctaw expression designating the people of this tribe as "warriors of the high bluff," from the Choctaw words *nakni,* "warrior," *sakti,* "bluff," and *chaha,* "high." It referred to the location of the tribe near the high bluff on the Mississippi River known as Natchez Bluff. The ending *ez* in the name was acquired through its pronunciation by the early French.

The Natchez are of the Muskhogean linguistic family, and were the largest tribe (nine villages with an estimated population of 6,000 in 1700) located directly on the lower Mississippi River. The tribe was almost annihilated in the bloody war that followed their massacre of the French settlers near Fort Rosalie at Natchez Bluff in 1729. Members of the tribe who managed to escape found refuge among the Chickasaw, Cherokee, and Creek.

There are a number of mixed-blood Natchez and Cherokee and Natchez and Creek in Oklahoma. Those within the limits of the former Cherokee Nation live some miles south of Fort Gibson, near Braggs, in Muskogee County. Some in the former Creek Nation live in the vicinity of Concharty Creek in Muskogee and Okmulgee counties.

Suggested Readings: Swanton, *Indian Tribes of the Lower Mississippi Valley;* ———, *Indians of Southeastern U. S.*

NEZ PERCÉ

The Nez Percé (the French name for the Sahaptini tribe) of the Shahaptian linguistic family were brought as prisoners of war with their famous leader, Chief Joseph, from their reservation in Oregon and Idaho, and settled on a reservation on the Chikaskia River in the Indian Territory in 1879. They were described as a most intelligent, religious, and industrious people. Because of their high death rate and unhappy condition in this southern climate and their constant plea to return to the Northwest, they were allowed to go to the Colville Reservation in Washington by an Act of Congress in 1885. Although the Nez Percé are no longer counted among the Oklahoma Indian tribes, it is said that some descendants by intermarriage with neighboring Indian families during the tribal sojourn in the Indian Territory are in the state. The Nez Percé reservation—a tract now included in Kay County—was assigned the Tonkawa (q.v.).

Suggested Readings: Clark, "The Nez Percés in Exile," *Pacific Northwest Quart.,* Vol. XXXVI, No. 3 (July, 1945); Grant Foreman, *Last Trek of the Indians;* Hodge, *Handbook of American Indians.*

OSAGE

The Osage are one of the five tribes in the Dhegiha group of the Siouan linguistic family (*see* Ponca). The name *Osage* is a French corruption of the tribal name *Wa-zha'zhe,* the derivation and meaning of which cannot now be conclusively determined. It may be analogous to the Omaha term *Wa-ba-zhi,* "one who carries a message," and probably had to do with some ancient ritual celebrating the return from a successful hunt for buffalo.

Among the old-time hunting tribes of the Great Plains, the Osage held high rank. Although they raised small crops of corn and squash near their permanent villages, located within what is now western Missouri, yet they depended largely upon the buffalo for food and clothing. When the buffalo disappeared from the Mississippi Valley after the coming of white traders, these Indians were forced to go west on hunting expeditions, thus coming into conflict with the tribes of the Plains, by whom they were greatly feared on account of their readiness for a fight, their prowess in battle, and their courage. The Osage generally set forth from their villages on foot, but returned well supplied with horses taken from their enemies as spoils of war. During the summer months, whole villages—men, women, and children—would resort to the plains of western Kansas and northern Oklahoma to hunt buffalo. Such expeditions afforded a season of pleasure, a visitor in a summer hunting camp in 1811 describing the scene as one of "mirth and merriment," for the Osage were living luxuriously on "fat buffalo meat, marrow bones, hominy, dried pumpkins, plums, and other dainties."

The tribal life of the Osage centered about their religious rites and ceremonials, which included a highly developed symbolism. Among themselves and their friends they have always been generous and hospitable, and they were known for their gentleness with children. Noticeably tall and well formed, they are dignified in their approach. They are reputed to have a haughty, sometimes arrogant air, arising from their importance in American Indian history from the earliest period of French and Spanish trading interests down to modern times when oil and gas discoveries on their tribal lands in Oklahoma brought them great wealth.

◆ **Present Location.** Most of the Osage live in Osage County, which was organized from their former reservation when Oklahoma was admitted to the Union as a state in 1907. Although some Osage families live elsewhere in the county or in the state, most of them have their homes in one of three special communities or "villages," each of which was originally settled by the members of one of three traditional groups within the tribal organization: "Dwellers-upon-the-Hilltop" at Gray Horse, "Dwellers-in-the-Upland-Forest" at Hominy, and "Dwellers-in-the-Thorny-Thicket" at Pawhuska.

◆ **Numbers.** The population of the Osage in Oklahoma, according to a census made by the Osage Agency at Pawhuska in 1950, is 4,972. There were 2,229 Osage on their reservation in 1906, this number comprising the completed tribal roll, or number of "head-rights," upon which all subsequent payments of tribal income or allotments of property have been based, the nearest of kin or descendants receiving proportional shares of a deceased allottee's head-right. Previously recorded enumerations or estimates of the Osage are 1,582 in 1886, 3,001 in 1877, 4,102 in 1843, and 5,000 in 1829. In 1804 the explorers Lewis and Clark reported that the Osage numbered

about 1,350 fighting men, which represented an approximate 6,500 total population for the tribe.

◆ **History.** Archaeologists believe that the Siouan peoples in prehistoric times migrated from the west to the Atlantic Coast. The Southern Siouan Division or Dhegiha group (Omaha, Ponca, Kansa, Osage, Quapaw, q.v.) occupied the Piedmont Plateau between the James and Savannah rivers in Virginia and the Carolinas for a long period, then began a westward migration, descending the Ohio River to its mouth, where they crossed the Mississippi River and eventually came to the Missouri River. In this region, the Southern Siouan Division or Dhegiha tribes separated, the Quapaw going downstream to the Arkansas River, the Osage remaining on the Osage River, and the Omaha, Ponca, and Kansa ascending the Missouri. The first recorded notice of the Osage was by Marquette in 1673, his map apparently showing their location on the Osage River. This is given as their principal location by subsequent writers until the removal of the tribe westward to their Kansas reservation between 1825 and 1836.

The tribe was geographically divided into two bands located on the Little Osage River in present Vernon County, Missouri: the Pahatsi or Great Osage living in a village near the mouth of the Marmaton River, and the Utsehta or Little Osage in a village about six miles west on the west side of the Little Osage River. These names had nothing to do with the physical appearance of the two bands, but had come from a legendary division of the tribe. Tribal life and ceremonials centered at these two villages for a long period, during which hunting and war expeditions set forth into the wide region now included in parts of Arkansas, Kansas, and Oklahoma. Visits of Spanish and French traders were common, even before 1719. In this year, the first official French visit was made among the Osage by Du Tisne; and La Harpe, on his first expedition to the

Oklahoma region to visit the Tawakoni
(q.v.) on the Arkansas, described meeting
some Osage war parties en route and related the terror they inspired among the
Caddoan tribes.

In the latter part of the eighteenth century, the Osage split into factions, difficulties arising from the trade rivalry in the
Missouri River region between Spanish
and French traders under the Spanish rule
of Louisiana. In this affair, the Chouteau
brothers, French traders of St. Louis who
had long identified their interests with the
Osage, persuaded a large part of the tribe
to locate permanently on the Arkansas
River in Oklahoma. This group became
known as the Santsukhdhi or Arkansas
Band, which comprised about half of the
Great Osage and some of the Little Osage,
generally young men and their families.
The move was made in 1802 under the
leadership of Cashesegra, "Big Track,"
who was in close alliance with the Chouteaus. Villages of the Arkansas Band were
located on the Arkansas near the mouth
of the Verdigris. Within sight of Claremore Mound near Sageeyah in Rogers
County, Oklahoma, was the village of
Clermont, the hereditary chief of the Osage,
whose name has been perpetuated by this
mound and the city of Claremore. In the
French trade rivalry, his right as chief had
been usurped by Pahuska, "White Hair,"
through the influence of the Chouteaus.
Clermont died in 1828 and was succeeded
by his son, also Clermont, whose portrait
was painted by George Catlin in 1834.

Before 1836, the government maintained
a subagency for the Osage at the Chouteau
trading post by the falls of the Verdigris
River, present site of Okay in Wagoner
County. Colonel Auguste P. Chouteau,
prominent in Indian affairs in Indian Territory, maintained a handsome residence
at the Grand Saline, a large salt spring near
present Salina, in Mayes County, where
his Osage wife and his children lived. A
number of other trading posts were established for the Osage trade at the "Three

Clermont (son of old Chief Clermont),
from the Catlin painting made in 1834,
now in the Smithsonian Institution

Forks," the region near the confluence of
the Verdigris and the Grand (or Neosho)
rivers with the Arkansas. One of the early
trading posts here was that of Nathaniel
Pryor, a Kentuckian who married an
Osage and for whom the town of Pryor,
in Mayes County, was named.

Union Mission, the first mission in Okla-
homa, was organized and established in
1820 among the Osage by the United For-
eign Missionary Society (Presbyterian–
Dutch Reformed). The first school in
Oklahoma was opened in 1821 at Union
Mission (about five miles northeast of
Maizie in Wagoner County), with four
French-Osage children as the first pupils.
Harmony Mission (near Papinsville, Bates
County, Missouri) was established at this
same time among the Osage of Missouri by
the American Board of Commissioners for
Foreign Missions. These early Protestant
missions were closed by 1834, and hence-

MURIEL H. WRIGHT

Bacon Rind

forth missionary efforts among the Osage
were carried on almost exclusively by the
Roman Catholic church.

For many years there was war between
the Osage and the Western Cherokee of
Arkansas, during which Chief Clermont's
village was wiped out by the enemy in the
Battle of Claremore Mound (1817). The
Osage were also generally at war with the
Kiowa and Comanche of the Southern
Plains, the hostilities coming to a climax
in the defeat and rout of the Kiowa in the
Battle of Cutthroat Gap in the Wichita
Mountain region in 1833. The return of
the Osage captives to their people and pro-

motion of peace on the Plains were the
main reasons for the famous Dragoon Expedition under the command of General
Henry Leavenworth and, later, Colonel
Henry Dodge, to the Wichita village in
southwestern Oklahoma in 1834 (*see*
Wichita). A year later, a delegation of
thirty-seven Osage, including the noted
leader Black Dog (Sho$^{n\prime}$-to^n-ça-be), along
with representative of eight other tribes of
the Indian Territory, signed the Camp
Holmes peace treaty sponsored by the
United States.

The Osage signed their first treaty with
the United States in 1808 at the recently
established Fort Clark (also known as Fort
Osage, present site of Sibley, Jackson County, Missouri), ceding to the federal government lands now comprising over half
the state of Missouri and northern Arkansas, including their old village locations on
the Little Osage River. After government
approval of this treaty some years later,
both the Great Osage and the Little Osage
moved west to the valley of the Neosho
River in Kansas. Pahuska, descendant of
the old Chief Pahuska in 1815 established
the Great Osage village near the present
town of Shaw, in Neosho County, while
the Little Osage made their settlements
just west of Chanute, in the same county.
Osage tribal life centered here for more
than half a century, these villages lying in
the eastern part of a reservation assigned
the Osage by treaty in 1825. This reservation tract in Kansas was fifty miles wide,
bordering present Oklahoma on the north
and extending west to the one-hundredth
meridian from a north-south line twenty-
five miles west of the Missouri state line.

When the Osage signed the treaty of
1825 at St. Louis, they had ceded all their
lands to the United States: all of Oklahoma north of the Arkansas and the Canadian rivers, northwestern Arkansas, western Missouri, and nearly half of Kansas.
When in 1828 the Western Cherokee (q.
v.) were given their country in northeastern and northern Oklahoma by the gov-

ernment, the Osage began leaving this region for their reservation to the north, all of the Arkansas Band having departed by 1836. From this time to 1872, the story of the Osage is a part of the history of Kansas. During this period the Osage Mission established by the Reverend Father John Schoenmakers, S. J., at the present site of St. Paul in Neosho County, Kansas, became the outstanding institution in the life of the tribe. It grew into one of the most influential Roman Catholic schools in the West and was attended by boys and girls from other tribes as well, including the Quapaw, Miami, and Cherokee.

After the outbreak of the Civil War, Commissioner Albert Pike secured a treaty in behalf of the Confederacy with the chiefs and leaders of the Great Osage Band in a council held at Park Hill in the Cherokee Nation, on October 2, 1861. Members of the Great Osage served in the Confederate Army, while the Little Osage furnished over four hundred men for the Second Indian Brigade of the Union Army, although provisions had been made in the Confederate treaty for the participation of the Little Osage. This cleavage caused great distress among the tribe, and the Osage also suffered great loss of property when the reservation was overrun by white guerilla bands in the Kansas border fighting. At the close of the war, the federal government secured the cession of a large part of the Osage lands in Kansas.

Soon the tribe faced intolerable conditions on account of the pressure to open all Indian lands in Kansas to white settlement, and an act of Congress on July 15, 1870, provided that the remainder of the lands in the Osage reservation be sold for the benefit of the tribe. From the proceeds a new reservation was purchased in the Indian Territory, the tract lying in the eastern end of the Cherokee Outlet and comprising all of present Osage County, together with a small tract—later sold to the Kansa (q. v.)—in northeastern Kay County.

By 1872 the Osage were settled on their new reservation. Agent Isaac Gibson (a Quaker) established their new agency, the village that later grew up about it being named Pawhuska in honor of old Chief Pahuska. The Osage Boarding School was soon opened near the agency, under government auspices, and its operation benefited the tribe for many years. In the eighteen seventies, under the auspices of the Society of Friends, two day schools were maintained on the reservation and field workers helped the Indians in the tribal camps or villages to raise their standard of living. Later, through the influence of some of the French-Osage families, a Catholic school for girls, St. Louis Mission, was established at Pawhuska, and one for boys, St. John's Mission, at Hominy.

Recovery from the difficulties suffered during their last decade in Kansas and their enforced removal from that state was slow, and the Osage had to make many adjustments to their new way of life. Indian Office reports from 1877 to 1884 show nearly a 50 per cent decline in the population of the tribe, caused partly by lack of adequate medical supplies and partly by the scarcity of food and clothing after the

Little Wing

disappearance of buffalo herds from the Plains. The Osage occupied themselves with small farming operations, some freighting of supplies to the agency from the railroad terminals in Kansas, and, later, with stock raising. Their reservation lands were the poorest for agricultural purposes of any in the Indian Territory, yet eventually the rich bluestem grass covering their acres proved to be among the best grazing. The growth of the range-cattle industry in the early eighteen eighties created a demand for the annual leasing by the Osage Council of hundreds of thousands of acres for pasture, the proceeds from the leases being divided on a per capita basis among the members of the tribe.

At the same time there was an increase in income from the interest on the tribal trust fund in the United States Treasury accumulating from the sale of the Osage lands in Kansas: in 1880, the total trust fund amounted to $1,992,972, producing an income of $90,648; in 1891, the total trust fund was $8,189,807, with an income of $409,490. Thus Osage affairs in the Indian Territory soon took on the aspect of "big business" and made the tribe unique in modern America. Today thriving cities in northern Oklahoma, located in the eastern part of the old Cherokee Strip (*see* Cherokee), owe their substantial beginnings to the wealth of the Osage.

Plans for the organization of a tribal government under a written constitution adopted by a convention held in Kansas in 1861 had been interrupted by the Civil War; twenty years later another constitution was adopted by the tribe in a convention held at Pawhuska. It provided for the organization of the Osage Nation, with a legislative council and a principal chief to

Osage chiefs in 1886

MURIEL H. WRIGHT

Osage Agency at Pawhuska about 1900

be elected by the people, and a supreme court to be chosen by the council. James Bigheart, a half-Osage who served as president of the convention, was later elected principal chief. The United States agent at Pawhuska at this time was Major Laban J. Miles (a Quaker), who proved to be a good friend and shrewd adviser. From the first, the most perplexing problem confronting the National Council was the proper enrollment of tribal members, for the increasing wealth of the Osage made citizenship in the nation a matter of great importance. As the years passed, bribes were offered to secure the enrollment as Osage by blood of persons with questionable rights to citizenship.

Since the Osage were exempted from the provisions for allotment of lands in severalty under the Congressional act of 1887, the matter of allotting lands to tribal members and of possible opening of surplus lands on the reservation to white settlement called for a special agreement between the United States and the Osage Nation. Members of the Cherokee Commission during June, 1893, in a series of meetings at the tribal "Round House" near Pawhuska, sought such an agreement. Black Dog and James Bigheart, heading a committee representing the fullblood members of the tribe, presented their objections in the form of an ultimatum, in which they stated that they could not consent to the allotment of lands and the division of tribal funds on the basis of the tribal roll as it then stood, since it bore the names of a number of persons who had no right to be on it. No agreement was ever made. Determining a correct roll of the Osage remained a vexatious problem for the United States Indian Office and was the cause of bitter factionalism among the tribe for many years.

Drilling for oil had already been begun elsewhere in the Indian Territory when a ten-year lease for oil and gas "mining" on the entire Osage Reservation was secured by Edwin B. Foster from the Osage Council and Chief James Bigheart in March, 1896. Under the terms of this lease, a royalty of one-tenth of the oil produced and the flat sum of fifty dollars annually for each gas well was to be paid the Osage Nation. Oil and gas discoveries in limited quantities in 1904–1905 at Avant, Okesa, and Osage City were an incentive to further drilling. The Foster lease, owned at this time by the Indian Territory Illuminating Oil Company, was renewed in 1905 by an act of Congress, which also covered subleases that had been made to other oil companies (including Barnsdall, Prairie Oil and Gas and Uncle Sam) and provided for a royalty of one-eighth of the oil and gas produced and one hundred dollars a year for each gas well in operation to be paid the Osage Nation. Oil produced on the reservation in 1906 totaled 5,219,106 barrels.

Aside from the income from oil and gas development, the Osage ranked as the richest Indian tribe in the United States. They were the owners of their reservation tract of 1,470,058 acres. By an act of Congress in 1905, five townsites (Pawhuska, Foraker, Bigheart, Hominy, and Fairfax) were established on the reservation and proceeds from the sale of town lots were soon being paid the nation. Outside cattlemen still leased the northern part of the reservation, where thousands of head of cattle were pastured. The majority of the Osage were capable in handling their own business affairs, and most families had several farms rented to white tenants. In 1906 the income from pasture leases amounted to $98,-376; the income from the tribal trust fund of $8,506,690 amounted to $428,134. The share of the individual Osage in these funds was reported as $3,928.50.

Meantime, there was great pressure for the opening of the Osage reservation preliminary to statehood for Oklahoma. The Osage themselves prepared a plan for the division of their tribal property interests in the form of a bill, which was approved in a tribal election and taken to Washington in the winter of 1906 by delegates representing all factions in the nation. This bill, introduced in Congress and passed on June 26, 1906, with some amendments, was known as the Osage Allotment Act. Its provision that all mineral rights on the reservation (including oil and gas) be retained as common property of the Osage Nation was different from any other provision made for other Indian tribes in Oklahoma. Royalties from these natural resources were to be divided on a per capita basis for a period of twenty-five years (to 1931, since extended to 1983). The act also provided for the allotment in severalty of the surface of the reservation, each Osage

to select a homestead of 160 acres and, subsequently, two tracts of 160 acres each, the remaining lands to be apportioned equally among the tribal members. The act stipulated that the final roll for the division of lands and funds should be the list of the enrolled Osage as of January 1, 1907 (necessary corrections to be allowed up to July 1, 1907). Three quarter-sections were set aside at each of the tribal village sites (near Pawhuska, Gray Horse, and Hominy, respectively) for the exclusive use of the Osage for dwellings. Allotment was completed in February, 1909, the per capita share of land amounting to approximately 657 acres.

Because of their shrewd arrangements for the leasing of their oil lands, the Osage became the wealthiest nation per capita in the world. In 1945 it was reported that their "barren" acres had produced 2 per cent of all the oil produced in the United States since 1859. The "blanket lease" system (the Foster lease was an example) was abandoned in 1916, the individual leasing of small tracts subsequently bringing in large revenues to the nation. The opening of the great Burbank oil pool in Osage County in 1920 was soon followed by petroleum leases that brought fabulous prices. In 1924 the total revenue to the Osage from oil and gas leases was $24,670,483, one 160-acre lease in the Burbank pool bringing the record breaking price of $1,990,000, and several other tracts more than $1,000,-000 each. In the forty-year period from 1905 to 1945, the Osage Nation received $300,000,000 which was divided pro rata among the 2,229 allottees whose names appear on the tribal roll, the heirs of any deceased allottee receiving proportionate shares of the head-right. In 1951, the income of the Osage from their mineral rights was lower than in former years, yet the employment of secondary recovery methods in oil production and the possibility of the discovery of new pools in Osage County before 1983 indicate additional potential wealth. In that year, the Osage

John Abbott and his wife, Grace, prominent fullblood Osage, in 1937

people will probably take over their mineral rights and operate as a business corporation under state and federal laws.

◆ **Government and Organization.** Tribal interests are governed by recommendations of the Tribal Council of eight members, together with the principal chief and the assistant chief, under the general supervisory control of the Indian Bureau in the United States Department of the Interior. Expenses of the tribal organization and all expenses of the Osage Agency at Pawhuska, with its superintendent and large office personnel, are paid out of tribal funds, a system that makes this Indian agency different from any other in Oklahoma. The principal chief of the Osage in 1951 was Warren Paul Pitts of Hominy, appointed by the Tribal Council to fill out the unexpired term of Chief John Oberly, who died on February 25, 1951. Chief Oberly had served since the death in 1949 of Chief Fred Lookout, who was first made chief in 1913.

◆ **Contemporary Life and Culture.** Full-blood Osage number approximately 11 per cent of the tribe. Many of the old mixed-blood families bear French names that have been handed down from intermarriages in the early period of the French traders in the West. There was great increase in the mixed-blood population by intermarriage with white people who came into the Osage country during the decade before allotment of lands.

The Osage are strongly Roman Catholic. Among the Protestant sects, the Baptist and the Methodist churches are active with growing memberships in the tribe.

The life of the Osage has been the most exciting and fantastic of any group in the history of modern America. Thirty years ago the public held the name Osage synonymous with profligate spending, big automobiles, expensive dress, and large residences with rich furnishings. Through these experiences, the Osage people generally have come to realize the necessity for moderation. The oil industry brought the Osage economic independence and the advantages of education, travel, and modernization of home and farm. About three-fifths of the Osage allotted lands have been sold, but much has been purchased by individuals in the tribe and is still owned by them. Aside from oil and gas development, the principal industry in Osage County is stock raising, in which some tribal members are engaged.

Among the outstanding Osage citizens of the state was the late Chief Fred Lookout, a graduate of Carlisle Indian School, who was revered by his tribe and admired by thousands of his fellow-citizens. Another distinguished member of the tribe is John Joseph Mathews, graduate of Oxford University in England and author of Wah' Kon-Tah and other notable books. Maria Tallchief is a solo ballerina of promise in the Ballet Russe de Monte Carlo. In World War II, Clarence L. Tinker of the Osage Nation was the commanding general of the air forces in Hawaii when he died in action in 1942 while personally leading his bomber command against the enemy. Tinker Air Force Base, Oklahoma City Air Materiel Area, is named in his honor and is the largest base in the United States Air Materiel Command.

◆ **Ceremonials and Public Dances.** Some of the old tribal ceremonials held at the Osage villages near Pawhuska, Hominy, and Gray Horse are open to the public on special occasions. These ceremonials have lost much of their old significance and are no longer really vital in the life of the people. Osage dancers participate in the historical pageantry of the annual American Indian Exposition at Anadarko.

Suggested Readings: Chapman, "Dissolution of the Osage Reservation," *Chron. of Okla.,* Vol. XX, Nos. 3 and 4 (1942), Vol. XXI, Nos. 2 and 3 (1943); Connelly, *History of Kansas;* Cutler, *History of Kansas;* Hargrett, *Laws of the American Indians;* Hodge, *Handbook of American Indians;* La Flesche, "The Osage Tribe," *36 Ann. Rep.,* Bur. Amer. Ethnol.; Mathews, *Wah' Kon-Tah;* Rister, *Oil!*

OTO AND MISSOURI

The Oto and the Missouri speak the same language and have been officially classed as one tribal group since their settlement in the Indian Territory. They are now referred to as the Oto, usually found spelled "Otoe" in Indian agency records, the Missouri having lost their separate tribal identity because of their comparatively small number. The two tribes, together with the Iowa (q.v.), are the Chiwere group of the Siouan linguistic family. The name Oto is from the Siouan term *wat'ota,* "lechers." White people on the frontier called the second tribe *Missouri,* "great muddy," because they were located on the Missouri River.

The Oto and the Missouri were primarily agriculturists. When they first made a treaty with the United States in 1817, they were a restless, contentious people living in several villages along the Platte River in what is now Nebraska, a small tribal group who had to maintain themselves in the midst of enemy forces. An army officer who visited them in 1844 wrote that they were unlike other Indians, for they lacked dignity, were given to levity, and were frivolous and careless. Their United States Indian agents, in contrast, generally spoke well of them for their loyalty, energy, and pleasant ways.

◆ **Present Location.** The Oto and Missouri live in rural communities centering at Red Rock and at the old "Otoe Subagency" (about six miles northeast) in the northeastern part of Noble County, Oklahoma.

◆ **Numbers.** There were 930 Oto and Missouri in Oklahoma in 1950. The Indian Office reported their total number in 1924 at 609. Allotments of land on the "Otoe and Missouria Reservation" were begun in 1891 and completed to 514 tribal members by 1907. Their total numbers as reported by the U. S. Indian Office at different periods were 377 in 1891, 438 (including 216

in Indian Territory) in 1880, 440 in 1869, 708 in 1862, and 931 in 1843.

◆ **History.** According to tribal tradition, people later known as the Oto, along with their relatives the Winnebago and the Iowa (q.v.), once lived in the Great Lakes region. In a prehistoric migration southwest in search of buffalo, they separated, the division that reached the mouth of the Grand River, a branch of the Missouri, calling themselves *Neutache* (or *Niu'-tache*), "those that arrive at the mouth." A personal quarrel between two of their chiefs led to a separation into two bands: the one that went up the Missouri became known as the Oto; the other that remained near their first settlement was called the Missouri. French explorers recorded the location of the Oto in the Des Moines River region, Iowa, about 1690–1700.

In the Oklahoma Historical Society is an original letter written in French by President Thomas Jefferson in 1806 to the chiefs of seven tribes, including the Oto and the Missouri. The President referred to them as "our red brothers" from west of the Mississippi River and promised them the care and protection of the United States.

The Oto and Missouri country lying south from the Platte River in eastern Nebraska was ceded by treaty to the United States in 1854, and a reservation (160,000 acres) was later established for the tribal group along the Big Blue River on the present Kansas-Nebraska line. Their diminished reserve on this tract (about 43,000 acres) was sold with their consent through an act of Congress in 1881, at which time they were promised a reservation in the Indian Territory. They subsequently purchased a reservation in the Cherokee Outlet with their own tribal funds, a tract of 129,113 acres located in the northeastern part of present Noble County and the western part of Pawnee County.

The opening of the Oto and Missouri reserve on the Kansas-Nebraska line to white settlement was pressed in 1874. Soon afterward, when the plan for their location in the Indian Territory was proposed, a few Oto families came south and encamped west of the Sac and Fox Agency. Voluntarily joined here later by others, they numbered nearly half the whole tribal group by 1880 and were generally referred to locally by the United States agents as the "Wild Otoes." The last of the tribesmen arrived from the north in 1883. Bitterness had arisen among the tribal members over the selection of their reservation in the Indian Territory. Frequent changes in their agency personnel and changes in government policies, especially the 1887 allotment policy which was violently opposed by the Oto and Missouri, retarded settled conditions and advancement among them. Their reservation lands were finally divided into equal allotments to tribal members, with 1,360 acres reserved for agency, church, and other tribal uses. The whole area was organized as parts of Noble and Pawnee counties when Oklahoma became a state in 1907.

◆ **Government and Organization.** The Oto Council and their chief—the 1951 chief was Ralph Dent — continue a nominal tribal organization for advisory purposes in their business affairs. Allotted lands in the restricted class (i.e., trust lands) are supervised by the Pawnee Subagency at Pawnee. About 35 per cent of the former reservation lands are still Indian owned, approximately 40,000 acres of which are leased annually and non-Indian operated.

◆ **Contemporary Life and Culture.** The full bloods are predominant in the Oto and Missouri tribal group. The mixed-bloods are descendants of intermarriages with closely associated tribes and with the early French and later white settlers. While the Oto and Missouri are generally a Christian rural people, a few of the older tribesmen still cling to some of the old ways and tribal dress. An annual Oto pow-wow is held in summer at the former Otoe Subagency in Noble County.

Suggested Readings: Chapman, "The Otoe and Missouria Reservation," *Chron. of Okla.,* Vol. XXVI, No. 2 (Summer, 1948); Grant Foreman, *Last Trek of the Indians;* Hodge, *Handbook of American Indians.*

OTTAWA

The name *Ottawa* is from the the Algonquian term *adawe,* "to trade" or "to buy and sell." It was first applied by the French to all the Indian tribes living on the shores of Lake Huron, in Upper Michigan, and west along Lake Superior, but was later given to that portion of the Algonquian linguistic family who had their villages in the southern part of what is now Michigan, in the vicinity of Grand River, and in Ohio and Indiana.

Some of the early French visitors described the Ottawa as one of the cruelest and most barbarous Indian tribes in Canada. Another Frenchman, who came later and knew them well, wrote that they were brave, intelligent, and respected by their allies. They were great hunters and were agriculturists as far as the climate in the north would permit. Both in traditional times and in the historic period they were noted as intertribal traders and barterers, dealing in furs and skins, cornmeal, sunflower-seed oil, rugs and mats, and medicinal herbs and roots. They were especially skillful in fine handwork and the invention of small toys and trinkets.

◆ **Present Location.** The name of Ottawa County, Oklahoma, perpetuates the name of this tribe whose descendants now are located within the boundaries of that county.

◆ **Numbers.** There are an estimated 480 Ottawa now in Oklahoma. In a special census made by the Quapaw Agency in 1941, they numbered 440, of whom 210 were living in the agency jurisdiction and 230 elsewhere. Their numbers as reported by the Office of Indian Affairs at different periods were 192 in 1905, 167 in 1902, 140 in 1875, and 149 in 1871, soon after their immigration to the Indian Territory from Kansas. Approximately 500 Ottawa moved from Ohio to Kansas in 1836. The total number of the Ottawa in 1906 was estimated at 4,700, which included, in addition to those in the Indian Territory, a large group living in Michigan and another on Manitoulin and Cockburn islands, Georgian Bay, Canada, where they are still located.

◆ **History.** At the beginning of their historic period about 1615, some of the Ottawa were located near the mouth of French River, Georgian Bay, where they were visited by the French explorer Samuel de Champlain. A large portion of the tribe were living on Manitoulin Island in 1635, indicating a westward migration under pressure from the Iroquois in their wars against the Huron (*see* Wyandot). About fifteen years later, an onslaught by the Iroquois drove the Ottawa to Green Bay, Wisconsin, where the Potawatomi (q.v.) received them as friends and allies. Some of the Ottawa later returned to Manitoulin Island, which they shared with the Chippewa. Four divisions of the Ottawa were represented in a treaty with the French at Montreal in 1700. Within a few years, some of the tribe were living near the lower end of Lake Michigan, from which the others spread out in every direction, the largest portion settling on the east shore of the lake as far south as the St. Joseph River, a few locating in southern Wisconsin and northern Illinois; still others settled on the shores of Lake Huron near the Chippewa and on the shores of Lake Erie near the Wyandot, from Detroit eastward to Pennsylvania. It was in the vicinity of Detroit that the celebrated Ottawa chief, Pontiac, waged war in 1763, an important event in the tribal history. Pontiac was bitterly opposed to further invasion of the Indian country by the British, but when his plan for an uprising of all the tribes against the British was unsuccessful, he finally made a peace treaty at Detroit on August 17, 1765.

The Ottawa concluded or are referred to in thirty-two different treaties with the United States. Under the terms of a treaty concluded on the Miami River of Lake Erie on August 30, 1831, three bands of Ottawa (Blanchards Fork, Oquanoxa's Village, and Roche de Boeuf) in Ohio ceded their lands in the state to the United States, and were granted a reservation of 74,000 acres in fee simple on the Marais des Cygnes River in what is now Franklin County, Kansas. These Ottawa resisted the removal west, but were finally moved from Ohio by government contractors under the direction of Colonel J. J. Abert, superintendent of Indian affairs in Ohio, arriving at the site of present Ottawa, Kansas, in December, 1836.

Dispirited and in a generally low condition after their enforced removal from Ohio, nearly half the Ottawa tribe died within five years. It was during this period that the Reverend Jotham Meeker, the well-known Baptist missionary who had planted the Shawanoe Mission Press among the Shawnee (q.v.) of Kansas, began his life's work among the Ottawa in that region. He knew their language and provided the inspiration that revived them, so that before many seasons had passed, they were reported a sober, industrious, and prosperous people.

Under pressure in Kansas for the opening and sale of all Indian lands, the Ottawa concluded a treaty at Washington, on June 24, 1862, providing for allotment in severalty to tribal members on the Kansas reservation and for the sale of the surplus lands to white settlers, the Ottawa to become citizens of the state and their tribal government to be dissolved within five years. An unusual provision in this treaty set aside 20,000 acres of the tribal domain as a foundation for a school for the Ottawa, which is now known as Ottawa College.

During the Civil War refugee bands of Quapaw, Seneca of Sandusky, Shawnee, and Osage (q.v.) were temporarily located on the Ottawa reservation. To provide for the protection and welfare of those Ottawa who were not ready to become citizens of Kansas, Chief John Wilson during this time made a contract with the Shawnee (q.v.) for the purchase a tribal tract on their reservation in the Indian Territory. The contract was confirmed in the Omnibus Treaty in 1867—the treaty that included provisions for remnants of several of the old Algonquian tribes to be settled on reservations in the Indian Territory (*see* Peoria).

The Ottawa moved to their new home, a reserve of approximately 14,860 acres bounded by the Neosho River on the west, and lying south and east of present Miami, in Ottawa County, Oklahoma. Under the Indian Allotment Act passed by Congress in 1887, 157 Ottawa were allotted lands in severalty by 1891. These people were prospering as farmers and businessmen when they became citizens of Oklahoma in 1907.

◆ **Government and Organization.** The Ottawa Tribe of Indians of Oklahoma, an organization in Ottawa County to promote the welfare of members of the tribe, was issued a charter of incorporation by the Office of the Secretary of the Interior in 1938, under the Oklahoma Indian Welfare Act of June 26, 1936. The certification of adoption of this charter was signed by members of the Ottawa Business Committee, Guy Jennison, chief; L. H. Dagenette, Fred S. King; Dave Geboe, second Chief; and Abe G. Williams, secretary-treasurer. On June 2, 1939, the adult members of the tribe ratified the charter for the organization by a vote of 79 for, and 1 against, in an election in which over 30 per cent of those entitled to vote (about 210 in the Quapaw Agency jurisdiction) cast ballots, as certified by Guy Jennison, chief, and Bronson Edwards, secretary-treasurer, Ottawa Tribe.

Suggested Readings: Grant Foreman, *Last Trek of the Indians;* Hodge, *Handbook of American Indians; Kansas Hist. Soc. Collections,* 1915; Wilson, *Quapaw Agency Indians.*

PAWNEE

The Pawnee belong to the Caddoan linguistic family. There are four confederated bands of the tribe: the *Chaui,* "Grand"; the *Kitkehahki,* "Republican"; the *Pitahauerat,* "Tappage"; and the *Skidi,* "Wolf." The Skidi (q.v.), Skedee or Skeedee, are the largest of the four bands, and have been closely associated and identified in their history with the Wichita (q.v.), who are called the "Black Pawnee" among the Sioux. The name *Chahiksi-chahiks,* "men of men," said to have been used by the Pawnee themselves, is not known in the tribe today.

The name *Pawnee,* found in historical records as *Pani, Pana, Panana, Panamaha* or *Panimaha,* was commonly applied to the group by the French of the eighteenth century. One study of the name has suggested its origin from the Pawnee word *pariki,* "horn," referring to their peculiar dressing of the scalp-lock with red ochre and buffalo fat until it stood erect and curved backward like a horn, although linguists have continued to point out the difficulty of harmonizing the phonetics of *pariķi* with *Panimaha, Pani, Pana,* and *Pawnee.* Furthermore, the concept of a horn, "pariki," does not have any association of ideas with the old-time hair dressing for members of the tribe. The designation or symbol of the Pawnee in pictograph painting was the scalp-lock standing erect and curved backward. It is more probable that the origin of the name is from the Choctaw words *pana,* "a braid" or "a twist," and *mahaia,* "to curve" or "to bend up." Like many other old names from the Choctaw, *pani mahaia,* "a braid or a twist (of hair) that curves or bends up," would be written and spoken in an abbreviated form: *Panamaha, Panimaha, Pana,* or *Pani.* The Pawnee and other Caddoan tribes once lived in the Lower Mississippi Valley according to tribal tradition. Marquette's map of 1673–74 shows their location along the lower Arkansas and the Missouri rivers. The names by which some of these tribes are now known were applied by the early Frenchmen, and in some instances by the Spaniards, from the languages of the tribes with whom they had had contact, especially the Choctaw (q.v.), whose speech was the trade language in a wide region eastward from the Lower Mississippi Valley through what are now the Southeastern states.

The Pawnee were notable for their tribal religion, rich in myth, symbolism, and poetic fancy, with elaborate rites and dramatic ceremonies connected with the cosmic forces and heavenly bodies. They believed that all these were created by the one deity, the all-powerful and all-present "Tirawa." Religious beliefs were highly integrated with most of the tribal institutions and practices—medicine, secret societies, war parties, buffalo hunting, construction of earth-covered lodges for dwellings, the planting and the growing of corn, marriage, games, feasts, and government. This background was significant in the development of the personal characteristics for which the Pawnee have always been known: courage, loyalty, and respect for authority. The men are robust and of good stature, and were noted in tribal days for their endurance. Runners traveling at a trot frequently made 100 miles in twenty-four hours without stopping for sleep or nourishment. Women are of smaller stature than the men; in tribal days, they were remarkable for their energy and their many accomplishments in the work of their homes and villages. From the time that their country was taken over in the Louisiana Purchase, the Pawnee never made war on the United States, and Pawnee scouts served faithfully and courageously in the United States Army in Indian

Pawnee earth-covered lodge, 1886

wars. Their young men made fine records in their country's service in both world wars.

◆ **Present Location.** The Pawnee live in or near the towns of Pawnee, Skedee, Lela, and Meramec in Pawnee County, and near Yale in Payne County.

◆ **Numbers.** Approximately 1,260 Pawnee lived in Oklahoma in 1950, a total of 1,213 having been reported on the tribal rolls in 1948. The Indian Office listed 784 members of the tribe in Oklahoma in 1924. Allotments in severalty were completed to 821 members of the tribe in 1893. Their numbers as reported by the Indian Office at different periods before this time were 1,306 in 1880, 2,398 in 1869, 3,414 in 1861, 4,500 in 1849 (after the loss of one-fourth of their numbers from cholera), and 10,-000, in 1838.

◆ **History.** The Pawnee were found in 1541 by the Spanish explorer, Coronado, on his expedition to Quivira, when he was led through what is now western Oklahoma by a Pawnee guide called "The Turk." At this time, their villages of earth-covered lodges were located near Quivira, the country of the Wichita (q.v.) in what is now central and northeastern Kansas. The Spanish settlements in New Mexico for two centuries (1600–1800) knew of the Pawnee through their raiding expeditions for horses, attempts to cultivate friendly relations with the tribe proving fruitless. However, French traders were established among the Pawnee before 1750. With the purchase of Louisiana, St. Louis became the American trading center for the Pawnee. Emigrant trails to the West through their country in the Platte River region brought many changes, principally decimation of their ranks from cholera and other diseases, which in turn meant great loss in power and prestige for the tribe.

Three treaties (in 1833, 1848, and 1857) provided for the cession of all Pawnee lands to the United States, with the exception of a reservation thirty miles long and ten miles wide along both banks of the Loup River, centering near present Fullerton (Nance County), Nebraska. Plans for their removal to the Indian Territory and the sale of their Nebraska reservation lands in 1872 caused great excitement among the Pawnee. When their delegations came south in search of a location, their meetings with the Kiowa and the Osage, their old enemies, and the gathering of all the Pawnee on their new reservation in 1875 provide some of most dramatic incidents in Indian history in Oklahoma. A party of 300 Pawnee from the Chaui and the Kitkehaki bands, under the leadership of their respective chiefs, Spotted Horse and Lone Chief, came to the Wichita Agency in the winter of 1873–74, where they remained as neighbors of the Wichita for more than a year, during this time joined by other bands of Pawnee who increased their number to 1,900 by the spring of 1875. Soon afterward, they left the Wichita Agency region for their new reservation.

In the autumn of 1874, the Pawnee chiefs and leaders and their agent, William Burgess, selected a location for the tribe between the Arkansas and the Cimarron

George H. Roberts, Sr., in 1917

MURIEL H. WRIGHT

Pawnee Business Council, with members of the Nasharo Council in 1947
Seated, left to right: Basil Chapman, James Marrington, George H. Roberts, Robert
Peters, Lawrence Goodfox, spokesman. Standing: Henry Chapman, Edwin Bayhylle,
James Sun Eagle, Charles Lone Chief, Harry D. Cummings, Phillip Jim, William Barker,
Jasper Hadley

rivers, a tract lying east of the ninety-seventh meridian which now forms Pawnee County (excepting the western townships; (*see* Oto) and the northeastern part of Payne County, Oklahoma. The purchase of this reservation of 283,020 acres by the Pawnee out of their tribal funds was confirmed by Congress in 1876. Within a year, the four bands of the Pawnee had come from Nebraska and the Wichita country and were establishing settlements on the new reservation: the Chaui, on Black Bear Creek, about three miles north and east of present Lela, in Pawnee County; the Kitkehahki, north of Black Bear Creek, about four miles west and north of present Pawnee; the Petahauerat, on Camp Creek about three miles south of Pawnee; the Skidi, on Skedee Creek about two miles north and west of Pawnee.

The new tribal agency was established and log buildings (dwellings for employees, mill, shops, stables, schoolhouses, and commissary) begun near the present Pawnee Subagency on Black Bear Creek in the summer of 1875. A boarding school near the Agency and two day schools on the reservation were soon in operation and well attended. Immediately after the defeat of General George Custer in the Battle of the Little Big Horn in 1876, one hundred Pawnee were enlisted by the United States army for the military campaign against the hostile Sioux in the North. Ten of these scouts were still living in Oklahoma in 1925: Rush Roberts, Dog Chief, Walking Sun, Wichita Blaine, Robert Taylor, Hisson, High Eagle, John Box, Billy Osborne, and John Leadingfox.

During reservation days, members of the tribe engaged principally in raising livestock, with small farming operations.

Clyde Atwood (Choctaw) sings and beats the drum for Alvin Jake (Pawnee) to dance, at Haskell Institute in 1941

Income from these sources and limited employment in day labor and freighting overland for the agency was very low. Open grass lands leased for a few seasons (1883–88) to white cattlemen of the Cherokee Strip Live Stock Association (*see* Cherokee) brought in a small revenue that meant a few dollars to each family when divided per capita. Fully two-thirds of the reservation was rough country—rocky hills, ravines, and scrub timber. Lack of supplies, poor crops, epidemics, uncertainties about the government's Indian policies, and outside demands for opening Indian lands to white settlement caused a struggle for mere existence and a great decline of population.

Commissioners for the United States government easily reached an agreement with the Pawnee in 1892 providing for the cession of the reservation to the United States with allotments of land in severalty to members of the tribe. Allotments were completed and the surplus lands (169,-320 acres) were opened to white settlement by a run starting at twelve o'clock noon on September 16, 1893.

◆ **Government and Organization.** Members of the confederated bands of Pawnee —Chaui, Kitkehahke, Petahauerat, and Skidi (or Skedee)—are organized under the title of "Pawnee Indian Tribe of Oklahoma," with a constitution and by-laws as provided in the Oklahoma Indian Welfare Act of 1936. The constitution provides for a Pawnee Business Council of eight members and a Nasharo Council of eight members selected from the chieftains of the four tribal bands. Meetings are held in the Pawnee Community Building quarterly. Those who have served on the Business Committee include George H. Roberts, Sr., James Mannington, Basil Chapman, Harry D. Cummings, James Sun Eagle, Charles Lone Chief, Henry Chapman, and Edwin Bayhylle. Members of the Nasharo Council have included Robert Peters, William Barker, Lawrence Good Fox, Sr., Phillip Jim, Rush Roberts, Sr., Jasper Hadley, and Tom Rice. A charter was issued to the Pawnee Tribe by the Department of the Interior and was ratified by a vote of the adult members of the tribe in an election on April 28, 1938.

◆ **Contemporary Life and Culture.** One-third of the Pawnee are fullblood members of the tribe. The mixed-bloods are descendants of intermarriages with the whites (French and English) and closely associated Indian tribes. There has been considerable intermarriage between the Skidi and Wichita, mixed descendants being found in both tribes today.

The Pawnee are a Christianized people, though no missions were established among them on their Indian Territory reservation.

Missionary work, begun in 1886 by the Methodist Episcopal church, later grew and gained many converts among them through the leadership of the Reverend Adolphur Carrion, an adopted Pawnee of French-Sioux descent, and his wife, Maggie C. Carrion, a Pawnee.

Members of the tribe are mostly engaged in farming and stock raising, with some of the young people found in business and other employment. Children attend the public schools in their home communities. The Pawnee Boarding School, located near the agency, about two miles east of Pawnee, was still in operation in 1951 under government supervision.

◆ **Ceremonials and Public Dances.** Old tribal ceremonials and dances are open to the public at the Pawnee pow-wow held at an announced time in summer in the vicinity of Pawnee. The Pawnees always take a prominent part in the pageant and tribal dance contests of the annual American Indian Exposition at Anadarko.

Suggested Readings: Dunbar, "The Pawnee Indians," *Magazine of American History,* Vol. IV, No. 4 (April, 1880); Grinnell, *Pawnee Hero Stories;* Moore, "Pawnee Traditions and Customs," *Chron. of Okla.,* Vol. XVII, No. 2 (June, 1939); Murie, *Pawnee Indian Societies;* Wedel, *Introduction to Pawnee Archeology.*

PEORIA

The name of the Peoria is from the name applied to the tribe by the French, a personal name rendered by them as *Peouarea,* from the Peoria tribal expression *piwares,* "he comes carrying a pack on his back."

The Peoria were formerly one of the principal tribes of the Illinois (q.v.) Confederacy belonging to the Algonquian linguistic family. At the beginning of the Historic period they lived near the mouth of the Wisconsin River in the general region of Prairie du Chien, Wisconsin, some

tribal bands being found in the latter part of the seventeenth century southward on the Mississippi in present Illinois and Iowa. Early records describe the Peoria as a genial people, tall and fine looking, general characteristics that hold to this day.

◆ **Present Location.** The Peoria are in Ottawa County, having been allotted lands in severalty in their reserve north and east of present Miami.

◆ **Numbers.** The peoria are listed by the Indian Office among the Confederated

Peoria (United Peoria and Miami) in the Quapaw Agency region, a 1945 census giving a total population of 413, of whom 150 were living within the agency jurisdiction and 260 living elsewhere, in Oklahoma and (a few) in other states. They were always recorded few in numbers as a single tribe, an estimate of their population being 250 in 1736. In 1800, after the close of the Indian wars north of the Ohio, it was said there were only four Peoria men living. This was an error since eleven Peoria made up the delegation that signed a treaty with the United States in 1818.

◆ **History.** The Peoria were moving southward from the Wisconsin River by 1670. Three years later a tribal band living near the Moingwena (q.v.) at the mouth of the Des Moines River moved over to the east side of the Mississippi in the vicinity of present Peoria, Illinois. After the French and Indian War when their enemies, including the Kickapoo and the Fox, began a war of extermination against the Illinois tribes, a part of the Peoria with some of the Wea (q.v.) settled on the Blackwater Fork near St. Genevieve, Missouri. The main part of the Peoria, however, remained on the Illinois River.

From their first treaty with the United States in 1818, the Peoria were united with the Kaskaskia (q.v.). By the terms of a treaty in 1832 the remnants of five tribes of the Illinois Confederacy (*see* Illinois) gave up their land claims in Illinois and Missouri to the United States. A reserved tract of 150 sections on the Osage River was assigned the Peoria and the Kaskaskia, extending east from the Wea and Piankashaw reserve in present Miami County, Kansas. Here, within a few years, the Peoria were prospering as a sober, industrious people under the influence of a Roman Catholic mission.

The great influx of white settlers on the Western frontier after the Gold Rush to California in 1849 soon saw the Peoria and Kaskaskia joining their neighbors, the Wea and Piankashaw, to form a confed-

erated tribe for mutual benefit and welfare. This confederation also counted among its members the descendants and last remnants of the Cahokia, Moingwena, Michigamea, and Tamaroa (q.v.), who had become a part of the Peoria many years before, as well as the Pepikokia, who had joined the Wea and Piankashaw in the latter part of the eighteenth century. An Indian agent in 1851 reported that the Peoria and Kaskaskia and their allied tribes had practically lost their tribal identity through intermarriage among themselves and with white people. A treaty with Commissioner Manypenny in behalf of the United States, at Washington, D. C., in 1854 officially recognized this union of tribes, henceforth usually referred to as the Confederated Peoria. This treaty, made in the same year that the Territory of Kansas was organized, provided for the opening of the Peoria-Kaskaskia and the Wea-Piankashaw reserves by sale of the surplus lands to white settlers after setting aside a reserve of ten sections to be held in common by the confederated tribes, in addition to an allotment of 160 acres to each tribal member.

The organization of the state of Kansas in 1861 found the Indian tribes harassed by illegal taxation of their property and inequalities under the state laws. Many of the Indians had lost their individual land holdings within a few years. At the close of the Civil War, the government pushed its plan to remove all the Indian tribes from Kansas to the Indian Territory. The terms of a complicated treaty, known as the Omnibus Treaty, which named ten tribes in Kansas, was signed at Washington on February 23, 1867. It provided, among other things, that the Confederated Peoria sell their remaining individual allotments and confederated land holdings in Kansas. The treaty also provided that the money received from the latter sales be applied to the purchase of a reservation tract for the benefit of the members of the Confederated Peoria who removed to the

Indian Territory. The new reservation of 72,000 acres lay west and south of the Quapaw in present Ottawa County, the land having been purchased partly from the Quapaw (q.v.) and partly from the Seneca and Shawnee (*see* Seneca). Fifty-five Peoria at this time decided to remain in Kansas to become citizens of that state.

The chief of the Confederated Peoria during this period was Baptiste Peoria (Lanepeshaw), of Wea-Peoria-French descent. A man of character and remarkable ability, able to speak French and several Indian languages, he was respected by United States officials and revered and loved as a leader by his people. He advised and helped them in their last treaties with the United States and moved with them to the Indian Territory. Before his death on the Peoria reservation in 1873, he saw his people prospering, their children attending school, and a church organization in their midst under the auspices of the Orthodox Friends.

After years of attempts on the part of the Indians, Congress enacted a law in 1873 providing for the union of the Miami (q.v.) of Kansas with the Confederated Peoria, under the title of "United Peoria and Miami." The members of this united group were predominantly of mixed-blood Indian and white descent. Allotment of lands in severalty (200 acres each) among these people was directed by a special act of Congress in 1889, and completed by 1893. In 1907, the members of the United Peoria and Miami became citizens of the new state of Oklahoma.

◆ **Government and Organization.** The tribe is incorporated as the "Peoria Indian Tribe of Oklahoma," under the Oklahoma Indian Welfare Act of June 26, 1936. The charter issued by the office of the Secretary of the Interior was approved by the Peoria Business Committee composed of George Skye, Leo Finley, Ada Moore Palmer, and Sherman Staton, members of the tribe. On June 1, 1940, the adult members of the tribe ratified the charter by a vote of 71 for, and none against, in an election in which over 30 per cent of those entitled to vote (147 in the Quapaw Agency jurisdiction) cast their ballots. The certification of this action was signed by George Skye, chief, and Alice O. Eversole, secretary-treasurer, Peoria Tribe.

Suggested Readings: Grant Foreman, "Illinois and Her Indians," in *Papers in Illinois History,* 1939; ———, *Last Trek of the Indians;* Hodge, *Handbook of American Indians;* Wilson, *Quapaw Agency Indians.*

PIANKASHAW

The name of the Piankashaw is from the Miami tribal term *payunggĭsh'ah,* signifying "those who separated and formed a tribe." They were once a sub-tribe of the Miami, of the Algonquian linguistic family, and looked on the deer as their totem.

◆ **Present Location.** The Piankashaw are a part of the Confederated Peoria (q.v.) located in Ottawa County, Oklahoma.

◆ **Numbers.** No separate census of Piankashaw has been made by the Quapaw Subagency in Ottawa County. In 1825, there were 234 members of the tribe. Previous estimates of their numbers were 800 1795, 950 in 1780, 1,250 in 1764, and 1,500 in 1759.

◆ **History.** The ancient village of the Piankashaw was near the present Illinois-Indiana boundary, on the Wabash River at the junction with the Vermillion. Later they settled farther down the Wabash at the site of present Vincennes, Indiana. About 1800, they began moving with the Wea (q.v.) into Missouri.

The Piankashaw are represented in ten different treaties with the United States.

A treaty concluded at Vincennes, Indiana Territory, on December 30, 1805, provided for the cession to the United States of all the Piankashaw tribal lands east of the Mississippi, approximately 26,000 acres in southeastern Illinois near the Wabash River. Two Piankashaw leaders represented their tribe in the treaty concluded at Castor Hill, St. Louis County, Missouri, on October 29, 1832, by which, in exchange for all their lands in "Missouri and Illinois," the Piankashaw together with the Wea (q.v.) were ceded by the United States 250 sections of land in present Miami County, Kansas. Early in the eighteen fifties the two tribes united with the Peoria and Kaskaskia, a confederation officially recognized in a treaty concluded at Washington, on May 30, 1854, by George W. Manypenny, United States commissioner. Thereafter the Piankashaw were a part of the Confederate Peoria (q.v.), who settled in the Quapaw Agency region in the Indian Territory in 1867.

Suggested Readings: Grant Foreman, "Illinois and Her Indians," in *Papers in Illinois History*, 1939; ———, *Last Trek of the Indians;* Hodge, *Handbook of American Indians;* Wilson, *Quapaw Agency Indians.*

PONCA

The Ponca are one of five tribes—Omaha, Ponca, Osage, Kansa, Quapaw (q.v.)—that form the group known as the Dhegiha in the Siouan linguistic family. The dialect of the Ponca is the same as that of the Omaha, with whom they were usually associated, and is similar to the Quapaw language. The name *Ponca* is apparently a mnemonic from these Siouan dialects, and has a symbolic connotation of "sacred head," from the term in these dialects *pa-ho^{n}ga,* from *pa,* "head" (including the face), and ho^{n}ga, "leader" or "that which is sacred." In the Osage, the term *pa-ho^n-gthe* signifies "in the first order of time" or "original." References to the Ponca in historical records include the variations "La Pong," "Panka," and "Punka."

The Ponca lived in earth-covered lodges built in permanent villages in Dakota. They were primarily agriculturists, yet engaged in seasonal expeditions hunting buffalo. One of their agents described them as a superior tribe mentally and morally, a kind, generous people who loved their children.

◆ **Present Location.** Ponca in Oklahoma live in Kay County, near Ponca City and White Eagle, and in the northeastern part of Noble County. A band of the tribe lives in northern Nebraska, where members were formerly allotted lands in severalty, some miles west of Niobrara.

◆ **Numbers.** Approximately 950 Ponca lived in Oklahoma in 1950. The United States Indian Office census for 1944 shows 916 members of the tribe in Oklahoma and 401 in Nebraska. The same office's report for 1907 shows that 784 Ponca had received allotments of land on their Indian Territory reservation. A report from Nebraska in the same year shows that 167 members of the tribe had been allotted lands in severalty on their reservation in that state. In 1876, the year before the Ponca moved south, the Ponca Agency then in South Dakota reported the total population of the tribe at 730. Previous estimates of their tribal population never exceeded 800.

◆ **History.** According to tribal tradition, the Dhegiha tribes divided when they came to the Mississippi during an ancient migration. The first division or Quapaw (q.v.) went downstream to the Arkansas. The other four tribes or Omaha division reached the mouth of the Osage River in present Missouri and then separated: The Osage remained on the Osage River, the Kansa ascended the Missouri, and the Omaha proper and the Ponca traveled together still farther up the Missouri.

Father Marquette supposedly heard of the Ponca on the Niobrara River in 1673. For a long period the Ponca were separated from the Omaha and were at war with the Sioux. During this time the Ponca villages were located in a number of places, including the pipestone quarry in southwestern Minnesota and the Black Hills of South Dakota. After many years the Omaha and Ponca rejoined, but finally separated, the Ponca remaining at the mouth of Niobrara River, near which they were assigned a reservation when they ceded all their land claims to the United States by treaty in 1858.

In 1865 the Ponca ceded nearly one-third of their reservation to the United States, but were guaranteed title to certain specified tracts (about 96,000 acres). De-

White Eagle, head chief of the Ponca for fifty years, in 1890

spite this guarantee by the government, the Ponca lands were ceded to the Sioux by a United States commission three years later, an act that amounted to criminal negligence in the treatment of the Indians. The Ponca soon saw their people being killed, their stock stolen and their lands overrun by the Sioux. All efforts by Standing Bear and other tribesmen to rectify these wrongs were of no avail for eight long years. Then an act of Congress in 1876 provided for the removal of the Ponca to the Indian Territory, a move of which they had no knowledge until an agent appeared to force them south. Most of the tribe refused to leave, saying that they would rather die in defense of their homes. Finally, with no alternative, a force of United States troops at their doors, the Ponca set out, and after great hardships and difficulties reached the Quapaw reservation, Indian Territory, in the summer of 1877. Here they numbered 681 persons, 36 having stayed in the North with the Omaha.

Convinced after several months' encampment near the Quapaw Agency that the Quapaw country and conditions there would never suit them, the Ponca leaders and a United States agent investigated the Arkansas River region west and selected a location for the tribe on the Salt Fork River. A tract of 101,894 acres lying at the mouth of and on both sides of the Salt Fork became the Ponca reservation, subsequently confirmed by Congress in 1881 though the deed for the tract was not made out until 1884. In the meantime, nationwide publicity had been given the plight of the Ponca.

All the members of the tribe left the Quapaw country with their agent for their new location on the Salt Fork, reaching their destination the latter part of July, 1878, after a week's travel overland in the terrific heat of summer. There were many deaths among them both during their stay at the Quapaw Agency and during their first year on the new reservation. Standing

MURIEL H. WRIGHT

Horse Chief Eagle, last hereditary chief of
the Ponca, who succeeded his father, White
Eagle, in 1914

Bear lost several members of his family. Thoroughly disheartened upon the death of his son, he decided to take the body back for burial in the old country of the Ponca on the Niobrara River. Without permission of the agent, Standing Bear, accompanied by some of his friends, left their encampment on the Chikaskia River in the Indian Territory during a blizzard in the winter of 1879, arriving overland several weeks later at the Omaha Agency. The little band of thirty Ponca were immediately arrested by a detachment of United States troops who had been ordered to return the Indians to the Indian Territory. Through the interest and efforts of citizens of Niobrara and Omaha, the case of Standing Bear was reviewed in the federal court, and he and his band were released from imprisonment at Fort Omaha in spite of the opposition of some officials in the Department of the Interior.

Soon afterward Standing Bear, sponsored by citizens of Omaha, made a lecture tour in the East, accompanied by Joseph La Flesche, an Omaha Indian, and his young daughter Susette, popularly known as "Bright Eyes." Dramatic programs presented the "plight of the Ponca" before audiences in many eastern cities, enlisting the interest of the poet Henry Wadsworth Longfellow and the novelist Helen Hunt Jackson. The unfair treatment of the Ponca and their enforced removal and settlement in the Indian Territory reached the proportions of a national scandal in Indian affairs. In 1880, President Hayes appointed a committee of army officers and prominent civilians to investigate conditions on the Ponca reservation in the Indian Territory, and the following spring Congress made a special appropriation to indemnify the Ponca for their losses and to secure better conditions for them.

Chief Standing Bear and his followers were granted homestead allotments on their old reservation on the Niobrara River, where they became known as the "Cold-country Ponca" or the "Nebraska Ponca." Standing Bear died in 1908 at the age of seventy-nine and was buried in the hills overlooking the old country of the Ponca on the Niobrara.

The Ponca in the Indian Territory became known as the "Hot-country Ponca." When conditions began improving in the early eighteen eighties, they became reconciled to their new location, guided by White Eagle, hereditary chief of the tribe, a quiet, forceful leader who made many trips to Washington in their behalf. The Ponca Boarding School was opened in 1883 near the Ponca Agency (later called White Eagle Agency) and was used for many years. A Methodist mission was also in operation in this vicinity in 1890.

Members of the Cherokee Commission who visited the reservation (in 1890 and 1893) for several weeks failed to secure an agreement with the Ponca for the sale of their reservation. The land in this tract was divided in severalty in equal allotments among the Ponca of White Eagle Agency, and became a part of Kay and Noble counties, Oklahoma, in 1907.

The Ponca were identified with the cattle-ranching interests in Oklahoma Territory through the annual leasing of large pastures on the reservation for grazing purposes. The West Ponca Pasture of 33,000 acres was leased in 1896 to George W. Miller of the famous 101 Ranch. Later,

U. S. ARMY SIGNAL CORPS

Delphine Cerre, Ponca, salutes at the Third WAAC Training Center, Fort Oglethorpe, Georgia, in World War II

some Ponca were among the Indians featured in the Miller Brothers Wild West Show.

Some of their old customs were observed by the Ponca at a comparatively late date. When Chief White Eagle died in 1914, he was dressed in his chieftain's regalia and his favorite horse was killed in the tribal ceremonies held at his graveside in the Ponca cemetery at White Eagle. A monument surmounted by a large white eagle, erected in 1927 to this chief who ruled his tribe for fifty years, can be seen on top of a hill near Marland, in Noble County. Chief White Eagle was succeeded by his eldest son, Horse Chief Eagle, who died in 1940, the last hereditary chief of the Ponca under their old tribal regime.

◆ **Government and Organization.** The Ponca still maintain their nominal government organization in the Ponca Tribal Council to promote their general interests and welfare, especially in relations with the Office of Indian Affairs. McKinley Eagle, son of Horse Chief Eagle, is chairman of the council and elected chief of the tribe. He is a respected citizen of the state and is employed by the Continental Oil Company at Ponca City. Others who have served on the Ponca Tribal Council include David Eagle, Hugh Eagle, Robert Little Dance, Perry LeClaire, Joey Primeaux, and Louis McDonald, all of whom have their homes near Ponca City.

◆ **Contemporary Life and Culture.** Approximately 40 per cent of the Ponca are fullblood members of the tribe. A number of families of mixed-blood descent have French names, by intermarriage with French traders of early days in the North.

The Ponca are generally Christianized, with the largest membership rolls in the Methodist and Baptist churches. They usually have comfortable homes, and their children attend the public schools of the state. Most of them are engaged in farming, with some employed in oil refinery and construction work. A few families became wealthy through the discovery of the Ponca City oil field.

◆ **Ceremonials and Public Dances.** The Ponca Tribal Council sponsors the Ponca Indian Pow-wow held annually at White Eagle, in Kay County, at an announced time in either August or early September. The exhibitions include tribal dances and ceremonials, open to the public. This pow-wow is a historical event among the Ponca in Oklahoma, celebrated in summer since about 1881. Ponca dancers also participate in the annual American Indian Exposition at Anadarko.

Suggested Readings: Stanley Clark, "Ponca Publicity," *Mississippi Valley Hist. Rev.,* Vol. XXIX (March, 1943); Fletcher and La Flesche, "The Omaha Tribe," *27 Ann. Rep., Bur. Amer. Ethnol.*; Grant Foreman, *Last Trek of the Indians;* Hodge, *Handbook of American Indians;* Zimmerman, *White Eagle.*

POTAWATOMI

This tribal name is from the Chippewa (Ojibway) term *potawatomink,* signifying "people of the place of the fire." The Potawatomi are of the Algonquian linguistic family and are ethnically closely related to the Chippewa and the Ottawa, the three having originally been one tribe, according to their traditions. They are described in early French records as "kindly disposed toward Christianity" and "more human and civilized than other tribes."

◆ **Present Location.** The Potawatomi in Oklahoma live near Shawnee, Tecumseh, Maud, and Wanette in Pottawatomie County. There is also a settlement near Lexington in Cleveland County. Members of the Oklahoma tribal group are known as "Citizen Potawatomi." Another group allied with them in pressing their old tribal claims before the United States Indian Claims Commission is the "Prairie Band," that part of the Potawatomi or "Fire Nation" referred to in early records as the *Maskotens.* Today the Prairie Band lived on a small reservation in Jackson County, Kansas. Other small groups of the tribe live in Michigan and Canada.

◆ **Numbers.** Approximately 3,100 Citizen Potawatomi are living in Oklahoma, and about 2,000 members of the Prairie Band in Kansas. In 1908 their numbers were, respectively, 1,768 in Oklahoma and 676 in Kansas. The Indian agency report for 1891 shows 1,469 Citizen Potawatomi allotted lands in severalty on their reservation in Oklahoma Territory. In 1880 there were 300 Citizen Potawatomi enumerated on this reservation in the Indian Territory. The total number of the whole tribe connected with their agency in Kansas in 1866 was 1,992. In previous periods, estimates of the total number in different years are 1,800 for 1843, 2,500 for 1812, 1,200 for 1795, and 2,000 for 1783.

◆ **History.** Traditional history records the Potawatomi, Chippewa, and Ottawa as one tribe living on the upper shores of Lake Huron. By 1700 the Potawatomi had moved southward and were located near the site of Chicago, in Illinois, and on the St. Joseph River in Michigan. When the Illinois tribes (q.v.) had been practically annihilated three-quarters of a century later, the Potawatomi took possession of the greater part of the Illinois country, their land claims extending into what is now Indiana.

During the French and Indian War and the Pontiac uprising, they were aligned against British interests. However, during the American Revolution, they were allied with the English against the American colonies, their hostility against the latter continuing until the treaty of Greenville (1795), which bears the names of twenty-four Potawatomi leaders, the largest number of any of the signatory tribes to that document. The Potawatomi were again allied with Great Britian in the War of 1812, the hostility of the tribe terminating in a treaty with the United States in 1815.

The Potawatomi as a tribe always lacked unity of action, and when the settlers on the American frontier crowded in upon them, they scattered in bands in different directions. The names of one or more of these tribal bands appear on fifty-three treaties between the Potawatomi and the United States (not counting the agreement for allotment in 1890), the first of these documents dated at Fort Hamar, Ohio, January 9, 1789, and the last at Washington, D. C., February 27, 1867. Probably the best known of these treaties was that signed at Chicago in 1833, under which the united Potawatomi, Chippewa, and Ottawa ceded five million acres of land to the United States. As a result, most of the Potawatomi were living west of the Mississippi by 1840.

The portion of the tribe that settled in Iowa became known as the Potawatomi of the Prairie, or Prairie Band, their principal settlement being near Council Bluffs, in Pottawatomie County, Iowa. Those who settled in Kansas were known as the Potawatomi of the Woods, their reservation in Kansas having resulted from the treaty of 1837 in which the tribe had ceded their lands in Indiana. The government, in an effort to unite all the Potawatomi with the Chippewa and the Ottawa, in 1846 provided a new reservation in Kansas, thirty miles square (576,000 acres), lying just west of present Topeka. Shortly afterward the Pawnee, who objected to the settlement of the Potawatomi in this region of the Kansas River valley, declared war on them. In a bloody battle between the two tribes, fought within the boundaries of present Pottawatomi County, Kansas, the Potawatomi were signally victorious. The anniversary of this battle was celebrated annually for many years by a Potawatomi chief, who, dressed in his finest war regalia, rode out to the western and the northern boundaries of the reservation to see for himself that the country was free of Pawnee.

In Kansas, the Potawatomi were subjected to grossly unfair treatment and were more often than not the victims of graft in the settlement of the state. The pressure of white settlement finally resulted in a treaty in 1861 providing for allotment of lands in severalty and the sale of the surplus reservation lands for the benefit of the tribe. Most of the tribe took their allotments, became citizens of the United States by terms of the treaty, and were hence-

MURIEL H. WRIGHT

Sacred Heart Mission, 1876–1901

forth known as the Citizen Potawatomi or Citizen Band. The Prairie Band, who refused allotments and withdrew from tribal relations with the other bands, were assigned a reservation eleven miles square in Jackson County, Kansas, where their descendants are living today.

The majority of the Citizen Potawatomi soon sold their allotments and joined in a plan to purchase a new reservation in the Indian Territory, where it was proposed to re-establish tribal relations. Those who did not dispose of their allotments were absorbed into the communities in Kansas where their lands were located. In 1867 a treaty provided for the registration of the Citizen Potawatomi who wished to go to the Indian Territory, under the direction of their agent and their own business com-

mittee, within two years after the ratification of the treaty.

The new reservation purchased by the Citizen Potawatomi extended from the Canadian River to the North Canadian River, between the western boundary of the Seminole Nation and the Indian meridian, a tract thirty miles square (about 575,000 acres) located in the recent Seminole cession, near the center of the Indian Territory. Soon after the close of the Civil War, this same tract, not then occupied, had been assigned by the government as a "location" for the Absentee Shawnee (q.v.). When the tract was sold to the Citizen Potawatomi, they asked the government to remove the Absentee Shawnee. Action was postponed, and matters drifted along for nearly twenty-five years until the allot-

U. S. INDIAN SERVICE

Two Ponca boys at Kickapoo Indian Day School prepare their school garden for planting, 1946

Mrs. Josie Green finds time for beadwork (1943)

ment of lands in severalty came under consideration. Since the Shawnee had settled in the northern part of the tract and the Potawatomi in the central and southern portions, there was never any clash between the two tribes, though some feeling arose among the Absentee Shawnee when the Citizen Potawatomi asked the United States to confirm their full possession of the reservation. An amicable and fair settlement was finally made in agreements with the two tribes and the government.

The Potawatomi agreement, entered into at Shawnee Town, near present Tecumseh, on June 25, 1890, between United States commissioners and the Citizen Potawatomi Business Committee (Alexander B. Peltier, Joseph Moose, John Anderson, Stephen Negahriquet, John B. Pambogo, Alexander Rhodd, and Davis Hardin), provided for allotment of land to each Citizen Potawatomi and payment in full to the Citizen Band for all surplus lands on the reservation, including those allotted to the Absentee Shawnee. The following day, an agreement made with the Absentee Shawnee (*see* Shawnee) and the United

States commissioners at Shawnee Town provided for allotment of lands in severalty to these Shawnee and a per capita payment of money equaling approximately that paid the Potawatomi. Allotments were completed in 1891, and the surplus lands (about 275,000 acres) became a part of Oklahoma Territory and were opened to white settlement by a run on September 22, 1891.

One of the best-known missions in Oklahoma was the Sacred Heart Mission and Abbey (near present Asher in Pottawatomie County), founded in 1876 by Father Isidore Robot of the Order of St. Benedict on reservation lands donated to the church by the Potawatomi. The mission flourished and later included St. Benedict's College and St. Mary's Convent, the latter notable in the education of Potawatomi and other girls from prominent and wealthy families of the nations and tribes in the Indian Territory. French Catholic missionaries had lived and labored among the Potawatomi long before, in Michigan, Illinois, and Indiana. Father Christian Hoecken began missionary work among the Potawatomi in Kansas in 1837, and ten years later St. Mary's Mission was established on the reservation in Kansas, the institution since growing into one of the leading Roman Catholic missions in the West.

Baptist mission work was begun among the Potawatomi and Ottawa at Carey Station, in Michigan, in 1822 by the Reverend Isaac McCoy, who was active in government surveys and settlement of many tribes in eastern Indian Territory in the eighteen thirties. In 1847, the Reverend Jonas Lykins established the Baptist mission on the Potawatomi reservation in Kansas, where the Reverend and Mrs. Simmerwell gave many years of service. Baptist mission work was also carried on among the Potawatomi after they came to the Indian Territory.

◆ **Government and Organization.** The Potawatomi in Oklahoma are organized as "The Citizen Band of Potawatomi Indians of Oklahoma," having voted their approval of a charter on December 18, 1948, under provisions of the Oklahoma Indian Welfare Act of 1936. Officers and members who have served on the tribal organization include Dan Nadeau, chairman, Iva Goodman, vice-chairman, Ozetta Jenks, and Audie Pecore. Regular meetings of the tribal council are held at the Shawnee Indian Subagency, Shawnee.

◆ **Contemporary Life and Culture.** A big

percentage of the mixed-blood Potawatomi are of French descent. Approximately 500 Potawatomi are reported fullblood members of the tribe. In Oklahoma, the Citizen Potawatomi have generally ranked as a progressive Indian group and are now so thoroughly Americanized that it is difficult to distinguish them as Indians in the population of the state. From the time that they began locating in the Indian Territory (1870–71), many families prospered in stock raising and farming. Tribal matters relating to the Citizen Potawatomi were reported for many years from the Sac and Fox Agency, the site of which was about five miles south of Stroud in Lincoln County.

One of the most talented and best-known American Indian artists, Woodrow Crumbo, is an Oklahoman of Potawatomi descent. A graduate of Shawnee High School and the University of Oklahoma, where he studied art, he has received critical recognition for his fine mural paintings, one of which is on the wall of the Department of the Interior Building at Washington. He is also successful as a craftsman in jewelry making and as an Indian dancer.

Suggested Readings: Connelly, *History of Kansas;* Grant Foreman, *Last Trek of the Indians;* Hodge, *Handbook of American Indians.*

QUAPAW

The name Quapaw is from the tribal term *Ugakhpa,* "downstream people." The Quapaw belong to the Southern Division of the Siouan linguistic family that migrated eastward in prehistoric times and located in the James and Savannah River regions on the Atlantic Coast, then after a long period began migrating back west. The Southern Division of the Siouan people traveled down the Ohio River, at the mouth of which they crossed the Missis-

sippi River and there divided. One band went downstream into present Arkansas, where it became known as the *Ugakhpa* or "downstream people"; the other band went northward and finally settled on the Missouri River in present Nebraska, where it became known as the *Omaha* or "upstream people." Early French explorers referred to the Quapaw as the *Akansea,* from which came the name of the Arkansas River and, later, the state of Arkansas. The name *Akansea,* found in some French records as *Akansa,* signifies "South Wind People," a mnemonic from the Siouan term *ak'a-koⁿce* (or *ak'a-kaⁿze*), in which the word *ak'a* means "south wind." The name *Akansa* is also found in early records applied to the closely related Kansa or Kaw (q.v.).

Early historical records describe the Quapaw as a peaceable people of liberal disposition and gay humor. They were agriculturists and noted as makers of beautiful pottery, which indicates their talent as artists. Their clothing and table and bed coverings were of deer and buffalo skins painted with designs of animals, birds, and calumets in different colors. They lived in pallisaded villages, where they built up high mounds of earth on which they erected long, dome-roofed, bark-covered houses, each the home of several families.

◆ **Present Location.** The Quapaw live in Ottawa County, their tribal interests within the jurisdiction of the Quapaw Subagency at Miami, Oklahoma.

◆ **Numbers.** There are approximately 625 Quapaw in Oklahoma. The Indian Office census in 1944 gives 593 members of the tribe listed by the Quapaw Agency, of which number 359 were in Ottawa County and 234 elsewhere. The population, including full bloods and mixed-bloods, was 305 in 1909, 284 in 1905, 198 in 1890, and 174 in 1885. Estimates of their numbers before 1860 were 476 in 1843 and 500 in 1829. A Roman Catholic missionary in 1750 estimated the "Arkansas" (Arkansea) population at about 1,600. At the time of the discovery of the Quapaw in 1541, the Spaniards reported that there were 5,000 or 6,000 members of the tribe.

◆ **History.** The chronicles of De Soto's expedition in 1541 report the Quapaw as the "Pacaha" or "Capaha," located on the west bank of the Mississippi River about forty or fifty miles north of the mouth of the Arkansas River. Their traditional history and evidences of their occupation indicate that they had lived in the lower Arkansas River region for a long period.

Jacques Marquette, the missionary in 1673 was the first French explorer to visit the Akansea village. The reoccupation of Arkansas Post (1722) and French trading activities in the Mississippi Valley broke up the tribal solidarity of the Quapaw, the main remnant of the tribe, joined by bands of the Illinois (q.v.), having gone farther up the Arkansas and located near the mouth of White River by 1780.

Soon after the purchase of Louisiana by the United States, the Quapaw were reported living in three villages on the south side of the Arkansas River, about twelve miles above Arkansas Post, claiming some lands north of the river and all the region on the south side, now included in southern Arkansas and Oklahoma and in northern Louisiana. They ceded this vast country to the United States in their first treaty, in 1818, with the exception of a tract of ap-

OKLAHOMA HISTORICAL SOCIETY

Chief Wa-sis-ta about 1890

proximately 1,225,000 acres on the south side of the Arkansas between Little Rock and Arkansas Post. The organization of Arkansas Territory brought demands for the opening of this Quapaw reserve to white settlement. As a result, another treaty, in 1824, provided for the cession of the reserve to the United States for $15,000 in cash and annuities, the members of the tribe agreeing to move to the country of the Caddo, on Red River in Louisiana. Floods made their new location uninhabitable; and within a few years they were drifting back to their old location in Arkansas—a homeless people who had lost one-fourth of their numbers through starvation and disease and had lost or abandoned most of their personal property.

The governor of Arkansas and the Indian agent called attention of officials at Washington to the dire condition of the Quapaw. The Quapaw themselves used some of their meager tribal funds to pay expenses of their chief, Heckaton, to Washington to plead for the return of some of their old home country, but the people of Arkansas were opposed to giving any land back to the tribe. Finally, a treaty made in 1833 at New Gascony, Arkansas Territory, with Chief Heckaton and ten other Quapaw leaders, provided the tribe with a reservation of 150 sections, under patent from the United States, near the Seneca in northeastern Indian Territory, the Quapaw on their part giving up any claims they might have in the Caddo country on Red River. About one-third (or 160) of the Quapaw came to the Indian Territory, but when the boundary line of their reserve was surveyed in 1838, they found they had built their homes and were farming on lands belonging to the Seneca. Most of the Quapaw left the country to join others of their tribe who were living in the Choctaw Nation and down Red River in Arkansas and Texas, about 250 of them locating on the Canadian River in the Creek Nation, near present Holdenville in Hughes County. In the midst of these uncertain

living conditions and wanderings, the ranks of the tribe were decimated by epidemics of measles and other diseases.

By 1852, a total of 314 Quapaw had located on their own reserve as surveyed and assigned by the government between the Neosho or Grand River and the Missouri line, north of the Seneca and Shawnee lands, in what is now northeastern Ottawa County. Their agent reported that their head chief, Wartoshe, their second chief, Joseph Vallier, and a few others were industrious men, had good farms and raised bountiful crops which they generously shared with the needy among their people. Crawford Seminary, established by the Methodist church in 1844 among the Quapaw, had been closed, but in 1853 twenty-seven boys and girls of the tribe were attending the Osage Manual Labor School operated by the Jesuits in southeastern Kansas.

At the beginning of the Civil War, Chief Wartoshe and ten other tribal leaders signed a treaty of alliance with the Confederate States; but despite this treaty more Quapaw, in proportion to their numbers, served in the Union Army than members of any other Indian tribe. The Quapaw reserve, bordering both Kansas and Missouri, was overrun early in the war by both the regular fighting forces and the guerrilla bands of both sides, making it impossible for members of the tribe to remain there. Consequently they moved en masse to Kansas, where they found refuge on the Ottawa reservation until the end of the war.

They returned to their reservation in the Indian Territory in 1865, but it was many years before they recovered from the effects of war. They were destitute and starving, and their numbers continued to decline under demoralizing elements from the states on their borders. They sought refuge from these conditions among the Osage, and all but thirty-five were reported in the Osage Nation in 1878. Within a few years, they were looked upon as intruders here.

Quapaw church at Devil's Hollow, near Quapaw, 1900

When allotment of lands was begun among the Indians of the Quapaw Agency region in 1887, the Quapaw began returning to their reserve, the western part of which (40,000 acres) had been sold to the Ottawa (q.v.) in 1867. The Quapaw protested receiving only 80 acres each, maintaining that their remaining 56,695 acres were enough land to allow an allotment of 200 acres each. Finally, after many disappointments and delays on the part of the government, they took matters into their own hands and carried on their own allotment program, thus differing from any other tribe in Indian history. The leader in this movement was Abner W. Abrams, a successful merchant in Kansas and member of the Stockbridge tribe, who, together with the members of his family, had been adopted by the Quapaw. The tribal officials, headed by Charley Quapaw, first chief, John Madison, second chief, James Silk, first councillor, George Land, second councillor, and Frank Vallier, interpreter, under an act and resolutions approved by the Quapaw Council on March 23, 1893, kept the necessary records and made allotments of 200 acres of land to each member of the tribe. To defray expenses in this important work, several white persons were adopted into the tribe upon payment of a nominal sum. These people received allotments of 200 acres each and thenceforth were referred to in official Indian records as the "fullblood white Quapaw." The acts of the Quapaw Council were ratified by Congress in 1895, making legal the allotments to 247 members of the tribe as reported by the United States Indian Office in 1905. A tract of 400 acres from the original reserve was set aside for school purposes and 40 acres for church purposes.

While there had been some surface lead mining in the Quapaw Agency region by 1890, the Quapaw did not know about the great wealth under their lands until the discovery of zinc ore in the drilling of a water well on the allotment of Felix Dardene, an adopted member of the tribe, soon

...e discovery of rich lead and zinc deposits near Commerce in 1905. The first extensive development of lead and zinc was carried on near Lincolnville, Ottawa County, by the Oklahoma and Iowa Mining Company organized by Abner W. Abrams and his associates. Many of the Quapaw were soon receiving incomes from mining leases that brought in more than $1,500,000 a year in royalties by 1926. John Quapaw, Sarah Staten, Alex Beaver, and others made generous donations for school and civic enterprises shared by both Indians and white people. In the flush days of lead and zinc mining in Ottawa County, many members of the tribe gained respect for their ability and character, making good use of their wealth, as seen in their substantial homes and general living conditions.

◆ **Government and Organization.** The Quapaw have retained their nominal tribal government since Oklahoma became a state. Their council reviews all matters relating to tribal business and welfare, its recommendations receiving careful consideration in any action taken by the United States Indian Office. Their last chief chosen under the old regime, referred to by some as "the last real chief of the Quapaw," was Louis Angel. Victor Griffin has also served as chief.

◆ **Contemporary Life and Culture.** The Quapaw are principally mixed-blood white and Indian, a number of families of predominantly French descent. The fullblood Indian group numbers about one-eighth of the tribe. Most of the tribe are in moderate circumstances, engaged in farming and business; some are poor, without property; and very few are wealthy. Yet the fortunes of the tribe as a whole from lead and zinc mining have had a large part in the development of northeastern Oklahoma. Today, the Quapaw are fully Americanized citizens of the state of Oklahoma, and young men of the tribe served in United States armed forces in both world wars.

Suggested Readings: Grant Foreman, *Last Trek of the Indians;* Hodge, *Handbook of American Indians;* Thoburn and Wright, *Oklahoma,* Vols. I and II; Wilson, *Quapaw Agency Indians.*

SAUK AND FOX

Originally closely related, independent tribes of the Algonquian linguistic family, the Sauk and the Fox have long been affiliated and allied. Since their settlement in the Indian Territory, they have been officially classed as one tribal group, the historical records in Oklahoma referring to them as the "Sac and Fox." The name *Sauk* is from their own name *Osa'kiwug,* "people of the outlet," which has also been interpreted "people of the yellow earth," to distinguish them from the Fox people, whose real name is *Mĕshkwa kihug,* "red earth people." The name *Fox* was applied by the early French to the latter tribe from one of their clan names, *Wagosh,* "Red Fox."

The Sauk and Fox, who were known for their conservatism, were endowed with native intelligence and at the same time slow to accept changes and new ways. Late in the reservation period in Oklahoma, some of their progressive leaders were still living in bark houses and wearing blankets with the tribal costume as an evidence of harmony and friendship with the old-time full bloods. Historical records describe the Sauk and Fox as formidable enemies in war, with the Fox especially noted for bravery, yet close and provident in their dealings. Both tribes were of the eastern Woodland People first found living in the Great Lakes region, where they used shells for utensils and were skilled in the mak-

Sauk and Fox wickiup, 1885

ing and the use of canoes. They retained the use of dugout canoes and learned about bull-boats after they left their early locations and settled along the rivers and streams west of the Mississippi. While some early records tell of their forays for horses as far west as Santa Fé, they did not generally use horses until a comparatively late date after their settlement in Kansas. They lived in fixed villages, but made long expeditions hunting buffalo. As agriculturists, they grew extensive crops of

Sauk and Fox bark house, 1890

corn, squash, and beans, and gathered wild rice. While the Sauk and Fox were one of the last Indian groups in Oklahoma to accept civilization, education, and the Christian religion, they produced some scholarly and eminent citizens in the state and nation.

◆ **Present Location.** The Sauk and Fox in Oklahoma live mostly in two groups centering around their community houses: The North Community house is about ten miles north of Stroud on the highway, in Lincoln County. The South Community house is about six miles northeast of Shawnee, in Pottawatomie County. A small band of Sauk and Fox live in Kansas, and a larger band near Tama City, Iowa.

◆ **Numbers.** 1,079 Sauk and Fox were in Oklahoma in 1950. In 1924, the United States Indian Office enumeration showed 686 tribal members in the state. Previous Indian Office reports for different periods show 536 in Oklahoma in 1909; 548 members allotted lands in severalty on their

Sauk and Fox chiefs in the eighties

reservation in 1891; and 421 living on this reservation in 1880. In the last year, the band in Iowa and a small band in Nebraska totaled 430. In the preceding half-century, they had rapidly decreased in numbers, estimated at a total of 6,400 in 1825. The total number of the Sauk and Fox in Oklahoma, Kansas, and Iowa in 1950 was about 1,800.

◆ **History.** The Sauk and the Fox were living in the Great Lakes region when found in 1667 by Father Allouez, who began his missionary work among some of the tribal bands at DePere Rapids, Wisconsin, two years later. Early in the eighteenth century, when they were being pushed southward by the French and the Chippewa, the two tribes formed a close alliance, though they kept their separate tribal identity. Part of them located in what is northwestern Illinois; still another part, mostly Fox, settled west of the Mississippi near the Des Moines River, in the country of the Iowa, with whom they formed a confederation. The groups that stayed near the Mississippi River became known as the "Sauk and Fox of the Mississippi," to distinguish them from the "Sauk and Fox of the Missouri," a large band that settled in the latter part of the eighteenth century along the Missouri River and its branch, the Osage River, in what is now the state of Missouri.

During the Indian wars in the Illinois country, the two tribes were allied with bands of the Potawatomi and the Kickapoo, who were their neighbors on adjoining reservations in the Indian Territory many years later. The Sauk and Fox were attached to the British interests during the American Revolution, and were a part of Tecumseh's Indian confederacy (*see* Shawnee) in 1811–13.

In 1804, the Sauk and Fox of Missouri signed a treaty at St. Louis providing for the cession of tribal lands on both sides of the Mississippi, a step that led to the relinquishment to the United States of all Sauk and Fox lands in Wisconsin, Illinois,

OKLAHOMA HISTORICAL SOCIETY

Grey Eyes (Ukquahoko)

and Missouri. When terms of the treaty of 1804 were made known, the rest of the Sauk and Fox were incensed with the Missouri band, the friction engendered finally culminating in the Black Hawk War in 1831–32. Black Hawk, a Sauk leader, rallied the tribal allies to stand on their rights and remain in Illinois when white men pushed to make the Indians leave Illinois and illegally seized the Fox lead mines at Dubuque west of the Mississippi. Black Hawk's forces were defeated by the

Chief Moses Keokuk about 1880

Illinois militia, and he himself was imprisoned by the United States War Department, but was later paroled and died in Iowa in 1838.

After the Black Hawk War, the Sauk and Fox went west to what is now Iowa, where the tribal bands rallied to make war on their old enemies, the Sioux, whom they defeated and forced out of that country. Sauk and Fox claims to most of the state of Iowa were established by their chief, Keokuk, in a debate in Washington before government officials and a delegation of Sioux. By a series of treaties (in 1842, 1854, 1859, and 1861), all Sauk and Fox lands in Iowa, Nebraska, and Kansas were ceded to the United States, leaving two of the tribal bands on diminished reserves: the Sauk and Fox of the Missouri, on a tract in present Doniphan County, Kansas; the Sauk and Fox of the Mississippi, on another larger tract in present Osage County, Kansas. Another group of the Sauk and Fox of the Mississippi, most-

ly Fox who refused to have any part in these treaties, joined the tribal band (mostly Fox) in Iowa, where with their own money they eventually purchased land upon which their descendants still live.

The history of the Sauk and Fox in Kansas was like that of all the Indians in that region: allotment of lands in severalty and unfairness in the state laws, with "diminished reserves" and surplus lands taken over by the white people, very often through sharp or fraudulent practices. In 1867 a treaty with the Sauk and Fox of the Mississippi provided for the sale of their Kansas lands to the United States and their removal to a reservation in the Indian Territory. This tract as surveyed, containing 479,667 acres, extended west from the Creek Nation, between the Cimarron and the North Canadian Rivers, an area now included in parts of Payne, Lincoln, and Pottawatomie counties.

A large part of the Sauk and Fox of the Mississippi arrived in the Indian Territory from Kansas with their United States agent in December, 1869. Their agency, referred to as the "Sac and Fox Agency," located about five miles south of present Stroud, in Lincoln County, was important in the history of Oklahoma. The Sac and Fox Boarding School, opened at this place in 1872, was in operation many years. No Christian missions were established on the reservation, though the Methodist and the Baptist churches carried on work that gained converts among the tribal members as the years passed. Most of the people engaged in stock raising, with some small-scale farming, depending principally upon the large annuities in cash paid them by the terms of their treaty with the government. These benefits had not been shared by that part of the Sauk and Fox of the Mississippi who had remained in Kansas under the leadership of their chief, Mokohoko. Disease and death having taken their toll among them, they were finally brought to the reservation under escort of United States cavalry in 1886.

The Sauk and Fox were organized as the "Sac and Fox Nation," in the spring of 1885, through the leadership of their chief, Ukquahoko. A written constitution and laws were adopted and later published, providing for the organization of tribal courts that were respected and carried on efficiently in the reservation area. Pressure for the opening of the Indian Territory to white settlement resulted in an agreement made by United States commissioners at the Sac and Fox Agency in June, 1890, signed by Principal Chief Mahkosahtoe and First Assistant Principal Chief Moses Keokuk in behalf of the Sac and Fox Nation, providing for the cession of their reservation to the United States. Allotments of 160 acres to each member of the nation were completed, and the surplus lands (about 385,000 acres) were opened to white settlement by run starting at twelve o'clock noon, Tuesday, September 22, 1891.

Eminent Sauk and Fox in the history of Oklahoma have included Moses Keokuk, son of Chief Keokuk (died 1848) to whose memory a monument was erected by the citizens of Keokuk, Iowa. Moses Keokuk was noted for his fine character and his eloquence in speaking the pure Sauk dialect. He was a member of the Baptist Church during his last years, and his death at the Sac and Fox Agency in 1903 was mourned as a calamity by his people. The well-known anthropologist William Jones was Sauk and Fox, born on the reservation in the Indian Territory, a graduate of both Harvard and Columbia University, and a member of the Field Columbian Museum at the time of his death in the Philippine Islands in 1909. The famous athlete Jim Thorpe, Pentathlon and Decathlon winner at the World's Olympic Games in Sweden in 1912, was born on the Sauk and Fox reservation.

◆ **Government and Organization.** The Sauk are organized with a constitution and bylaws as "Sac and Fox Tribe of Indians of Oklahoma," under provisions of the Oklahoma Indian Welfare Act of 1936. A

prominent citizen of Norman, Don Whistler, was principal chief of the Sac and Fox Tribe at the time of his death in 1951. Members of the Business Committee of the tribal organization have included Edward Mack and Mrs. O. D. Lewis, both of Shawnee; Guy Whistler of Stroud; and Dixon Duncan of Cushing.

◆ **Contemporary Life and Culture.** The Sauk and Fox in Oklahoma are mainly of Sauk descent, members of the division formerly referred to as the Sauk and Fox of the Mississippi. Mixed-bloods in the tribal group are increasing by intermarriage with white people. An estimated 100 persons are fullblood Sauk and Fox. Most of the Sauk and Fox are engaged in farming and stock raising. The discovery of oil in the Cushing field in 1912 brought wealth to some of the Sauk and Fox whose allotments were located in the Cimarron River region. Members of the tribe are generally Christians, with the largest memberships in the Methodist and Baptist churches.

◆ **Ceremonials and Public Dances.** Sauk and Fox hold an annual celebration of

OKLAHOMA HISTORICAL SOCIETY

Mrs. Mary Keokuk, wife of Chief Moses Keokuk

their tribal ceremonials and dances in the vicinity of the South Community House northeast of Shawnee, in Pottawatomie County, at an announced time late in the summer.

Suggested Readings: Grant Foreman, *Last Trek of the Indians;* Hargrett, *Laws of the American Indians;* Hodge, *Handbook of American Indians;* Jones, *Fox Texts;* Michelson, *Fox Ethnology;* Rideout, *William Jones;* Skinner, *Ethnology of the Sauk Indians.*

SEMINOLE

The Seminole are classified among the Muskhogean peoples, a group of remnant tribes having joined in forming this division in Florida during the border wars between the Spanish and the English colonists on the Florida-Carolina frontier in the eighteenth century. The name *Seminole,* first generally applied to the tribe about 1778, is from the Creek word *seminō'lē,* "runaway," signifying emigrants, or those who left the main body and settled in another part of the country.

The Seminole are one of the Five Civilized Tribes in Oklahoma. More than any other of these tribes, they are a cosmopolitan Indian group. Both their men and their women have always been remarkable in their appearance. The men, particularly of the Tiger Clan, have a dark, copper-colored complexion. They are well developed in muscle and limb, and are capable of great physical endurance, A large head, square face, and slightly aquiline nose are tribal characteristics. The women generally tend to average height or less. One ethnologist has stated that the three representative types of a handsome, a pretty, and a comely woman could be selected from the Seminole as the first tribe in rank among the American Indians for fine-looking women. The people of this tribe are amiable in disposition, brave, and truthful. Seminole are among the leading families in the state of Oklahoma, highly respected in the professions and in business.

◆ **Present Location.** In Oklahoma, the Seminole live mostly in Seminole County, which comprises their former tribal lands from 1866 to statehood in 1907. A small part of the tribe that remained in the swamps of Florida after the great Seminole War never came west. Their descendants still dwell in the Brighton and the Big Cypress Swamp reservations in Southern Florida.

◆ **Numbers.** 2,070 Seminole lived in Oklahoma in 1950. Their entire population reported in 1924 by the United States Indian Office was 2,141. Allotment of lands in severalty had been completed to 2,138 members of the tribe in Oklahoma in 1907. In 1875 their numbers were reported from the Union Agency in the Indian Territory at 2,438. An enumeration of the tribe in the Indian Territory in 1836 shows 3,765 in this region, this number falling to about 3,000 in 1845. The first official census of the tribe in Florida was made in 1823, reporting their total population at 4,883. There were about 800 Seminole in Florida in 1950, previous census reports from the United States Indian Office showing an increase in their numbers from 476 in 1924.

◆ **History.** The nucleus of the Seminole Indians was a tribe called the Oconee who lived on the Oconee River, near the present town of Milledgeville, Georgia, in the seventeenth century. The Oconee were a part of the Hitchiti (q.v.), the most important of the native Indian peoples discovered in what is now southern Georgia. The victory of the English colonists on the Carolina frontier in the Indian war of 1715, called the Yamassee Uprising, was soon followed by the departure of some of the tribes from this region, the Oconee emigrating from the Oconee River location westward to the Chattahoochee River, where they became identified with the Lower Creek (*see* Creek). Rivalries between the Spanish and the English trading interests soon after the Yamassee Uprising caused two factions among the Coweta of the Lower Creek. Bands of these people belonging to the Spanish faction began moving south and settling in Florida, in the vicinities of the present cities of Pensacola and Tallahassee, a region that had been vacated by the recently defeated Apalachee tribe. The old country of the Apalachee was included in the "neutral ground" lying between the Altamaha and the St. Johns rivers westward along the present Florida-Georgia border, as provided in a "treaty of friendship" between the English and the Spanish colonial officials in 1736. The neutral ground became a haven for the Oconee and allied remnant tribes, including the Yamassee, Apalachicola, Yuchi, and others, who migrated to this region about 1750 under the leadership of Secoffee of the Lower Creek. These tribal groups living in the neutral ground were the beginning of the Seminole.

The Oconee and their Hitchiti-speaking allies became known as the Mikasuki, the warrior or "Red Stick" division of the Seminole, that bitterly opposed any dealings with the white colonial interests (Spanish, French, or English). After the Creek or Red Stick war in 1813–14, the population of the Seminole was tripled by refugees from the Upper Creek towns (*see* Creek). From this time on, the Creek language predominated, and, indeed, is used today by the Seminole. The Oconee- and Hitchiti-speaking groups, however, were powerful and supplied the leading chiefs in the tribe.

In colonial times, Negro slaves who had run away from their Spanish masters sought refuge in the Seminole country, where they made themselves useful and eventually formed a large element of the population. After the organization of the state of Georgia, runaway Negro slaves from that state were the cause of trouble between the whites and the Indians. Georgia citizens armed themselves and entered the Indian country searching for their slaves among the Seminole. Unprincipled white men even boldly seized Negro slaves belonging to some of the leading Indians. Indeed, the accusation that they had harbored runaway slaves was the main cause of the first Seminole war in 1817–18, during which nearly three thousand American troops under the command of Andrew Jackson attacked and burned the town of Mikasuki, located near the lake that bears this name in present Jefferson County, Florida.

The treaty of 1819 by which Spain ceded Florida to the United States also brought the Seminole under the jurisdiction of the United States. And thereafter the Georgia citizens, already incensed by the runaway-slave issue, demanded that the Seminole and their Negroes move off the fertile agricultural lands, where they had long lived, to another part of Florida. These demands culminated in the first treaty between the

Osceola, from the portrait made by Catlin in 1834, now in the Smithsonian Institution

United States and the Seminole (referred to as the "Florida Indians"), on Moultrie Creek, Florida Territory, September 18, 1823, providing the tribe with a reserved tract in the interior of the country east of Tampa Bay. This was generally a swamp country, and most of the Seminole were soon nearly starving. They were also subject to raids by white men ostensibly seeking their runaway slaves with the permission of the United States secretary of war.

The Indian Removal Act in May, 1830, signed by President Andrew Jackson, was followed by treaties with the eastern tribes for the cession of all their lands and their removal and settlement in the Indian Territory. Commissioner James Gadsden secured a treaty with the Seminole on May 9, 1832, at Payne's Landing on the Ocklawaha River, Florida Territory, for the relinquishment of their land claims in Florida, their removal to the Indian Territory, and their settlement among the Creek. An exploring party composed of seven of the leading Seminole signers came west to find a location in the Creek Nation, accompanied by their agent, John Phagan, and "their faithful interpreter," the Negro Abraham, who in his role as interpreter was quite a character in Seminole history. Among the members of this delegation of "confidential chiefs" were John Blunt, John Hicks, Holahte Emathla, Charley Emathla, and Jumper. They arrived at Fort Gibson in November, 1832, examined the western part of the Creek country, and reported to their people in Florida that they liked the western country but objected to settling near the wild Indians of the Plains in the midst of tribal wars. Jumper, in particular, was bitterly opposed to his people's settling near the "roguish" Plains tribes, as this would imply that the Seminole were of the same character, which they were not.

The treaty of Payne's Landing had contained the statement that the Seminole delegation should examine the Creek country west of the Mississippi "and should

they be satisfied with the character of that country, and of the favorable disposition of the Creeks to reunite with the Seminole as one people," the articles of the treaty should "be binding on the respective parties." While the Seminole delegates were examining the Creek country, United States Commissioners Montfort Stokes, Henry L. Ellsworth, and J. F. Schermerhorn secured a treaty with the Creek Nation at Fort Gibson on February 14, 1833, purporting to settle the boundary lines of the Creek country west and agreeing that the Seminole should henceforth be considered a constituent part of the Creek Nation and be located in some part of the Creek country to be selected by the commissioners. Agent John Phagan maneuvered the Seminole delegation into signing a treaty with the same commissioners at Fort Gibson two months later (April 12, 1833), despite the fact that the members of the delegation were merely an exploring party and not authorized to enter into treaty negotiations. The new treaty stated that as this Seminole delegation was satisfied with the Creek country, the commissioners designated and assigned the "Seminole tribe of Indians, for their separate future residence, forever," a tract of country between the main Canadian and the North Fork, extending west to a line twenty-five miles west of the mouth of Little River.

When the delegation arrived home in Florida and reported what had taken place during their western tour, there was great concern among all the Seminole. They opposed being merged within the Creek Nation (q.v.), torn as it was by factionalism and bloodshed. They objected to settling in a new country where they might be drawn into a war among the Plains tribes, for at this very time there was bloody fighting between the Kiowa and the Osage (q.v.). The Seminole would not recognize the treaty made by their delegation at Fort Gibson, and urged Agent Phagan to call a council where all the chiefs and the people could confer on the difficulties confronting them. The council was refused, Agent Phagan stating that nothing could be done, that all the Seminole must leave Florida for the West. Shortly afterward, charges against him in connection with the handling of tribal funds caused his removal from office.

Ratification of the treaty of Payne's Landing and the treaty of Fort Gibson (both on April 12, 1834) found the Seminole waiting, for the first of these treaties allowed three years before the removal should take place and the second provided that arrangements for the emigration satisfactory to the Seminole would be made by the government. However, Chief John Blunt and his followers of the Apalachicola band had left Florida and were encountering many difficulties en route to join a kinsman who had lived on the Trinity River in Texas for many years. Chief Blunt (or Blount), a friend of Andrew Jackson in the first Seminole war, had received special consideration in the treaty of 1823, with payments in cash to be made later by the government, whenever he removed his people from Florida.

In 1834 the Seminole had a goodly share of intelligent and resourceful leaders. Prominent among them was Mikanopi ("Top Chief"), hereditary ruler and descendant of the ancient Oconee, recognized as head chief of the whole tribe, owner of considerable personal property and Negro slaves, and a man to be reckoned with for

Seminole capitol at Wewoka

his native ability as well as his prestige. Jumper, a descendant of the Yamassee (in their line of chiefs), was highly intelligent and the most influential leader in the tribal council. John Hicks (Takos Emathla), a chief of the Mikasuki, was strongly in favor of removal, as were Holahte Emathla, chief of the Mikasuki, and his son, Charley Emathla, the latter known for his practical common sense and strong personality. Alligator, a descendant of the Yamassee, a shrewd, sensible man, was recognized as one of the real leaders in the council. Osceola (one-fourth Scot, also known by the name of Palmer), a native of the Upper Creek town of Tulsi, was something of a politician among the Mikasuki, yet famous for his undaunted courage. Coa Coochee (Wild Cat), son of the chief of the Seminole in the St. Johns River region called King Phillip, was a young man of promise with an unusual personality.

The year 1835 ended the three-year period prior to the beginning of the Seminole removal according to government officials' interpretation of the treaty of Payne's Landing. When United States Agent Wiley Thompson announced this fact, Holati Emathla and other tribal leaders met him in council in May, agreeing to a time for the departure in the late autumn and early winter of 1835. Bitter opposition to these plans spread among the Seminole under the influence of Osceola, in alliance with Chief Mikanopi and other powerful leaders. In November, threats by opponents resulted in the killing of Charley Emathla, who had steadily supported the removal plans. Agent Thompson then issued an ultimatum that if the Seminole were not ready to leave Florida on the date set, troops would be sent to enforce the order. Soon afterward, Agent Thompson, a young army officer, and some employees at the agency were fired upon and killed by a band of Mikasuki led by Osceola. On the same day (December 28, 1835), a battle took place near the Great Wahoo Swamp north of the Withlacoochee River, in which a large party of Seminole and their Negro allies attacked and killed all but three of a company of 110 United States troops on their way to Fort King (present site of Ocola, Florida) to aid in the removal of the tribe. This was the beginning of the second or great Seminole war that lasted almost seven years at a cost to the United States of the lives of nearly 1,500 soldiers and many civilians and twenty million dollars in money.

The great Seminole war and the removal of the tribal bands to the Indian Territory from time to time during that period form the worst chapters in the history of the whole Indian removal. The war itself was one of attrition. In the campaign carried on in the fall and winter of 1837 under the command of General Thomas Jesup, Indian towns and provisions were burned and destroyed, cattle were killed, and ponies were captured. Negro slaves were captured and promised their freedom to track down the Indians. Families scattered, hiding deep in the Florida swamps while the warriors fought with coolness and courage. Disappointed and perplexed by their failure to conquer the Seminole, the United States forces resorted to questionable tactics. Osceola and Wild Cat were captured under a flag of truce, but Wild Cat escaped from the prison in which Osceola later died. Chief Mikanopi, with a number of subchiefs and warriors, was taken prisoner during a peace parley at army headquarters in December, 1837. The Seminole renewed the fighting, but in the following spring Alligator and Jumper surrendered to Colonel Zachary Taylor. The war came to a close only in 1842 when General W. J. Worth agreed that several hundred members of the tribe might remain in Florida under certain conditions. They stayed in the Florida swamps but never surrendered. As late as 1856, when visited by some of their tribesmen from the Indian Territory and approached on the subject of going west, they refused. Their descendants are the Seminole in Florida today.

As the tribal leaders surrendered at different times during the war, their followers immigrated to the Indian Territory under military escort, experiencing great hardships and suffering, and arriving in their new country destitute, sick, and dying. The first of the immigrant Seminole were led by Chief Holahti Emathla, who died en route a few miles west of the Choctaw Agency in the summer of 1836. His party, who had lost many of their number by death during their two months' journey, located north of the Canadian River near Little River, in present Hughes County, where their settlement became known by the name of their most influential leader, Black Dirt (Fukeluste Harjo). In the spring of 1838, Jumper died of tuberculosis in the army barracks at New Orleans while awaiting transportation to the Indian Territory.

In June, soon after the arrival of Chief Mikanopi at Fort Gibson, a friendly council was held with the Creek of the Lower Towns, headed by Chief Roly McIntosh. At this time there was a cleavage, an almost hostile feeling, between the Lower Creek and the Upper Creek settlements (*see* Creek). When the matter of the location of the Seminole was discussed in the council, Chief Mikanopi and the Seminole leaders refused to settle in any part of the Creek Nation other than the tract assigned them between the Canadian and the North Fork under the treaty of 1833. Since the Upper Creek towns were occupying the best locations in this tract, the Seminole remained near Fort Gibson, some of them in the Cherokee Nation.

The plight of the Seminole presented a difficult problem, impoverished as they were, without the solidarity of their old tribal organization, and with the added complications of disputes and trouble with the Creek, who claimed some of the Negro slaves and free Negroes who had come with the Seminole from Florida. One historian has pointed out that in order to understand Seminole history in the first half of the nineteenth century, one must bear in mind the affection between the Indian master and his Negro slave who was with him in perilous times and who greatly feared the hand of a strange, new owner. In 1845 a treaty signed by United States commissioners and delegations of the Creek and the Seminole nations paved the way for adjustment of the trouble that had arisen between the two tribes. Provision was made for the settlement of the Seminole in a compact body, if they so desired, anywhere in the Creek country, where they could have their own town government under the general laws of the Creek Nation. The Seminole, however, were never reconciled to this provision. A treaty between the United States and the Creek in 1856 ceded a part of the Creek country to the Seminole, in which they were to establish their own government and laws. This tract lay north of the main Canadian River, beginning at the point where this stream crosses the ninety-seventh parallel, a few miles east of the mouth of Pond Creek (in present Pottawatomie County, Oklahoma), thence on a line due north to the North Canadian, and along this river to the south boundary of the Cherokee Outlet, and thence west to the one hundredth meridian.

By 1849 the Seminole settlements had been located in the valley of the Deep Fork south to the main Canadian in what is now the western part of Okfuskee and Hughes counties and adjoining parts of Seminole County. The revered Chief Mikanopi, who represented the power of the ancient Oconee, died in 1849. He was succeeded in the chieftaincy by his nephew, Jim Jumper, who in turn was soon succeeded by John Jumper, nephew of the famous Chief Jumper. John Jumper, who had come as a prisoner of war to the Indian Territory, was one of the great men in Seminole history and ruled as chief until 1877, when he resigned to devote his remaining days to the ministry of the Baptist church. Wild Cat, the principal adviser of Chief Mikan-

opi during his last years, never accepted rule under the laws of the Creek Nation. Although his views prevailed in the end under the treaty of 1856, he did not profit by it, for he had left the Indian Territory in 1850 to plant a Seminole colony in Mexico.

Settlement of the Seminole on the tract ceded by the Creek in 1856 and organization of their tribal government were under way by 1859, although their plans were interrupted a little later by the Civil War. There were other difficulties also. The war waged on the Comanche (q.v.) on the Plains by the Texas Rangers and United States troops in 1858 was followed by threats of trouble with the Plains Indians on the borders of the Seminole country. Nevertheless, the new agency for the Seminole, with Samuel Rutherford as agent, was erected in 1859 at a location that approximates the present site of Wanette in Pottawatomie County.

Confederate Commissioner Albert Pike concluded a treaty with the Seminole at the tribal Council House on August 1, 1861, signed by John Jumper, principal chief of the nation, and town chiefs (*sic*) Pascofa, George Cloud, Foshutchi Tustinukki, Foshutchi Hachochi, Ochisi Chofotoa, Tustinuk Chochoconi, Satoa Hacho, Chofotop Hacho, Sunuk Micco, Tacosa Ficsico, Halpata, and Imathla. Town chiefs Billy Bowlegs and John Chupco refused to sign the Confederate treaty; and before the close of the year, with their followers and their families, they joined the forces of the Creek leader Opothleyahola (*see* Creek) in Kansas, where their men later were enlisted in the Indian Home Guard Brigade of the Union Army. John Jumper immediately organized the Seminole Battalion of the Confederate Army, which served with distinction throughout the war and in which he attained the rank of colonel.

At the close of the war, United States Agent G. J. Reynolds was instructed to select a delegation from the Northern faction and the Southern faction of the Seminole to discuss a treaty at Washington. The Northern Seminole were still in the vicinity of Fort Gibson, where they had been living as refugees for two years; and the Southern Seminole were located on the Washita River in the Chickasaw Nation —thus making it difficult for the tribe, acting as a unit, to select the delegates. Agent Reynolds therefore compelled the selection of the delegates by the two groups separately and hurried them off to Washington, this action giving John Chupco, of the Northern faction, first place during the negotiations. He was recognized by United States commissioners and signed the new treaty on March 21, 1866, as principal chief of the Seminole. John F. Brown, son-in-law of Chief John Jumper and a lieutenant in the Confederate Indian forces, represented the Southern Seminole and signed the treaty in their behalf.

This treaty provided for the cession to the United States of the entire Seminole domain (1856 lands, estimated at 2,169,080 acres), for which the Indians received about fifteen cents an acre, or a total of $325,362. Out of this sum, they were to pay fifty cents an acre to the Creek Nation for a 200,000-acre tract. Through an unfortunate error in the government survey of the western boundary of the Creek Nation, many Seminole discovered some years later that they had settled and made improvements in the Creek country. This necessitated the purchase of approximately 175,000 additional acres from the Creek, adjoining the first tract, at one dollar an acre, making a total of 365,851 acres which comprised the lands of the Seminole Nation until 1907, when Seminole County was organized under the Oklahoma constitution. The treaty of 1866 also renewed the annuities due the Seminole under earlier treaties. Certain sums were apportioned out of the tribal funds to establish the Seminole people in their new country, $50,000 to be used to reimburse the "loyal" or Northern Seminole for losses sustained during the war.

OKLAHOMA HISTORICAL SOCIETY

Governor John Brown about 1888

Prior to the Civil War, religious teaching had been carried on among the Seminole by the Presbyterian and the Baptist mission boards. When the war began, the Presbyterian missionary, the Reverend J. R. Ramsey, went north, and eventually most of the people who had joined the Presbyterian church found their way to Kansas as refugees. The Baptist missionary, the Reverend J. S. Murrow, on the other hand was a Southern man, and was appointed as the Seminole tribal agent by the Confederate government. All the Baptist Seminole are said to have sided with the Confederacy and were joined by the Presbyterian Seminole who were Southern in sympathy. When the war ended, the lines of partisan cleavage in the Seminole Nation were roughly those of these two denominations.

Until the late eighteen seventies, there were two head chiefs in the nation: John

Chupco (died 1881), chief of the "loyal" or Northern faction of the Seminole; and John Jumper (died 1896), chief of the Southern or majority group. When Chief Jumper resigned his office in 1877, he was succeeded by John F. Brown, who served as principal chief until the dissolution of the Seminole government, except for the term 1902–1904 when Hulputta Micco was the elected principal chief. Chief Jumper had been the leader in the Spring Baptist Church that is said to have been organized and located about 1850 among the Seminole living on Buckhorn Creek, east of present Lexington, in Cleveland County. He was ordained in the Baptist ministry and served as pastor of the Spring Church until 1894, when he was succeeded by John F. Brown, who served as pastor until his death in 1919. Spring Baptist Church was moved at an early date and was finally located on its present site, about one mile west of Sasakwa, in Seminole County, where it remains one of the interesting Baptist Indian churches in Oklahoma.

John F. Brown, always referred to and addressed as Governor Brown, the son of a Scottish physician and his Seminole wife, was one of the most influential and prominent Indian leaders in Oklahoma during a period of over forty years. He was a member of the Wewoka Trading Company, one of the largest commercial firms in the Southwest, once rated by Dunn & Bradstreet in the million-dollar class. The interest, welfare, and education of the Seminole were the objectives of Governor Brown's thirty-year service as their principal chief. His sister, Alice Brown Davis, well known for her executive ability and for her activities as an interpreter of her native language, was appointed in 1922 by the President of the United States as chief of the Seminole.

By 1868, the tribal bands had left their refuge locations elsewhere in the Indian Territory and settled in the area that became known as the Seminole Nation. Here, for the first time in a third of a century, they had the opportunity of establishing tribal solidarity. Their council house was erected at Wewoka, which was designated the capital of the nation. The government consisted of a principal chief, a second chief, a national council, and a company of lighthorsemen. The principal chief and the second chief were elected every four years by the majority vote of the male citizens. The council of forty-two members, three each for the fourteen bands or "towns" in the nation, constituted the legislative and the judicial departments, all civil and criminal cases being tried in the latter. Homicide and larceny were the two capital offenses. All other offenses were punishable by whipping. The company of

Governor Brown's home at Sasakwa

MURIEL H. WRIGHT

Emhaka Academy for Girls, established in 1893

ten lighthorsemen, headed by an elected captain, was the law-enforcing body which won distinction as the best police force among the nations of the Indian Territory. More isolated than any other of the Five Civilized Tribes until the building of the first railroad in their country about 1895, the Seminole had the reputation of being a law-abiding, peaceful people. There were twelve Indian towns in the nation and two separate towns for Negro freedmen, these people having full rights as citizens of the nation through the treaty of 1866.

The Seminole had asked for schools for their children when they began locating in the Indian Territory. The first school was opened in 1844, under government auspices, with John D. Bemo as teacher, a Seminole with a remarkable career and advantages of schooling in the East. The first mission school was Oak Ridge Mission, opened in 1848 about three miles southeast of present Holdenville, in Hughes County, under the auspices of the Reverend John Lilley, a Presbyterian. Four schools had been established in the nation by 1868, under the superintendence of the Presby-

terian missionary James R. Ramsey, who also opened a boarding school for Seminole girls, known as the Wewoka Mission, about two miles north of Wewoka. By 1884 missionaries of the Methodist Mission Conference were operating the Sasakwa Female Academy. Two large boarding schools were erected and equipped by the Seminole Nation at a cost of $65,000 each: the first was Mekasukey Academy for boys, opened in 1891 and located about three miles southwest of present Seminole, in Seminole County; the second, Emahaka Academy for girls, opened in 1893, five miles south of the City of Wewoka. This period saw all the Seminole become Christians, generally engaging in small farming operations and stock raising for their livelihood. The Seminole Baptist church had even established a mission church among the Kichai (q.v.) by the early eighteen eighties in the vicinity of Gracemont, in Caddo County, which is still maintained by the Seminole Baptists.

Allotment of lands in severalty was completed among the Seminole by 1907, under an agreement between the Dawes Commission and the nation which had been signed on December 16, 1897, by Seminole representatives John F. Brown, Okchan Harjo, William Cully, K. N. Kinkehee, Thomas West, and Thomas Factor.

The most important event in the history of the Seminole after statehood was the opening of the Greater Seminole oil field near Wewoka in 1923. Within three years Seminole County was world famous for the production of oil. Drilling for oil and gas had been carried on without appreciable results as early as 1902 in this vicinity by the Wewoka Trading Company. At the opening of the Greater Seminole field, only about one-fifth of the original Seminole lands were owned by tribal members. Most of this property was in small acreages, but brought good returns, even great wealth in some instances to the Indian owners. Many of the Seminole also made money in other enterprises through the industrial development in Seminole County.

◆ **Government and Organization.** The Seminole have a nominal tribal government consisting of a chief and a council of thirty-six members, three members elected by each of the former twelve Indian "towns" or bands. The council meets on call of the chief at the County Court House in Wewoka, and serves as an advisory body to the United States Indian Office in matters relating to the general tribal interests and welfare. The chief in 1951 was George Harjo, of Sasakwa.

◆ **Contemporary Life and Culture.** Approximately 50 per cent of the Seminole are fullblood Indian, including descendants by intermarriage with other tribes, principally the Creek. The mixed-blood white and Seminole families are increasing and comprise a generally educated and cultured group. Some admixture with Negro is found, but has not been socially recognized, these people mostly living among the freedmen, descendants of former Negro slaves in the Seminole Nation.

When the Seminole people made their last settlement in the Indian Territory, eight tribal square grounds (*see* Creek) were established in different parts of the nation where the old ceremonials, dances, and ball games were held. There were thirty clans (Swanton's list), in which descent was matrilineal, whose members had certain offices and positions in these ceremonials. Only two of these square grounds are now used, Tallahasutci (or Tallahasse) and Thliwathli (or Therwarthle), where tribal groups sometimes assemble in summer for the old ceremonials and ball games. There is still a loose organization of the twelve Seminole "towns" or bands that were organized for politico-geographical purposes in re-establishing the tribal government along the lines that had formerly existed during the development of the tribe in Florida. However, the close organization of the clans, square-grounds, and "towns" are no longer a vital part of Seminole life in Oklahoma.

Suggested Readings: Grant Foreman, *Five Civilized Tribes*; ———, *Indian Removal*; Hodge, *Handbook of American Indians*; Porter, "The Seminole in Mexico," *Hispanic Hist. Rev.,* Vol. XXXI, No. 1; Spoehr, *Kinship System of the Seminole;* Swanton, "Social Organization, Creek," *42 Ann. Rep.,* Bur. Amer. Ethnol.

SENECA

The name of this tribe is from the Iroquoian term which means "people of the standing or projecting rock or stone," derived originally from *Onĕñiute'roñ'no^n*, rendered in the Mohegan dialect *Onĕñiute'a'kă'* which, in turn, was Anglicized from the Dutch enunciation to *Seneca*. The tribe belongs to the Iroquoian linguistic family, the largest division of the Five Nations or League of the Iroquois, who were first found occupying western New York.

Some researchers believe that the Seneca in Oklahoma are not Seneca proper. They were known as the Seneca of Sandusky when they moved from Ohio to the Indian Territory in 1832, a people called Mingo in colonial times who moved early in the eighteenth century from Pennsylvania to the Ohio and thence to the Sandusky River region, where they became known as Seneca of Sandusky. As the years passed, other bands or remnants of tribes united with them so that they came to include some of the people of the Erie, Conestoga, Cayuga, Oneida, Mohawk, Onondaga, Tuscarora, and Wyandot. It is inferred that the nucleus was largely Erie and Conestoga who were dependent upon the Seneca and lived on Seneca territory along the Ohio and Sandusky rivers whence the name Seneca of Sandusky. Doubtless, however, there was some early intermarriage in these groups with the Seneca proper that gives the Oklahoma Seneca relationship with this well-known Iroquoian tribe of New York.

◆ **Present Location.** The Seneca are principally located in Ottawa County, having been allotted lands in severalty on their reservation in the southern part of the county east of the Neosho or Grand River.

◆ **Numbers.** Approximately 875 members of the Seneca tribe are connected with the Quapaw Subagency in Oklahoma, the largest tribal group in Ottawa County. The census report by the United States Indian Office in 1944 gives 861 under the name Seneca at the Quapaw Agency, of whom 476 are listed in Ottawa County and 385 elsewhere in Oklahoma and other states, these numbers including the descendants of other tribal bands (Erie, Conestoga, Oneida, Cayuga, Onondaga, Tuscarawa), among whom the Cayuga form the largest single group. A total of 372 Seneca were finally allotted lands in severalty at the Quapaw Agency before

Oklahoma became a state. A total of 352 Seneca of Sandusky (including Cayuga, etc., q.v.) arrived from Ohio in the Indian Territory in the summer of 1832. An enumeration at the close of 1832 shows 275 Seneca of Sandusky at their new location on the Cowskin River.

◆ **History.** The Seneca tribe of Sandusky ceded Ohio lands (40,000 acres in present Sandusky and Seneca counties) and agreed to move to the Indian Territory by the terms of a treaty concluded at Washington on February 28, 1831, by James B. Gardner, United States commissioner from Ohio, and the tribal chiefs and warriors, Comstick, Small Cloud Spicer, Seneca Steel, Hard Hickory, and Captain Good Hunter. They received in exchange for their Ohio lands 67,000 acres in the Indian Territory, bounded on the east by the Missouri state line and on the south by the north line of the Cherokee Nation, making a tract that extended west 15 miles and north 7 miles.

The removal from Ohio was delayed until late in the fall of 1831 owing to the slowness of the coming of government supplies promised by the treaty and the reluctance of the Seneca to leave their country. They were a provident people who worked and planned to take with them articles of clothing, household goods, farming implements, and quantities of seeds for planting their new land. Heavily loaded with baggage, they finally left their village on the Sandusky River, embarked by steamboat from Dayton, and arrived on November 16 at St. Louis. They reached their destination on the Cowskin River, northeastern Indian Territory, on July 4, 1832. Their journey had taken eight months and was beset by long delays and great suffering from winter storms, floods, sickness, and death. On their arrival, they found their new country with western boundaries that overlapped those of the Cherokee, who had also been ceded their lands by United States treaty.

Another band of Seneca who had been

long confederated with a band of Shawnee (q.v.), known as the Mixed Band of
Seneca and Shawnee, owned a tract of
land near Lewiston, in Logan County,
Ohio. This Mixed Band (including a band
of Wyandot, q.v.) concluded a treaty with
the United States on July 20, 1832, providing for an exchange of their Ohio lands
for 60,000 acres in the Indian Territory,
with their east boundary lying two miles
west of the western boundary of the country ceded to the Seneca of Sandusky. The
tract ceded the Mixed Band of Seneca and
Shawnee was thus wholly within the limits
of the Cherokee Nation. Members of the
Mixed Band left Ohio in September; and,
after many hardships and deaths from
cholera that was raging in the white settlements along the rivers, a part of this Indian tribal group (258 persons) arrived at
the Seneca Agency on the Cowskin on December 13, 1832. To their dismay, they
found themselves without a country, for
the Cherokee objected to their settlement
on the tract assigned them by the government under the recent treaty.

In the meantime, to secure the removal
of all the Indian tribes from east of the
Mississippi River to the Indian Territory,
in keeping with the Congressional act of
May 30, 1830, President Andrew Jackson
appointed a special commission in July,
1832, to treat with the Indians, the commission members being Governor Montfort Stokes of North Carolina, Henry Ellsworth of Connecticut, and the Reverend
John F. Schermerhorn of New York. The
first work of this commission in Oklahoma
was the adjustment of the lands assigned
the Seneca from Ohio. A treaty made at the
Seneca Agency near Buffalo Creek (branch
of the Cowskin River) on December 29,
1832, signed by Chief Comstick together
with thirteen leaders of the Seneca of Sandusky, and by Chief Methomea or "Civil
John" with eleven leaders of the Mixed
Band of Seneca and Shawnee, provided for
the confederation of the two groups under the title of the "United Nation of

Senecas and Shawnees." The two tribal
groups gave up to the United States all
claims to lands lying west of the Neosho
or Grand River (i.e., overlapping lands
in the Cherokee Nation). As the United
Nation, they were to occupy and hold in
common a tract lying east of the Neosho
or Grand River, bounded on the south by
the Cherokee line and on the east by the
Missouri state line, the north half, or 60,-
000 acres, to be granted in fee simple to
the Mixed Band of Seneca and Shawnee,
and the south half to the Seneca of Sandusky. This treaty, the first made by the
United States with the immigrant Indians
within the boundaries of Oklahoma, thus
provided for the basic title of Seneca lands
in this region, much of which was years
later sold in small tracts to other Indian
tribes.

An official report in 1837 shows the general condition of the Seneca Agency tribes
in the Indian Territory, from which there
was little change during the next twenty-
five years. A census report (1837) gives
200 Seneca of Sandusky, with Comstick,
first civil chief; 211 Mixed Band Seneca
and Shawnee, with Civil John, first civil
chief; and 50 Mohawk (q.v.). These people were civilized according to frontier
standards, were generally steady in deportment, and most of them could speak English, although they were not interested in
a school for their children. They did not
live in villages, but settled in chosen locations over the country where they farmed
and raised livestock. Their homes were
neat log cabins furnished with homemade
furniture, all constructed by themselves.
One of the natives—John Brown—was a
merchant who had a store near the agency.
There was also a miller, a tailor, and a
cooper among them. Under treaty provisions, the government maintained two
blacksmith shops and a grist and saw mill.
When the Methodist Episcopal church,
South, was organized in 1844, the Seneca
were included in the Cherokee District of
the Indian Mission Conference, John F.

Boot serving as Indian pastor on a circuit in 1846.

In October, 1861, following the outbreak of the Civil War, Commissioner Albert Pike secured a treaty with the Seneca in behalf of the Confederate States, signed at Park Hill, Cherokee Nation, by Little Town Spicer, principal chief, and Small Cloud Spicer, second chief, of the Seneca of Sandusky; and Lewis Davis, principal chief, and Joseph Mohawk, second chief, of the Mixed Band Seneca and Shawnee. Their country, located as it was bordering Missouri near both the Kansas and the Arkansas lines, was ruthlessly plundered of horses and cattle and other supplies for the army when Federal forces from Kansas made their first invasion of the Indian Territory in the spring and summer of 1862. More than two-thirds of the Seneca and Shawnee, having suffered great losses in the property and livestock, left for Kansas where they remained with the Ottawa on their reserve until after the close of the war. At this time, the Seneca and Shawnee, together with the Quapaw (q.v.), were listed at the Neosho Agency at Baldwin City, Kansas.

The last treaty with the Seneca and Shawnee of northeastern Indian Territory, referred to as the "Omnibus Treaty," was concluded at Washington on February 23, 1867, providing for the sale of part of their lands for the settlement of several small tribes that had been located in Kansas: Wyandot, Ottawa, Peoria, Kaskaskia, Wea, Piankashaw, and their affiliated tribal bands included under these names (q.v.). The treaty provided for the separation of the Seneca from the Shawnee, the latter to be known as the Eastern Shawnee (*see* Shawnee); all the Seneca (the Sandusky and the Mixed Band) to be joined as one tribe under the name Seneca. Beginning with 1871, the affairs of the two tribes were reported from the Quapaw Agency, now a subagency located at Miami, Oklahoma. The Seneca School, still in operation near Wyandotte in Ottawa County, was established in 1869–70 as a mission by the Friends Orthodox).

The Seneca were allotted their reservation lands in severalty and their tribal affairs generally settled and approved by Congress on May 27, 1902.

◆ **Government and Organization.** The Seneca are incorporated as "Seneca-Cayuga Tribe of Oklahoma," under the provisions of the Oklahoma Indian Welfare Act of June 26, 1936. Their charter, issued by the Secretary of the Interior, was ratified by the adult members of the tribe on June 26, 1937, by a vote of 161 for and none against, in an election in which over 30 per cent of those entitled to vote (450 in the Quapaw Agency area) cast their ballots. Certification of the election was signed by Thomas Armstrong, chief, and Grover C. Splitlog, secretary-treasurer of the Seneca-Cayuga Tribe. The election of officers for the next two-year term was held at the annual meeting of the Council in June, 1947, when tribal members selected David Charloe, chief; Peter Buck, Roy Fisher, and Thomas Peacock, councilmen; and Ruby Charloe, secretary-treasurer.

◆ **Ceremonials and Public Dances.** The Green Corn Feast with its ceremonials and dances is held by the Seneca-Cayuga on an announced date in summer, generally at Turkey Ford on the Cowskin River, near the Ottawa-Delaware County line.

Suggested Readings: Grant Foreman, *Last Trek of the Indians;* Hodge, *Handbook of American Indians;* Wilson, *Quapaw Agency Indians.*

SHAWNEE

The Shawnee are one of the most important tribes of the Algonquian linguistic family.

The accepted form of their name *Shawnee* is from the Algonquian term *shawun,* "south," or *shawunogi,* "southerners." They call themselves *Shawano.* Since they were always in the van of the voluntary migration of Indian tribes from the Atlantic Coast westward in the historic period, their name *Shawnee* or *Shawneetown* is found in many different states where they once had their village homes.

The Shawnee in the old tribal days were noted for their courage and prowess. They were faithful and trustworthy as hunters, scouts, and guards, and as herders for cattle and horses in the trade with Santa Fé along the famous trail that lay through their reservation when they settled in Kansas. During their migrations and the many changes in their fortunes, they clung to their old tribal customs and ceremonies. They have many beautiful legends, and their native language is expressive and eloquent.

◊ **Present Location.** Three main groups of Shawnee Indians live in Oklahoma: the Eastern Shawnee in Ottawa County (*see* Seneca); a large group living among the Cherokee in Craig, Rogers, and other northern counties who formerly were a part of the Cherokee Nation; and the Absentee Shawnee near the city of Shawnee in Pottawatomie County and east of Norman in Cleveland County.

◊ **Numbers.** An estimated 2,250 Shawnee were in Oklahoma in 1951, comprising the three main groups in the state with a few descendants among the Delaware and the tribes known under the name Caddo in southwestern Oklahoma. The Indian Office census for 1944 gives 308 Eastern Shawnee listed by the Quapaw Agency in Ottawa County and 731 Absentee Shawnee listed at the Shawnee Agency in Pottawatomie County. With an estimated 1,100 Shawnee among the Cherokee, the total population of the tribe in Oklahoma in 1944, was 2,139. In 1902, there were 820 Shawnee listed on the Cherokee rolls for allotments of land in the Cherokee Nation. A total of 563 Absentee Shawnee had been allotted lands in severalty on the Potawa-

tomi reservation in 1891. Allotments were completed to 84 Eastern Shawnee on their reservation under the supervision of the Quapaw Agency, in present Ottawa County, by 1893. In 1909, their numbers were reported 107 Eastern Shawnee, 481 Shawnee, and about 800 Shawnee among the Cherokee, making a total of 1,388 in Oklahoma—a decrease in their population during the preceding twenty years. The highest estimate of their numbers in their previous history was given in 1817 when the total population of the Shawnee tribe was reported at 2,000.

◊ **History.** Traditional history and archaeological studies of the Shawnee point to their location on the Ohio River in prehistoric times. Wars with the Iroquois forced them to leave this region and migrate southeastward. The first English colonists found the Shawnee in South Carolina and Georgia, with a few bands living as far south as the Gulf Coast. One small band, whose village was called Sawanogi, settled at a very early period among the Muskokee or Creek people on the Tallapoosa River in Alabama. Even while living in the South, the Shawnee seem to have kept up friendly communication with their kindred Northern Algonquian tribes, especially the Delaware and Mahican. By 1692 the main part of the Shawnee had migrated northward to settle near the Delaware in the valleys of the Delaware and the Susquehanna rivers in northeastern Pennsylvania. Another large branch of the tribe settled in the valley of the Cumberland River in Tennessee, but these Shawnee were driven out in a war with the Cherokee and the Chickasaw about 1714, and migrated northward into Kentucky. About 1730 they began settling north of the Ohio River, where they were united about twenty-five years later with the main body of the tribe that moved westward from Pennsylvania.

The Shawnee were allied with the French against the British in the French and Indian War. They took an active part with the Ottawa (q.v.), Potawatomi, and

Miami in Chief Pontiac's uprising. During the Revolutionary War the Shawnee supported the British forces. Some years after the Revolution, a large band of the tribe joined a band of Delaware west of the Mississippi in Spanish territory, and settled at Cape Girardeau, in what is now Missouri, where they were granted a tract of land by Governor Carondelet in 1793.

The Shawnee of Ohio were openly hostile to the United States until the defeat of the Ohio tribes by General Anthony Wayne, who secured the treaty of Greenville in 1795. Among the nine Shawnee who signed this treaty was their famous Chief Bluejacket.

When Tenskwatawa (The Prophet), their medicine man, and his brother, the great war chief Tecumseh, began spreading the doctrine that all the Indian tribes should unite against the white man's civilization, the Shawnee took to the warpath. Tecumseh took command of the Northwestern tribes on the side of the British in the War of 1812, during which he proved his talents as a military commander and was regularly commissioned a brigadier general in the British Army. His death in the front ranks of his warriors in the Battle of the Thames, Canada, in 1813, before the victorious American forces, broke the spirit of the tribes of the Ohio region. The Shawnee were among those who soon made peace with the United States.

The Shawnee of Missouri, known as the Black Bob band, ceded their lands at Cape Girardeau by treaty in 1825 to the United States, at which time they were promised a reservation west of Missouri. The tract finally selected was in the beautiful, fertile country lying south of the Kansas River in what is now eastern Kansas. During a period of ten years, bands of Shawnee from different parts of the country came to this reservation and established their farms and homes in present Wyandotte and Johnson counties, Kansas. Among them were the tribal members from Ohio, who sold their lands in that state, at Wapakoneta and on the Ottawa River (formerly Hog Creek), to the United States in 1831. The emigration of some of the bands from Ohio was made with much difficulty, in which they suffered loss of life and property. That part of the tribe known as the Mixed Band of Seneca and Shawnee of Ohio settled in present Ottawa County, Oklahoma, in 1832, where they later became known as the Eastern Shawnee (*see* Seneca).

About 1800 some of the Shawnee in Missouri voluntarily migrated from Cape Girardeau southwest, bands of them living at different times in Arkansas, Louisiana, Oklahoma, and Texas. The name of the Shawneetown community near Idabel recalls an early Shawnee settlement in McCurtain County, Oklahoma. These southwestern bands became known as the Absentee Shawnee, some of them settling along the Canadian River in the Creek and Choctaw nations in 1836, near Edwards Store (located at the mouth of Little River in Hughes County). Others came to this region with the Texas Cherokee from the Sabine reservation when the Cherokee and their allies were defeated by the Texans in 1839 (*see* Cherokee). Another band of Absentee Shawnee, with a band of Delaware, located among the remnant Caddoan tribes on the Brazos Reserve in Texas, were removed in 1859 under supervision of United States Indian agents to the Washita River, where they came under the supervision of the new Wichita Agency (*see* Anadarko and Caddo). In 1844, the Choctaw General Council granted some Shawnee families the right to remain in the Choctaw country, the name of Shawnee Creek in Hughes County and that of the Shawnee Hills near the Hughes-Pittsburg County line recalling their thriving settlement in the vicinity, well-known on the California Road through this region. In 1846 many Shawnee left their reservation in Kansas to join their Absentee tribesmen along the Canadian River, following their leaders, who were Southern in their sympathies, in the secession movement that resulted in the organization of the Methodist Episcopal church, South.

The Shawnee ceded their reservation (1,600,000 acres) in Kansas to the United States by a treaty concluded at Washington in 1854, which was signed by their principal chiefs Joseph Parks and Black Hoof, in addition to delegates representing various bands: George McDougal, Longtail, George Blue Jacket, Graham Rogers, Black Bob, and Henry Blue Jacket. Payment for the reservation included $829,000 to be paid out in tribal annuities over a period of years, and a reserve tract of 200,000 acres of their reservation bordering the Missouri state line. The reserve tract was divided in severalty, 200 acres to each member, the members of Black Bob's band and of Longtail's band continuing to hold their pro rata share in common in two separate tracts. The surplus reservation lands (24,138 acres) were to be allotted in severalty to the Absentee Shawnee if they came to Kansas within five years after the ratification of the treaty. Certain tracts were set aside for each of three missions in operation on the reservation: Methodist, Baptist, and Society of Friends, the latter having been interested in the Shawnee since the time of William Penn in Pennsylvania.

During the Civil War the Shawnee in Kansas suffered great losses in property and inequalities under the state laws, yet the able-bodied men of the tribe enlisted and gave valiant service in the Union Army. When Kansas demanded the opening of Indian-owned lands to white settlers after the war, the Shawnee entered into

Shawnee girls, 1853, from the original drawing by H. B. Möllhausen in the Whipple Collection, Oklahoma Historical Society

an agreement with the Cherokee (on June 6, 1869) whereby 722 members of the tribe were admitted to citizenship in the Cherokee Nation. By 1871 they had located in the northern part of the nation, where their children attended the Cherokee schools. The Reverend Charles Bluejacket, the grandson of Chief Bluejacket, was the faithful Methodist preacher and leader of the people who settled in present Craig County, where the village of Bluejacket commemorates this prominent Shawnee family. At the time of allotment of lands in the Cherokee Nation, Vinita was the headquarters of the Shawnee Business Committee that sought a settlement of affairs relating to tribal annuities and claims under the old treaties with the government.

The Absentee Shawnee living on the Wichita-Caddo reservation were represented by their chief, John Linney, among the eleven tribes that made a treaty of alliance in August, 1861, with the Confederacy at the Wichita Agency. Some of the Absentee Shawnee served in the Confederate Army. Most of the Absentee bands, however, left the Indian Territory for the valley of the Walnut River, Kansas, where they remained as refugees during the war. By the terms of a treaty with the United States in 1867, which was never ratified, the Absentee Shawnee were granted the right of selecting lands in the Indian Territory west of the Seminole Nation. They came to this region in 1868 and established their farm homes on land that was subsequently found by survey to be within the reservation assigned the Potawatomi (q.v.), now included in Pottawatomie and the eastern parts of Cleveland and Oklahoma counties. They were eventually joined here by most of Black Bob's band, whose ranks had been decimated during the war and its aftermath, their land tract in Kansas having been practically confiscated and sold under a bill passed by Congress.

While the affairs of the Absentee Shaw-

nee for many years were under the supervision of the Sac and Fox Agency near present Stroud, their principal trading post was Shawnee Town, about one and one-half miles south of the North Canadian River, near present Tecumseh in Pottawatomie County. Mission work by the Society of Friends was carried on here as early as 1875. The post office Shawneetown was established at this point in January, 1876, with Thomas Deer, a native, as postmaster. The same year saw the opening in the vicinity of the Shawnee boarding school, of which Thomas Wildcat Alford, great-grandson of Tecumseh, was superintendent for a number of years.

The rights of the Absentee Shawnee to lands within the Potawatomi country were recognized by the act of Congress of May 23, 1872. However, since the allotments in severalty were to be much smaller than those allowed the individual Potawatomi, life for the Shawnee was one of uncertainty and dissatisfaction for nearly two decades. There were two bands among them: the followers of Big Jim, the grandson of Tecumseh, reported to be conservative and stubborn, yet honorable and industrious, making their own way independent of government supervision; and the larger number, followers of Chief White Turkey, energetic, progressive, and tractable. An agreement with the Potawatomi and Absentee Shawnee secured by the Cherokee Commission on June 26, 1890, provided for the cession of their tribal lands to the United States, settlement of their property rights, and the opening of the surplus lands to white settlement (*see* Potawatomi).

◆ **Government and Organization.** The Shawnee kept their tribal organization according to bands until allotment of lands in severalty in the Indian Territory, each band governed by a chief and council members.

The Eastern Shawnee organized in 1939 as the "Eastern Shawnee Tribe of Oklahoma," under the Oklahoma Indian Welfare Act of June 26, 1936, with a constitution and by-laws approved by a vote of the members, as certified by the Eastern Shawnee Business Committee, composed of Walter Bluejacket, Thomas A. Captain, Ora S. Hampton, Edward H. Bluejacket, and Edward Dushane. The charter issued to the organization by the Secretary of the Interior was approved by a vote of the adult members in an election held on December 12, 1940, certification of the election being signed by Walter L. Bluejacket, chief, and T. A. Captain, secretary-treasurer, Eastern Shawnee Tribe.

The Absentee Shawnee are also organized as the "Absentee Shawnee Tribe of Indians of Oklahoma," under the Oklahoma Indian Welfare Act. This organization is governed by a tribal council, headed by the Absentee Shawnee Business Committee, whose members in 1949 were: Harold Abraham, chairman, Thomas B. Hood, vice-chairman: Sallie H. Tyner, secretary-treasurer: Arthur Rolette and Charley Switch, members. The Council meets annually and the Business Committee quarterly at the Indian Subagency at Shawnee.

◆ **Contemporary Life and Culture.** The Shawnee are predominantly mixed blood by intermarriage with the Delaware, the Cherokee, and white people. The largest number of fullblood Indians is found among the Absentee Shawnee. Throughout the state, members of the tribe are respected citizens, engaged in farming, livestock raising, and professional and business life.

The Baptist church and the Society of Friends have the largest membership rolls among the Absentee Shawnee.

◆ **Ceremonials and Public Dances.** Big Jim Band of Absentee Shawnee have kept up some of their old ceremonials, holding tribal thanksgiving dances in early spring and fall and an annual war dance in August. These dances are held at the home of Little Jim, about one-quarter of a mile south of Little Axe on State Highway 9, east of Norman. The public may attend these dances, but no pictures may be taken. Suggested Readings: Alford, *Civilization;* Connelly, *History of of Kansas;* Grant Foreman, *Last Trek of the Indians;* Hodge, *Handbook of American Indians.*

SKIDI

The Skidi, the largest of the four confederated bands of the Pawnee (q.v.), are generally considered a separate tribe since they speak a distinct dialect of their own (Caddoan family). They are looked upon as the original tribal group from which the other three Pawnee bands came. Their name Skidi, from the Pawnee word *tsikri,* "wolf," was applied from the location of their villages on the Wolf, or Loup, River in Nebraska. For this same reason they were called *Loups* by the French traders. One of the most important ceremonies held by the Skidi every year in old tribal times was the sacrifice of a captive girl to the Morning Star. The celebrated Pawnee

brave, Petalesharo, whose father was much opposed to the practice, rescued a captive Comanche girl from the sacrifice, after which the Skidi abolished the ceremony. A band of Skidi fought a battle with the Wichita in western Oklahoma in 1837 and later were at war with the Comanche in this region. As a tribe, however, the Skidi were usually closely associated and intermarried with the Wichita. The Skidi are a part of the Pawnee in Pawnee County. Suggested Readings: Dunbar, "The Pawnee Indians," *Magazine of American History,* Vol. IV, No. 4 (April, 1880); Hodge, *Handbook of American Indians;* Wedel, *Introduction to Pawnee Archeology.*

STOCKBRIDGE

The Stockbridge were originally known as the Housatonic, but became known by this new name when the village of Stockbridge, Massachusetts, was founded near their tribal settlement. In their early history, they occupied the Housatonic Valley in what is now the southern part of Berkshire County, Massachusetts. The Housatonic or Stockbridge belonged to the Mahican Confederacy of the Algonquian linguistic family.

At the close of the American Revolution, the dispirited remnant of the Stockbridge joined the Oneida and located on a tract of tribal land in Madison and Oneida counties, New York. Here they prospered and increased, numbering 300 in 1796. In 1832 the Stockbridge with a band of Oneida confederated with the Munsee (q.v.) in the purchase of a reservation tract near Lake Winnebago, Wisconsin, where a large group still live. A part of the Confederated Stockbridge and Munsee, later known as "Christian Indians," moved to Kansas in 1839 and subsequently, in 1867, by special agreement with the Cherokee, settled in the Indian Territory as citizens of the Cherokee Nation. Members of a family of Stockbridge were also adopted by the Quapaw (q.v.) in 1893.

Suggested Readings: Grant Foreman, *The Last Trek of the Indians* (Chicago, 1946); Hodge, *Handbook of American Indians.*

TAMAROA

The name of the Tamaroa is said to be from the Illinois term *tamarowa,* "cut tail," probably having reference to a totemic animal, perhaps the bear or the wildcat.

The Tamaroa were one of the tribes of the Illinois Confederacy (q.v.) of the Algonquian linguistic family. In 1680 their population was estimated at about 1,000 living on both sides of the Mississippi River at the mouths of the Illinois and the Missouri rivers. They were friendly to the French, who always stopped at their villages on the way to and from Canada and Louisiana. This friendship with the French made the Chickasaw and the Shawnee their enemies, both tribes waging a continual war on the Tamaroa. They were greatly weakened in the general extermina-

tion of the Indian tribes north of the Ohio River in the latter half of the eighteenth century. Two Tamaroa leaders signed the treaty of 1818 by which the Illinois tribes, including the Peoria, ceded approximately half of present Illinois to the United States. The name of the Tamaroa as a tribe is listed in the treaty made with the Kaskaskia and the Peoria at Castor Hill, St. Louis County, Missouri, on October 27, 1832. Henceforth the Tamaroa were a part of the Peoria (q.v.), whose descendants may be found in Ottawa County, Oklahoma. Suggested Readings: Grant Foreman, "Illinois and Her Indians," in *Papers in Illinois History,* 1939; ———, *Last Trek of the Indians;* Hodge, *Handbook of American Indians.*

TAWAKONI

The name *Tawakoni* (varying to *Tawakani* or *Towakani*) is found interpreted "river bend among red sand hills," the term probably having reference to the location of some village of this tribe near a stream. The historical records for 150 years, beginning early in the eighteenth century, report the Tawakoni villages near some river, first in Oklahoma and later in Texas, before the final settlement of the tribe in Oklahoma. The earliest of these records refers to the tribe as the Touacara, later variations of the name appearing as Tahwaccaro, Tahuacaro, or Towoccaro.

The Tawakoni belong to the southern group of the Caddoan linguistic family. They and their closely allied tribe, the Waco (q.v.), speak a dialect of the Wichita language.

Up until the middle of the nineteenth century, the Tawakoni were noted traders, their villages serving as markets especially for the Tonkawa (q.v.), who brought in large quantities of buffalo robes, deerskins, tallow, dried buffalo tongue, and other products. Among their allied tribes, the Tawakoni were esteemed as friends and leaders. When they came under agency supervision in Texas, they were reported energetic in their building and farming operations. They were raising tobacco and corn in large quantities when first reported in Oklahoma by the French in 1719.

◆ **Present Location.** The Tawakoni are counted as part of the Wichita in Caddo County, Oklahoma.

◆ **Numbers.** About 190 Tawakoni live in Oklahoma. The last separate census of the Tawakoni in 1894 gave their number at 126, their tribal population having diminished from 162 in 1883. The agent's report for 1875 listed a total of 102 members. About 258 Tawakoni located on the Washita River in 1859 under the supervision of the Wichita Agency, after their removal with the Caddo (q.v.) from the Brazos Reserve in Texas. In 1772 approximately 750 tribal members were living in two Tawakoni villages on the Brazos and Trinity rivers in Texas. La Harpe in 1719 reported nine allied Caddoan tribes among whom the Tawakoni were the leaders, with a total population of 6,000 members living in villages along the Arkansas River in Oklahoma.

◆ **History.** The main Tawakoni (or Touacara) village on the Arkansas River, near the present site of Haskell in Muskogee County, was visited by the French commandant, La Harpe, on his first expedition in Oklahoma in 1719. Members of the tribe had many fine horses and were already in possession of Spanish saddles and bridles secured in the Spanish trade in the Southwest. A throng of Indians, including the chiefs of nine different tribes living in the vicinity on the Arkansas, attended La Harpe's council in the Tawakoni village. After a week of Indian ceremonials, singing, dancing, and feasting, the French set up a post carved with the coat-of-arms of the king of France and the date, September 10, 1719, perhaps thus marking the first agreement between a European nation and the Indian tribes in Oklahoma.

At the close of the French and Indian war in 1763, the Tawakoni drifted south into Texas with other Caddoan tribes, pushed southwest by their enemies, the Osage, from the northeast. The Tawakoni were usually at peace with the Hainai (Ionie), the Kadohadacho (Caddo proper), and the Tonkawa, but were enemies of the Apache and were reported to have sold many of their hated Apache captives as slaves to the French in Louisiana.

The Tawakoni with their allies, the Waco (q.v.), were living in two villages on the Brazos River in the vicinity of present Waco, Texas, when they were visited in 1778–79 by De Mézières on behalf of the Spanish government.

The importance and prestige of the Tawakoni among the western tribes were recognized in a number of peace councils and treaties in the nineteenth century. Their chiefs, Daquiarique (or Tauacaquerie) and Tacahehue, made a treaty alliance with the Mexican government in 1821. The Tawakoni had a leading part in bringing the Comanche and the Wichita (q.v.) to Camp Holmes on the Canadian River in 1835, when these two tribes signed their first treaty with the United States in the Indian Territory. The Tawakoni, referred to as "Tawakaro," were among the three tribes whose leaders signed the peace treaty at Fort Gibson, on April 7, 1837, with Montfort Stokes and Auguste P. Chouteau, commissioners for the United States. In May, 1846, the name of the tribe appeared among those that signed the treaty with United States commissioners at Council Springs, Texas, which brought about the establishment some years later of the Lower Reserve on the Brazos River, in Young County, for the remnant Texas tribes.

The Tawakoni settled on the Lower Reserve in 1855 (*see* Anadarko). They prospered in their new location, built good houses in their village, cared for their livestock, raised large crops of corn, some wheat, and a plentiful supply of vegetables.

MURIEL H. WRIGHT

Tawakoni Jim, chief of the Wichita, about
1901

The United States agent commended them for their advancement and peaceable conduct, remarking that they were particularly interested in sending their children to the government school on the reservation.

Among the Tawakoni children on the Lower Reserve was a lad named Kor-sid-awas-er-date, who became well known many years later as Jim Tehuacana or "Tawakoni Jim," one of the Indian leaders in the area of the Wichita Agency and Fort Sill, Oklahoma. He once said that as a small boy he had lived among the Wichita (q.v.) on Rush Creek, but returned with his family to their people on the Brazos River, where their chief, Ochillas, took him by the hand and told him to go to school and learn the white man's ways.

In July, 1859, Chief Ochillas represented the Tawakoni in the intertribal council of nine tribes held at Fort Arbuckle with United States officials preparatory to the location of these tribes in western Indian Territory. A month later, the Tawakoni came north from the Lower Reserve with the Caddo (q.v.) and other Texas tribes, and settled on the Washita River, where they were under the supervision of the Wichita Agency.

With the outbreak of the Civil War, Commissioner Albert Pike secured a treaty for the Confederate States with the tribes at the Wichita Agency on July 12, 1861, among the signers of which appeared the name of "Ochiras" (Ochillas), principal chief of the "Tahuacaros" (Tawakoni), Subsequently, a large part of the tribe went north to Kansas, where they remained as refugees with the Wichita and other Union Indians until the end of the war. On their way back to their former locations on the Washita River in 1867, many of them were stricken and died during an epidemic of cholera that swept their ranks.

The Wichita Agency was re-established in 1868 near the present site of Anadarko, where the Tawakoni were afterward listed as a part of the Wichita and Affiliated Tribes. Within this associated tribal group, the Tawakoni were closely allied with the Wichita, Tawakoni Jim serving as chief of the Wichita in 1898. When the Court of Indian Offenses was established at the Wichita Agency in 1888, he served as one of the Indian judges with Lone Wolf of the Kiowa and Quanah Parker of the Comanche (q.v.)

Under an agreement between United States commissioners and the Wichita and Affiliated Tribes, ratified by Congress on March 2, 1895, the Tawakoni were allotted lands in severalty on the Wichita-Caddo reservation in 1901, their lands generally located north of the Washita River in Caddo County. Since then they have been counted as a part of the Wichita (q.v.) in their tribal interests and activities, and have been a rural people living on their farms.

Suggested Readings: Bolton, *Athanase de Mézières;* Grant Foreman, *Last Trek of the Indians;* Hodge, *Handbook of American Indians;* Lewis, "La Harpe's First Expedition in Oklahoma," *Chron. of Okla.,* Vol. II, No. 4.

TONKAWA

The name *Tonkawa* is from the Waco term *tonkaweya,* meaning "they all stay together."

The Tonkawa belong to the Tonkawan linguistic family that was once composed of a number of small subtribes formerly living west from central Texas and western Oklahoma to eastern New Mexico. The Tonkawa had a distinct language, and their name as that of the leading tribe was applied to their linguistic family.

They were one of the most warlike tribes during nearly two centuries of conflict with their enemy tribes on the Western plains and with the Spanish and the later American settlers in the Southwest. Their men were famous warriors, their chiefs bearing many scars of battle. The Tonkawa women were also strong physically and vindictive in disposition. These characteristics of the tribe may have been the reason for their name among the Kiowa and the Comanche, signifying "man-eating men" or "cannibals." The Caddo and other tribes believed that the Tonkawa were cannibals when they settled on the Washita River before the Civil War. The truth of such stories about the Tonkawa has long been a matter of dispute.

The people of this tribe were nomadic in their habits in the early historic period, moving their tipi villages according to the wishes of the chiefs of the different bands. They planted few crops, but were well known as great hunters of buffalo and deer, using bows and arrows and spears for weapons, also some firearms secured from early Spanish traders. They became skilled riders and owned many good horses in the eighteenth century.

Early historical records show that the Tonkawa were an industrious people. A list of articles that they manufactured and used in their daily life, besides some of their weapons, included saddles, bridles, tether ropes, shields, tipis, blankets, shirts, moccasins, girths, belts and ornaments, horn spoons and drinking cups, sinew thread, and glue (all made from the bones, skins, and hair of buffalo and deer).

They were known among the Spanish and the later American traders for the large quantities of tallow, deerskins, buffalo robes, and tongues which they had to sell. In their earlier trading relations, the Tonkawa brought in thousands of buffalo and deer hides every year to barter with the Tawakoni (q.v.).

◆ **Present Location.** The Tonkawa live in the vicinity of the town of Tonkawa, in Kay County.

◆ **Numbers.** According to the most recent

enumeration by the Office of Indian Affairs (1944), there are 56 Tonkawa in the state, including some Lipan (q.v.) who have been identified with the tribe in Oklahoma since 1885. In that year, 92 members of this Indian group were brought from Fort Griffin, Texas, where they had numbered 115 (including 17 Lipan) in 1880. Their numbers declined from that time, indicating the possible extinction of the tribe. There were 85 Tonkawa (including the few Lipan) in 1887, 73 in 1890, 53 in 1910, 48 in 1924, and 46 in 1936.

It was reported that about 350 Tonkawa were brought by the government from Texas to the Washita River with the Caddo in 1859. An official report in 1847 numbered the Tonkawa at 150 fighting men, indicating a total population of 600 to 750 in the tribe in Texas. In 1805 an Indian Office report estimated 800 to 1,000 Tonkawa in Texas. In 1778 De Mézières reported their numbers at 300 fighting men, indicating a possible 1,500 total population for the whole tribe.

◆ **History.** Luis de Moscoso, who succeeded De Soto as governor of the surviving Spaniards on his famous expedition, visited the Tonkawa on the Trinity River in Texas in 1542. Specific mention of the tribe was made in the records of southwestern government relations—French and Spanish—in 1691. The French commandant, La Harpe, on his first expedition in Oklahoma in 1719 mentioned the Tonkawa (Tancaoye) as one of the "roving nations" in the upper Red River region. Until the close of the eighteenth century, they were hostile to the Lipan and Apache in the Texas-Oklahoma country, a condition which kept them generally friendly with the Comanche and the Caddo tribes. Tonkawa warriors were with the Comanche who destroyed the Catholic mission on the San Saba River, Texas, in 1758 (*see* Apache). From about 1800 the Tonkawa were allied with the Lipan and were friendly to the Texans and other southern divisions. By 1837 they had for the most part drifted

toward the southwestern frontier of Texas and were among the tribes identified in Mexican territory.

A treaty of peace and commercial alliance was secured and signed by United States commissioners at Council Springs on the Brazos River, in Robertson County, Texas, the Tonkawa appearing among the tribes signing on May 15, 1846. Through subsequent activities of government agents in Texas, the tribe settled on the Lower Reserve on the Brazos River in Young County in 1855 with the Caddo and Anadarko.

In the late summer of 1858, some Tonkawa were employed among the Indian scouts who accompanied several companies of the Second Cavalry under the command of Captain (Brevet Major) Earl Van Dorn on an expedition against the Comanche north of Red River in the Indian Territory. Just before Van Dorn's forces attacked a Comanche encampment near the Wichita Village (*see* Wichita) on Rush Creek, in present Grady County, Oklahoma, the Tonkawa scouts were active in locating and driving off the Indian horses in the vicinity of the encampment and the village, leaving the Comanche and the Wichita on foot during the ensuing fight. For their part in this battle the scouts incurred the hatred of the Comanche, Wichita, and Caddo bands in the Indian Territory toward the whole Tonkawa tribe.

When in the summer of 1859 the Texans adopted the policy of exterminating all the Indian tribes within the borders of their state, the Tonkawa were brought north from the Brazos Reserve (*see* Caddo *and* Anadarko) and settled on the Washita River in the Leased District (*see* Choctaw) under the supervision of the Wichita Agency established in August, 1859, near the site of Fort Cobb in Caddo County. They located in the Washita Valley a few miles south of the agency and soon began farming operations.

After the beginning of the Civil War, a "Treaty with the Comanches and other

Tribes and Bands," negotiated at the Wichita Agency on August 12, 1861, by Albert Pike for the Confederate States, included the Tonkawa. From this time, they were the most loyal to the Confederate alliance of all the tribes on the Washita River, consistently following their old ties with the Southern people in Texas.

A band of Delaware and Shawnee, well armed with guns and ammunition by the Federal forces in Kansas, attacked the Wichita Agency, killed some of the employees, and burned the building during the afternoon of October 23, 1862. Immediately afterward, a report was circulated that the Tonkawa had recently killed a Caddo boy and had been seen cooking his body in preparation for a cannibalistic feast. In the meantime, hearing that their friends at the agency had been killed, the Tonkawa, armed only with bows and arrows, set out from their homes for Fort Arbuckle, seeking protection of the Confederate troops. Early in the morning on October 24, 1862, the Tonkawa encampment about four miles south of present Anadarko was attacked by the infuriated Northern Delaware and Shawnee, who were aided by bands of Wichita, Caddo, and other tribes. A total of 167 Tonkawa men, women, and children were brutally massacred. Their chief, Plicido, who had always been counted a good, sensible man, was killed in the fighting. Undoubtedly the whole tribe would have been exterminated if a band of them had not been away from the reservation on a buffalo hunt.

Soon after the massacre, the surviving Tonkawa arrived at Fort Arbuckle in a pitiable condition. In November, 1862, Governor Winchester Colbert of the Chickasaw Nation granted them permission to locate temporarily on Rock Creek, about halfway between Fort Arbuckle and Fort Washita, provided they observed the Chickasaw laws and furnished guides to the Chickasaw Battalion in the Confederate service. After the war, bands of Tonkawa were seen in southwestern Texas in

the vicinity of San Antonio. Some were involved in the last Indian wars in this region and were generally regarded as outcasts.

The Tonkawa were finally gathered around Fort Griffin, Texas, where they were placed under the supervision of the acting Indian agent, Captain J. B. Irvine of the Twenty-second Infantry, who pleaded for aid for them from Washington in 1879. He said that these starving Indians deserved better treatment, for they had always been friendly to the whites and had served the government well as guides and scouts.

The Indian Appropriation Act passed by Congress in 1884 provided for the support, civilization, and instruction of the Tonkawa. The following autumn, members of the tribe left Fort Griffin, Texas, for the Indian Territory, arriving on October 22, 1884. They were in a destitute condition throughout the winter, during which most of their ponies starved to death. In the spring of 1885 the tract of approximately 91,000 acres recently occupied by the Nez Percé (q.v.) in present Kay County was assigned by the Department of the Interior as the Tonkawa reservation. The last remnant of the Tonkawa—a total of 92 persons, including a few Lipan (q.v.)— arrived here in an exhausted condition on June 30, 1885, from the Sac and Fox Agency.

The report from the Indian agency at Oakland in 1886 stated that the able-bodied among the Tonkawa had worked together and, with "four old horses," two or three plows, and some hoes, had produced excellent crops on thirty-five acres. Within a few seasons, the members of the tribe had generally improved in their living conditions.

In the summer of 1891 the Tonkawa (and Lipan, q.v.) selected allotments of lands in severalty (about 160 acres each) on their reservation through the work of Helen P. Clark, a member of the Blackfoot tribe in Montana who was serving as allotting agent for the government. An agreement with the Tonkawa made by the Cherokee Commission on October 21, 1891, secured the cession of the whole Tonkawa reservation (90,760 acres) to the United States for $30,600. All allotments of land in severalty were confirmed to the individual allottees by the terms of the agreement. The surplus lands (79,276.60 acres) were opened to white settlement at the opening of the Cherokee Outlet on September 16, 1893.

In 1905, the Tonkawa were reported contented and generally prospering on their farms, a total of 73 having received allotments. A Methodist mission had been established among them. Their children attended the agency school at old Oakland, located in the midst of a grove of trees, on good land on the west bank of the Chikaskia River, about two and one-half miles southeast of present Tonkawa in Kay County. The Tonkawa Indian Agency at Oakland was closed about 1910; but the Tonkawa, together with the few Lipan, became citizens of the state of Oklahoma in 1907.

◊ **Government and Organization.** An election committee, composed of John Rush Buffalo, Paul Allen, and Walter Jefferson, certified the adoption of the constitution and bylaws of the "Tonkawa Tribe of Indians of Oklahoma" under the provisions of the Oklahoma Indian Welfare Act of 1936. There had been 9 votes for and 7 against organizing the tribe in an election held on April 21, 1938, the number voting representing more than 30 per cent of the Tonkawa entitled to vote in such an election. The preamble of their new tribal constitution set forth that the organization was to promote the "common welfare and to secure" to the Tonkawa and their descendants the "rights, powers, and privileges offered by the Thomas-Rogers Oklahoma Indian Welfare Act."

◊ **Contemporary Life and Culture.** The Tonkawa are so few in number they are not noticeable in the general population of Tonkawa. Some have intermarried among white people, yet the tendency is to keep to the Indian group in the vicinity. Most of them live on their farms and are engaged in rural occupations and day labor. Their children attend the public schools, though some at high-school age are sent to Chilocco Indian Agricultural School. The Tonkawa are generally members of Protestant denominations.

Suggested Readings: Abel, *The American Indian in the Civil War;* Bolton, *Athanase de Mézières;* Hodge, *Handbook of American Indians;* Nye, *Carbine and Lance.*

TUSCARORA

The Tuscarora are of the Iroquian linguistic family, their name derived from the the tribal term *Skaru'rĕⁿ*, "hemp gatherers," referring to the many uses these Indians made of the plant called Indian hemp. When reported by English colonial officers at the beginning of the eighteenth century, the Tuscarora were a powerful tribe living toward the Atlantic Coast in North Carolina. Though they were known for their generosity and friendliness to the early colonists, war and massacre by the settlers in North Carolina against them forced the Tuscarora out of their country. Most of the tribal remnant went north to New York, where through the influence of the friends, the Oneida, they were permanently adopted by the League of the Iroquois in 1712–15. The largest groups of the Tuscarora now live in New York and Canada.

As one of the tribes called New York Indians, the chiefs of the Tuscarora signed a treaty with the United States at Buffalo

Creek, New York, in 1838, providing for their removal west to the forks of the Neosho River. A party of New York Indians, among whom were a band of Tuscarora, came to this region in 1846, having suffered many hardships that permanently weakened their tribal entity. A total of thirty-two Tuscorora were eventually allotted lands in severalty on a small reservation tract near the Cherokee and the Osage lands in eastern Kansas. Pressure by white settlers after the Civil War forced them to sell their lands as provided in the Congressional act of February 19, 1873. Some of their descendants are reported among the mixed-blood members of the Shawnee and the Seneca in northeastern Oklahoma.

Suggested Readings: Grant Foreman, *Last Trek of the Indians;* Hodge, *Handbook of American Indians;* Johnson, *Legends, Traditions, and Laws, Iroquois;* Swanton, *Indians of Southeastern U. S.*

TUSKEGEE

The name of the Tuskegee, also spelled "Taskigi," signifies "one who has received a war name," the meaning of the Creek word *Tv'seki'yv,* from which the name probably originated. The Tuskegee were an ancient tribe of the Muskhogean linguistic family, discovered by De Soto in 1540 living in what is now northern Alabama. They subsequently separated into two divisions: the Tuskegee living on the Tennessee River became a part of the Cherokee; those living at the junction of the Coosa and Tallapoosa rivers were counted among the Upper Creek in the Creek Confederacy (*see* Creek). When the latter came to the Indian Territory, they lived for a period in the southeastern part of the Creek Nation, in the vicinity of present Eufaula, later settling between the North Canadian River and Pole Cat Creek in the western part of present Creek County. Tuskegee in this region was one of the largest "towns" (population 401 in 1891) of the Creek Nation from the close of the Civil War until 1907, represented by one member in the House of Kings and two members in the House of Warriors of the Creek National Council. Roly McIntosh, second chief of the Creek Nation (1895–99) was of Tuskegee Town. He was the namesake and protégé of old Chief Roly McIntosh and was considered the outstanding orator in his nation during his active life.

Suggested Readings: Debo, *The Road to Disappearance;* Speck, *Creek Indians of Taskigi Town;* Swanton, *Early History of the Creek.*

WACO

The Waco were referred to by several different names including *Huanchane, Houechas,* and *Honeches,* in early French records. The name *Waco,* by which the tribe is commonly known in Oklahoma, is probably an abbreviation of one of the early names applied to the tribe. It did not appear in the form *Waco* until after 1820 and then in the writings of the Anglo-Americans in Texas.

The Waco are of the Caddoan linguistic family and are closely related to the Tawakoni, with whom they were closely associated to the end of their tribal days. The two tribes spoke a dialect of the Wichita language.

Primarily an agricultural people, the Waco were also good hunters and were well known for their readiness and courage on expeditions for both peace and war.

They were highly commended for their industry in cultivating extensive crops and building good houses when they were under the authority of the United States agency on the Brazos Reserve, Texas, in 1858.

◆ **Present Location.** The Waco are now counted as part of the Wichita living in Caddo County, Oklahoma.

◆ **Numbers.** Approximately 60 Waco are now living in Oklahoma. Their last separate census as a tribe in 1894 gave 37 members. An enumeration in 1874 reported 140 Waco at the Wichita Agency. Jesse Stem's careful estimate of the Indians in Texas in 1851 reported 114 Waco, which number did not include bands of the tribe with some of the Tawakoni and the Hainai north of Red River in the Indian Territory. Earlier estimates of their numbers are indefinite, since the Waco were usually reported with the Tawakoni, Kadohadacho, and Hainai in Texas.

◆ **History.** The Waco, called by one or another of the early tribal names applied to them by the French, were reported among the Caddoan tribes living on the Arkansas River in Oklahoma in 1719 when La Harpe visited the Tawakoni (q.v.) village on the Arkansas. Except for seasonal hunting expeditions north of Red River, the main part of the Waco had migrated from the Arkansas River region with other Caddoan tribes and were living in Texas by 1779. In that year, the Waco village was reported west of the Brazos River, near the present site of Waco, Texas. Nearly half a century later, this same Waco village on the Brazos was described as having a population of about 400 persons, who cultivated in the vicinity extensive fields of corn enclosed with brush fences.

Relations of the United States government with the Waco began in 1834 when the Dragoon Expedition, under the command of Colonel Henry Dodge, visited the Wichita (q.v.) in their village on North Fork of Red River, in present Kiowa County, Oklahoma. The Wichita chief and Chief Wetarauyah of the Waco accompanied Colonel Dodge to Fort Gibson where a meeting was held with delegations of other tribes which paved the way for the Camp Holmes treaty of 1835 (*see* Wichita). Subsequent to this time, the Waco were associated with the Tawakoni (q.v.) in Texas. They were moved by United States agents from the Brazos Reserve in Texas to the Washita River in the Indian Territory in 1859, and were henceforth under the supervision of the Wichita Agency. As a part of the Wichita and Affiliated Tribes, the Waco were allotted lands in severalty on the Wichita-Caddo reservation in 1902.

Suggested Readings: Grant Foreman, *Last Trek of the Indians;* Hodge, *Handbook of American Indians;* Swanton, *Source Material, Caddo.*

WEA

The name of the Wea apparently has reference to the location of the tribe at an eddy in a curve or bend of a stream, the name probably being a contraction of *Wawiaq-tenang,* "place of the round or curved channel," or of *Wayah-tonuki,* "eddy people." These place names suggest a possible relationship, if not a close connection, between the Wea and Wawyach- tonoc, "eddy people," one of the five divisions of the Mahican, "wolf," who once lived on the upper Hudson River in present New York and were known to the Dutch as "River Indians." As a subtribe of the Miami (q.v.), the Wea are of the Algonquian linguistic family, to which the Mahican also belong.

◆ **Present Location.** The Wea are located

in Ottawa County, Oklahoma, having been allotted lands in severalty among the Confederated Peoria (*see* Peoria) in the Indian Territory.

◆ **Numbers.** It is thought that there are less than 100 Wea descendants in Oklahoma, none of whom are fullblood members of the tribe. A French memoir of 1718 records the Wea living in five contiguous villages on the Wabash River, their men being "very numerous—fully a thousand or twelve hundred," undoubtedly an exaggeration since other reliable records at different periods reported the Wea few in numbers. In 1680–82 an estimated 140 members of the tribe were living in the vicinity of present Peoria, Illinois, and another band was located on the St. Joseph River, near the Indiana-Michigan boundary.

◆ **History.** A French memoir of 1718 describes the Wea as being different from other tribes, keeping their fort or stockade enclosure at their main village extremely clean, with a sanded floor where not a blade of grass was allowed to grow. This village, called Ouiatenon, was near the Wabash river, located on a high hill in the midst of extensive prairies where herds of buffalo could be seen grazing in the distance. In the immediate vicinity were extensive fields of corn, pumpkins, and melons grown by the Wea. Ouiatenon became the location of the principal headquarters of the French traders.

In 1757 the Wea and their allied tribe, the Piankashaw (q.v.) endeavored to establish friendly relations with the Anglo-American colonists, yet the earlier French influence brought the tribes into conflict with the English interests and the later Anglo-American frontiersmen. The Wea villages on the Wabash were destroyed by United States troops in 1791. Four years later, the treaty of Greenville between the United States and the tribes of the Ohio country bore the names of Amacunsa ("Little Beaver"), Acoolatha ("Little Fox"), and Francis in behalf of the Wea and the Piankashaw.

The Wea sold the last of their tribal lands in Indiana in 1818. They settled with the Piankashaw in Kansas in 1832, where the government granted them 250 sections of land in what is now Miami County. Their reserve was adjacent to that of the Kaskaskia and the Peoria, with whom they were confederated in 1854. Thereafter the history of the Wea, including their removal to the Indian Territory under the treaty of 1867, is the same as that of the Confederated Peoria (*see* Peoria).

Suggested Readings: Cutler, *History of Kansas;* Dillon, *History of Indiana;* Grant Forman, "Illinois and Her Indians," in *Papers in Illinois History,* 1939; ———, *Last Trek of the Indians;* Hodge, *Handbook of American Indians.*

WICHITA

The name Wichita seems to have originated from the Choctaw term *wia chitoh,* "big arbor," from the Choctaw words *wia,* "arbor" or "loft-like platform," and *chitoh,* "big," descriptive of the large grass-thatched arbors, drying platforms, and houses for which the people now commonly known as the Wichita have been noted. This name, like some others of tribes and

streams west of the Mississippi River, was undoubtedly first carried westward by French explorers and traders from the lower Mississippi, Alabama, and lower Louisiana. The tribe was officially called Wichita (or Wichitaw) in government records beginning with the Camp Holmes treaty of 1835, in which the Choctaw had a prominent part since the Wichita were living at that time within the boundaries of the Choctaw Nation.

Early Spanish records of the Southwest refer to the Wichita proper as the Jumano (pronounced "Shumano"). One tribal interpreter has rendered *Jumano* to mean "drummer," from the old custom of summoning the tribe for council by means of a drum. The Wichita Mountains in southwestern Oklahoma are referred to as the "Jumano Mountains" in some old records. Spanish traders from San Antonio and Santa Fé called the Wichita proper *Taovayas,* in later history also known as the *Tawe'hash,* which, it has been said, means "traders."

The Siouan tribes to the north called the Southern Pawnee, who were closely allied with the Wichita, the *Paniwassaba,* "Black Pawnee," whence comes the name *Panioussa* found in French accounts of the Wichita. French traders from the Illinois country called them *Pani Pique,* "Tatooed Pawnee," a name applied to the Wichita in publications descriptive of the tribes in the region of the Plains as late as the eighteen fifties.

The Wichita call themselves *Kitikiti'sh* (or *Kidi-kit-tashe*), which has been given the interpretation of "raccoon-eyed," probably referring to their face painting in primitive times. They are of the Caddoan linguistic family, though their dialect formerly was distinct from that of the Caddo proper. They were more warlike and roving than the Caddo.

The Wichita were generally described in tribal days as hospitable and reliable. Their villages were distinguished by their large, dome-shaped houses covered with grass thatch; large arbors and drying platforms near the houses were shaded with grass-thatched roofs. The Wichita were primarily agriculturists, their well-cultivated fields in which they raised corn, melons, squash, pumpkins, and tobacco extending out from their villages. They were also known as good hunters, depending largely on the buffalo for meat, tallow, and robes.

◊ **Present Location.** The Wichita live in rural areas in the vicinity of Gracemont, north of the Washita River, in Caddo County, within the jurisdiction of the Anadarko Area Office of the Bureau of Indian Affairs.

◊ **Numbers.** Exclusive of affiliated tribes, the Wichita number approximately 242 in the state today. After 1894, the tribal groups enumerated by the United States Indian Office as "Wichita" included the Wichita proper (Tawehash), Tawakoni, Waco, Kichai, Hainai, and Delaware, under the supervision of the Indian agency at Anadar-

MURIEL H. WRIGHT

Wichita grass-thatched house in Caddo County

ko. (In recent years, the Indian Office census records have enumerated these Delaware, q.v., separately.) The 153 Wichita proper as recorded in the last separate tribal census in 1894 increased to approximately 180 at the time of allotment of lands in severalty, in 1901. Their number was reported to be 300 in 1873, and 228 in 1875. In 1864 the refugee Wichita in Kansas, who remained loyal to the Union during the Civil War, numbered 271. There is no accurate census of the tribe available for the preceding half-century. In 1809 their estimated number was 2,800. The official report of Sibley in 1805 gave the number of "Pani or Towiaches" men at 400 living in two tribal villages on upper Red River, which would indicate a total of 1,600 to 2,000 members of the tribe. These same villages in 1778, reported belonging to the Taovayas, were described in their locations on both sides of Red River, below the mouth of the Wichita River of Texas, with an estimated number of 800 men. This would indicate a total population of about 3,200 at that time.

◆ **History.** At the start of the eighteenth century, the Wichita were a southern confederacy of Caddoan tribes living along the Arkansas River in Oklahoma and south along the Red River and the Brazos River in Texas. This tribal confederacy included the Taovayas (or Tawehash), Touacara (or Tawakoni, q.v.), Waco, and Kichai. Their hated enemies were the Apache, who lived westward from central Texas and Oklahoma, the Comanche, from the Northwest, and the Osage, from the Osage River region in western Missouri.

Wichita tradition indicates the migration of the tribe southward from the north and east, a prehistoric movement that seems to have been from an early tribal location in south central Missouri, under pressure of the Osage and the Kaw of the Southern Siouan division. In 1541 the expedition of Coronado to Quivira, which covered a wide region from northeastern Kansas into northern Oklahoma, discovered that the natives belonged to a related tribe if they were not the Wichita proper. The chroniclers of this first Spanish expedition northward from the plains of Texas, on through western Oklahoma into Kansas, recorded that Coronado's *Teyas* (Texas) guide from south of Red River had no difficulty conversing with the Quiviran people since their languages were almost identical. Subsequently, the migration of the Quiviran people southward—which had probably already begun under pressure from the Southern Siouan division—was hastened by the coming of the Comanche from the northwest in the seventeenth and eighteenth centuries.

When the French commandant, Bernard de la Harpe, made his first expedition in Oklahoma in 1719, he listed *Ousita* (*Wusita,* i.e., Wichita) as an important tribe among the nine Caddoan tribes represented in the great council that he held at the Touacara (Tawakoni, q.v.) village on the Arkansas River, near the present town of Haskell, in Muskogee County. These Caddoan tribes, also known collectively as the *Pani Pique* among the French traders from the Illinois country, had their villages along the Arkansas River in Oklahoma, from the mouth of the Canadian River to the vicinity of the southern boundary of Kansas.

At the same time that La Harpe was on his expedition north from Red River to the Touacara village on the Arkansas, another Caddoan village farther up the same river was visited by the French officer and trader, Lieutenant Claude Charles du Tisne, coming south from Kaskaskia in the Illinois country.

French activities along the Arkansas and the Red River in the period, after the La Harpe and Du Tisne expeditions, succeeded in securing a treaty of friendly alliance between the Jumano (Taovayas or Wichita) and the Comanche in 1746. From this time on, the two tribes were generally united in hostilities against the Apache and the Osage. A strong force of

Comanche (q.v.) and Wichita attacked and destroyed the Apache mission on the upper San Saba River, Texas, soon after its establishment by the Spaniards in 1758.

Extensive trade was carried on between the Comanche and the people of the Taovayas (Wichita) village on Red River in Texas, at which place there was a big supply of French arms and the French flag was seen flying in 1759. This village site was later referred to as the "Spanish Fort," a name seen on modern maps of Montague County, Texas. This and another Taovayas village on the opposite side of Red River, in present Jefferson County, Oklahoma, were visited in 1778 by Athanase de Mézières, Indian agent under the Spanish regime of Louisiana.

In 1805 the United States Indian agent at Natchitoches, Louisiana, reported two villages of the "Pani or Towiaches" about eight hundred miles up Red River, the lower village called "Wicheta" (later known as Spanish Fort) and the upper, "Towaahack" (*k* error for *h*). The tribal chief was called Great Bear. The people of these villages raised large crops of corn, pumpkins, beans, and tobacco, and traded the surplus of their crops to the Comanche for horses and mules and buffalo robes. Pumpkins cut into strands and dried were woven into mats for trade with the Comanche. Tobacco cut as fine as tea was tied up in leather bags of a certain size as articles of trade.

The mountain region west of present Fort Sill was the scene of war between the Kiowa and the Osage in 1833, in which the Tawehash or Wichita were on the side of the Kiowa (q.v.). United States government relations with the Wichita in Oklahoma began the following year when the Dragoon Expedition, organized at Fort Gibson by General Henry Leavenworth, was sent to the Southwest under the command of Colonel Henry Dodge to hold a council and promote peace among the Indian tribes. The expedition visited the Wichita village of some two hundred grass-thatched houses located on the meadow floor of the granite-walled canyon, now called "Devil's Canyon," on the North Fork of Red River in present Kiowa County. A reliable Wichita leader reported that the village had been in this location for seventy years and that the people were originally from south of Red River (probably from the tribal group known as the Jumano or Taovayas).

During a three-day council attended by more than two thousand Wichita, Comanche, and Kiowa, Colonel Dodge urged an end of the war with the Osage and friendly alliance with the tribes of eastern Indian Territory, the plan finally gaining the approval of the council largely through the leadership of the venerable Wichita chief, We-tar-ra-shah-ro. As a result of the council, the first treaty with the Plains tribes in Oklahoma was made in a meeting with United States commissioners at Camp Holmes on August 25, 1835, near the Canadian River in the vicinity of present Lexington in Cleveland County. The Camp Holmes treaty, promising peace and perpetual friendship among the tribes and nations represented at the meeting, was signed by delegations from the Cherokee, Muscogee (Creek), Choctaw, Osage, Seneca, and Quapaw from eastern Indian Territory; and by the Comanche and the "Witchetaw" from the West. From this time, the people of this tribe are referred to as Wichita in government records.

In 1850 the Wichita had mostly moved from their locations near Red River and were living in the Wichita Mountain region, with their principal villages a short distance north of the present site of Fort Sill. Later they established their new village and cultivated large fields of corn and melons on Rush Creek, about four miles southeast of present Rush Springs in Grady County.

It was at the village on Rush Creek that the unfortunate event, known in Oklahoma history as the "Battle of the Wichita village," took place on October, 1858, when a band of Comanche who had encamped near by were suddenly attacked by four companies of the Second United States Cavalry and their Indian allies under the command of Captain Earl Van Dorn, who had come north from Texas to wipe out the "wild" Comanche tribe. Unknown to Van Dorn, the band of Comanche in the encampment had just come from a friendly council with United States officials at Fort Arbuckle and had stopped on their way west to visit the Wichita. With Van Dorn's attack, a furious fight took place, during which a large number of Indians were killed, including some Wichita women. Captain Van Dorn himself was severely wounded, and Lieutenant Cornelius Van Camp was killed, struck in the heart by an Indian arrow. Though the Wichita were involved in the battle totally by chance, some of the Comanche looked upon them as enemies for many years, blaming them and suspecting them of treachery in the attack. With their village destroyed, their fields and crops laid waste, and their horses lost in the battle, the Wichita fled to Fort Arbuckle for protection, near which they encamped in an impoverished condition for nearly a year.

Early in the summer of 1859, the Wichita chief, Isadowa (recorded as "Ausodawats"), represented his people among delegations from nine tribes that attended a council with United States officials at Fort Arbuckle to discuss the permanent settlement of these tribes in the Leased District (see Choctaw). Soon afterward, the Wichita moved to reserves assigned them south of the Canadian River near the present Caddo-Grady County line. In August the tribes from the Brazos Reserve in Texas (see Caddo) were located in the same region along the Washita River. A new agency, called the Wichita Agency, the first in western Oklahoma, was established by the Indian Office on Leeper Creek, north of the Washita, in present Caddo County. Within a few weeks, Fort Cobb was established about four miles southwest

of the Wichita Agency for the protection of the tribes in this region.

With the outbreak of the Civil War, Confederate Commissioner Albert Pike secured a treaty with the chiefs and leaders of eleven Indian tribes at the Wichita Agency on August 12, 1861. Principal Chief Isadowa and two sub-chiefs were among these signers in behalf of the people referred to in the treaty as "the Ta-wa-ihash people of Indians, now called by the white men Wichitaws." Failure of Confederate authorities to carry out the terms of the treaty in 1862 caused the greater part of the Wichita to leave the country for Kansas, where they remained as refugees until their return to the Indian Territory in 1867. Some were enlisted in the organized Indian troops in the Union Army. The site of their village in Kansas during the war is now that of the city of Wichita, which perpetuates the name of the tribe in that state.

When the Wichita returned to the Indian Territory, their agency was re-established by the United States Indian Office at a new location about two miles north of present Anadarko in Caddo County. Government agents encouraged the consolidation of the related Caddoan tribes here, and at a later period they were recorded as the "Wichita and Affiliated Tribes," namely the Tawehash (Wichita), Tawakoni, Waco, and Kichai, together with the Caddo, Anadarko, and Hainai; and included also the Penateka Comanche and some Delaware and Shawnee. These soon lost their old tribal identification in government records.

A tragedy that nearly ended in a tribal war, with the angry Kiowa and Comanche on the side of their old allies, the Wichita, was the killing of Chief Isadowa by a band of Osage in June, 1873, while he was on a buffalo hunt. In 1883 Ches-tedi-lessah was reported as chief of the Wichita. He was succeeded in this position by Jim Tehuacana or Tawakoni Jim (see Tawakoni), prominent in tribal affairs up to the time of allotment of lands in severalty.

In the beginning of this period in their history, the Wichita were in a weakened and impoverished condition from loss of their livestock, lack of proper food supplies, and epidemics during and after the Civil War. A boarding school was opened near the agency for the Indian children in 1873. The people of the old Wichita tribal confederacy in western Indian Territory did not come under missionary influence until the eighteen seventies, but by 1900 both Catholic and Protestant missionaries were among them.

The greatest concern of the tribe prior to allotment was the matter of a government title to the lands that they had long claimed. The reservation tracts nominally assigned them in the Indian Territory before the Civil War were included in the large reservation granted the Cheyenne and Arapaho (q.v.) in 1869. Discussions between government agents and Wichita leaders at the agency finally resulted in an agreement under which the United States granted the tribe a reservation between the Canadian and the Washita rivers. This agreement was never ratified by Congress. The reservation tract of 743,610 acres, known locally as the Wichita-Caddo reservation, was designated on maps of the Indian Territory as "Wichitaws Unratified Agreement, Oct. 19, 1872." The question of the Wichita land title was a serious one for many years and necessitated the employment of counsel by the tribe.

On June 4, 1894, United States commissioners made an agreement with the Wichita and Affiliated Tribes, signed by 152 chiefs and headmen, providing that these tribes relinquish to the United States all claims to any lands in the Indian Territory. The Wichita protested the agreement, claiming coercion on the part of the government representatives. The case was carried to the United States Court of Claims, which entered judgment in favor of the Wichita. Unlike any others among the reservation tribes in Oklahoma before statehood, the Wichita and their affiliated tribes were allotted lands in severalty which they had held by right of occupancy only. Allotments to 965 Indians on the Wichita-Caddo reservation were completed and the surplus lands opened to white settlement on August 6, 1901, a region now included in adjoining portions of Caddo, Grady, Canadian, Blaine, Custer, and Washita counties in Oklahoma.

◆ **Government and Organization.**   The Wichita are closely associated with the Caddo (q.v.) and no longer have a separate tribal organization.

◆ **Contemporary Life and Culture.**   The Wichita have given up their tribal customs, and are Christianized, living generally as any rural people. Their children attend the public schools in their home communities. Some attend the Riverside Indian School at Anadarko, a well-equipped institution offering many advantages.

◆ **Ceremonials and Public Dances.** Some of the best Indian dancers in western Oklahoma are found among the Wichita. The most interesting of the old tribal dances is the "Horn Dance." The Wichita form a prominent group in the pageantry, ceremonials, and dances that are a part of the American Indian Exposition held annually in August at Anadarko.

Suggested Readings: Bolton, *Athanase de Mézières;* Chapman, "Establishment of Wichita Reservation," *Chron. of Okla.,* Vol. XI, No. 4; ———, "Dissolution of Wichita Reservation," *Chron. of Okla.,* Vol. XXII, Nos. 2 and 3; Grant Foreman, *Last Trek of the Indians;* Hodge, *Handbook of American Indians;* Mooney, "Calendar History of the Kiowa," *17 Ann. Rep.,* Bur. Amer. Ethnol.; Nye, *Carbine and Lance.*

WYANDOT

The name *Wyandot* is the approved form of the tribal term *Wendat,* which signifies "islanders" or "dwellers on a peninsula." The Wyandot people belong to the Iroquoian linguistic family, at the time of their discovery by the French comprising a confederacy of four tribes located in the present province of Ontario, Canada, east of Lake Huron. The French about 1600 began calling them *Huron,* signifying "rough" or "uncouth," from the French word *hure,* "head of the wild boar," referring to the roached hair of the tribal warriors which resembled the rough bristles on the head of a wild boar. The Wyandot themselves never accepted the French name *Huron,* which, however, is frequently found in historical records and official documents in reference to this confederacy of Iroquian tribes.

Early writers described the Wyandot or Huron as agriculturists who grew fine crops of corn, squash, beans, tobacco, and sunflowers, extracting from the seeds of the last an oil which they used for many purposes. The tribal government showed an advanced development, with the women voting to choose the executive officers, who were thereupon organized into legislative and judicial councils. The titles of chieftaincy of several grades were hereditary in the family, a candidate for such an office being chosen by the mothers in his family.

◆ **Present Location.** The Wyandot live in Ottawa County, having been allotted lands in severalty east of the Grand or Neosho River, on their reservation in the vicinity of the present town of Wyandotte eastward to the Missouri line.

◆ **Numbers.** An estimated 850 Wyandot reside in Oklahoma. The Indian Office census for 1944 gives 826 members of the tribe listed at the Quapaw Agency at Miami, with 305 within Ottawa County and 521 living elsewhere. Their numbers reported at various periods were 342 in 1901, 310 in 1893, 251 in 1885, 247 in 1875, 222 in 1872, and 435 in 1863. About 700 Wyandot settled in Kansas in 1843. Their population was reported as 1,250 in 1812. The Jesuits made the first estimate of their numbers in 1639 at 20,000 (Huron).

◆ **History.** When French explorer Jacques Cartier made his voyages up the St. Lawrence River in 1536–43, he found Huron or Wendat on the present sites of Montreal and Quebec in a fierce war with the Iroquois of New York, better known in history as the Five Nations. This was a war of extermination against the Huron that brought their utter defeat by the Iroquois in 1649, after which the surviving Huron fled westward from their country east of Lake Huron, some going to Michilimakinac at the head of Lake Michigan, and others to Green Bay, where they were given refuge by the Potawatomi. The Five Nations relentlessly pursued them, but the French Catholic missionaries followed the refugees, befriending and helping them in their distress. About 1700 the Huron were established at Sandusky, Ohio; Detroit, Michigan; and Sandwich, Ontario.

The Huron war chief, Orontony, with a large party of followers led a conspiracy entered into by many of the Middle Western tribes—including the Ottawa, Potawatomi, Sioux, Sauk, Fox, Shawnee, and Miami—against the French. When his villages and stockade were destroyed in 1748, the conspiracy was broken, from which time the Huron at Detroit and Sandusky became definitely known as the Wyandot. Though comparatively few in number, they gained great influence among the other tribes living between the Great Lakes and the Ohio River, despite the fact that most of these were of the Algonquian family.

The Wyandot claimed the greater part of present Ohio and a part of Indiana.

They took part in the conspiracy of the great Ottawa chief, Pontiac (*see* Ottawa); sided with the French in the French and Indian War, and with the British in the American Revolution. They were divided in the War of 1812, part being allied with England and part with the United States. Beginning in 1795, they ceded their lands to the United States in various treaties, giving up their last tracts near Upper Sandusky and Detroit in 1842. They agreed at this time to move to a reservation of 148,000 acres west of the Mississippi River.

Under the leadership of their chief, Francis A. Hicks, the Wyandot left Ohio in 1843 and settled at the forks of the Kansas and Missouri rivers, in the eastern part of present Wyandotte County, Kansas, where they purchased a reserve of about thirty-nine sections from the Delaware. Already advanced in civilization, they continued to make progress in their new country. The Wyandot Mission at Upper Sandusky, the first mission ever founded by the Methodist Episcopal church, was brought

B. N. O. Walker, Wyandot, who served as clerk in the Quapaw Agency

west and many years later became the Washington Avenue Methodist Episcopal Church of Kansas City, Kansas.

There had been many intermarriages with white people in Ohio, and such marriages increased after the tribe came west. Among the prominent mixed-blood members were families by the names of Armstrong, Clark, Northrup, and Walker. In 1854, William Walker, one of the leaders of the tribe, was chosen as the provisional governor of the Territory of Nebraska. The Walker family is still well known among the Wyandot in Oklahoma. Governor Walker was the great-uncle of the late B. N. O. Walker who served as chief clerk in the Quapaw Agency at Miami for many years, a talented musician, singer, and poet. Under the pen name "Hentoh," he wrote *Tales of the Bark Lodges,* one of the classics of early Oklahoma literature.

A treaty concluded at Washington in January, 1855, between George W. Manypenny, United States commissioner, and a delegation of Wyandot, provided for allotment of their reservation lands in severalty, members of the tribe to become citizens of the United States, with the exception of those who made application for such protection and assistance from the government as they had formerly possessed. The great tide of white immigrants in Kansas and the inequalities the Indians suffered under the Kansas laws meant that many of the Wyandot soon lost their allotments and became impoverished. A band of two hundred of them came to the Indian Territory in 1857 to live among the Seneca (q.v.). Fifty years before this, the Wyandot had befriended the Seneca in Ohio when they were in need, granting them 40,000 acres on the Sandusky River for a reserve. In 1859, Chief Little Tom Spicer of the Seneca and his councilmen, remembering the kindness of their old friends the Wyandot, entered into an agreement with their chief, Matthew Mudeater, and his councilmen, assigning them 33,000 acres across the north side of the Seneca reservation.

Catholic church built by Matthias Splitlog at Cayuga, Delaware County

When regular army forces and guerrilla bands overran this region in the first part of the Civil War, both tribes went north to Kansas, where they remained until the end of the war in 1865. By the terms of the Omnibus Treaty with the United States in 1867, the agreement between the Seneca and the Wyandot was confirmed, the latter being granted a reserve of 20,000 acres (surveyed 21,246 acres) on the north side of the Seneca lands.

The surviving 110 Wyandot in the Indian Territory, joined by their kinsmen from Kansas who had lost their allotments there, reorganized their tribal government in 1871, continuing their annual meetings and elections, with a first and a second chief and council members. They were poor and without tribal annuities, but through their own energy and enterprise became the owners of good farms and generally prospered before many seasons had passed. Their children attended a school operated by the Friends (Orthodox), still maintained in 1951 by the government as the Seneca Boarding School, near Wyandotte in Ottawa County.

Allotments of land in severalty on their reservation to 241 Wyandot were completed under the supervision of the Quapaw Agency by 1893. About 70 other Wyandot had recently joined them, mostly from Kansas, but were too late to share in the allotment of lands. Provisions were made by Congressional acts between 1894 and 1896 to purchase locations for them elsewhere. It has been reported that some of these people went to Ohio and others to Canada.

◆ Government and Organization. The Wyandot of Ottawa County were organized in 1937 as the "Wyandotte Tribe of Oklahoma" under provisions of the Oklahoma Indian Welfare Act of 1936. A charter issued to the organization by the Secretary of the Interior was ratified by a vote of 148 for and none against in an election in October, 1937, in which over 30 per cent of those entitled to vote cast ballots. The election was certified by L. N. Cotter, chief, and Bertha Cheek, secretary-treasurer, of the Wyandotte Tribe.

◆ **Contemporary Life and Culture.** The Wyandot have many leading citizens in Ottawa County. They are predominantly mixed-blood white and Indian. An enumeration made by the Quapaw Agency about 1940 shows only 3 fullblood Indians out of a total of 799 Wyandot, of whom 688 had less than one-quarter Indian blood. Members of the tribe who had been living in northeastern Indian Territory became citizens of Oklahoma at statehood in 1907.

Suggested Readings: Connelly, *History of Kansas;* Grant Foreman, *Last Trek of the Indians;* Hodge, *Handbook of American Indians;* Merwin, "The Wyandot Indians," *Trans.* Kansas Hist. Soc., Vol. IX (1906); Wilson, *Quapaw Agency Indians.*

YUCHI

The people of this tribe call themselves *Tsoya'ha,* pronounced nearly *Chōyä'hä,* "children of the sun." The name *Yuchi* is usually found in Oklahoma historical records spelled phonetically *Euchee* or *Uchee.* A recent ethnological study has suggested that it originated from the Hitchiti term *Ochesse,* signifying "people of another language" (*see* Creek). Another study gives its origin in the expression *Yu'tci,* signifying "a settlement at a distance," from the Yuchi words *Yu,* "at a distance," and *tci,* "sitting down," the name thought to have been applied to the tribe from a reply given by one of its members to an early Spanish explorer in answer to the question, "Where are you from?"

The Yuchi have a distinct language and are classified as the Uchean linguistic family, the name of the family being that of this leading tribe. In Oklahoma, the Yuchi have been counted as a part of the Creek Nation, continuing their identification with the old Creek Confederacy in the Southeastern states. The earliest known location of the Yuchi was in the southernmost region of the Appalachian Highland, lying in adjoining portions of what are now western South Carolina, northern Georgia, and eastern Tennessee.

Early Spanish records described the Yuchi as a rebellious mountain tribe given to fighting and war expeditions. They have always been noted for their independence and pride in their own customs. As early as 1729, they were reported an orderly agricultural people who dwelt in permanent villages along the southern streams in South Carolina, Georgia, and Florida. The men were good hunters, erected the dwellings, and shared in cultivating the fields. The women were industrious and modest. Tradition has it that the tribe was gladly admitted to the Creek Confederacy because of the beauty of the Yuchi women. In appearance, members of the tribe are above medium height, slender, and lithe, with well-developed muscles; they usually have a light complexion and gray eyes and are fair in comparison with persons of the dark fullblood groups in the Creek Nation.

◆ **Present Location.** The Yuchi generally live south and east of Sapulpa and Mounds, Creek County, and south into Okmulgee County. There is a community east of Mounds on Duck Creek, in the vicinity of Bixby in Tulsa County. This whole area was in the Okmulgee District, or northwestern part of the Creek Nation before statehood, where members of the tribe were mostly arbitrarily allotted 160-acre tracts when the Creek lands were divided in severalty under the supervision of the Dawes Commission, circumstances that indicate their conservatism in tribal matters and alignment with the so-called "Snake" group among the Creek.

◆ **Numbers.** A report from Chief S. W. Brown, who represents the Yuchi on the Creek Tribal Council, stated that there were 1,216 Yuchi in Oklahoma in 1949. The official census of the Creek Nation, made by authority of the National Council in 1891, gave a total of 580 Yuchi, the percentage of increase since that time being the equivalent of that of many other tribal groups living in the state today. An estimate of the Yuchi population in 1909 was 500. In 1910 a report from the Five Civilized Tribes Agency listed 78 Yuchi, this number undoubtedly being an error for some unexplained reason. An official report in 1832 listed a total Indian population of 1,139 in two Yuchi settlements in the Creek country before the removal from Alabama, which did not include a part of the tribe that had come to the Indian Territory with the McIntosh Creek. In 1778 the well-known Yuchi settlement on the Chattahoochie River, in what is now Alabama, was estimated to have a population of from 1,000 to 1,500 persons.

◆ **History.** One version of the traditional Creek migration legend indicates that the Yuchi were living in what is now the southeastern part of the United States before the Creek came into this region in prehistoric times. The Creek say that the Yuchi language is unintelligible and that they conquered the Yuchi long ago, a claim that has never been allowed by the Yuchi themselves. It is true that they have their own distinct language and have continued a nominal, separate tribal organization down through the centuries. In the light of these facts, it seems that the Yuchi tribe gradually left the old location under pressure in colonial Indian wars, and joined the Creek confederacy for mutual protection, a movement accelerated by

European settlement on the Atlantic and the Gulf coasts.

De Soto in 1540 learned of the tribe under the name of Chisca. For two hundred years after his time, many different names, including *Chisca, Cisca, Chichimecs, Hogologe, Tahogole, Tickohockan, Uchee, Westo,* and others, are found in one or more of the Spanish, French, or English records to designate the Yuchi. The Spaniards and the English often reported them a warlike people in league with other tribes halting the advance of European expeditions and settlements, and sometimes defeating them and their Indian allies. In 1567 the chief of the Chisca (Yuchi), with many warriors of his own and allied tribes, threatened the Spaniards in the vicinity of Port Royal, South Carolina.

Local colonial wars throughout the coastal region against different tribes brought about the migration of the Yuchi from the southern part of the Appalachian Highland. In 1656 some of the tribe were living in a settlement (estimated population, 600 to 700) on the James River, Virginia, where they defeated the English in battle. The Yuchi are never heard of again in Virginia, this band from the James River probably having moved away after the battle and joined some of their kinsmen in eastern Tennessee, where the present town of Euchee on the Tennessee River, in Meigs County, has perpetuated the name of the tribe in this region. In 1677 a successful campaign was made against another part of the Yuchi by the Spaniards and their Apalachee Indian allies in what is now northwestern Florida. La Salle reported meeting a band of Yuchi on his voyage down the Mississippi River in 1682, at Fort St. Louis near the present site of Utica, Illinois, members of the band saying that they had left their easternmost settlement in "English Florida" (Carolina) after one of their villages had been burned by another tribe "aided by the English."

In 1715 there was a Yuchi settlement on the Savannah River above the present site of Augusta, Georgia. This part of the tribe later joined a band of friendly Shawnee and moved to the Tallapoosa River, where they became identified with the Upper Creek people and served as allies in the Creek or Red Stick War of 1813–14.

The organized resistance of the South Carolina tribes against the English in the Yamassee War brought defeat to these Indians in 1715, after which bands of Yuchi eventually formed settlements on the lower Savannah River and on other streams in southeastern Georgia—Ogeechee, Cannuchee, and Satilla rivers.

In 1729, Chief Ellick of the Kasihta (Creek tribal division), who had married a Yuchi, moved to the Chattahoochee River and induced others of his wife's people to join his settlement. This became the largest and best known of the Yuchi "towns," its people identified with the Lower Creek. Referred to as "Uche" in the trading records of the time, it consisted of three vil-

lages located on the right bank of the Chattahoochee River near the mouth of Big Uchee Creek in present Alabama. William Bartram, of Philadelphia, visited this place in 1778 and described it as "the largest, most compact, and best situated Indian town" that he had even seen.

Another band of Yuchi lived for a time near the Mikasuki (Seminole, q.v.) in western Florida. Afterward they moved east to Dexters Lake in Valusia County, Florida, where they were allied with the Seminole in the war against the United States from 1835 to 1843. A few of this band of Yuchi were living among the Seminole in 1847.

A notable family among the Yuchi were the children of Timothy Barnard from the British Isles, who became a man of political influence in Indian affairs and prominent in the history of Macon County, Georgia. He married a Yuchi girl before the time of the American Revolution and was the first white settler in Macon County, where his home on the Flint River was well known for many years before his death in 1820. He had a large estate in England and owned most of Macon County, along with many Negro slaves and large herds of cattle and horses. A man of unusual intellect and ability, he learned the Yuchi language and other Indian languages, served as interpreter for many government commissions, and was at one time appointed temporary Indian superintendent south of the Ohio. He and his Yuchi wife were the parents of eleven children who were famous for their good looks.

Three sons—Timpoochee, Michee, and Cosenna—were in command of a company of Yuchi who served as allies of the American forces in the Creek War of 1813–14. Timpoochee served as captain at this time, his name appearing in behalf of the Yuchi among the signers of three Creek treaties with the United States—1814, 1826, and 1827. His grandson, Timothy Barnard (sometimes spelled "Barnett"), was prominent in the Creek Nation, West. He was a

Timpoochee Barnard, from a painting made about 1830

special delegate in a meeting at North Fork Town, in 1861, when the United Nations of the Indian Territory was founded, an organization that was active in its alignment with the Confederate States to the end of the Civil War in 1865. He was one of the five delegates from the Muskokee Nation in 1870, when the General Council of the Indian Territory drafted the Okmulgee Constitution. Cosena Barnard was a prominent Yuchi leader in the Creek Nation, West, having emigrated from Alabama with his children and grandchildren in a self-emigrating party in 1834. His home was on the present site of the town of Slick, in Creek County, where he died and was buried before the Civil War. His great-grandson, the late Jesse Allen, who lived five miles east of Bristow, served for a time as deputy United States marshal.

The Yuchi as a tribe came west to the Indian Territory in two main groups: The first group, which had been identified with the Lower Creek (McIntosh party, *see* Creek)) arrived in the vicinity of Fort Gibson in 1829; the second, larger, group came with the main removal of the Creek people from Alabama in 1836.

During the Civil War, the Yuchi were divided in sentiment, those recently aligned with the Lower Creek or McIntosh party siding with the Confederacy, although 140 others served with the Union forces. After the war the main settlements of the Yuchi were on Pole Cat Creek southward to tributaries of the Deep Fork, a generally hilly, well-watered, and thinly wooded region in the western parts of present Creek and Okfuskee counties. There were four of these Yuchi settlements: Big Pond, about six miles southeast of the town of Depew; Pole Cat, near Kelleyville; Sand Creek (a new name and part of Big Pond group), south of Bristow; Snake Creek and Duck Creek, east of Mounds (and south of Bixby). A small group of the tribe located on Salt Creek in western Creek County, where they refined salt for a living and were in friendly association with the Sac and Fox

people who became their neighbors on the west in 1870. Other small groups of Yuchi lived near Paden and on Buckeye Creek in Okfuskee County.

When the Creek Nation was organized under a written constitution in 1867, these Yuchi settlements were together designated Yuchi Town, or the fifteenth of the forty-four towns comprising the whole nation. The constitution provided for the representation of Yuchi Town in the National Council of the Creek Nation, one member in the House of Kings and four members in the House of Warriors (*see* Creek). Representatives were elected on the basis of population, one each for the three large settlements of Yuchi Town and one additional representative for the 200 extra residents in the largest settlement, on Pole Cat Creek. In 1867, Samuel W. Brown, whose mother, Suttah, was a sister of Chief Tissoso, was elected chief of the Yuchi and member of the House of Kings from Yuchi Town. Prominent in the affairs of the Creek Nation for many years, he was later elected to serve a term as national treasurer.

Plans for a school among the Yuchi were begun by the Presbyterian Mission Board in 1891 and culminated in the founding of

ELLA BURGESS

SPAR June Townsend

ELLA BURGESS

Army nurse Ann Alice Townsend

Euchee Boarding School about a mile from Sapulpa. Buildings were erected and the school opened in 1894, an appropriation for the school having been made by the Creek Council from tribal funds through the work of Chief Brown and other leaders. The Council appointed a Yuchi as the first superintendent of this school—Noah Gregory, a Methodist minister and a descendant of Cosena Barnard. New buildings were erected, and Euchee Boarding School was improved, enlarged, and maintained by appropriations from Creek funds until 1928 when it was taken over and supported entirely by federal appropriations under supervision of the United States Indian Office. In 1947 the school was closed and the tract within the city limits, together with a number of substantial buildings, was sold to Sapulpa for the use of the public schools.

◆ **Government and Organization.** The Yuchi have a nominal tribal organization

along the lines of the old clan system and the town system. The tribal rolls are checked annually by the chief, who is elected and holds office for life. Special officials conduct the annual town-square ceremonials in summer. The chief in 1951 was S. W. Brown, son of the late Chief Samuel W. Brown. He also serves as member of the present Creek Council in the interests of the Yuchi (*see* Creek). As a part of the Creek organization, business matters relating to the tribe are under the supervision of the Five Civilized Tribes Agency at Muskogee.

◆ **Contemporary Life and Culture.** There has been some admixture with the Anglo-American among the Yuchi. The full-bloods comprise about one-half of the tribe. Some of these fullbloods are of Creek-Yuchi descent through intermarriage with the Creek, with whom there has been more admixture than with any other racial or tribal group.

The Yuchi are remarkable for having retained their own tribal language and much of their lore, even though they were a part of the old Creek Confederacy and of the Creek Nation, West, during a period of two hundred years. Few outsiders, if any, have ever mastered the Yuchi language, the Creek people having always ridiculed it as too difficult. The Yuchi were formerly noted for their pottery, an industry in the hands of the women; clay pipes were made by the men. Some of the tribe living near the old Wetumka school (about five miles from the present town of Wetumka) used to make pottery of blue and brownish-yellow clay.

◆ **Ceremonials and Public Dances.** The Yuchi still have two square-grounds where they hold the Green Corn Dance ceremonials in summer: on Duck Creek, south of Bixby, and on Pole Cat Creek, west of Kellyville. The square-ground, called the "Rainbow" or "Big House" (*Yu-ah*), is a plot about seventy-five feet square, the four sides facing the points of the compass—north, west, south, and east. During the ceremonials, the dances continue near the four sides of the square, in the center of which a sacred fire is kept burning. A lack of colorful pageantry now makes the rituals and dances monotonous to the visitor unless he is familiar with their symbolism. There is much mystery in the story of the Yuchi people.

Suggested Readings: Speck, *Ceremonial Songs, Creek and Yuchi;* ———, *Ethnology of the Yuchi Indians;* Swanton, *Early History of the Creek* (see "The Yuchi").

Complete List of Suggested Readings

Full titles of and complete publication information for all books and articles listed in the suggested readings following the individual tribal histories are given below. These titles are not repeated in the bibliography.

Abel, Annie Heloise. *The American Indian as Participant in the Civil War*. Cleveland, 1915.

Alford, Thomas Wildcat. *Civilization*. As Told to Florence Drake. Norman, 1936.

Alvord, Clarence Walworth (ed.). *Kaskaskia Records, 1778–79*. Illinois State Historical Society, 1909.

Barrett, Stephen M. (ed.). *Geronimo's Story of His Life*. New York, 1906.

Benson, Rev. Henry C. *Life Among the Choctaw Indians*. Cincinnati, 1860.

Bolton, Herbert Eugene (ed.). *Athanase de Mézières and the Louisiana-Texas Frontier, 1768–1780*. Cleveland, 1914.

———. "The Native Tribes about the East Texas Missions," *The Quarterly,* Texas State Historical Association, Vol. XI, No. 4 (1908).

Boyd, Julian P. (ed.). *Indian Treaties Printed by Benjamin Franklin, 1736–1762*. Philadelphia, 1938.

Bradford, W. R. *The Catawba Indians of South Carolina*. Columbia, S. C., 1946.

Brinton, Daniel G., m. d. *The Lenape and Their Legends, with the Complete Text and Symbols of the Walum Olum*. Philadelphia, 1885.

Brown, John P. *Old Frontiers*. Kingsport, Tenn., 1938.

Buntin, Martha. "The Mexican Kickapoos," *Chronicles of Oklahoma*, Vol. XI, Nos. 1 and 2 (1933).

Chapman, Berlin B. "Charles Curtis and the Kaw Reservation," *The Kansas Historical Quarterly*, Vol. XV (1947).

———. "The Cherokee Commission at the Kickapoo Village," *Chronicles of Oklahoma*, Vol. XVII, No. 1 (1939).

———. "Dissolution of the Iowa Reservation," *Chronicles of Oklahoma*, Vol. XIV, No. 4 (1936).

———. "Dissolution of the Osage Reservation," *Chronicles of Oklahoma*, Vol. XX, Nos. 1 and 2 (1942); Vol. XXI, Nos. 2 and 3 (1943).

———. "Dissolution of the Wichita Reservation," *Chronicles of Oklahoma*, Vol. XXII, Nos. 2 and 3 (1944).

———. "Establishment of the Iowa Reservation," *Chronicles of Oklahoma*, Vol. XXI, No. 4 (1943).

———. "Establishment of the Wichita Reservation," *Chronicles of Oklahoma*, Vol. XI, No. 4 (1933).

———. "The Otoe and Missouria Reservation," *Chronicles of Oklahoma*, Vol. XXVI, No. 2 (1948).

Chronicles of Oklahoma. A quarterly published by the Oklahoma Historical Society, Oklahoma City, 1921–.

Clark, J. Stanley. "The Nez Percés in Exile," *The Pacific Northwest Quarterly*, Vol. XXXVI, No. 3 (1945).

———. "Ponca Publicity," *The Mississippi Valley Historical Review*, Vol. XXIX, No. 4 (1943).

Commissioner of Indian Affairs, Department of the Interior. *Report, 1859.*

Connelly, William E. *A Standard History of Kansas and Kansans.* 5 vols. New York, 1918.

Curtin, Jeremiah. *Myths of the Modoc.* Boston, 1912.

Cutler, William G. *History of the State of Kansas.* Chicago, 1883.

Dale, Edward Everett, and Gaston Litton. *Cherokee Cavaliers.* Norman, 1939.

Debo, Angie. *The Rise and Fall of the Choctaw Republic.* Norman, 1934.

———. *The Road to Disappearance.* Norman, 1941.

Dillon, John B. *A History of Indiana.* Indianapolis, 1859.

Dorsey, George Amos. *Traditions of the Caddo.* Washington, 1904.

Dorsey, James Owen. "A Study of Siouan Cults," in *Eleventh Annual Report*, Bureau of American Ethnology. Washington, 1894.

Dunbar, John B. "The Pawnee Indians," *Magazine of American History*, Vol. IV, No. 4 (1880).

Dunn, William Edward. "Apache Relations in Texas, 1718–1750," *The Quarterly*, Texas State Historical Association, Vol. XIV, No. 3 (1911).

Fletcher, Alice C., and Francis La Flesche, "The Omaha Tribe," in *Twenty-seventh Annual Report*, Bureau of American Ethnology. Washington, 1911.

Foreman, Carolyn Thomas. "Black Beaver," *Chronicles of Oklahoma*, Vol. XXIV, No. 3 (1946).

Foreman, Grant. *Advancing the Frontier.* Norman, 1933.

———. *The Five Civilized Tribes.* Norman, 1934.

———. *History of Oklahoma.* Norman, 1942.

———. "Illinois and Her Indians," in *Papers in Illinois History, Transactions* of the Illinois State Historical Society, 1939. Springfield, Ill., 1940.

———. *Indian Removal.* Norman, 1932.

———. *The Last Trek of the Indians.* Chicago, 1946.

Grinnell, George Bird. *The Cheyenne Indians.* 2 vols. New Haven, 1923.

———. *The Fighting Cheyennes.* New York, 1915.

———. *Pawnee Hero Stories and Folk-Tales.* New York, 1920.

Gue, Benjamin F. *History of Iowa.* New York, 1903.

Hargrett, Lester. *A Bibliography of the Constitutions and Laws of the American Indians.* Cambridge, Mass., 1947.

Hebard, Grace Raymond. *Sacajawea.* Glendale, 1933.

Hodge, Frederick Webb (ed.). *Handbook of American Indians North of Mexico. Bulletin No. 30*, Bureau of American Ethnology. 2 vols. Washington, 1910–11.

Illinois Historical Society *Journal*, 1908–.

James, Thomas. *Three Years Among the Indians and Mexicans.* St. Louis, 1916.

Johnson, Elias. *Legends, Traditions, and Laws of the Iroquois . . . and History of the Tuscarora Indians.* Lockport, N. Y., 1881.

Jones, William. *Fox Texts.* Leyden, 1907.

Kansas State Historical Society *Collections, 1915.* Topeka, 1915.

Kroeber, A. L. *Handbook of Indians of California. Bulletin No. 78*, Bureau of American Ethnology. Washington, 1925.

La Flesche, Francis. "The Osage Tribe," in *Thirty-sixth Annual Report,* Bureau of American Ethnology. Washington, 1921.

Lewis, Anna. "La Harpe's First Expedition in Oklahoma," with editorial notes by Joseph B. Thoburn, *Chronicles of Oklahoma,* Vol. II, No. 4 (1924).

Llewellyn, Karl N., and E. Adamson Hoebel. *The Cheyenne Way: Conflict and Case Law in Primitive Jurisprudence.* Norman, 1941.

Malone, James H. *The Chickasaw Nation.* Louisville, 1922.

Marriott, Alice. *The Ten Grandmothers.* Norman, 1945.

Mathews, John Joseph. *Wah'Kon-Tah.* Norman, 1932.

Meacham, A. B. *Wi-ne-ma and Her People.* Hartford, 1876.

Merwin, Ray E. "The Wyandot Indians," in *Transactions* of the Kansas State Historical Society, Vol. IX (1906). Topeka, 1906.

Meserve, John Bartlett. "Chief Samuel Checote, with Sketches of Chiefs Locher Harjo and Ward Coachman," *Chronicles of Oklahoma,* Vol. XVI, No. 4 (1938).

———. "Chief Pleasant Porter," *Chronicles of Oklahoma,* Vol. IX, No. 3 (1931).

———. "The Perrymans," *Chronicles of Oklahoma,* Vol. XV, No. (???) (1937).

Michelson, Truman. *Fox Ethnology. Bulletin No. 114,* Bureau of American Ethnology. Washington, 1937.

Milling, Chapman J. *Red Carolinians.* Chapel Hill, 1940.

Miner, William Harvey. *The Iowa.* Cedar Rapids, 1911.

Mooney, James. "Calendar History of the Kiowa Indians," in *Seventeenth Annual Report,* Bureau of American Ethnology. Washington, 1898.

———. "Ghost Dance Religion," in *Fourteenth Annual Report,* Part II, Bureau of American Ethnology. Washington, 1896.

———. "Myths of the Cherokee," in *Nineteenth Annual Report,* Bureau of American Ethnology. Washington, 1900.

Moore, George Rowley. "Pawnee Traditions and Customs," *Chronicles of Oklahoma,* Vol. XVII, No. 2 (1939).

Murie, James R. *Pawnee Indian Societies.* Anthropological Papers of the American Museum of Natural History, Vol. XI, Part VII. New York, 1914.

Nelson, Al B. "Juan de Ugalde and Picax-Ande Ins-Tinsle, 1787–1788," *The Southwestern Historical Quarterly,* Vol. XLIII, No. 4 (1940).

Nye, Colonel W. S. *Carbine and Lance: The Story of Old Fort Sill.* Norman, 1943.

Opler, Morris Edward. *Myths and Legends of the Lipan Apache Indians.* New York, 1940.

Page, Elizabeth M. *In Camp and Teepee.* New York, 1915.

Peery, Dan W. "The Indians' Friend, John H. Seger," *Chronicles of Oklahoma,* Vols. X and XI (1932 and 1933).

Porter, Kenneth W. "The Seminole in Mexico, 1850–1861," *The Hispanic American Historical Review,* Vol. XXXI, No. 1, Part I (1951).

Reeve, Frank D. "The Apache Indians in Texas," *The Southwestern Historical Quarterly,* Vol. L, No. 2 (1946).

Richardson, Rupert N. *The Comanche Barrier to South Plains Settlement.* Glendale, 1933.

Riddle, Jeff C. *The Indian History of the Modoc War.* San Francisco, 1914.

Rideout, Henry Milner. *William Jones.* New York, 1912.

Rister, Carl Coke. *Border Command: General Phil Sheridan in the West.* Norman, 1944.

———. *Oil! Titan of the Southwest.* Norman, 1949.

Royce, Charles C. "The Cherokee Nation of Indians," in *Fifth Annual Report,* Bureau of American Ethnology. Washington, 1887.

Schoolcraft, Henry R. *Historical and Statistical Information Regarding the History, Condition and Prospects of the Indian Tribes of the United States.* Philadelphia, 1855.

Seger, John H. *Early Days Among the Cheyenne and Arapahoe Indians.* Edited by Stanley Vestal. Norman, 1934.

Senate Document No. 144, 54 Cong., 2 sess.

Skinner, Alanson. *The Ioway Indians. Bulletin* of Milkaukee Museum. Milwaukee, 1926.

———. *Observations on the Ethnology of the Sauk Indians.* Milwaukee, 1923.

Speck, Frank G. *Ceremonial Songs of the Creek and Yuchi Indians.* Philadelphia, 1911.

———. *The Creek Indians of Taskigi Town.* Lancaster, Pa., 1907.

———. *Ethnology of the Yuchi Indians.* Philadelphia, 1911.

———. *Oklahoma Delaware Ceremonies, Feasts, and Dances,* 59 Cong., I sess., *Sen. Doc. No. 501.*

———. *A Study of the Delaware Indian Big House Ceremony.* Harrisburg, Pa., 1931.

Spier, Leslie. *Klamath Ethnography.* Berkeley, 1930.

Spoehr, Alexander. *Kinship System of the Seminole.* Publication No. 513, Field Museum of Natural History. Anthropological Series, Vol. XXXIII, No. 2. Chicago, 1942.

Swanton, John R. *Early History of the Creek Indians and Their Neighbors. Bulletin No. 73,* Bureau of American Ethnology. Washington, 1922.

———. *The Indians of the Southeastern United States. Bulletin No. 137,* Bureau of American Ethnology. Washington, 1946.

———. *Indian Tribes of the Lower Mississippi Valley and Adjacent Coast of the Gulf of Mexico. Bulletin No. 43,* Bureau of American Ethnology. Washington, 1911.

———. "Social Organization and Social Usages of the Indians of the Creek Confederacy," in *Forty-second Annual Report,* Bureau of American Ethnology. Washington, 1928.

———. "Social and Religious Beliefs and Usages of the Chickasaw Indians," in *Forty-fourth Annual Report,* Bureau of American Ethnology. Washington, 1927.

———. *Source Material on the History and Ethnology of the Caddo Indians. Bulletin No. 132,* Bureau of American Ethnology. Washington, 1942.

———. *Source Material for the Social and Ceremonial Life of the Choctaw Indians. Bulletin No. 103,* Bureau of American Ethnology. Washington, 1931.

Thoburn, Joseph B., and Muriel H. Wright. *Oklahoma: A History of the State and Its People.* 4 vols. New York, 1929.

Wardell, Morris L. *A Political History of the Cherokee Nation, 1838–1907.* Norman, 1938.

Wedel, Waldo Rudolph. *An Introduction to Pawnee Archeology. Bulletin No. 112,* Bureau of American Ethnology. Washington, 1925.

Williams, Samuel Cole (ed.). *The History of the American Indian,* by James Adair. Johnson City, Tenn., 1930. First printed in London, 1775.

Wilson, Charles Banks. *Quapaw Agency Indians.* Miami, Okla., 1947.

Zimmerman, Charles LeRoy. *White Eagle.* Harrisburg, Pa., 1941.

Bibliography

MANUSCRIPTS

In the Grant Foreman Collection, Muskogee, Oklahoma:

Letter, report relating to Indian administration, Office of Indian Affairs, C. J. Rhoades, commissioner, to Hon. William H. King, U. S. Senate, Washington, D. C., January 18, 1933.

In the Oklahoma Historical Society, Oklahoma City:

Allotment Records of the Cheyenne and Arapaho Agency, June 30, 1891. By O. S. Rice. (Library)
Byington, Rev. Cyrus. Letters, Missionary to the Choctaw Indians, 1820–68. 2 vols. (Library)
Caddo Indians—Texas, 1841–54. (Library)
Cherokee Census Roll, 1835. By Daniel Henderson, copy made by G. W. Curry, 1836. (Library)
Cherokee Indians, Life and Customs. By W. B. Alberty, 1933. (Library)
Cherokee Indian Records. (Indian Archives)
Cherokee Nation. Cherokee Citizenship—Authenticated Rolls of 1880. (Indian Archives)
Cherokee Nation, Vol. 251. (Indian Archives)
Cheyenne-Arapaho Agents' Reports. (Indian Archives)
Chickasaw Indian Records. (Indian Archives)
Chickasaw Nation. Constitution, 1848, Manuscript Acts of the Chickasaw Nation, No. 64. (Indian Archives)
Choctaw Indian Records. (Indian Archives)
Creek Indian Records. (Indian Archives)
Foreman, Grant. Transcripts compiled from Manuscripts in the Office of the Commissioner of Indian Affairs, Washington, D. C., 1829–55. 20 vols. (Indian Archives)
———. Transcripts from Public Record Office, London, Colonial Office, Class 5, Vols. 12 and 67, 1725–67. 3 vols. (MS subjects including Catawba, Cherokee, Chickasaw, Choctaw, Creek, Ottawa, Potawatomi, Huron, Chippewa.) (Indian Archives)
———. Indian-Pioneer History. Works Progress Administration Project S–149. 112 vols. (Indian Archives)
———. Tobias Fitch's Journal to the Creeks. Transcripts from Public Record Office, London, Colonial Office, Class 5, Vol. 12, 1726. (Library)
International Council File. (Indian Archives)
Keel, Alice James, and Hudson, Peter J. A Dictionary of the Chickasaw Language. Compiled under the direction of Muriel H. Wright. 1930. (Library)
Kiowa Agents' Reports. (Indian Archives)
Litton, Gaston. Litton Papers. Transcripts of Newspaper Articles on Cherokee, Chickasaw, Choctaw, Creek, Seminole, 1815–1937. 8 vols. (Indian Archives)

Loughridge, Rev. Robert M. History of Mission Work Among the Creek Indians, Presbyterian Church, U. S. A., Wealaka, I. T., 1887. (Library)

Moore, Guy Rowley. History of the Pawnee Indians, Thoburn Collection. (Library)

Pawnee Agents' Reports. (Indian Archives)

Quapaw Agents' Reports. (Indian Archives)

Robertson, Mrs. W. S. Creek Dictionary, 1870. (Library)

Sac and Fox Agency—Tonkawa Indians, Fort Griffin, Texas, 1880. (Indian Archives)

Sac and Fox—Kickapoo Indians. (Indian Archives)

Sac and Fox and Shawnee Agents' Reports. (Indian Archives)

Seminole Indian Records. (Indian Archives)

Seminole Laws, 1897–1903. Trans. by G. W. Grayson. (Indian Archives)

Thoburn, Joseph B. Brief Histories: Comanche, Delaware, Kansa or Kaw, Pawnee,
Wichita, Wyandotte or Huron. Thoburn Collection. (Library)

———. The Northern Caddoan Peoples of Prehistoric Times and the Human Origin of
the Natural Mounds, So Called, of Oklahoma and Neighboring States, 1930. (Library)

Tonkawa. Letter, Captain J. B. Irvine. (Indian Archives)

Union Mission Journal, 1820–26. By Rev. Wm. F. Vaill, superintendent of Union Mission
to the Osages. (Library)

Volume Kaw–2. (Indian Archives)

Volume Sac and Fox–5, and Volume Sac and Fox–13B. (Indian Archives)

Whipple, Amiel Weeks. Journal, 1853–54, Field Notes Pacific Railroad Survey. 28 Note-
books. (Library)

Wright, Rev. Alfred. Letters, 1820–37. Missionary Work Among Choctaw Indians.
(Library)

In the University of Oklahoma, Norman:

Acts of the Choctaw Nation, 1857, 1869–1910. (Phillips Collection)

Parsons, David. Removal of the Osage Indians from Kansas. Ph.D. thesis, 1940.

In the Muriel H. Wright Collection, Oklahoma City:

Chickasaw Laws, 1871, 1872.

Choctaw Documents, Laws, Letters, Reports in the Allen Wright Papers (1856–85) and
in the Dr. E. N. Wright Papers (1885–1931).

Delegate Convention of Choctaws at Goodland, Oklahoma, June 5–8, 1934, Minutes and
Resolutions.

*In the Office of the Superintendent of the Five Civilized Tribes, Muskogee, Okla-
homa:*

Union Agency Files.

GOVERNMENT DOCUMENTS

*American State Papers. Documents, Legislative and Executive, of the Congress of the
United States,* Class II, Vols. 7 and 8 (*Indian Affairs,* 2 vols.), 1789–1828; Class V,
Vols. 18–22 (*Military Affairs,* 5 vols.), 1823–37. Washington, 1832–.

Annals of Congress. The Debates and Proceedings in the Congress of the United States.
New York and Washington, 1851–56.

Constitutions and By-laws of Indian Tribes, drafted under the Department of the Interior Office of Indian Affairs:

Absentee-Shawnee Tribe of Indians of Oklahoma, ratified December 5, 1938. Washington, 1939.

Alabama-Quassarte Tribal Town, Oklahoma, ratified January 10, 1939. Washington, 1939.

Caddo Indian Tribe of Oklahoma, ratified January 17, 1938. Washington, 1938.

Cheyenne-Arapaho Tribes of Oklahoma, ratified September 18, 1937. Washington, 1938.

Eastern Shawnee Tribe of Oklahoma, ratified December 22, 1939. Washington, 1940.

Iowa Tribe of Oklahoma, ratified October 23, 1937. Washington, 1938.

Kickapoo Tribe of Oklahoma, ratified September 18, 1937. Washington, 1938.

Kialegee Tribal Town, ratified June 12, 1941. Washington, 1942.

Miami Tribe of Oklahoma, ratified October 10, 1939. Washington, 1940.

Ottawa Tribe of Oklahoma, ratified November 30, 1938. Washington, 1939.

Pawnee Indians of Oklahoma, ratified January 6, 1938.

Peoria Tribe of Indians of Oklahoma, ratified June 1, 1940. Washington, 1940.

Citizen and Potawatomi Indians, Oklahoma, ratified December 12, 1938. Washington, 1939.

Sac and Fox Tribe of Indians of Oklahoma, ratified December 7, 1937. Washington, 1938.

Seneca-Cayuga Tribe of Oklahoma, approved April 26, 1937. Washington, 1937.

Thlopthlocco Tribal Town, Oklahoma, ratified December 27, 1938. Washington, 1939.

Tonkawa Tribe of Indians of Oklahoma, ratified April 21, 1938. Washington, 1938.

Wyandotte Tribe of Oklahoma, ratified July 24, 1937. Washington, 1937.

Constitutions and Laws of Five Civilized Tribes before 1900:

Cherokee Nation. *Laws of the Cherokee Nation*: Passed at the Annual Sessions of the National Council, 1854–55. Tahlequah, 1855.

———. *Constitution and Laws of the Cherokee Nation*. St. Louis, 1875.

———. *Compiled Laws of the Cherokee Nation*. Tahlequah, 1881.

Chickasaw Nation. *Constitution, Laws, and Treaties of the Chickasaws*. Tishomingo City, 1860.

———. *Constitution and Laws of the Chickasaw Nation*. Compiled by Davis Homer. Parsons, Kan., 1899.

Choctaw Nation. *Constitution and Laws of the Choctaw Nation*. Doaksville, 1852.

———. *Constitution and Laws of the Choctaw Nation*. Compiled by Joseph P. Folsom. New York, 1869.

———. *Constitution, Treaties, and Laws of the Choctaw Nation*, Sedalia, Mo., 1887.

———. *Constitution and Laws of the Choctaw Nation*. Dallas, 1894.

Creek (or Muskogee) Nation. *Constitution and Laws of the Muskogee Nation*. Compiled by L. C. Perryman. Muskogee, 1890.

———. *Constitution and Laws of the Muskogee Nation*. Compiled by A. P. McKellop. Muskogee, 1893.

Commissioner of Indian Affairs. *Annual Reports, 1830–1949.*

———. *Treaties between the United States of America and the Several Indian Tribes, from 1778 to 1837*. Washington, 1837.

Indian Corporate Charters Issued under the Department of Interior Office of Indian Affairs:

Alabama-Quassarte Tribal Town, Oklahoma, ratified May 24, 1939. Washington, 1939.

Caddo Indian Tribe of Oklahoma, ratified November 15, 1938. Washington, 1939.

Eastern Shawnee Tribe of Oklahoma, ratified December 12, 1940. Washington, 1941.

Iowa Tribe of Oklahoma, ratified February 5, 1938. Washington, 1938.

Kialegee Tribal Town, Oklahoma, ratified September 17, 1942. Washington, 1943.

Kickapoo Tribe of Oklahoma, ratified January 18, 1938. Washington, 1938.

Miami Tribe of Oklahoma, ratified June 1, 1940. Washington, 1940.

Ottawa Tribe of Oklahoma, ratified June 2, 1939. Washington, 1939.

Pawnee Tribe of Oklahoma, ratified April 28, 1938. Washington, 1938.

Peoria Tribe of Indians, Oklahoma, ratified June 1, 1940. Washington, 1940.

Seneca-Cayuga Tribe of Oklahoma, ratified June 26, 1937. Washington, 1938.

Thlopthlocco Tribal Town, Oklahoma, ratified April 13, 1939. Washington, 1941.

Wyandotte Tribe of Oklahoma, ratified October 30, 1937. Washington, 1938.

Laws Relating to the Five Civilized Tribes in Oklahoma, 1890–1914. Printed by order of the Committee on Indian Affairs, House of Rep., 63 Cong., 3 sess. Washington, n.d.

Miscellaneous Indian Documents, some from U. S. Department of Interior. 52 vols. Emmet Starr Collection, Oklahoma Historical Society, Oklahoma City.

U. S. Census Office. *Indians Taxed and Indians Not Taxed, 11th Census, 1890,* X.

U. S. Commission and Commissioner to the Five Civilized Tribes. *The Final Rolls of the Citizens and Freedmen of the Five Civilized Tribes in the Indian Territory,* 1906. Washington.

U. S. Commission to the Five Civilized Tribes. *Annual Reports,* 1894–1905.

U. S. Commissioner to the Five Civilized Tribes. *Annual Reports,* 1905–14.

U. S. Congress. *Conditions of the Indian Tribes, Report* of Joint Special Committee. Joint Resolution of March 3, 1865. Washington, 1867.

U. S. Court of Claims. *The Choctaw Nation of Indians v. the United States.* 1881, 2 vols. No. 12,742.

——. *The Creek Nation v. the United States.* 1926, 1930, 1933, 3 vols. No. F–205, No. H–510, No. L–168.

——. *The Choctaw and Chickasaw Nation v. the United States of America.* 1934. No. F–181.

——. *The Wichita and Affiliated Bands of Indians in Oklahoma, the Tawaconies, Wacos, Keechis, Ionies and the Delaware Band of the Wichita, and the Individual Members of Said Wichita and Affiliated Bands of Indians v. the United States of America.* 1927. No. E–542.

U. S. Indian Inspector. *Reports,* 1899–1900, 1904–1905.

U. S. Indian Office. *Oklahoma Indian Tribes, Brief Historical Sketches.* Organization Division, A. C. Monahan, regional co-ordinator. Oklahoma City, 1940.

U. S. Department of the Interior. *The Five Civilized Tribes in the Indian Territory. Extra Census Bulletin.* Washington, 1894.

——. *Indian Administration since July 1, 1929.* Office of Indian Affairs *Report,* C. J. Rhoades, commissioner; J. Henry Scattergood, assistant commissioner. March 3, 1933.

——. *The Indian Bureau from 1824 to 1924.* Board of Indian Commissioners, *Bulletin No. 242.* Washington, 1924.

——. *Pamphlet III—Tables on Hospitals, Schools, Population, and School Census,* 1945, 1950. Indian Service.

——. *Statistical Supplement to the Annual Report* of the Commissioner of Indian Affairs, June 30, 1944.

U. S. President. *Messages and Papers of the Presidents, 1789–1897.* Washington, 1896–99.
U. S. Senate *Doc. 512,* 23 Cong., 1 sess. Vols. I–V (Indian Removal). Washington, 1834–35.
—— *Doc. 501,* 59 Cong., 1 sess. (Delaware Indian History.)
—— *Doc. 215,* 60 Cong., 1 sess., 3 vols. (Kickapoo Indian Hearings.)
—— Committee on Indian Affairs. "The Condition of the Indian Tribes in the Indian Territory, and upon other Reservations," Resolution, June 11 And December 3, 1884, and February 23, 1885. *Sen. Rep. 1278—I. T.–1.*
—— *Report* of the Select Committee to Investigate Matters Connected with Affairs in the Indian Territory. Hearings. 59 Cong., 2 sess, *Sen. Rep. 5013,* Part I, II, Vols. I, II. Washington, 1907.
—— Survey of Conditions of the Indians of the United States, Hearings before a Subcommittee of the Committee on Indian Affairs, *Sen. Rep. 79* (70 Cong.), *Sen. Rep. 308* (70 Cong.), *Sen. Rep. 263* (71 Cong.), 71 Cong., 2 sess. *Oklahoma,* Part 14 (Five Civilized Tribes). Washington, 1931.
—— *ibid., Sen. Rep. 79* (70 Cong.), *Sen. Rep. 308* (70 Cong.), *Sen. Rep. 263* (71 Cong.), *Sen. Rep. 416* (71 Cong.), 72 Cong., 1 sess. *Indian Claims Against the Government,* Part 25 (Oklahoma, etc.). Washington, 1932.
War of the Rebellion. Compilation of the Official Records of the Union and Confederate Armies, Series I, Vols. III, XIII, XXII; Series IV, Vol. I. Washington, 1880–1901.
Wells, George C., supervisor of Indian education for Oklahoma. *Fourth Annual Report to the Commissioner of Indian Affairs.* June 30, 1935.
Whipple, Lieut. A. W. *Reports of Explorations and Surveys to Ascertain the Most Practicable Route for a Railroad from the Mississippi River to the Pacific Ocean.* Ex. Doc. No. 78, 33 Cong., 2 sess., 1853–54. Washington, 1856.

NEWSPAPERS

Cherokee Advocate (Tahlequah).
Cherokee Phoenix (New Echota, Georgia).
Cheyenne Transporter (Darlington).
Fort Smith Elevator (Fort Smith).
Muskogee Phoenix (Muskogee).
Muskogee Times-Democrat (Muskogee).
Niles Weekly Register (Baltimore).
The Arkansas Gazette (Little Rock).
The Kingfisher Times (Kingfisher).
The Indian Champion (Atoka).
The Indian Citizen (Atoka).
The Indian Journal (Muskogee, Eufaula).
Purcell Register (Purcell).

BOOKS

See also Complete List of Suggested Readings on pages 270–73. Books listed there are not repeated in this section.
Abel, Annie [Anna] Heloise. *The American Indian as Secessionist.* Cleveland, 1915.
——. *The American Indian Under Reconstruction.* Cleveland, 1925.
——. *Cherokee Negotiations of 1822–1823.* Cleveland, 1916.

————. *History of Events Resulting in Indian Consolidation West of the Mississippi.* Washington, 1908.

Adams, Richard C. *Ancient Religion of the Delaware Indian.* Washington, 1904.

Anderson, Mabel Washbourne. *Life of General Stand Watie.* Pryor, Okla., 1915.

Babcock, Sidney H., and John Y. Bryce. *History of Methodism in Oklahoma.* N. p., 1935.

Bancroft, Hubert Howe. *History of Arizona and New Mexico.* Vol. XVII, *Works.* San Francisco, 1889.

Bandelier, Adolph F. A. *Hemenway Southwestern Archeological Expedition.* Cambridge, Mass., 1890.

————. *Final Report of Investigations Among the Indians of the Southwestern United States.* Cambridge, Mass., 1890.

Bartram, William. *Travels Through North and South Carolina . . . the Cherokee Country . . . and the Country of the Choctaws.* Philadelphia, 1791.

Bass, Althea. *Cherokee Messenger.* Norman, 1936.

Beatty, Thomas C. *A Quaker Among the Indians.* Boston, 1875.

Boas, Franz. *Handbook of American Indian Languages. Bulletin No. 40,* Bureau of American Ethnology, Parts I and II. Washington, 1911, 1922.

Bolton, Herbert Eugene. *Coronado on the Turquoise Trail.* Albuquerque, 1949.

————. *Spanish Explorations in the Southwest, 1542–1706.* New York, 1916.

————. *Texas in the Middle Eighteenth Century.* Berkeley, 1915.

Brady, Cyrus Townsend. *Indian Fights and Fighters.* New York, 1908.

Brill, Charles J. *Conquest of the Southern Plains.* Oklahoma City, 1938.

Brinton, Daniel G., and Anthony Albert Seqaqkin. *A Lenape-English Dictionary.* Philadelphia, 1888.

Britton, Wiley. *The Civil War on the Border.* New York, 1904.

————. *Union Army Brigade in the Civil War.* Kansas City, 1922.

Brown, John Henry. *Indian Wars and Pioneers of Texas.* Austin, 1890.

Brown, John P. *Old Frontiers.* Kingsport, Tenn., 1938.

Byington, Cyrus. *Grammar of the Choctaw Language.* Philadelphia, 1870.

————. *Dictionary of the Choctaw Language. Bulletin No. 46,* Bureau of American Ethnology. Washington, 1915.

Catlin, George. *North American Indians.* New York, 1842.

Caughey, John Walton. *McGillivray of the Creeks.* Norman, 1938.

Chahta Holisso Ai Isht Ia Vmmona. The Choctaw Spelling Book. Eighth Edition. Richmond [n.d.].

Claiborne, J. F. H. *Mississippi as a Province, Territory, and State.* Jackson, 1880.

Clum, Woodworth. *Apache Agent—The Story of John P. Clum.* New York, 1936.

Coblenz, Catherine. *Sequoya.* New York, 1946.

Coe, Charles H. *Red Patriots: The Story of the Seminoles.* Cincinnati, 1898.

Collins, Dennis. *The Indians' Last Fight, or the Dull Knife Raid.* Girard, Kan., 1915.

Collins, Hubert E. *Warpath and Cattle Trail.* New York, 1928.

Conkling, Roscoe P. and Margaret B. *The Butterfield Overland Mail, 1857–1869.* Glendale, 1947.

Cook, John R. *The Border and the Buffalo.* Topeka, 1907.

Coues, Elliott. *The Expeditions of Zebulon Montgomery Pike.* New York, 1895.

Culin, Stewart. *Games of the North American Indians. Twenty-fourth Annual Report,* Bureau of American Ethnology. Washington, 1907.

Cushman, H. B. *History of the Choctaw, Chickasaw, and Natchez Indians.* Greenville, Texas, 1899.

Dale, Edward Everett. *Oklahoma: The Story of a State*. New York, 1950.

———, and Morris L. Wardell. *History of Oklahoma*. New York, 1946.

Debo, Angie. *The Five Civilized Tribes*. Report on Social and Economic Conditions. Philadelphia, 1951.

———. *Oklahoma: Foot-loose and Fancy-free*. Norman, 1949.

———. *Prairie City*. New York, 1944.

———. *Tulsa: From Creek Town to Oil Capital*. Norman, 1943.

Densmore, Frances. *Pawnee Music. Bulletin No. 93,* Bureau of American Ethnology. Washington, 1929.

Dixon, Mrs. Olive K. *The Life and Adventures of Billy Dixon*. Dallas, 1927.

Dodge, Colonel Richard Irving. *The Hunting Grounds of the Great West*. London, 1878.

———. *Our Wild Indians*. Chicago, 1882.

Dorsey, George Amos. *The Traditions of the Osage*. Field Columbian Museum *Publication No. 88,* Anthropological Series, Vol. VII, No. 1. Chicago, 1904.

———. *The Mythology of the Wichita*. Washington, 1904.

———. *The Pawnee Mythology*. Part I. Washington, 1906.

Dorsey, James Owen. "On the Comparative Phonology of the Four Siouan Languages," in *Annual Report, 1883,* of the Smithsonian Institution. Washington, 1885.

———. "Siouan Sociology," in *Fifteenth Annual Report,* Bureau of American Ethnology. Washington, 1897.

———, and Swanton, John R. *A Dictionary of the Biloxi* and *Oto Languages. Bulletin 47,* Bureau of American Ethnology. Washington, 1912.

Drake, Samuel G. *The Book of the Indians*. Boston, 1841.

Eastman, Elaine Goodale. *Pratt: The Red Man's Moses*. Norman, 1935.

Eaton, Rachel Caroline. *John Ross and the Cherokee Indians*. Menasha, 1914.

Foreman, Carolyn Thomas. *Indians Abroad*. Norman, 1943.

———. *Oklahoma Imprints*. Norman, 1936.

———. *Park Hill*. Muskogee, Okla., 1948.

Foreman, Grant. *Indians and Pioneers*. New Haven, 1930.

———. *Pioneer Days in the Early Southwest*. Cleveland, 1926.

Foster, Laurence. *Negro-Indian Relationships in the Southeast*. Philadelphia, 1935.

Gabriel, Ralph Henry. *Elias Boudinot, Cherokee, and His America*. Norman, 1941.

Gatschet, Albert S. *A Migration Legend of the Creek Indians*. Philadelphia, 1884.

Gayarre, Charles. *History of Louisiana*. 2 vols. New Orleans, 1903. 4th ed.

Gittinger, Roy. *The Formation of the State of Oklahoma*. Norman, 1939.

Gipson, Lawrence (ed.). *The Moravian Indian Mission on White River. Indiana Historical Collections,* Vol. XXIII. Indianapolis, 1938.

Glisan, R. *Journal of Army Life*. San Francisco, 1874.

Goode, Rev. William H. *Outposts of Zion*. Cincinnati, 1863.

Gould, Charles N. *Oklahoma Place Names*. Norman, 1933.

Gregg, Josiah. *Commerce of the Prairies*. Philadelphia, 1844.

Gridley, Marion E. *Indians of Today*. Chicago, 1947.

Grinnell, George Bird. *The Story of the Indian*. London, 1896.

———. *Two Great Scouts and Their Pawnee Battalion*. Cleveland, 1928.

———. *When Buffalo Ran*. New Haven, 1920.

Hallenbeck, Cleve. *Spanish Missions of the Old Southwest*. Garden City, 1926.

Hargrett, Lester. *Oklahoma Imprints, 1835–1890*. New York, 1951.

Harlow, Rex F. and Victor. *Makers of Government in Oklahoma*. Oklahoma City, 1930.

Harrington, Mark Raymond. *Sacred Bundles of the Sac and Fox Indians*. Philadelphia, 1914.

Haywood, John. *The Civil and Political History of the State of Tennessee*. Nashville, 1891.

Heckewelder, John G. E. *History, Manners, and Customs of the Indian Nations . . . Pennsylvania and Neighboring States*. Philadelphia, 1876.

Heusser, Albert H. *Homes and Haunts of the Indians*. Paterson, N. J., 1923.

History of American Missions to the Heathen. Worcester (Spooner and Howland), 1840.

Hitchcock, Ethan Allen. *A Traveler in Indian Territory*. Edited by Grant Foreman. Cedar Rapids, 1930.

Hodge, Frederick Webb. *Indian Notes and Monographs*. New York, 1919.

————. *Spanish Explorers in the Southern United States*. New York, 1907.

Hornaday, William T. *Extermination of the American Bison*. Annual Report, U. S. National Museum, 1887. Washington, 1889.

Hrdlička, Aleš. *Physical Anthropology of the Lenape or Delawares*. Bulletin No. 62, Bureau of American Ethnology. Washington, 1916.

Hunter, John Dunn. *Manners and Customs of Several Indian Tribes West of the Mississippi*. Philadelphia, 1823.

Hyde, George H. *The Pawnee Indians*. Denver, 1934.

Irving, Washington. *A Tour on the Prairies*. Oklahoma Edition, with Notes from Irving's Journal, edited by Joseph B. Thoburn and George C. Wells. Oklahoma City, 1930.

James, George W. *New Mexico, the Land of the Delight Makers*. Boston, 1920.

Jones, Jonathan H. *A Condensed History of the Apache and Comanche Indian Tribes*. San Antonio, 1899.

Jones, William. *Ethnography of the Fox Indians*. Bulletin No. *125*, Bureau of American Ethnology. Washington, 1939.

Kappler, Charles J. *Indian Affairs, Laws, and Treaties*, Vols. I–IV. Washington, 1903–29.

Keim, DeB. Randolph. *Sheridan's Troopers on the Border*. Philadelphia, 1885.

La Flesche, Francis. *Dictionary of the Osage Language*. Bulletin *109*, Bureau of American Ethnology. Washington, 1932.

Loughridge, R. M., and Hodge, David M. *English and Muskokee Dictionary*. Philadelphia, 1914.

Manypenny, George W. *Our Indian Wards*. Cincinnati, 1880.

Marable, Mary Hays, and Elaine Boylan. *A Handbook of Oklahoma Writers*. Norman, 1937.

Marcy, Captain Randolph B. *Exploration of the Red River in the Year 1852*. Washington, 1854.

Mazzanovich, Anton. *Trailing Geronimo*. Edited by E. A. Brininstool. Los Angeles, 1926.

Methvin, J. J. *In the Limelight, History of Anadarko* [*Caddo, Co.*] *and Vicinity from the Earliest Days*. [Anadarko, Okla.? n.d.]

Mooney, James. *Swimmer Manuscript—Cherokee Sacred Formulas and Medicinal Prescriptions*. Bulletin No. *99*, Bureau of American Ethnology. Washington, 1932.

Moorehead, Warren King. *Archeology of the Arkansas River Valley*. With a Supplementary Paper by Joseph B. Thoburn, "The Prehistoric Cultures of Oklahoma." New Haven, 1931.

Morrison, William B. *The Red Man's Trail*. Richmond, 1932.

————. *Military Posts and Camps in Oklahoma*. Oklahoma City, 1936.

Myer, William E. "Indian Trails of the Southwest," in *Forty-second Annual Report*, Bureau of American Ethnology. Washington, 1928.

Nuttall, Thomas. *Travels to the Arkansas Territory, 1819.* Vols. XIV–XVII in Reuben Gold Thwaites' *Early Western Travels.* Cleveland, 1905.

O'Beirne, H. F. *Leaders and Leading Men of the Indian Territory.* 2 vols. Chicago, 1891.

——— and E. S. *Indian Territory, Its Chiefs, Legislators, and Leading Men.* St. Louis, 1892.

Otis, Colonel Elwell S. *The Indian Question.* New York, 1878.

Pickett, Albert James. *History of Alabama.* With "Annals of Alabama," by Thomas A. Owen. Birmingham, 1900.

Pilling, James C. *Bibliography of the Muskhogean Languages.* Washington, 1889.

Posey, Alexander. *Poems.* With a Memoir by William Elsey Connelly. Topeka, 1910.

Rister, Carl Coke. *Baptist Missions Among the American Indians.* Atlanta, 1944.

Rowland, Dunbar, A. G. and Sanders. *Mississippi Provincial Archives, 1729–1740. French Dominion,* Vol. I (only vol. published). Jackson, 1927.

Royce, Charles C. "Indian Land Cessions in the United States," in *Eighteenth Annual Report,* Bureau of American Ethnology. Washington, 1899.

Schmeckebier, Laurence F. *Office of Indian Affairs.* Washington, 1925.

Schoolcraft, Henry R. *Indian Tribes of North America.* Philadelphia, 1860.

Speck, Frank G. *Decorative Art and Basketry of the Cherokee. Bulletin* of the Milwaukee Public Museum. Milwaukee, 1920.

Starr, Emmet. *Early History of the Cherokees.* [Kansas City, 1916?]

———. *History of the Cherokee Indians.* Oklahoma City, 1921.

Stone, William L. *The Life and Times of Red Jacket or Sa-Go-Ye-Wat-Ha.* New York and London, 1841.

Swanton, John R. *Social and Ceremonial Life of the Choctaw Indians. Bulletin No. 103,* Bureau of American Ethnology. Washington, 1931.

Swett, Morris. *Fort Sill, a History.* Fort Sill, Okla., 1921.

Thomas, Alfred B. (ed.). *After Coronado: Spanish Exploration Northeast of New Mexico, 1696–1727.* Norman, 1935.

———. *The Plains Indians and New Mexico, 1751–1788.* Albuquerque, 1940.

Thomas, Cyrus. "Burial Mounds of the Northern Sections of the United States" and "Burial Ceremonies of the Hurons," in *Fifth Annual Report,* Bureau of American Ethnology. Washington, 1887.

Thoburn, Joseph B. *A Standard History of Oklahoma.* 5 vols. Chicago and New York, 1916.

Twitchell, Ralph E. *The Leading Facts of New Mexican History.* Cedar Rapids, 1911–17.

Vestal, Stanley (ed.). *New Sources of Indian History, 1850–1891: A Miscellany.* Norman, 1934.

Walker, Robert Sparks. *Torchlights of the Cherokees.* New York, 1931.

Watkins, Ben. *Complete Choctaw Definer, English with Choctaw Definition.* Van Buren, Ark., 1892.

Whipple, A. W. *A Pathfinder in the Southwest.* Edited and Annotated by Grant Foreman. Norman, 1941.

Winship, George Parker. *Journey of Coronado, 1540–1542.* New York, 1922.

Wright, Allen. *A Chahta Leksikon.* Richmond, 1880.

———. *Chikasha Oklai Kvnstitushvn Mich i Nan Vlhpisa.* New York, 1873.

Wright, Muriel H. *Springplace, Moravian Mission, Cherokee Nation.* Guthrie, 1940.

———. *The Story of Oklahoma.* Guthrie, 1949. 4th ed.

ARTICLES

See also Complete List of Suggested Readings on page 270. Articles listed there are not repeated in this section.

In *Chronicles of Oklahoma*:

Antle, H. R. "Excavation of a Caddoan Earth Lodge," Vol. XII, No. 4 (1934).
———. "Interpretation of Seminole Clan Relationship Terms," Vol. XIV, No. 3 (1936).
Becker, Daniel A. "Comanche Civilization with History of Quanah Parker," Vol. I, No. 3 (1923).
Becker, W. J. "The Comanche Indian and His Language," Vol. XIV, No. 3 (1936).
Brown, Loren N. "The Choctaw-Chickasaw Court Citizens," Vol. XVI, No. 4 (1938).
———. "The Appraisal of the Lands of the Choctaws and Chickasaws by the Dawes Commission," Vol. XXII, No. 2 (1944).
Caldwell, Norman W. "The Chickasaw Threat to French Control of the Mississippi in the 1740's," Vol. XVI, No. 4 (1938).
Campbell, W. S. (Stanley Vestal). "The Cheyenne Dog Soldiers," Vol. I, No. 1 (1921).
Chapman, Berlin B. "How the Cherokees Acquired the Outlet," Vol. XV, No. 1 (1937); "How the Cherokees Acquired and Disposed of the Outlet"(Part II), Vol. XV, No. 1 (1937); "How the Cherokees Acquired and Disposed of the Outlet, the Fairchild Failure" (Part III), Vol. XV, No. 3 (1937); "How the Cherokees Acquired and Disposed of the Outlet" (Part IV), Vol. XVI, No. 1 (1938).
Clark, J. Stanley. "A Pawnee Buffalo Hunt," Vol. XX, No. 4 (1942).
Covington, James Warren. "Causes of the Dull Knife Raid," Vol. XXVI, No. 1 (1948).
Dale, Edward Everett. "The Cheyenne-Arapaho Country," Vol. XX, No. 4 (1942).
———. "Some Letters of General Stand Watie," Vol. I, No. 1 (1921).
———. "Two Mississippi Valley Frontiers," Vol. XXVI, No. 4 (1948).
Evans, Charles. "The Heritage of the Oklahoma Child," Vol. XXII, No. 4 (1944).
Forbes, Gerald. "History of the Osage Blanket Lease," Vol. XIX, No. 1 (1941).
———. "The International Conflict for the Lands of the Creek Confederacy," Vol. XIV, No. 4 (1936).
———. "The Origin of the Seminole Indians," Vol. XV, No. 1 (1937).
Foreman, Carolyn Thomas. "Dutch, the Cherokee," Vol. XXVII, No. 3 (1949).
———. "Education Among the Chickasaw Indians," Vol. XV, No. 2 (1937).
———. "Education Among the Quapaws," Vol. XXV, No. 1 (1947).
Foreman, Grant. "Historical Background of the Kiowa-Comanche Reservation," Vol. XIX, No. 2 (1941).
———. "The Story of Sequoyah's Last Days," Vol. XII, No. 1 (1934).
Hall, Arthur H. "The Red Stick War," Vol. XII, No. 3 (1934).
Hewes, Leslie. "Cherokee Occupance in the Oklahoma Ozarks and Prairie Plains," Vol. XXII, No. 3 (1944).
Keith, Harold. "Memories of George Mayes," Vol. XXIV, No. 1 (1946).
Lambert, O. A. "Historical Sketch of Col. Samuel Checote, Once Chief of the Creek Nation," Vol. IV, No. 3 (1926).
Laracy, John, O.S.B. "Sacred Heart Mission and Abbey," Vol. V, No. 2 (1927).
Lewis, Anna. "French Interests and Activities in Oklahoma," Vol. II, No. 3 (1924).
———. "Oklahoma as a Part of the Spanish Dominion, 1763–1803," Vol. III, No. 1 (1925).
Martin, Robert G., Jr. "The Cherokee Phoenix: Pioneer of Indian Journalism," Vol. XXV, No. 2 (1947).

Meserve, John Bartlett. "Chief Lewis Downing and Chief Charles Thompson (Oocha-lata)," Vol. XVI, No. 3 (1938).

——. "Chief Opothleyahola," Vol. IX, No. 4 (1931).

——. "The McCurtains," Vol. XIII, No. 3 (1935).

——. "The MacIntoshes," Vol. X, No. 3 (1932).

Morrison, James D. "News for the Choctaws," Vol. XXVII, No. 2 (1949).

Morrison, William B. "Diary of Rev. Cyrus Kingsbury," Vol. III, No. 2 (1925).

——. "The Saga of Skullyville," Vol. XVI, No. 2 (1938).

Nye, Wilbur S. "The Battle of the Wichita Village," Vol. XV, No. 2 (1937).

——. "Kiowa Sun Dance," Vol. XII, No. 3 (1934).

Porter, Kenneth W. "Wild Cat's Death and Burial," Vol. XXI, No. 1 (1943).

Schmitt, Karl. "Wichita-Kiowa Relations and the 1874 Outbreak," Vol. XXVIII, No. 2 (1950).

Spoehr, Alexander. " 'Friends' Among the Seminole," Vol. XIX, No. 3 (1941).

——. "Oklahoma Seminole Towns," Vol. XIX, No. 4 (1941).

Swett, Morris. "Sergeant I-see-o, Kiowa Indian Scout," Vol. XIII, No. 3 (1935).

Thoburn, Joseph B. "Ancient Irrigation Ditches on the Plains," Vol. IX, No. 1 (1931).

——. "An Important Archeological Discovery," Vol. VI, No. 4 (1927).

——. "Notes on Archeology," Vol. XV, No. 1 (1937).

——. "Oklahoma Archeological Explorations in 1925–26," Vol. IV, No. 2 (1926).

——. "The Origin of the 'Natural' Mounds of Oklahoma and Adjacent States," Vol. XV, No. 3 (1937).

——. "Prehistoric Cultures of Oklahoma," Vol. VII, No. 3 (1929).

——. "The Tropical and Subtropical Origin of Mound-Builder Mounds," Vol. XVI, No. 1 (1938).

Thomas, A. B. "Spanish Exploration of Oklahoma, 1599–1792," Vol. VI, No. 2 (1928).

Wardell, M. L. "Protestant Missions Among the Osages, 1820 to 1838," Vol. II, No. 3 (1924).

Williams, Samuel C. "The Father of Sequoyah: Nathaniel Gist," Vol. XV, No. 1 (1937).

Woldert, Albert, M. D. "The Last of the Cherokee in Texas, and the Life and Death of Chief Bowles," Vol. I, No. 3 (1923).

Wright, Muriel H. "Official Seals of the Five Civilized Tribes," Vol. XVIII, No. 4 (1940).

——. "The Removal of the Choctaws to the Indian Territory, 1830–1833," Vol. VI, No. 2 (1928).

In other sources:

Abel, Anna [Annie] Heloise. "Indian Reservations in Kansas and the Extinguishment of Their Title," *Transactions* of the Kansas State Historical Society, Vol. VIII 1903–1904.

Allen, Henry Easton. "The Parilla Expedition to the Red River," *The Southwestern Historical Quarterly,* Vol. XLIII, No. 1 (1939).

Burnett, E. K. "The Spiro Mound Collection in the Museum," *Contributions* from the Museum of the American Indian, Heye Foundation, Vol. XIV (1945).

Clements, Forrest E. "Historical Sketch of the Spiro Mound," *Contributions* from the Museum of the American Indian, Heye Foundation, Vol. XIV (1945).

Debo, Angie. "John Rollin Ridge," *Southwest Review,* Vol. XVII, No. 1 (1931).

Dunbar, Rev. John. "The Presbyterian Mission Among the Pawnee Indians in Nebraska, 1834–1836," *Collections* of the Kansas State Historical Society, Vol. XI (1909–10).

Ferris, Mrs. Ida M. "The Sauks and Foxes in Franklin and Osage Counties, Kansas," *Collections* of the Kansas State Historical Society, Vol. XI (1909–10).

Goodwin, Grenville. "The Social Divisions and Economic Life of the Western Apache," *American Anthropologist,* new series, Vol. XXXVII, No. 1 (1935).

Haggard, J. Villasana. "Letters and Documents, Spain's Indian Policy in Texas," *The Southwestern Historical Quarterly,* Vol. XLIII, No. 4 (1940).

Morehouse, George F. "History of Kansa or Kaw," *Transactions* of the Kansas State Historical Society, Vol. X (1910).

Opler, M. E. "The Concept of Supernatural Power Among the Chiricahua and Mescalero Apache," *American Anthropologist,* new series, Vol. XXXVII, No. 1 (1935).

Rister, C. C. "Satanta, Orator of the Plains," *Southwest Review,* Vol. XVII, No. 1 (1931).

Romig, Rev. Joseph. "The Chippewa and Munsee (or Christian Indians) of Franklin County, Kansas," *Collections* of the Kansas State Historical Society, Vol. XI (1909–10).

Rouse, Mrs. Shelley D. "Colonel Dick Johnson's Choctaw Academy," Ohio Archeological and Historical Society *Publications,* Vol. XXV (n.d.).

Index

Baptist Indian churches and missions: 26, 52, 84, 105, 106, 117, 137, 149, 166, 177, 180, 198, 201, 213, 218, 227, 233, 235, 243, 245
Barker, William: 131, 207
Barnard, Cosena: 266, 267
Barnard, Michee: 266
Barnard (or Barnett), Timothy: 138, 266
Barnard, Timpoochee: 266
Bartles, Jacob B.: 152
Bartles, Joe: 153
Bartles, Nannie Journeycake: 152
Bates, George: 165
Battey, Thomas C.: 52, 174
Battles: Little Big Horn (Mont.), 17, 80, 81, 205; Washita, 17, 88, 125, 173; Talina, 59; Ackia, 86, 101; Horseshoe (Tallapoosa River), 133; Fallen Timbers (Ohio), 149; Claremore Mound, 150, 192; Wichita Village (Ind. Ter.), 165, 250, 258; Cut Throat Gap, 1833, 171, 192; Great Wahoo Swamp (Fla.), 231; Thames (Canada), 242
Bayhylle, Edwin: 407
Bear, Turner, 140
Beaver, Alex: 222
Bedoka, Maurice: 53
Bell, John A.: 64
Bell, Rev. Robert: 89
Belvin, Harry J. H.: 115
Bemo, John D.: 236
Bent and St. Vrain Trading Co.: 149
Berry, Tennyson: 178
Big Bow, Woody (Kiowa): 177
Bigheart, James: 195
Big Jim: 244
Big Jim Band (Shawnee): 245
Big Pasture (Kiowa-Comanche lands): 127, 175
Big Tree: 173
Binger: 48
Bird's Fort Treaty (Texas): 50
Birdshead, Saul: 46
Black Beaver: 148, 152
Black Bob's Band (Shawnee): 242, 243, 244
Black Dirt (Fukeluste Harjo): 232
Black Dog (Shoⁿ-toⁿ-ça-be): 192, 195
Black drink (Creek): 144
Blackfoot tribe: 146
Black Hawk, Chief (Sauk): 167, 225
Black Hawk War: 167, 225, 226
Black Hoof (Shawnee chief): 243
Blackhorse, Dan: 46
Black Kettle (Cheyenne chief): 15, 43, 79, 173
Black Pawnee: 202
Bloomfield Academy (Chickasaw): 91
Blue-Cloud Men (Arapaho): 42
Blue Jacket, George: 243
Blue Jacket, Henry: 243
Bluejacket, Chief (Shawnee): 242, 244
Bluejacket, Edward H.: 245
Bluejacket, Walter: 245
Blunt, John: 230, 231
Bob, Chief Jim (Delaware): 153
Boggy Depot: 107
Boiling Spring (Chickasaw council): 90
Bond, Henry J.: 114
Bond, Reford: 94

"Boomers": 17
Boot, Rev. John F.: 240
Boudinot, Elias: 64
Boudinot, Elias C.: 71
Bougie, Joseph (or Bogy): 104
Bowl (Cherokee chief): 50
Bowlegs, Billy: 233
Box, John (Pawnee scout): 205
Brainerd Mission: 62
Brant, Joseph: 149
Brazos Agency: 34
Brazos Reserve (Lower Reserve, Texas): 31, 51, 123, 146, 147, 165, 242, 254
Brewer, Judge O. H. P.: 73
Bringing Good, Luther: 46
Brown, John (Cherokee): 66
Brown, John (Seneca of Sandusky): 239
Brown, John F. (Seminole chief): 234, 235, 237
Brown, S. W. (Yuchi chief): 268
Brown, Samuel W., Sr. (Yuchi chief): 267, 268
Brown, W. P.: 95
Bryant, William: 115
Buck, Peter: 240
Buffalo, Ben: 46
Buffalo, John Rush: 252
Buffalo Creek (N. Y.) treaty, 1838: 238, 252, 253
Buffalo Hump: 119
Buffalo Wallow fight: 124
Buffington, Chief T. M. (Cherokee): 73, 74
Burbank pool (Osage oil discovery): 196
Bureau of Indian Affairs, organizations of: 10, 22
Burgess, William: 204
Burke Act, 1906: 21
Burney, B. C.: 95
Burney Institute (Chickasaw): 91, 92
Bushyhead, Chief D. W. (Cherokee): 72, 74
Bushyhead, Fred: 83
Butler, Pierce M.: 50, 51, 68
Butterfield Overland Mail route: 107
Byington, Rev. Cyrus: 106
Bynum, John: 87
Byrd, William L. (Chickasaw governor): 94, 95

Cache Creek Mission (Dutch Reformed): 175
Caddo (or Kadohadocho): 31, 32, 47 ff., 108, 156, 249, 259; name, 47; history, numbers, present location, 48; government and organization, 52; contemporary life and culture, 53; ceremonials and public dances, 53
Caddo Battalion in Civil War: 52
"Caddo George Washington" (Showetat or Little Boy): 52
Caddo Hills, battle of (Ind. Ter.): 49, 104
Caddo Indian Tribe of Oklahoma: 25, 52
Caddo Nation: 32
Caddo Tribal Council: 53
Caddoan Confederacy: 164
Caddoan linguistic family: 8, 155, 164, 202, 245, 247, 253, 256
Cahokia: 11, 53 ff., 157, 160, 208; history, 53; present location, 54
Cahokia Mound: 53
Calbert (or Colbert), James: 87
California Road: 242
Camp Harris (Chickasaw Nation): 92